LOCAL HEROES

About the Authors

Jim Gray joined the *Sligo Champion* as a junior reporter in 1973. He later worked for the *Western and Sligo Journal*, the *Roscommon Champion* and the *Longford Leader*, before returning to Sligo in the mid-1980s. Twice named Journalist of the Year in annual national media awards, he became editor of the *Champion* in the latter part of his career. As a broadcaster, Jim was a regular contributor to RTE sports programmes over several years.

Recovering from cancer, he took up fiction-writing and has had winning stories published in *Ireland's Own Anthology of Short Stories* and in the RTE Ray D'Arcy book, *A Page from My Life*.

Jim is married to Mary, and they have three grown-up daughters, Emma, Ciara and Lisa, and three grandchildren, Daniel, Amber and Lauren.

Leo Gray began his career in journalism in 1974 when he joined the *Sligo Champion* as a junior reporter. He was appointed the paper's first sports editor five years later and served in that role until his retirement in 2014.

He has the rare distinction of having won prestigious national media awards for his coverage of GAA and soccer. He received a coveted GAA MacNamee Award for his coverage of Sligo's Connacht Championship triumph in 2007 and an FAI Kantar Media Communications Award for his writings on Sligo Rovers' League of Ireland success in 2012.

During the course of a decorated 40-year career in local journalism, Leo reported on Sligo sports stories for national print and broadcast media.

He lives in Sligo with his wife, Suzanne, and the couple have two children, Ruth and Keith, and two grandchildren, Cara and Eoin.

Local Heroes

A Celebration of Sligo Sport

Jim Gray & Leo Gray

Red Stripe Press

Published by
Red Stripe Press
an imprint of
Orpen Press
Upper Floor, Unit B3
Hume Centre
Hume Avenue
Park West Industrial Estate
Dublin 12
Ireland

email: info@orpenpress.com
www.orpenpress.com

Paperback ISBN 978-1-78605-179-0
ePub ISBN 978-1-78605-180-6

A catalogue record for this book is available from the British Library.

Printed in Dublin by SprintPrint Ltd

To our parents, Leo and Vera

ACKNOWLEDGEMENTS

The authors sincerely acknowledge and thank the following people who, each in their own way, contributed valuable assistance in the preparation of this book: Pádraig Boylan, Ann Bradshaw, Carl Brennan, Tom Callanan, Una Callanan, Ita Calligy, Darren Carr, Susie Carr, Marie Casserly, Kevin Colreavy, Gerry Conway, Darragh Cox, Seán Cunningham, Paul Deering, Michael Devins, James Fallon, Colin Feehily, Pádraig Feehily, Kevin Flanagan, Zola Flynn, Mary Forte, Jeffrey Fox, Tommie Gorman, Niall Gray, Tommy Higgins, Eileen Keenan, John Kent, Anthony Kilfeather, Kevin Lydon, Brenda McCallion, Jean McConnell, Colm McGee, Mary McGowan, Pádraig McKeon, Kevin McMorrow, Eamonn McMunn, Viola McSharry, Myra Merrick, Glen Monaghan, Gerry Monaghan, Gerry Nicholson, Paul O'Donnell, Barry O'Flynn, Conor O'Grady, Martin O'Hara, Shane O'Meara, Wendy Pugh, Rory Raftery, Sligo County Council, Sligo Credit Union, Sligo GAA, Sligo Rovers FC, Stephen Reid, Seán Reynolds, Gary Rooney, Martin Seery, the *Sligo Champion*. And also Michael Brennan and Eileen O'Brien of Red Stripe Press.

They also wish to sincerely thank all of the wonderful sportsmen and sportswomen who agreed to be interviewed for the book and who trusted them to tell their stories.

Foreword

Nobody is better suited to write a book about the heroic figures and episodes of Sligo sport than Jim and Leo Gray. Love of their Sligo homeplace is a defining theme of their lives.

We first met in Sister Annette's 'low babies' class in Sligo's Scoil Fatima national school. We have been friends for the 62 years since. We appeared together as sailors in Sister Veronica's second-class action song, 'The Saucey Sue', wearing costumes produced by Mrs Hopper, in her house on Riverside.

In third class, we transferred to Saint John's national school in Temple Street. With their cousin John Quinn, and neighbours including the Hartes, Declan Coen and Martin Callaghan, they came with a team from Saint Brigid's to play against our crowd from the Pearse Road area. The match took place in the Nun's Field in Cleveragh, long since replaced by the Cranmore housing development.

They both left Sligo Technical School in their early teens, armed with useful shorthand and typing skills to begin their reporting careers with the *Sligo Champion*, owned by the Townsend family. As with the *Champion*'s editor, the late Seamus Finn, they could easily have moved to jobs in Dublin or beyond. But like their sister, Imelda, and brothers, Eddie and Philip, Jim and Leo had that inbuilt belief that Sligo is as good as it gets.

I'm indebted to them for the help they gave me early in my working life. Part of my two-year training in the Rathmines College of Journalism involved a six-week placement in the *Sligo Champion*. Jim and Leo had a sideline, providing brief summaries of the Sligo Rovers home games for the four national newspapers, the *Irish Independent*, *Irish Press*, *Irish Times* and *Cork Examiner*. When I returned to studies in Dublin, they handed over the nixer to me. It paid for the weekend train ticket home, with a few quid left over, and, crucially, it allowed me to gather a portfolio of published work.

Jim met his Kilkenny-born wife, Mary, at a dance in the Imperial Hotel. She was part of the intake of student nurses at the new training school at Sligo General Hospital. Leo's wife, Sue, is from Dublin. She came to Sligo, working in one of the banks. Like Mary, she realised the Grays would not be uprooted.

I complicated Jim's life for a number of years. In the late 1970s I persuaded him to join a new venture, the *Western Journal and Sligo Journal*. We had great fun together. But after the project folded, Jim had to travel to Roscommon and later to Longford for a number of years for work as a reporter. Thankfully Seamus Finn and the Townsends had the good sense to rehire him and the Gray twins spent the rest of their working lives as the spine of the Sligo Champion, Leo as sports editor and Jim as senior reporter and later editor. Jim was also a polished broadcaster, and his summaries of Sligo Rovers and Sligo GAA matches on RTÉ radio were always on the money.

In national school it took a while to learn how to distinguish one twin from the other. They've always been exceptionally close. At weddings and other celebrations, they are easily persuaded to sing a Beatles number. Their relationship is reflected in the harmonies and perfect timing.

They are also creatures of habit. For years they'd go to the same pub on the same night and the ritual always included detailed conversations about sport and quiz questions from their friend, the late Michael McGowan. Some of the knowledge acquired in those gatherings is shared in these pages.

True to their generous nature, this book is Jim and Leo's way of giving back something to the place they love. In that spirit, enjoy it.

Tommie Gorman
May 2022

Contents

ATHLETICS

BASKETBALL

BOXING

COMMUNITY GAMES

CYCLING

GAA (All Stars)

RACING

RACKETBALL SPORTS

RUGBY

SOCCER (Junior)

SOCCER (Ladies)

SOCCER (Sligo Rovers)

SOCCER (Youth)

SURFING

SWIMMING

MEDIA

ETERNAL STARS

Athletics

Lucy Brennan

Sport has been my therapy

Somewhere in the hallowed halls of academia, a bevy of busy boffins are feverishly ruminating over the therapeutic values of sport. They should consult with Lucy Brennan.

"Sport has been my therapy," confirms Sligo's most decorated athlete. Lucy's impressive haul of silverware as one of the country's top long-distance runners would embarrass any pirate's cove. But the real glory is her courageous fortitude in recovering from a life riddled with heartache and sadness.

A super-fit athlete at the top of her game, Lucy was diagnosed with breast cancer in 2010, only weeks after winning the Cork Marathon. Two years later, her partner of eight years, Dermot Cronin, was diagnosed with pancreatic cancer. She married the love of her life in February 2013; he died aged 65, three months later.

> Dermot's death floored me. I'd come through cancer, he'd been by my side every step of the way, and then he became ill, dreadfully ill. It had been his idea to get married. It had always been on our to do list, but we were always so busy with everything. Then Dermot just said one day, "time is short, let's get married", so we did. We knew we wouldn't have long.
>
> But knowing the end is coming doesn't make it any easier, it doesn't lessen the pain. He needed constant care throughout his illness. Pancreatic cancer is so horrific. I was so involved in caring for him that I didn't look beyond that. We just coped hour by hour, day by day.

Sadly, she was already well versed in the trauma of cancer, having dealt with her own diagnosis just three years earlier. It came out of the blue, at the peak of her athletics prowess. The notion of invincibility engendered by elite athleticism was brutally shattered.

> I'd won the Cork Marathon for the third year in a row in June 2010, so how could I possibly be unwell? Two months later, I went for a routine mammogram check. I almost didn't go to be honest, because I was so busy at work, I thought I wouldn't bother. I was feeling so well.

Luckily, she kept her appointment, although the result came as a major shock. She was called to Galway where her worst fears were confirmed.

> Even sitting in the waiting room, I was thinking this is no big deal, this can't be happening. Then I rather frighteningly realised this was more than just a routine call. But after the initial shock, I was quite positive about it. It was just another challenge to be overcome.

She had her lumpectomy surgery in September of that year, followed by seven weeks of radiotherapy treatment, during which she continued to run around the fields close to University Hospital, Galway.

> They probably thought I was a bit loco. I'd run 10k every day after radiotherapy. It was just a natural thing to do.

Given the all-clear in 2011, Lucy returned to her running career and her job as a horticulturist with Sligo County Council, where she is parks foreperson. But fate had yet another cruel twist in store. Dealing with Dermot's death was much more traumatic than her own recovery process had been.

> Honestly, I just felt I'd had enough at that stage. I lost my love of running, competing. I didn't want to know. I was physically and emotionally exhausted. But gradually, I came to realise I had to shake myself, to get back out there, to re-establish contact with friends, with the life I'd lived. I found it very difficult to go back at first. I had gone for some grief counselling, but it was my re-engagement with athletics which was my real therapy. I knew this is what Dermot would have wanted.

Having somehow found the will to assemble and re-fit the shattered pieces with the delicate precision of a watchmaker, Lucy returned to running, pounding familiar roads and fields, surprising even herself with the fresh enjoyment she derived from it. Her love of and dedication to athletics was her coping mechanism.

By the following July, the old spark had been reignited with a fourth-place finish in the women's race in the gruelling Warrior's Run in Strandhill, an event she'd already won on six previous occasions. Renewed by the thrill of competitive activity, she set her sights on the Dublin Marathon that October. In total, she's competed in the event ten times since her first attempt at the age of 36 in 1996, but this one was coloured by poignancy.

> Whatever else I've achieved in my career, crossing the finishing line in Dublin that year was the best moment of all, considering all I'd been through and after such a long absence. It was the most emotional moment of my life. I honestly felt Dermot was with me all the way. From a position where I thought I'd never run again, here I was completing the Dublin marathon. I knew Dermot was with me, looking after me. I felt very close to him during the race.

Born in Tubbercurry and reared in Bunninadden in South Sligo, Lucy was a latecomer to athletics. She remembers playing basketball in the Marist Convent Secondary School, but has no memory of sport being a central part of her life.

That all changed in 1985 after participation in a few mini-marathons with friends spiked her interest. Striking up friendships with members of the Sligo Triathlon Club was to change the course of her life.

Instantly taking to the rigorous training as swimmer, cyclist and road runner, Lucy carved out a reputation as one of the country's top triathletes. The pinnacle of that phase of her career was representing Ireland at the European Masters Triathlon in Holland 2000, where she helped the Irish team to gold and picked up an individual silver medal.

In retrospect, she feels the grounding she got from the ultra-competitive triathlon circuit proved hugely beneficial when she began to concentrate exclusively on cross-country and marathon running. The tangible evidence came in a remarkable six victories in the demanding Warriors Run in her home county, and a litany of similar successes throughout the country.

Her jaw-dropping treasure trove of honours includes five National Marathon silver medals; two silvers and team gold at the British Masters Home Countries Cross Country Championships in 2004 and again in 2016; a record-breaking three-in-a row gold at the Cork City Marathon; victories in marathons in Belfast, Derry and Longford, which she won five times; and the female 55 first in the Dublin City Marathon in 2003, a feat which earned her a ranking at that time of sixth in the world. There has also been an endless list of record-breaking runs at smaller events throughout the length and breadth of the country and beyond.

Of her incredible success rate, she modestly remarks:

> All I can say is that it's a wonderful feeling crossing the finishing line, knowing the rest of the field is behind you. It doesn't get much better than that.

Like most athletes who take their sport seriously, the Olympic Games was always an aspiration for Lucy. And there was a very realistic chance she might achieve that ambition in 2004, before the fates once again conspired against her. She explains:

> Following the Dublin Marathon in 2003, where I'd posted a time of 2.43, about four minutes short of the Olympic qualifying time, I was approached by the late Ray Flynn, a high-performance coach, who reckoned that with better quality training and more specific training, I might have a chance of making the Athens Olympics the following year.
>
> He put me in touch with the late Jerry Kiernan, then a top coach and mentor to so many great athletes. We met Jerry, he drew up a training programme and he would phone me every day to check on how things were going. He was very positive about the chances of achieving the qualifying time. I convinced myself that I could give this a real shot.
>
> The plan was to go to the London Marathon in April in an attempt to clock the qualifying time. I was fairly confident I could do it. But in February, I picked up a troublesome foot injury, a stress fracture, and I was out for weeks. All our plans had to be abandoned.
>
> It was a bad blow, and I suppose one of the biggest regrets is that I'll never know if I could have made it. There is so much hard work off the track, so much preparation, so many lonely nights on the dark roads, and in the end, it can sometimes come down to just how you feel on the day. Some days it just might not happen. In the heat of battle, you lose sight of those things, so if I could do it all again, I think I would be a bit smarter. But, I suppose, that applies to all walks of life.

Post-Covid, she intends to resume her career, but with a marked difference in attitude.

"I'm working on losing my competitive edge," she offers, somewhat surprisingly.

> There's a part of me that wants to go into an event without pressure, just for the pure enjoyment. I've always enjoyed it, of course, but in a different way. I don't want to get uptight or anxious or nervous about the expectations I placed on myself. You haven't heard the last of me, not by a long way, but I think people will see a different Lucy from now on.

Her healthy mental attitude is fortified by her job, where she designs, shapes and enhances the urban landscape with eye-catching, uplifting floral explosions.

Despite walking so much of her life in the shadow of heartbreak and pain, Lucy Brennan, supreme athlete and gifted horticulturalist, continues to bloom. Mother Nature's child.

Mary Cullen

Courageous athlete won her biggest race

She's pounding familiar territory. To her left, the pale blue Atlantic Ocean sprawls towards a far distant horizon. Across her right shoulder, majestic Benbulben reaches for the sky like a protective comfort blanket. The hedgerows are decorated with burgeoning spring colours and the only twitters are those emitted from little birds in over-hanging trees. She breathes heavily, checks her stopwatch. Seven miles behind and one to go. Almost home. Oh, the privilege.

For Mary Cullen, a European Indoor 3000m bronze medalist and Irish indoor record holder, this is a privilege hard won. When the dream of representing your country at an Olympics Games is cruelly snatched from you not once but for three consecutive events, you're entitled to wonder if the guy charged by the gods with throwing the curveballs is having a laugh. When you optimistically convince yourself life couldn't possibly get any worse, an even more crushing blow comes hurtling your direction in the form of a rare cancer which threatens not only your own life but that of your unborn child.

In her fortieth year of a life marked by impressive highs but far too many lows, Mary Cullen is entitled to the luxury of carefree running on the roads around her native North Sligo. She has stared down the barrel of adversity on the track and off, she has shed too many tears, and yet retains the ability to light up any room with the radiance of her engaging smile.

Hers is an epic story, enough detail, glorious and grim, to dazzle even the most adept screenwriter. It's tempting to be drawn first to the final act, the most courageous victory of all, beating the socks of a life-threatening cancer. But in many ways, the resilience and dogged determination which saw her win that battle can be best understood in the context of her fascinating athletics career.

As a youngster playing soccer and Gaelic football she stood out mainly for the speed with which she travelled the length of the pitches, so athletics people like Marie Mullen, Christine Gallagher, Paddy Brennan, Danny McGinley and Michael Carney took her under their collective wing at North Sligo A.C.

In time, she was good enough to represent Ireland at junior cross-country championships, the World Youth Olympics and the World Cross Country Championships. Offers from the big American colleges began to pour in, and she chose a sports scholarship to Providence College, Rhode Island, where her introduction to American culture coincided with the 9/11 attacks.

> I remember being on a pay-phone at the side of the street ringing home just to let my family know I was safe. We were three hours from New York, but it was still a worrying time. I remember Mum asking if we were under attack. Parents of some of the American athletes were going to New York just to see if they could help out, if there was anything they could do.
>
> I suppose it made the adjustment that much more difficult. We are a very close tight-knit family. There was no social media or mobile phones back then so contact with home was limited. It wasn't easy, but thankfully I settled in well as time went on.

Her potential was underlined in 2006 when winning a major NCAA title, the US Colleges 5,000 meters in Boston, leading to a four-year contract with Reebok and teaming up with agent Ray Flynn, the former Olympian athlete from Longford.

> That was my last race for Providence, and it was so good to go out on such a high. The contract with Reebok meant I was now earning a living from my passion, which is the ultimate dream. Everything was going in the right direction.

She broke Sonia O'Sullivan's 3,000m indoor Irish record at Boston University in February 2009 and shortly afterwards claimed bronze at the European Indoor Championships in Turin. Her record of 8.43 over the distance remains untouched.

But, when it came to the Olympics, the rollercoaster was destined to go into reverse. Beijing in 2008 looked promising, but a calf injury disrupted preparations. Then, four years later, she failed to make the qualifying time for London, although somewhat cruelly, she discovered too late that her B standard time would have been sufficient. If injuries didn't spoil the plot, then there was always a technicality to do the job.

Disaster struck again when Rio 2016 rolled around. This time, she had enjoyed an injury-free run-in. Mentally and physically, she was in good shape. In April, at an invitation tournament, she recorded a time just two seconds shy of the coveted qualifying mark. Surely, this was the Sligo athlete's turn. But fate decreed differently. A hamstring injury intervened and as time ran out one final bid was mounted to reach the required standard.

A local athletics coach, Dermot McDermott, had a brainwave. Two weeks before the cut-off date for Rio qualification he organised a special track event at IT Sligo in the hope Mary would finally get over the line. A massive crowd of well-wishers, young and old, turned up to roar her home, hell-bent on playing their part in making her the county's first female Olympian. It was within touching distance, but the effort ultimately proved futile.

Two weeks later, she had to pull out of the European Championships because of more worrying injury issues. It was time to face the unpalatable reality that she would never be an Olympian.

> That hurt. I'm not denying it. I wanted to run in the Olympics so badly. And while I'm proud of what I've achieved, I can never say I'm an Olympian. It took me a while to process that. I remember being at Mona McSharry's homecoming after she had done so well in Tokyo, and while I was crying tears of joy for her, part of me was saying 'oh my God, imagine if that was me'.

The hurt manifested itself in periods of lonely reflection. Looking back, Mary concedes a hint of depression and anxiety began to invade her mindset.

> There were days when I really didn't want to get out of bed. There was self-examination, feeling sorry for myself. Why did I have to get all those injuries? Then you feel pressure from sponsors to get out there, to be visible.
>
> And nobody really understands the hurt, because they haven't seen the sacrifice. People might see you in a race, but they have no idea about the months and years of training, gym work, recovery, up to 100 miles a week running, training. And then an injury puts an end to it all.
>
> Luckily, I come from a great family, always there to support me. Tough love, if you like. They got me through those dark times.

The reflection amounted ultimately to a straight choice:

> I'm in my 30s. Do I want to continue to chase a dream that may never be realised, continue all those sacrifices, or do I want a family? Is having a child more important than the Olympics? My mindset began to shift. I knew the answer.

Along with her partner, Sligoman Mark Smith, himself a noted athlete, Mary Cullen's greatest challenge was about to unfold.

In September 2018, during a holiday in Portugal with her sister, she began to experience deafness in her right ear. The search for answers included a series of tests locally and in Dublin, before a range of ultrasounds, biopsies, scans and scopes confirmed the worst: she was suffering from a rare form of head and neck cancer.

Mary takes up the story:

> As an athlete, I was so in tune with the rhythm of my body. I instinctively knew there was something very wrong about this. I looked my doctor straight in the eye and asked: 'are you considering cancer here?'
>
> Further tests brought confirmation of what we already knew. My godmother and dad had both died from cancer, so that added to the worry.
>
> But the big concern for me was that I was eight weeks pregnant. Nobody apart from Mark knew. My priority was the baby. I couldn't get the necessary PET and CT scans to establish if or how much the cancer had spread because I didn't want my baby exposed to radiation. Although surgery carried a risk of miscarriage if I bled too much, they said it had to be done. Both lives were at risk otherwise.

So, on 15 December 2019, the tumour was removed through her nose. There was also need for neck dissection, where the surgeon literally slit her throat to remove 90 lymph nodes from her head and neck.

Further treatment would be required, she was told, because a cancerous node still resided menacingly beside her brain stem. But, by now, only her unborn baby mattered.

> My only thought was to get as healthy a gestation period for my baby as possible and then I could deal with whatever I needed to do for my

> own safety. So, I postponed treatment until the baby was born, and we didn't have a clue whether the cancer was growing in that time. It was a balancing act, but the baby was the priority.

Ellis Frankie Smith arrived into the world in May 2020, a few weeks early but weighing in at a healthy five pounds.

Now, the new mum was able to resume her cancer battle. Accompanied by Mark, her mum and the newborn baby, Mary travelled to Essen in Germany for proton radiation and chemotherapy. It was an exhausting regime, radiation every day for seven weeks and four hours of chemotherapy once a week.

Typical of the warrior she has always been, she continued running for the first four weeks.

> Maybe it was an act of defiance. I wasn't going to let it beat me, so I ran every day for the first four weeks, four or five miles just to keep me sane. I had to give in for the last two weeks, though. It finally floored me.

She's convinced the resilience which fuelled her world class athletics career dragged her through the worst period of her life.

> As an athlete, it's all about setting goals, doing the hard work to get a good return, recovering from setbacks. So that's how I approached the cancer. I took it day by day, did whatever they said would make me better, and kept focused on getting through.

She is now three years post-surgery and although regular check-ups will be required for some time yet, she can sense the finishing line.

These days, she works as a Special Needs Assistant at the Mercy College secondary school, where girls not even born when she was scorching Irish records get excited and inquisitive when the penny finally drops. She would regard it as a worthy legacy if her story could inspire them to do good things in their lives.

In the school's main concourse, there's a pictorial Hall of Fame, a monument to past pupils who've made their mark. Mary Cullen always smiles back at the image of herself beaming out from an old school photograph. Life is good. The loneliness of the long-distance runner has long since morphed into a contented, fulfilled young mother.

The daily eight mile run through the scenic beauty of her native terrain is both a nod to the past and a reach for the future. The leg muscles often burn, the breathing gets heavy, the road unforgiving, but she keeps going, keeps pushing herself. She's running away from the worst and towards the best.

"I always love a challenge," says the lady who's had more than her fair share.

Martin Gordon

"I'm not what happened to me, I'm what I chose to become"

The cruelty of sudden sight loss at just 17 years of age plunged Martin Gordon's world into utter darkness. But his life has been illuminated by awesome depths of resilience and an extraordinarily indomitable spirit which has propelled him to become one of the country's top athletes.

A tandem track sprinter, the Hazelwood native is officially the fastest cyclist in Ireland, having gone within tantalising seconds of claiming a bronze medal in the 1,000 metre time trial event at the Paralympics in Tokyo last year with his tandem pilot, Eamonn Byrne. The pair have also claimed silver in the tandem sprint at the UCI World Cup in London in 2018, and Martin is a realistic medal contender for the next Paralympics in Paris in 2024.

But behind the impressive statistics of Sligo's Paralympic hero is an inspirational story of a young man's refusal to wallow in self-pity, to courageously recover from a devastating body blow which would have floored most people his age, and to hone towering achievement from the most excruciating trauma.

On 15 June 2002, Martin went to sleep in a London hotel room 'a happy and healthy teenager'. He woke up blind the next day. His sight has never returned. It was the end of life as he knew it, but the beginning of an incredible journey. Not only has he become an elite athlete, but has skillfully navigated a path through university and law school to carve out a successful career in the legal profession. He has become a family man, too, sharing a Dublin home with his partner, Louise, and six-year-old daughter, Nora. He is the living embodiment of Swiss psychologist Carl Jung's pronunciation: "I'm not what happened to me, I'm what I chose to become."

He had suffered sight problems from early in life due to a rare complication associated with glaucoma but the prospect of complete blindness was never considered a danger. It was while on a visit to London for routine treatment that the worst happened, without warning and without reprieve. As he recalls:

> When it first happened, it was a case of sink or swim. They were the only choices. It would have been easier to sink but I chose to swim. And I was blessed that I had a very supportive family, great friends, and terrific backing from the school community at Sligo Grammar School. That made all the difference.
>
> It wasn't as if I'd been born blind. I'd seen the world, I'd seen my parents, my brother, my extended family. I'd played golf and rugby, I'd cycled through Hazelwood near my home. I'd often do my homework on a bench overlooking Lough Gill. What a wonderful life I had. Suddenly all that was snatched from me. Of course, I'd love to have it back, but I thank God I had those 17 years of full sight.
>
> I had to grow up very fast and mature years ahead of my peers. There's a certain sadness to that because I had to grow up before my time and I had to learn to take some severe body-blows. A 17-year-old shouldn't have to do that, and my parents, Ronnie and Margaret, shouldn't have had to deal with that trauma. But it was their amazing strength which carried me.

With the loyal assistance of his guide dog, Jake, who was by his side for eight years – the first of three Labradors who have been his essential guides – Martin obtained an impressive Leaving Cert at Sligo Grammar School, went on to do Legal Studies and Sociology at University College Galway, then to Trinity College and on to King's Inns law school, where he qualified as a barrister. He realised early on that education would be the key to unlocking a better future.

His university experience wasn't much different from any other student. He had the pressure of exams, a hectic social life, fun and games, no inhibitions or restrictions but there was one highly significant moment along the way, and it involved his faithful Jake.

Martin explains:

> Jake was lying on the floor in the canteen area in King's Inns while I was having coffee one afternoon when a very clumsy girl tripped over him. She came over to apologise and we got chatting, and twelve years later,

> Louise and I are still together and have our lovely daughter, Nora. It was the biggest favour Jake ever did for me.

He is refreshingly candid about the sensitivity of the heartbreak of having never seen his partner or their daughter.

> I have a mind's eye view of them. I know in my heart what they're like but it's not easy. However, I don't focus on not being able to see them, only on how lucky I am to have them in my life. My attitude never revolves around what I can't have. It revolves around enjoying and appreciating what I do have. Although she's only six, my daughter's concept of it is not about Daddy not being able to see her, rather it's about her seeing me live my life like everybody else and doing the things everybody else does. Her big thing is that her daddy is the fastest cyclist in Ireland.

Martin's cycling career was ignited by a 2007 tandem trek across Ireland from Mizen to Malin, a charity cycle to raise funds for the Irish Guide Dog Association, of which he has been a director for over five years.

On the same cycle in 2016, a conversation with strength and conditioning coach Conor Kennedy led to an introduction to Garda Eamonn Byrne, an established track sprinter who was to become Martin's tandem partner.

Together, they were selected for Ireland for the World Track Championships in Los Angeles in 2017 and the following year took sixth position at the Worlds, clocking the times necessary to secure a place on the Cycling Ireland high performance programme which opened the doors for valuable funding. In 2018 they won silver in the tandem sprint at the UCI World Cup in London. Targets were now firmly set on the Tokyo Paralympics.

> We went there with a reasonable shout of a medal, and we came within seconds of the bronze. Our time in Tokyo for the Kilo (1k time trial over four laps) was the fastest ever recorded by Irish cyclists, faster than any able-bodied cyclist. We would have been travelling an average of 60 kilometres an hour, peaking at 72 kilometres an hour, and between us generating 4,000 watts of power. It's such an adrenalin rush, one minute of ferocious speed. Tandem bikes are the fastest in the world. The speed is insane, but it's such an incredible buzz and so much fun.

Now 37 years old, his next target is the Paralympics in Paris in 2024, and although he'll have a new pilot as Eamonn Byrne has retired, he's quietly confident of getting amongst the medals.

> The margins are very tight. A matter of seconds or even fractions of seconds can make a difference. But we'll prepare well and give ourselves every chance. It's an honour to be able to represent my country, so I'll give it one more shot and see what happens.

Having dedicated so much of his life to his chosen sport, Martin is happy that the Paralympics is now being perceived on equal footing with the Olympic Games.

> The more exposure it gets the more people see us as genuine athletes. There's a growing awareness that there's no difference between the Olympics and Paralympics. They're both now THE GAMES. That's hugely encouraging. The reality for me is that I'm as much an Olympian as, say, Sonia O'Sullivan, and vice versa, and the same goes for all Paralympic athletes. That perception will grow as more events are held.

Outside the world of sport, where his daily job is as an in-house barrister for An Garda Síochána, he's not as convinced about the equality afforded disabled people, offering this forthright view:

> Ireland is a cruel country for people with disability. There is a discrimination against disabled people. Simple things like getting taxis or access to restaurants, for example, can be bad experiences. Employment figures for visually impaired people in Ireland are the lowest in the EU. That's not because people are uneducated or unable to work, it's because of a negative perception of people with disabilities. There's a lot of talk about equal opportunity, but a lot of time employers don't follow that through. It would be hard to prove that contention, of course, but it's definitely there. I'm not bitter about it, but I am a realist.

Realistic enough to know, too, that the backdrop to his story will always be that fateful day in June 2002.

> What happened that day was the most intimate thing in my life, for myself and for my parents and family. I know it's a background and a context for what happened afterwards, but that day is mine and mine alone.
>
> Of course, there are days when it's utterly frustrating and days when there are challenges. Days when I know I just have to get on with it.

> There's always the potential for it to be a dark place, but I've crammed so much into my life and I have so much to be thankful for. I'm at peace with it.

Martin Gordon, the fastest cyclist in Ireland, is definitely not what happened to him; he is, unquestionably, what he chose to become. And what he has become is something truly special.

Bridie Nicholson

Double transplant recipient became world champion

She once had a passing encounter with Muhammad Ali. Had he known who was standing next to him, the greatest boxer in the history of the sport might well have recognised in her the living embodiment of one of his famous motivational quotes.

Ali once declared: "Suffer now and live the rest of your life as a champion."

The woman with whom he shared a lift in a Durban hotel in 2013 could have told him a thing or two about the agony and ecstasy of that monumental journey.

A double pancreas and kidney transplant recipient, 61-year-old Bridie Nicholson has faced adversity with stoic defiance, battered it into the ground, and emerged as an all-conquering European and world champion at the Transplant Games.

The courageous Sligowoman, who acquired a prosthetic limb in2022 after the amputation of her right leg, refuses to compromise her lifelong adherence to the power of positivity, a trait which has seen her carve out a spectacular medal-laden career.

Raised in Calry with her six siblings, she inherited a love of community from her parents, Kate and the late Paddy. They were both at the core of everything in the Parish. Her father was a driving force behind many local initiatives while her mother was an active member of the Irish Countrywomen's Association, excelling in craftwork.

There was a strong sporting tradition in the family too. Her grand-uncle Tom Fox won a gold medal at a national athletics event in 1903. Her brothers, Leo and Roger, were also accomplished athletes.

Despite developing diabetes as a child, which required daily insulin injections, Bridie shared the family's passion for sport. She was a high achiever academically too. After completing a data processing and computer course at Sligo IT, she began writing computer programmes in several languages. She secured a job at Sligo Library – a position she held for 37 years, becoming a familiar and popular personality with service users.

Her life changed forever when she suffered kidney failure in her mid-30s. She was on dialysis for three years before undergoing a double kidney and pancreas transplant at Beaumont Hospital. As she recalls:

> The double transplant literally gave me a new life. I felt as if I had climbed Mount Everest.
>
> Even in the tough days when I was very ill, I refused to let things get me down. I vividly remember lying in my bed and watching the sun streaming into the room and just thinking how wonderful it was to be alive.

Gripped by an almost obsessive desire to conquer the difficulties ill-health had visited upon her, Bridie rekindled her love of walking, a pursuit which gave her so much pleasure during her carefree childhood. Day by day, week by week, she stepped up her training regime. The prospect of representing Ireland in the Transplant Games was a powerful stimulant.

She made her debut at the Games in the European Championships in Ljubljana, Slovenia, in 2004, competing in the 1500m walk. It was an uplifting experience. She didn't manage to finish among the medals but she revelled in the competitive environment, testing herself against transplant athletes from all over Europe, witnessing at first hand the bravery of her opponents, forging improbable friendships which would last forever. She was fascinated by the culture and traditions of the host country too. She promised herself she would absorb all there was to know about every country she visited during her career.

Much as she enjoyed the peripheral trappings of the various championships, the competitive streak was never more than thinly disguised.

When she was selected for the World Games in Thailand in 2007, she embraced the challenge with fervent enthusiasm. She prioritised Pétanque as her number one sport. Luckily, Sligo County Council had developed a

Pétanque course at Mitchell Curley Park close to Sligo town and this became her personal training camp.

"I practically lived there," she laughs.

The international coaches suggested she had an outside chance of making the semi-finals. Bridie's aspirations were more ambitious. She struck gold, defeating more experienced opponents from Australia and the Phillippines on a relentless march to glory.

The sense of achievement was overwhelming. She reflected on the dark days and the long, weary road to recovery after her double transplant. She thought about her donor. How that person's selfless organ donation had given her the chance to live a full and active life. She was a world champion. It would never have been possible without her donor, the medical experts at Beaumont Hospital, the care of former Dublin GAA star David Hickey, who was head of transplantation at the hospital, and the support of her family.

All those things crossed her mind as she stood on the medal podium. The Irish flag fluttered in the breeze and the national anthem rang out triumphantly. She felt she would dissolve in tears.

> I was overjoyed. Winning a gold medal for Ireland was beyond my wildest dreams. It was as much an honour for my donor as it was for me. And I remembered all the people at home who had given me so much love and support. I knew they would be so proud of what I achieved. It was all very emotional.

Bridie assumed the role of 'golden girl' again at the World Games in Durban, South Africa, 2013, this time winning the Pétanque pairs championship with her partner, Catherine Murphy from Cork.

The Sligo woman was among the medals at the European Championships in Finland in 2016, claiming a gold in the Pétanque doubles, silver in the individual Pétanque competition and bronze in darts.

Throughout her career, Bridie was happy to take on board the advice of the high-profile motivational speakers who turned out to support the Transplant Games athletes before their departure to the major championships. She remembers inspirational contributions from GAA personalities Alan Brogan, Jim Gavin and Mickey Harte; soccer star Niall Quinn; and athlete Eamonn Coughlan.

But the most restorative tonic she ever received came from the childish affection of her young nephew, Eoin, following her double transplant all those years ago. She was out for a short walk on the lonely roads near her home. The little boy spotted her in the distance and cried out to his mum: "We can stop praying for Auntie Bridie now. She's out walking and she's doing fine."

"That gave me such a lift," she confirms. "It's one of those lovely memories that stay with you forever. It meant more than all the medals."

Another treasured memory is a visit to Áras An Uachtaráin where she met President Mary McAleese.

Bridie's transplanted kidney failed in 2017 and she went back on dialysis. Her right leg was amputated in 2021. But as she asserts,

> I don't regard myself as disabled. I am abled. I lost one of my limbs, not my brain. I get wonderful assistance from the Centre for Independent Living in Sligo, and I have a very supportive family. I have a lot of interesting hobbies, such as reading, crafts and photography. And I've been writing a diary about my life. I try to be as positive as possible.

She believes the Transplant Games play an important role in highlighting organ donation.

> It's vital that the message goes out to those on the difficult journey of organ failure that there is light at the end of the tunnel. Hopefully, more people will be encouraged to carry donor cards and consider organ donation. The impact of my transplant was enormous. It opened a whole new world for me. There's always hope.

Bridie's indomitable spirit is a glowing beacon of inspiration.

Chris O'Donnell

From fledgling soccer star to Olympics finalist

The Japan National Stadium, Tokyo, 31 July 2021.

Chris O'Donnell from Grange in North Sligo is on the starting line for the 4 x 400m mixed relay final. Not just an Olympian but an Olympic finalist.

Life is what happens to you when you're making other plans, according to John Lennon. O'Donnell would surely concur.

When he was a young boy, he dreamed of being a professional footballer, thrilling an adoring audience at the Aviva Stadium or the fabled arenas across Europe with his spellbinding skill. He would make the breakthrough at his beloved Sligo Rovers, earn a move to a top club in England, graduate to the Irish team and set about conquering the world.

As he lined up alongside teammates Cillín Greene, Sophie Becker and Phil Healy in Tokyo, it felt like he was living a dream, only not the one of his boyhood fantasies.

The Irish team was on the cusp of history. The country had enjoyed many celebrated moments of outstanding achievement at the Olympics but this was the first time a mixed relay team had reached a final. Now four young sprinters were ready to earn a treasured place among the elite of modern-day athletics.

Whatever transpired, they had already re-written the story of Ireland's Olympic record. Running in the final against the most powerful nations in sprinting was a bonus. The real victory was earned the previous evening with a stunning semi-final performance.

Roll back the saga a little further to the qualifiers in Poland in 2021. Emerging from the soul-destroying uncertainty unleashed by the Covid 19 pandemic, the Irish team sent out an emphatic statement of intent. The team defied all expectations, finished in fourth place and announced their arrival as serious contenders.

Confirmation of the make-up of the team for Tokyo would come later. O'Donnell took nothing for granted. It wasn't until three weeks before the Games that he got the nod. There was a mixture of relief and elation at the news.

The intervention of Covid delayed the qualifiers, pushed the Olympics back a year. There was frustration and uncertainty. For a while, there was a real possibility that the Games mightn't take place at all. As the Sligo athlete admits:

> It was demoralising not knowing what was happening from week to week. The challenge was to stay focused and keep training as hard as ever. It was crucial to be ready whenever things stabilised.

Despite their superb effort in the qualifiers, the Irish mixed-relay team was slightly underrated going into the Olympics. But the athletes were confident of doing well, happy to operate under the radar and spared the pressure which comes with high expectation.

"We each set a target of achieving a PB in the semi-final," reveals O'Donnell. "That's exactly how it turned out. It was enough to qualify us for the final. It was an extraordinary achievement."

The scheduling of the final the following day left little time for rest or preparation. Also, the semi-final outcome generated a degree of controversy when the USA and the Dominican Republic were disqualified on technicalities. This led to appeals and the disqualified countries were re-admitted. It was messy and chaotic. It didn't directly impact the Irish team but it created a distraction they could have done without.

For young athletes still high on the adrenalin of their semi-final effort, it was a step too far.

> We found it hard to sleep after the semi-final. The emotion of it all was a bit overwhelming. It caught up with us. Still, we finished eighth of nine in the final. It meant we were eighth best in the world, an amazing achievement.

For 23-year-old O'Donnell, it was the high point of a stunning odyssey which had taken him from the mud-splattered pitches in the local soccer league, through a glittering domestic athletics career to the very pinnacle of elite sport.

The context is interesting. He was a relative latecomer to athletics, introduced to running more by accident than design. Once he discovered a talent for sprinting, it required relentless determination and selfless sacrifice to maximise his potential. It was his obsessive devotion to the sport which set him apart.

The modest soccer pitches dotted around Sligo were where the dreams of a sporting career were fleshed out. Inheriting a love of football from his father, Philip, and with the encouragement of mum, Heidi, he enthusiastically embraced the beautiful game, lining out for local team Benbulben Rangers. He played on the wing. There were many weary full-backs on opposing teams who would testify to his blistering pace.

The North Sligo youngster soon caught the attention of the Sligo–Leitrim selectors, earning a place on the League representative team for the prestigious Kennedy Cup in 2012. His soccer coaches, Maurice Monaghan, Ryan Casey and Marcel Gordon, suggested specialised speed training at his local athletics club in Grange.

Up to that point, O'Donnell had never considered running as a sporting option, but he went along with the idea, dropping into the North Sligo Athletic Club once or twice a week. Almost immediately, his explosive speed on the track marked him out as something special. Before long, he was winning Connacht medals and earning a place on the Irish under-16 schools' team. He recalls:

> I loved soccer, but I couldn't ignore what was happening on the athletics side of things. Suddenly, I had a big decision to make. I would have been thinking more about a football career, but the pathway just wasn't there at the time.
>
> When I initially took up running on the advice of my soccer coaches, my plan was to give it a year or two. It wasn't a long-term plan but then I got on the Irish team and there was no going back.

Rosemary McGowan was an instructive coach at North Sligo AC and later O'Donnell came under the tutelage of former national 800m champion Roddy Gaynor.

Gaynor, who excelled on the track during his own career, winning the national 800m title in 1982, was well-qualified to spot untapped talent and quickly concluded the young Grange runner was something out of the ordinary.

He proved an invaluable mentor, not just in encouraging and coaching O'Donnell in the art of running but also introducing him to the equally important aspects of appropriate lifestyle, dietary considerations and proper rest and sleep schedules.

Gaynor's faith in his protégé, not to mention his coaching expertise, gave O'Donnell the direction his career needed. Drawing on the enthusiastic encouragement of his part-time coach, the young athlete quickly transitioned from a somewhat reluctant runner into a confident sprinter, equipped with the talent and skillset to make a telling impact at national and international level.

He registered eye-catching victories on the track. In 2017, he broke the Irish record for the Under 20 400m at the European Championships in Italy and followed up with three senior national 400m titles in a row, 2018, 2019 and 2020.

His impressive form in competition was matched by a strict adherence to a healthy lifestyle:

> I've never been much of a social animal. Diet, sleep, recovery techniques, discipline. These are the priorities in my life. It's all about giving me the best chance possible of making the most of my talent. In over eight years of competitive running, I've never had a single muscle injury. That's the payback for the way I live.

Becoming an Olympian defines O'Donnell now. He shares the honour with his neighbour, Mona McSharry, the exceptional young swimmer who also captivated the heart of the nation with her superb performances in Tokyo.

Whatever happens in the future, treasured recollections of the Olympics will reside in a special corner of his memory bank. He'll reflect on the glory of reaching an athletics final and of the extraordinary coincidence of fate which brought two young athletes from a small rural village in Sligo to the epicentre of global sport.

They shot the breeze on a few occasions in the Olympic Village. The talk was of home and the generosity of the people of Grange and further afield. They were proud of each other, proud of their home place. They both understood they were at the heart of a novel story. The unspoken aspiration was that there would be many more adventures ahead of them.

"Athletes from the other countries thought it was amazing that two Olympians had grown up in the same small village in Ireland," reports O'Donnell. "It was nice that it got so much recognition."

The North Sligo AC sprinter continued to burn up the track in 2022. He became the second fastest Irishman over 400m, when he recorded a personal best 45.26 at the Continental Tour Silver meeting in Madrid. Only Irish record holder David Gillick has registered a faster time. He followed that up by winning the Irish national 400m title for a fourth time.

Coached by renowned Swede Benke Blomkvist, O'Donnell continued his breathtaking form at the World Athletics Championships in Oregon, USA. He helped the Irish 4 x 400m mixed relay team to qualify for the final, where they finished a respectable eighth overall, before producing eye-catching displays in the individual events.

He finished fourth in the 400m heats in a time of 46.01, reaching the semi-finals as one of the fastest runners outside automatic qualification. At the end of a demanding week, he somehow conjured up another heroic performance to take seventh place in the final.

O'Donnell has been studying at the famous Loughborough University, close to Leicester in the UK for the past few years. The College, which is the base for the British athletics and swimming national training centre, boasts a glittering list of high-achievers among its graduates, including Seb Coe and Paula Radcliffe. He's studying for a degree in sports science.

Now, everything is geared towards the Paris Olympics in 2024.

> That's the target. This time around, my family and friends will be able to make the trip. They missed out on Tokyo so it would be wonderful to have them in Paris if I qualify.

Warriors Run

Landmark in county's sporting calendar

It germinated, as a lot of good ideas do, in a pub, over a few pints. Knowledgeable locals in Sonny Bree's popular hostelry in Strandhill were discussing the best way to climb to the top of Knocknarea, which towered above them literally across the road. A German tourist overheard the conversation and wagered that his 17-year-old son could scale the mountain quicker than any of them. So off he went, this brash young boy scout, hopping over the back wall of the pub and scurrying up the face of the rugged mountain in a staggering time of 19 minutes. Peering through the back window, the pint-drinkers watched in gobsmacked admiration, like a scene from Killinaskully. Something was stirring.

Nestled at the foot of Knocknarea, the reputed burial place of the legendary Queen Maeve of Connacht, the bustling Strandhill seaside village is steeped in legend, mythology and history. Whether the tale of the mountain-conquering German youth belongs in any of those categories is debatable, but it planted the seeds for what has become a landmark event in the county's sporting calendar, an institution in its own right, which draws over 1,000 competitors and up to 5,000 spectators to Strandhill on the last Saturday of every August.

The Warriors Run, first contested in 1985 as part of a local festival aimed at boosting tourism figures, has become one of the country's foremost athletics events, attracting runners from all over Ireland and many parts of the world, as an incongruous mix of elite and recreational runners converge to follow in the footsteps of Queen Maeve's ancient warriors.

The gruelling 15km run takes competitors from the cannon gun at the beachfront in Strandhill to the top of Knocknarea, around Queen Maeve's Cairn at the summit and back to the scenic starting point. Classified as a multi-terrained race, 9km of the route are on paved roads, but it is the middle six kilometres which give the event its real bite. As the organising committee PRO, Micki Murray, explains:

> For the uninitiated, a 15km race might seem relatively easy, but that's not the case with the Warriors Run. The middle six kilometres include a 700-foot climb through fields, loose gravel, unsurfaced and heather paths. At its steepest incline on the way up, even the most professional athletes have to slow to a walk before bracing themselves to face the equally daunting descent, running downhill across often slippy and potentially dangerous slopes.

Initially conceived as a road and hill running race, and one of the first of its kind in the country, the inaugural event in June 1985, took its 160 competitors from the beachfront to the mountain top.

While the early races finished at Maeve's tomb, competitors and spectators soon began to request even more excitement, so the course was extended to return to the starting point at the beachfront. More challenging for participants and enhanced accessibility for spectators, the Warriors Run has become synonymous with Strandhill summers and a major tourist attraction in its own right. Its 5,000 spectators, crammed into the village in a carnival-like atmosphere, make it the single most popular event in the county. As Murray confirms:

> Its popularity has grown to such an extent that each year runners from around Ireland and the world vie to gain a place in the limited race field. In the early years, runners could just rock up on the day, but now they have to pre-book their place and we're always sold out months in advance. For safety reasons, we have to put a limit of 1,200 participants. There's always a waiting list.

While the warriors are not as fast as our 19-minute German friend – it is a much longer course these days – there have been some highly impressive times recorded over the years. Usually, the winner is home in under the hour mark. Kenya's Josphat Boit from the Clonliffe Harriers club posted one of the fastest times on record when winning the 25th anniversary event in 53.04 in 2009. World champion mountain runner, Kerry's John Lenihan, is the record holder for most wins, being first across the line from 1985 to 1989.

The stragglers, meanwhile, normally droop past the finishing line about two-and-a-half hours after they set off.

"If they're not home by then we send out the mercy mission to give them a lift home," quips Murray.

While records show the event has attracted competitors from the US, Canada, the UK, Germany and Spain, local runners have always been hugely supportive, too. Local winners include Lucy Brennan, Damien McSharry, Danny Hannon, Catherine Bradley, Gary Higgins, Seamus Somers, Marie McCambridge, and Emmett Dunleavy, while Turlough Conway has featured regularly as the first local across the line. Well-known local traffic warden Tony Fox has the distinction of competing in most Warriors Run events since its inception.

The first local male and female home are presented with perpetual trophies named in honour of the event's founders, the late Pat Curley and Tom Staunton. Little could those innovators have known back in 1985 that their creation would become such a phenomenal event, destined for a place amongst Sligo's sports legends.

Basketball

Michael Bree

All Stars kid who became top professional

It is the soccer equivalent of Sir Alex Ferguson sitting in your front room, offering an enticing contract to join Manchester United's academy while showering your parents with serene assurances.

In the 'good' room in the Bree family home at Treacy Avenue in the Maugherboy area of Sligo, it wasn't a football legend delivering the soothing sales pitch, but one of America's top collegiate basketball coaches with a reputation as awesome as any top-notch soccer manager.

A dozen Coach of the Year awards and over 30 major titles to his name, Bob McKillop is an astute fisher of talent. Over 30 years as coach of North Carolina's Division One college team, Davidsons Wildcats, he has spread his net not only throughout his native America but in less likely waters such as Turkey, Croatia, Sierra Leone and Nigeria. Now, he is sitting in a council housing estate in Sligo, offering a skinny 17-year-old Summerhill College student the opportunity of a lifetime.

Listening intently, with the giddy excitement of a child on his first visit to Santa, Michael Bree can scarcely believe what he's hearing. Upstairs, his bedroom walls are plastered with posters of his basketball idols. While most of his friends swooned to the artistry of Keane or Cantona or Giggs, Bree only had eyes for Michael Jordan, Magic Johnson or Larry Bird. He'd catch what little there was of televised basketball on Channel 4 and devour whatever basketball magazines and newspapers he could get hold of. He knew all there was to know about the NBA, its quaintly named teams and its larger-than-life superstars. He vowed this is what he wanted his future to look like.

Now, with his Leaving Cert just completed, he is being offered a four-year scholarship worth $24,000 a year at one of America's most elite sports and academic colleges, becoming the first Irishman ever to be given such a deal.

But his mum, Rita, isn't so sure. Michael is her 'baby', the youngest of seven children she'd reared with her husband, Pádraig. Two of her daughters had already emigrated and were settled in New York and New Hampshire, but her mother's intuition is gnawing at her. Was Michael too young, too shy, lacking the wherewithal for this momentous step into the unknown? She gave McKillop the type of cross-examination normally reserved for tense courtroom battles.

Bree can afford to laugh now at his mother's reticence on that fateful night in 1996. Now a parent of two young children, he appreciates the parental concern McKillop encountered but is supremely relieved that the coach's charm and easy hustle won the day.

> I vividly recall the conversation. This top coach had flown all the way from America to offer me a dream come true, but Mum gave him a bit of a grilling. She just wanted to be sure that I'd be safe and that I'd be looked after, that I'd get a good education and that there would be something at the end of it. Natural worries, really. But what impressed her, and myself at the time, was how honest Bob was with us. He made it clear all he was offering was an opportunity. The rest was up to me. Mum was also very straight with him, and for years after, he would always ask me how she was doing.

The sealing of the deal was the springboard for a remarkable journey, taking the Sligo youngster through four successful years on the Division One American College circuit with Davidsons Wildcats, onto a ten-year professional playing career in Europe, degrees in Economics and Sociology, and his current job as programme director with the Swedish National Basketball Academy. He has played for and captained his country at every level from under-16 to senior. He is not only Sligo's most illustrious basketballer, but is generally regarded as one of the best ever to come out of Ireland.

Growing up, he lived almost directly opposite the Merville Youth Centre, so access to sport was never a problem, and he showed an early aptitude for both soccer and Gaelic football, representing Merville in the soccer leagues and St Mary's in GAA. But his older twin brothers, Paschal and Robert, had found a niche with the All-Stars Basketball Club, and that's where his heart lay. He recounts:

> I'd say I fell in love with basketball as early as six years old. Basketball was big in Sligo at the time, and the All Stars had great coaches like Monty Monaghan and John McGowan. Great people. They would have been early influences.

Tall, lean and lightning-fast, Bree played as an elegant and fearless point guard, the 'playmaker' or 'quarter-back', who made things happen, controlled the pace of a game, and chipped in with some sensational scores. His prodigious talent shone like a beacon in an under-19 international tournament in Portugal, when Ireland unexpectedly reached the semi-final. He won the tournament's Most Valuable Player (MVP) award and earned a place at the Nike Camp in Paris, an annual showcase for the best 70 players in Europe.

> Everything changed after that. I'd been planning to go to Florida on an exchange programme organised by Summerhill College, but suddenly I had about 16 offers of scholarships from America. It was crazy. Although it was something I always wanted, it came out of the blue.

And so, in July 1997, he found himself in the college town of Davidson in North Carolina, the first Irish player on a Division One basketball scholarship, a fact which barely troubled him. The new and strange environment wasn't much of a problem either.

> Of course, it was difficult leaving home. We're a very close family, and I was homesick for about three months, and I always knew I could go home at any time with no regrets. But I wanted to stick it out, this was my dream, and after the first year I was quite at home really. Davidson is a small enough town, very affluent, lovely, relaxed way of life. It was relatively easy for me to adapt, and people both inside and out of college were very accepting and accommodating.

The basketball court presented different challenges, however. By his own admission, his physique at the time was 'skin and bone'. He was at least two stone lighter than he needed to be, and while his natural skill and intelligent play proved invaluable, he was often betrayed by his slight frame. So academic pursuits were regularly spiced with intensive gym work. By his fourth and final year, his unwavering self-belief, allied to relentless hard work, was rewarded with the college's MVP.

Bree's decision to opt for Davidsons, with its 6,000-seater stadium, its Division One NCAA status, prime time television and *Sports Illustrated* exposure, was made deliberately because it offered a shot at an NBA career. But maturity brought with it the realisation that the dream, while tantalisingly close, was just out of reach. As he admits:

> Even though I was 6 foot tall, I was small compared to other players, and I was maybe knocked off the ball more easily than I should have been. So, there was a lot of gym work and I did develop physically. But my game was never about physicality, and there are some things you just can't control. There comes a certain point where you know that while you're a very good player, that level of physicality will always be beyond you.

After graduation, the Sligoman targeted a professional career in the rarified air of European basketball. He became a bit of a drifter, chasing the next contract, striving to earn a living from the sport he loved. His first engagement was three months with the Beauvais club in France, followed by a further two months with Spanish club Rosalía, based in Santiago De Campostella, before signing a three-year contract with top Bundesliga club ULM Ratiopharm. One-year deals followed in Sweden and Poland.

When recurring knee injuries brought a premature end to his playing career at the age of 30, Bree turned his attention to coaching. He returned to America to become assistant coach at NBA D-League team, Bakersfield Jam in Los Angeles, a feeder club for the LA Lakers and LA Clippers. If his dream of playing in the NBA had failed to materialise, here he was now preparing youngsters for their shot at the big time. It was, he reports, a job which brought him terrific satisfaction.

Married to college sweetheart Jamye, an accomplished sprinter and soccer player, and with two young children, Mikaela and Cillian, it was time to put down roots.

The family opted for a return to the Swedish town of Kinna where, for the last seven years, Bree has been working as the progamme director with the RIG Mark Swedish Basketball Academy, coaching the country's elite boys and girls players, passing on the lessons and experiences gleaned from his own adventurous career. As he explains:

> I've earned a comfortable living from the game, and my current job keeps me involved at a professional level. But it's also about giving something back, and if I can help young players to become better at their game and help them develop as young adults then that's as much as I could hope for.

He is a regular visitor to his native Sligo, where he always makes time to catch up with old pals, sip a few beers and maybe take in a game. He also conducts training camps for local youngsters, perhaps seeing in them a glimpse of the skinny young lad with a head full of dreams and dynamite in his sneakers. And he harbours the hope that if a top coach comes calling someday, their mums will listen, just as his did.

***

Basketball has been played in Sligo since the early 1960s, with Summerhill College teams making an early impact by winning both the junior and senior Connacht titles in 1962. The following year, Joe Palmer became the county's first basketball international when selected on the national under-15 squad. Other prominent personalities in those early years included Summerhill and Sligo Boys club players John McGowan, Stan Burns, Jim Eccles, and Brian 'Boots' O'Hara, who were members of the Sligo minor team which won the Connacht Championship for three successive years in the mid-60s.

Sligo All-Stars was formed in 1965 under the inspirational leadership of American coach Tom O'Brien. Shortly afterwards, Stan Burns became the first Sligo player to be capped at senior level by Ireland, as the club became one of the most dominant basketball forces in the country. Throughout the 60s and 70s, more than 20 players were capped for Ireland at every level from juvenile to senior. Other senior internationals included Tom Hickey, who played professionally in England for Crystal Palace, the late John McGowan, Gerry Monaghan and Anthony Cronnolly, while a crop of underage internationals include Cillian Gallagher, Philip Hamilton, Jack Moran and Oisin O'Reilly.

The club also has a proud record in the ladies' game, where Therese Kiernan and Louise Harte have been stalwarts for many years. Ladies internationals include Lorainne Dolan, Stephanie O'Reilly and Bernice Beirne.

Dedicated administrators whose selfless work has kept the club alive for over 50 years include Brendan Crowne, Francis Rodgers, Bernard Brennan, Fergal Kelly, John Mulligan, Jim Lawlor and Glen Monaghan.

The club currently has over 400 players and 14 teams at all age levels. Its senior team, EJs All-Stars, won promotion to the National Super League in 2022 as well as reaching the National League final, under the tuition of head coach Shane O'Meara, while the under-20 team made it a notable double by reaching their league final. An indication of the growing interest in basketball locally is that the All-Stars were the best supported team at the national finals in the National Basketball Arena in Tallaght that year while their home games at the Mercy College gym regularly attract crowds of multiple hundreds.

A major success in local ladies basketball occurred in the early 1970s with the ground-breaking success of the Mercy College team. They won the European Cadette Championship in 1971 and a year later lifted the European Senior Championship in Maastricht, Holland, defeating Belgium 57–42 in the final. The heroic squad included Barbara Kielty, Collette Kielty, Ann McLoughlin, Ann Keaveney, Catherine Foley, Martha Kivlehan, Jennifer Cawley, RoseAnn Barr and Geraldine Mannion; and coach Tom O'Brien.

Boxing

Alan and Stephen Reynolds

Punching with panache

Alan Reynolds will never forget the embarrassment of his first experience in a boxing ring. He was seventeen years old and possessed neither the discipline nor physicality for the gruelling demands of the sport.

He'd seen his older brother, Stephen, come from nowhere to win a Connacht title and thought he'd like some of the action.

He had a job in Sligo town and would often skip along to the St Joseph's Boxing Club in Ballytivnan after work to get a lift home.

One day, he plucked up the courage to have a sparring match with one of the young lads in the club.

"I hadn't a clue what I was letting myself in for," he recalls with more than a hint of dismay. "I was a heavy smoker at the time. I was out on my feet after about thirty seconds. I got absolutely battered. My initial reaction was that I was never going back there again. It was humiliating."

He says he needed some direction in his life at the time. He was often subjected to bullying among his peers and lacked self-esteem. He was lost in admiration for his brother and wondered if boxing might offer him redemption.

Mercedes Taaffe, a former European kickboxing champion, was coaching the boxers at the St Joseph's Club. She was one of the best in the country. Stephen was the stable star. Maybe his younger brother had the heart of a fighter too. She'd take him on, push him as hard as she could, see if she could transform the rough diamond into an all-conquering gem.

Alan was up for the challenge. An easy-going and passive personality outside the ring, he developed into a merciless warrior inside it. Ambition replaced ambivalence. Like his brother before him, he was hot-wired for the top. The Reynolds boys were ready to rumble.

Stephen had a head start, although he too was a relative latecomer to the sport. He says he stumbled into it more by accident than design. There was no tradition of boxing in the family.

Growing up in Ballinacarrow in South Sligo, the brothers, along with their siblings, Kenny, Debbie and Karen, dabbled a bit in a few sports and their parents, Kenneth and Helen, encouraged them in any pursuit they chose.

There was always great excitement in the family when the annual Community Games finals came around every Summer. Alan, a skinny and athletic kid, was a bit of a flyer. He qualified for the national finals a few times, even won a couple of medals in the sprints. But Karen was the real star. She won a gold medal at Mosney one year.

Stephen remembers how proud they all were when Karen came up with the gold. There was a bit of a fuss and her photograph was in the local paper.

Stephen and Alan would later steal the headlines locally and nationally for their incredible boxing feats – they won a stunning total of twelve senior national titles between them during a phenomenal run of success in the 1990s and 2000s – but there was little hint of such awesome achievement in their teenage years.

"We were carefree young men," admits Stephen. "Smoking, drinking, going to dances. All the stuff young lads of our age were into. Sport wasn't on the radar, certainly not in a serious way."

The lightbulb moment for Stephen came when his friend Francis Durcan took up weight training. He explains:

> I couldn't believe the difference it made to him physically. It was just something that caught my imagination. I followed his lead, and the transformation was dramatic. I went from 13 stone to 18-and-a-half stone within a few years.

He did a course in weight and fitness instruction and was invited to do some coaching at a new boxing club in Sligo town. Based in a community hall at St Joseph's Church in Ballytivnan, it was part of a FAS scheme. The coach, Mercedes Taaffe, was an impassioned custodian of fledgling young talent.

On his first night at the club, Stephen marvelled at the enthusiasm of the young fighters and the brilliance of their coach.

"I was hooked straight away," he remembers. "I had no experience of boxing but once I saw the passion with which Mercedes coached those kids, and how they responded to her, I knew it was something I had to try."

He wasted no time in establishing himself as one of the big players on the regional and national circuit. In only his second fight at the National Stadium, he won the Irish Intermediate title and his third appearance at the famous venue resulted in victory in the senior super heavyweight division.

Alan observed his brother's remarkable progress. The prospect of carving out a similar trajectory in his own career was all the motivation he needed. As he admits:

> I was in awe of what Stephen achieved, the respect he earned from it, not just in boxing circles but in the wider community. Up to that point, I was a bit of a joker, never took anything too seriously. That all changed when I took up boxing.

The brothers were fiercely competitive, each using the other's success as a springboard for their own career. As Stephen says:

> We were good together. We'd often get into the ring and knock lumps out of each other. It was good fun but there was a serious side to it as well. We inspired each other. I don't think any of us would have achieved so much if we hadn't had that relationship between us.

Their commitment to training bordered on lunacy at times. It was all-consuming. Stephen explains:

> We couldn't get enough of it. Even on nights when there wasn't scheduled training at the club, we'd go down to Mercedes Taaffe's home place in Coolaney. We'd put together a makeshift ring and get in there for a few hours. Sometimes we would end up rolling around on the ground like two washed-up wrestlers, totally exhausted. Then we'd go home shattered and be back at it again the following evening.
>
> There was a healthy rivalry between us. Alan had fierce power, that was his greatest strength. I was a bit more tactical, a counter-attacker. We learned from each other. There was a great dynamic between us.

Despite their multiple titles, the brothers remained admirably grounded. As Alan insists:

> The success never went to our heads. To us, it was just doing something we loved. Sure, it was hard work and required massive commitment. We put our lives on hold for many years because boxing consumed

> everything. Success was the reward for all we put into the sport, but we took it all in our stride. We never got too far ahead of ourselves.

Stephen won five national senior championships, two at super heavyweight and three at heavyweight, while Alan's impressive haul of national titles included six senior light heavyweight crowns and one heavyweight title. Between 1999 and 2010, Alan fought in ten Irish senior finals, winning seven of them.

They both came agonisingly close to Olympic qualification.

Stephen could have claimed a place in the 2000 Sydney Olympics on a technicality when his Russian opponent turned up late for a qualification bout in Ukraine. The fight eventually went ahead, and the Russian boxer won decisively.

"That was as close as I came to making the Olympics but, in fairness, the better fighter qualified so I've no regrets," he says.

Alan's experience in the qualification bouts for Sydney was more controversial:

> I fought an Italian in Venice and most observers felt I won decisively. Unfortunately, the decision went against me. There's not much you can do when things happen outside your control. It was frustrating to say the least.

Domestically and internationally, the Ballinacarrow brothers represented their county and country with enormous pride. As Alan enthuses:

> Boxing took me all over the world. I put my foot in every ocean. It was like a drug. You were always looking for something more, whether it be national or European titles or Olympic qualification. There was always something to aim for. Even now, I'm still addicted to it. I was seventeen years old when I had my first fight. I'm 44 now and I don't consider myself retired. I'm just taking a break.

After a decorated career on the amateur circuit, Stephen stepped into the professional ranks when he was 39 years old. He laughs:

> Some people thought I was crazy. I wanted to test myself at that level.

Those who doubted his sanity had cause to reassess their judgement. He impressively dismissed the challenge of Moses 'The Black Mamba' Matovu in his first pro fight before flooring a Lithuanian opponent four times on the way to a facile victory in his next outing. The swan song was a pulsating showdown with Declan Trainor, fifteen years his junior, in the Celtic Nations cruiserweight title fight in Belfast in 2013. Stephen triumphed in the sixth round. Battered, bruised but undefeated, he unlaced his gloves for the last time. It was the perfect finale to a compelling career.

The Ballinacarrow brothers forged success beyond their wildest expectations during a whirlwind adventure, and they put it all down to the influence of one person – Mercedes Taaffe.

Stephen insists:

> I'd never have taken up boxing if it wasn't for Mercedes. She was a wonderful role model, having enjoyed such a brilliant career in kick-boxing, and a fantastic coach. I owe everything to her.

Alan believes Taaffe's pioneering work in the early days of female boxing paved the way for the current crop of brilliant boxers, including Katie Taylor and Kellie Harrington. He declares:

> Mercedes was promoting female boxing when nobody wanted to know. Without her, there would be no Katie or Kellie. That's a fact.

Although they've hung up their gloves, Stephen and Alan are still active in boxing, running the Ballinacarrow Boxing club at a few locations in Sligo town and county. As Stephen confirms:

> It's wonderful to have the opportunity to pass on our knowledge and expertise to the next generation of young local boxers. Watching the joy on the faces of young fighters gives me as much satisfaction as anything I achieved in the ring. It's a privilege to still be involved in the sport.

Community Games

Ann Kelly

Bringing Games to the community

Most of the high achievers featured in this book were infused with a passion for sport through the local Community Games movement.

The Sligo Games, which celebrated their fiftieth birthday in 2022, are run by a network of selfless volunteers. Despite the ravages of the Covid-19 pandemic, they are as strong as ever, with 22 areas affiliated to the county association.

Few epitomise the steadfast commitment to the movement as much as Riverstown native Ann Kelly, who retired as county secretary in 2022 after 37 years of loyal service.

Along with John McGetrick, who has been an inspirational figure in the county for over six decades, Ann is synonymous with Community Games, and is regarded throughout the country as one of the most efficient and unsparing officials in the movement.

The first Sligo committee was formed on 24 April 1972, at a meeting in Kelly's Hotel in Sligo town. The first chairman was Fr Michael Donnelly, while Gerry Bourke took on the role of secretary with John McGetrick serving as treasurer.

Initially, most of the areas attracted to the new movement were from Sligo town and surrounding localities but soon the lure of the Games spread throughout the county. Within two years, over 20 areas were affiliated, among them Riverstown, where Ann and her late husband, Paddy, were among the founding members. Paddy was at the heart of community activity in the village and was particularly associated with Arrow Harps soccer club.

Ann's energy and meticulous organisational skills made her a perfect candidate for the county executive, but she managed to stay clear of any official role until the inevitable call to duty arrived in 1985.

She attended the Annual General Meeting with fellow Riverstown delegate Breege McKeon, and neither had ambition for high office. As Ann recalls, laughing:

> We actually hid in the toilet. We had no desire to join the executive but there wasn't a big queue forming to take any of the officer positions so we were eventually persuaded to step forward. I became secretary with Breege as my assistant. Little did I know I would be doing the job for 37 years.

Her reluctance to take the role was quickly replaced with almost obsessive dedication to the job. Ann confirms:

> I loved every minute of it. There were times when the workload was overwhelming, but I just kept the head down and got on with the job. I've always had a passion for sport and I enjoy working with children. The two combined in Community Games so it was a labour of love.

Sligo earned a reputation as one of the most progressive associations in the country. Many initiatives introduced in the county were taken on at national level.

> We led the way in terms of structure. Other counties saw how successful we were and followed suit. Sligo was the template for the rest of the country. The movement is hugely successful all over Ireland and Sligo can be proud of the role it played in establishing Community Games as the powerful force it is nationally.

At administrative level, many officers from Sligo have served with distinction at national level and the county also boasts a proud record of achievement across a range of sports.

> We've always tried to be innovative in our programme. GAA, soccer and athletics are always popular, but we've endeavoured to be as inclusive as possible. In the early years, fishing and show jumping were included in the Sligo Games and over the years the schedule has expanded to include activities such as model making and art. A lot of cultural

> disciplines have been added as well. The objective is to give as many children as possible the opportunity to take part in positive recreational activities. The fact we've achieved that in Sligo is our greatest success.

Several local sports stars came through the Community Games ranks to forge successful careers in their chosen disciplines. They are quick to acknowledge the influence of the Games in giving them a solid grounding in sport. As Ann explains:

> It's lovely to see kids who were involved in Community Games doing well in later life. A lot of them come back and pay their own tribute to the people involved. Aoife McDermott, the Irish rugby and basketball international, took time out from a busy schedule to present medals to the children at the Riverstown finals for example. That sort of connection is great. It highlights the value of Games to the local communities.

Ann is the essence of what volunteerism is all about. She's invested a lifetime of faithful work to the Games but insists she's got more in return than she ever contributed.

> I've made friends for life through my involvement with Community Games. I've had the opportunity to share some magical moments with young children and I've been able to pursue my personal passion for sport. You can't ask for much more than that.

Although officially retired, she continues to assist the county executive and runs a skittles team in the Riverstown area.

"It keeps me ticking over," she jokes.

Her love of sport was passed on to her children. Her son, Johnny, is an enthusiastic Community Games volunteer in Riverstown while his brother, Shay, is involved with Castlebar Celtic soccer club. Her daughter, Tanya, served as National Games Director with Community Games for a number of years.

Widely acknowledged as one of the county's most resourceful sports administrators, Ann deflects credit for the success of Community Games to the colleagues who have served with her over the years.

John McGetrick is renowned throughout the country for his outstanding contribution at local and national level for the past 50 years while an army of unsparing volunteers have kept the wheels well-oiled throughout county Sligo.

Among those who have served the Games with distinction are Ina Monaghan, Sr. Gabrielle, Maura McMoreland, Rosaleen Holland, Noreen

Jinks, Mary Leydon, Michael Curley, Anthony Leonard, Kay Crocock, Paddy Kearns, Martin Davey, Evelyn Gallagher, Margaret Bolton, Anne Taaffe, Noreen McDermott, Bernadette Melly, Tom O'Brien, Pete Cooney and Eileen Brennan.

There are many others in every area in the county who helped create a vibrant Community Games organisation which continues to be at the core of Sligo's sporting culture.

Cycling

Mark Scanlon

Cycle of success for world champion

Not even the lingering suspicion of unfulfilled potential can diminish the phenomenal career of Mark Scanlon, one the greatest sports stars Sligo has ever produced.

By the time of his premature retirement from professional cycling at the age of 27 in 2007, he had clocked up a staggering run of success which defined him as one of the genuine superstars of his era.

There are many shrewd judges of the cycling game who believe the Sligoman still had his best years ahead of him when he turned his back on the sport. Speculation regarding the heights he could have reached in one of the most demanding sports of all makes for interesting contemplation but what is in no doubt is his awesome record of achievement.

The shy young boy from Sligo town rose from the ranks of local race riding to become one of the outstanding personalities of his generation, claiming a string of coveted titles at national and international level along the way.

A breathtaking victory in the World Junior Championship in Holland in 1998 catapulted him to international fame, his heroic performance in the Tour De France in 2004 confirmed his status as one of the sport's leading competitors and his participation in the Athens Olympics the same year assured him of a special place in the annals of Sligo sporting history. He's one of only four Olympians from Sligo.

While those highlights illustrate the towering scale of his accomplishments, they are but a sparkling sample of just some of the classic performances he produced in an all-too brief career. At a time when cycling was devalued by a sinister narrative of wrongdoing and cynicism, Scanlon's inspiring story was an illuminating exception.

It all began on the streets of Cranmore, a proud working-class area on the edge of Sligo town. The council housing estate produced an impressive host of budding young sports stars. Mark Rossiter was signed by Sunderland; his brother, Ian, won a European youth soccer medal with Ireland; Alan Cawley got a move to Leeds United. Scanlon's brother, Trevor, represented the Sligo GAA underage and senior teams.

Scanlon kicked a ball too, but nothing provided as much stimulation as getting up on a bike and pounding the highways and byways, stretching from Sligo town around Lough Gill, out the Dublin road, north towards Donegal, wherever there was a long stretch of road and a few challenging hills. The tougher the better.

He was just twelve years old when he won the Sligo Traders Cup. His opponents probably rode on bikes that had seen more years. The event held a revered place in the town's sporting calendar since it was first held in 1966. Some great locals had their name carved on the roll of honour, but nobody could remember anybody as sensational as Scanlon.

In the years that followed, the Sligo teenager blitzed the top youth and under-18 races in Ireland.

Soon he was being hailed as the next big thing in Irish cycling. The hype would have been an irritation for a young man content with life away from the limelight. He couldn't operate in the shadows for long, however.

His explosive performance in the World Junior Championships in Valkenberg changed everything. No longer was he Mark Scanlon, the unknown hopeful from Sligo; he was Mark Scanlon, world champion. Ireland's latest cycling superhero. Public property.

The Valkenberg success was fairytale stuff. The date is etched in Sligo sports folklore: 10 October 1998. It was Scanlon's eighteenth birthday. His parents, Michael and Mary, who were unstinting in their support of their son's career from the day he first sat on a bicycle, were there to witness the unfolding drama.

The race, a 137.6km test of endurance, courage and tactical awareness, was attritional and uncompromising. Scanlon was in the thick of it, alert to the menacing manoeuvres of his opponents, making the right decisions, calculating with maturity beyond his years. He was part of an 18-man breakaway group at the 120km mark. Briefly, he dropped off the pace, but it proved to be no more than an energy-saving strategy. The destination of the title boiled down to a frantic dash to the line. It called for ice-cool composure and fearless determination in equal measure. The Sligo teenager had an abundance of both. In one last lung-bursting surge to the finishing line, he sprinted past local hero, Coen Loos, and accelerated so powerfully he was able to withstand the relentless effort of the fast-finishing pair of Italy's Phillipo Pozzato and Russia's Edward Kivichev.

"It's the best birthday present I could have wished for," beamed the new world champion in a post-race interview with the *Sligo Champion*.

Proudly displaying his gold medal and rainbow jersey, he reflected on the fluctuating pattern of a gripping race:

> There was one scary moment when I got caught behind a crash. Thankfully, I was able to make up lost ground over the next 5k. With 1km to go, the Dutch rider went on and I sat in behind him. I knew he was tiring but I had to hold my nerve and wait for the right moment to make my move. I was aware there were one or two riders coming strong near the finish but there was no way I was going to be overtaken in the dash to the line.

The President of Ireland, Mary McAleese, and cycling legend Seán Kelly led tributes to the young star. A few days later, thousands of well-wishers turned out to welcome the new world champion home to Sligo.

Having conquered the world at junior level, Scanlon transitioned to the senior division with all the panache of a young man destined for greatness. After finishing third and second in successive years in the elite Irish National Senior Championship, he finally claimed the crown for the first time at Stramullen in 2002. Despite having just recovered from an ankle injury, the Sligo rider stormed to a pulsating win, dashing home well clear of Ciarán Power, who was the highest ranked professional in Ireland at the time.

The following year, he won the national title again. This time, the success came with a bonus. The race was staged in his hometown and huge crowds turned out to enjoy another devastating performance by the local hero, who by now had teamed up with French professional outfit Ag2r.

Just weeks after thrilling his Sligo fans, Scanlon recorded another landmark victory, taking the opening stage in the prestigious Tour of Denmark. He held the lead in the race for three days before finishing a highly credible fifth overall.

His scintillating form earned him a place on Ag2r's team for the Tour De France in 2004. He was the first Irishman in eleven years to take part in the gruelling event. An extremely busy season, during which he raced on 53 occasions, probably took a heavy toll but the Sligoman persevered with typical courage and fortitude to complete the race. He finished eight-ninth overall and fourteenth in the young rider category, an excellent achievement for a 23-year-old competitor.

Later that summer, Scanlon represented Ireland at the Olympics in Athens, competing in the road race on the opening day of the Games.

Although nobody could have guessed it at the time, the hectic 2004 season proved to be the peak of Scanlon's extraordinary career. In an interview with *Sligo Champion* journalist Michael Moran, during a well-deserved holiday in Sligo, the rider reflected on one of the busiest years in his life.

He described how it was always his ambition to ride in the Tour de France and how the relentless exertion of the season finally caught up with him at the Olympics. He regarded his achievement in completing the Tour as one of the highlights of his career, noting he had played a key role in stage wins by two of his Ag2r teammates.

At the Olympics, Scanlon was among several Tour de France competitors who failed to complete the road race. Slightly disappointed not to finish the event, the Sligo rider was proud to have represented his country on the biggest stage of all in world sport.

His legacy is a thriving local cycling scene where young riders, who weren't even born when he conquered the world in Holland in 1998, draw inspiration from his awesome career.

Scanlon still takes to the roads in local and regional races. Registered with the Sligo-based Bottecchia club, he regularly competes in the Sligo League, adding novelty and nostalgia, not to mention sheer class, to the popular event.

"It's a great thrill for young riders to line-up alongside a legend like Mark Scanlon in a local race," agrees Kevin McMorrow, chairman of the Yeats Country Cycling Club.

The club join forces with Bottecchia and the Innisfree Wheelers to organise the Sligo League, an event which has grown in stature over the years. The competition runs from April to September and comprises ten rounds of competitive races. The schedule includes road races, time trials and hill climbs and attracts riders from Sligo and neighbouring counties.

A range of sportives and seasonal classics are also prominent features of the Sligo cycling calendar.

"The cycling scene in Sligo is buzzing again," confirms McMorrow. "The county has produced some exceptional riders over the years and hopefully that trend will continue."

Sligo's first cycling club, Eire Óg, was established in 1955 with Ronan McEvilly, Jack Mahon and Jack Mooney among the founding members. The tradition was carried on by enthusiasts such as Martin O'Hara, Philip McCaffrey, Michael Mooney, Francie McGovern, Gary Rooney and Noel Davey. Another prominent personality in the cycling community was Tony Mooney, who passed away in 2022. He competed successfully at events all over the country and maintained a strong affection for the sport right up to the time of his passing. One of his happiest moments was cheering on his son, Óisin, to a thrilling victory in a round of the Sligo League shortly before his death.

The Traders' Cup, the Markievicz Cup and the Michael Mooney trophy were popular races in the town for decades, attracting top riders from Ireland and abroad. Donegalman Philip Deignan won the Markievicz Cup before forging a successful professional career. His wife, Lizzie, is one of the top women riders in the world, counting the world road race championship among her many high-profile victories.

Brian McMorrow, Matthew Devins and Daire Mooney are among a host of talented local riders competing on the national and international circuit at present.

Sligo boasts eight first-class cycling clubs: Ballisodare Bay, Bottecchia, Eire Óg, Innisfree Wheelers, IT Sligo, North-West Mountain Biking, Ox Mountain and Yeats Country.

GAA (All Stars)

Charlie Harrison

The reluctant footballer who became an All Star

By his own admission, Charlie Harrison, one of only four Sligo All Stars, was a reluctant convert to the joys of Gaelic football. If it wasn't for the persuasive powers of the underage coaches at his local club, St John's, he would happily have concentrated exclusively on rugby, the sport which absorbed his boyhood affection.

It was out of a sense of neighbourly courtesy rather than any craving to play football that he accepted an invitation from the manager of St John's juvenile squads, Mick Barrett, to tog out for the GAA team.

Harrison's recollection is that they must have been short of players. Why else would they bother with a skinny kid who displayed none of the conventional attributes required to be a useful Gaelic footballer? Barrett's judgement proved more perceptive than anybody could have imagined. He unearthed a gem.

The young rugby player remained unconvinced. Harrison testifies:

> I was a bit awkward. Even the basics of kicking a football properly was a bit of a challenge. I had plenty of pace but little else. Fortunately, the coaches at St John's saw something in me.

Throughout his career, there were moments when Harrison required the restorative affirmation of supportive managers. He recalls what he describes as disastrous debuts with the county minor and senior teams and wonders if he would have packed it in if it wasn't for the faith shown in him by the respective mentors, Leo Boland and Tommy Breheny.

"There were many days when I doubted myself but somebody was always there with a word of encouragement," he says.

His first game for the minors in 1999 was a case in point. It was a Championship match against Galway at Markievicz Park. He was marking Matthew Clancy and spent most of the game chasing shadows.

> I got an absolute roasting. The abuse from the fans was so cruel my five sisters had to leave the game early. As debuts go, it was a nightmare.

Boland took him to one side after the game, offered a few timely words of encouragement and promised to include him in the minor panel the following year. When the 2000 season came around, the manager promoted Harrison to captain. The decision had little to do with sentiment. It was a resounding acknowledgement of the player's leadership qualities.

Harrison's debut for the Sligo seniors in 2005 was traumatic too. He was a student at Strawberry Hill College in London, with whom he won a Trench Cup medal, and was thrilled to get the call to report for duty for a league game against Down at Newcastle.

Seventeen minutes in, he misjudged the flight of a ball. A grateful Down forward finished to the net. Harrison was hauled off.

"I was so excited to make my senior debut and it was all over after seventeen minutes," is his rueful recollection of the demoralising experience. "It was hardly worth getting the flight from London."

This time, Sligo selector Tommy Breheny offered reassurance, convincing Harrison to soldier on. The following year, Breheny took over as manager. He quickly identified the young St John's defender as one of the key building blocks in an evolving team which would go on to win the Connacht Championship in 2007.

As he warmed up in the dressing room at Hyde Park on the day of the Provincial final, Harrison contemplated the eventful odyssey which had taken him from the training field at Cuilbeg to the cusp of an historic victory with Sligo. Among the men ready to go into the trenches with him on this defining day for Sligo football were a 'Band of Brothers' from his days at St John's National School.

Michael McNamara, Johnny Davey, Johnny Martyn and Mark Breheny were buzzing for the heat of battle. They had all played together in the school leagues, their heads filled with dreams and ambitions, hanging on to every inspiring word and informative advice from their teacher, Bernard Mulhern, himself a former county player of note. The last time Sligo won the Nestor Cup, none of them were born. Now here they were, sharing a momentous mission, determined to bring a Connacht title back to their native county for the first time in 32 years.

It was the carefree footballing environment at St John's NS which tipped the balance for Harrison. He enjoyed rugby and was good enough to get called up for the Connacht development squad and Irish schoolboy trials. But his love of Gaelic games was cultivated at the Temple Street school and there was no turning back.

Leaving rugby behind was a difficult decision, he admits. His uncle Seamus Scanlon introduced him to the game when he was just six years old. Despite his slight frame, he adapted to the peculiar demands of rugby with surprising ease. He was quick and agile and possessed boundless energy. Sligo Rugby Club was where he found stimulation. He was highly regarded there.

"I was totally engrossed in rugby," he explains. "All my friends played the game. It was the only sport on my radar and I loved it."

He was eleven years old when St John's came calling. The club's intervention in his sporting pursuits was, literally, a game changer. Even if nobody could have anticipated it at the time, Harrison's first tentative, nervous steps on to the GAA field in Carraroe were the beginning of a journey which would mark him out as one of the outstanding footballers of his generation.

The 2007 provincial final was the dividend from all he invested in transitioning from a clumsy young footballer into one of Sligo's most dependable players, a stylish corner-back blessed with explosive speed and a fearless appetite for the big hits. Harrison points out:

> Once I committed to football, I was determined to give myself every chance of fulfilling my potential. Everything in my life revolved around that objective, my lifestyle, diet, rest patterns, training routines. It was almost obsessive.

His selfless devotion was rewarded with a Connacht medal. The 2007 campaign, which culminated with a pulsating win over Galway in the decider, has passed into legend. Harrison is rightly acclaimed as one of the great adventure's superheroes.

> We were a very tight group on and off the pitch. Our manager believed in us; we believed in each other. We set ourselves a target of winning a Connacht title and never stopped believing we could achieve it.

The provincial medal rests proudly alongside Trench Cup and Sigerson Cup medals in his trophy cabinet. The Sigerson was won with a star-studded

University of Ulster team. Playing with the top players in Ulster was an invaluable learning curve.

The crowning glory came later, a richly-deserved All Star award in 2010.

Ironically, the accolade came at the end of a year of bitter disappointment. A Sligo team, astutely constructed under the shrewd guidance of Kevin Walsh, smashed the record books by beating heavyweights Galway and Mayo in the Championship but were ambushed by Roscommon in the final.

As team captain, Harrison felt the devastation more than most:

> We left that one behind us. We had come up through Division Four and Division Three in the National League and a Connacht title would have confirmed our arrival as a serious team. For whatever reason, we underperformed in the final. It was a crushing blow.

His contribution to an exciting season was acknowledged by the All Star judges. It was categoric affirmation of his status as one of the top players in the country. The honour meant everything to his parents, Anne and Charlie. They weren't of traditional GAA stock but were immensely proud of their son's outstanding career.

Harrison viewed the award as an honour for his teammates as much as for himself. He reasons that Sligo's exposure on TV and in the print media that season brought him to national prominence but insists the team's dynamic run to the provincial final was a collective effort:

> That group of players was exceptional. For three years, from 2007 to 2010, they gave everything to the cause. Lads like Mark Breheny, David Kelly, Brendan Egan, Keelan Cawley, Philip Greene and Noel McGuire virtually put their lives on hold. We all did. On a personal level, I was proud to receive the All Star award but I genuinely believed it was due recognition for the whole squad.

A serious student of the game, Harrison doesn't discount the possibility of taking up a managerial role at some point in the future.

He observed how Tommy Breheny and Kevin Walsh went about the job and was lost in admiration for both. He was fascinated by that side of the game. He would talk to Walsh for hours on end about management, tactics, dealing with players, making the hard calls.

> It's not an option now because of work and family commitments but maybe further down the line it's something I'd consider. I've always been interested in that aspect of the game.

A full-time employee of the GAA, where he works as international manager responsible for overseas promotion and development, Harrison lives in Sligo with his wife, Aisling, and the couple's two young children, Benjamin and Harper Jane.

Mickey Kearins

An illuminating star on the football landscape

The legendary GAA broadcaster Mícheál Ó Muircheartaigh nailed it.

"Some players are consistent," he observed. "Others are brilliant. Mickey Kearins was consistently brilliant."

Over the course of a spellbinding career which spanned more than two decades and illuminated the football landscape way beyond the boundaries of his native county, Kearins was the very personification of football magic.

A master in the art of score-taking, from any distance with either foot, from play or from frees, the Dromard man was Sligo's unfailing talisman, often carrying the county single-handedly to unprecedented heights.

He gave success-starved supporters reason to reach for the stars, to dare dream of competing at the top table, of consigning to history years of heartbreak and despair. If, at the end of it all, an All Star award, two Railway Cup medals and one Connacht Championship amounted to meagre reward for such a prodigious talent, there was no concealing the joy and excitement generated by Kearins' irresistible talent.

Frequently among the top scorers in club and county football, his stats are mouth-watering. In 215 games for Sligo, he clocked up an astounding 36 goals and 1,158 points.

All this from a man who was consigned to the role of fringe player during his days at St Muirdeach's College, Ballina. As he concedes:

> I wasn't good enough to make the college team. I had a few tricks, and the priests would often take me to training with the older lads and ask me to show them how to sidestep an opponent. I told them it wasn't

> possible to coach that skill. You either had it or you didn't. It all came naturally to me.

Kearins' transition from moderate college footballer to one of the greatest players of his era illustrates the indestructible character of a man who was inspired rather than inhibited by adversity. In his football career, he turned the challenge of battling against the odds into an art form while his devotion to his professional life as a cattle trader was so passionate that even now at 79 years of age he refuses to entertain thoughts of retirement.

He devoted seventeen years to Sligo's senior team and candidly admits he was 'sick of it' by the time he played his last game as a favour to his long-time friend Nace O'Dowd in 1978. He recalls:

> I sat out the 1977 season and had no intention of going back. I had enough of it. I wasn't enjoying the training and the matches didn't excite me either. Then Nace O'Dowd took over the Sligo team and asked me to go back. He was a legend; I didn't want to disappoint him. So, I returned to the squad. It was a huge mistake. I was too slow and too heavy. I had nothing left to give. Galway beat us by three points in Tuam in the Championship. It was the last time I turned out for Sligo. As I trooped off the pitch, I was relieved it was all over.

If there was a hint of frustration at the way his inter-county career came to an end, nothing overshadows the immense contribution the Dromard man made to his native county.

He played in three Connacht finals and contends the teams that lost the 1965 and 1971 deciders were better than the one which finally ended the county's famine in 1975.

> I was thrilled to win a Connacht medal and it was a huge thing for the county. But it was the end of an era rather than the start of something special. The edge had gone off the team by then. Had we made the breakthrough a few years earlier, we might have won a few Connacht titles and maybe even had a serious go at an All-Ireland.

The 1965 team, which contained such outstanding players as Noel Mullaney, Bill Shannon, Cathal Cawley, Danny McHugh and Mickey Durkin, was a serious outfit but was derailed by the juggernaut that was Galway's famous three-in-a-row All-Ireland squad. The multi-talented Tribesmen were pushed to the pin of their collar to survive Sligo's gallant challenge in the Connacht final.

Kearins believes the 1971 team was the best he ever played with. It was the year Sligo brought soccer stars David Pugh and Gerry Mitchell into the panel, becoming the first county to take advantage of the removal of the infamous ban. Only months earlier, Sligo was one of only two counties in favour of retaining the contentious rule. The irony wasn't lost on anybody, but Kearins doesn't recall any acrimony within the squad. He insists:

> The soccer lads were welcomed with open arms. Pugh was very strong and gave us added physical presence in attack. Mitchell had different qualities. He was a very intelligent footballer. They were great players.

Kearins was in his prime then. In the Connacht final against Galway, he clocked up a staggering twenty-seven points over two games, the initial match and the replay. It earned him a place on the inaugural All Stars team, an appropriate acknowledgement of his extraordinary talent.

The elusive Connacht medal landed in 1975. But the seeds of weariness were already taking root for Sligo's star forward:

> I wouldn't have played at all that year if it wasn't for a sense of loyalty to our player-coach, Barnes Murphy. I was on the verge of walking away, but Barnes encouraged me to stick with it. He was the driving force behind the team. I couldn't let him down.

Sligo lost heavily to Kerry in the All-Ireland semi-final, a missed penalty by Kearins in the early stages serving as a prelude to a disastrous afternoon for the Connacht champions.

The memory of the spot-kick still leaves a bitter taste, he admits, although he credits Kerry keeper Paudie Mahoney for a great save.

> I got too much height on the kick but the keeper still did well to get to it. He told me later he studied the way I took a penalty in the Connacht final. Fair play to him, he had his homework done. In the end, the miss didn't make much difference. Kerry ran riot in the second half. We didn't help ourselves by making some senseless changes, but Kerry went on to prove themselves as one of the greatest teams ever, so we had to take it on the chin.

Having made his first senior appearance in a League game against Cavan in 1961, his Championship debut the following year and played on Connacht Railway Cup teams for 13 successive seasons, Kearins sensed the final act was close at hand. The curtain finally came down on his inter-county career in 1978.

> I played senior football for Sligo for seventeen years. The time had come to walk away. It wasn't a difficult decision. I gave it everything and I was happy to leave it behind.

If the county scene offered him the platform to showcase his breathtaking skillset, club football was the heart and soul of all that was important to him.

He was still only a wisp of a boy when he turned out for Ballisodare in the senior championship in the early 1960s. He vividly remembers the titanic clashes between Ballisodare and their great rivals, Collooney Harps. He recalls:

> Collooney had a star-studded team, many of them Railway Cup players, and we had some great battles with them. There was massive interest in club football in the county at the time. I was only starting out in senior football and I was in awe of some of those lads. It was rough and tumble stuff, but it was a great learning curve for a young lad. It certainly toughened me up.

Kearins won his first senior championship medal with Ballisodare in 1962 and by the time he hung up his boots he had added six further county senior championships to his CV, five of them with his beloved St Pat's.

He was 39 years of age when he played his last game in the county final in 1982. He went out without fuss or fanfare. Tourlestrane won the title. Sligo's greatest ever footballer was denied the fairytale farewell his awesome talent deserved. He bowed out with few regrets, however.

"We had a great run with St Pat's, winning five county titles between 1968 and 1974. Then we went to America on an end-of-season trip and that finished us," he jokes.

Born into a farming family in West Sligo, Kearins was engrossed in football from a very young age. His father, Jimmy, was a crafty player, lining out for Dromard, and his mother, Mabel, was of GAA stock too.

"We didn't have a lot, but we had football," he recalls. "It was the only entertainment we had, and it was more than enough for me."

There was no underage team in the parish so a local teacher, Master Mulligan, arranged for him to play at under-12 and under-14 level with Dromore West. He was a nippy forward and was obsessively devoted to football. A natural right-footer, he would spend endless hours kicking a ball against a wall with his left foot. He took to pounding the highways and byways around West

Sligo and would go on punishing runs along the beach at Dunmoran Strand. He knew he had to be stronger, more athletic. He had to develop a harder edge.

Football took priority over everything. He was falling behind academically so he made a deal with his father. If he failed his Inter Cert, he would give up school and go into the livestock business. That's how things turned out. Over sixty years later, he's still on the road, savouring every minute of it.

He made his debut for Sligo minors in 1960 and was fast-tracked to the senior team. His growing reputation came with a heavy price tag, however. The young forward had a target on his back. He recounts:

> I used to get hammered, particularly in the club games. I was in good shape so I could handle it but some weeks it would be a Tuesday or a Wednesday before I could walk properly, such was the attention I was getting.
>
> It was never a big issue. It's just the way it was, and it never spilled over. I used to get kicked around the field but I'd meet my opponents afterwards at a dance or some social event and there was never a problem. We greeted each other like long lost friends. It was all a bit of craic really.

Widely acclaimed as one of the greatest players never to win an All-Ireland medal, the Sligo star was inducted into the GAA Hall of Fame at Croke Park in 2014.

He lives in Dromard with his wife, Frances. The couple have four grown-up children, Karl, Adrian, Valerie and Evanna.

Top left: Sligo paralympic competitor Martin Gordon.

Top right: Mary Cullen pictured with her son, Ellis, who was born during her treatment for cancer. Pic Brian Farrell.

Bottom left: Sligo's highly successful athlete Lucy Brennan. Pic *Sligo Champion*

Bottom right: Bridie Nicholson displays some of the medals she's won at European and World Transplant Games

Left: Sligo Olympian Chris O'Donnelll in full stride

Right top: Competitors setting off from Strandhill for the 2022 Warriors Run

Right middle: Multiple national boxing champions Stephen and Alan Reynolds

Right bottom: Sligo All Stars team 1981. Back row (l-r): Gerry Monaghan, Joe Palmer, Scott McCarthy, Eugene Monaghan, Tom Hickey, Stan Burns (coach). Front row (l-r): John McGowan (RIP), Michael Delorey, Francis Rogers, Brian O'Hara, John Burns (RIP)

Top left: One of Sligo's all-time greats, Mickey Kearins, winner of an All Star award in 1971 and a Connacht Championship medal in 1975. Pic Eamonn McMunn

Top right: Sligo GAA legend Barnes Murphy, a GAA All Star in 1974. Pic Eamonn McMunn

Bottom left: Charlie Harrison, one of four Sligo GAA All Stars. Pic *Sligo Champion*

Bottom right: World junior cycling champion Mark Scanlon. Pic courtesy *Sligo Champion*

1975

Top: Sligo Connacht Champions 1975. Pic courtesy Tom Callanan

Bottom left: Sligo GAA All Star Eamonn O'Hara. Pic: *Sligo Champion*

Bottom right: Sligo Ladies' All-Ireland-winning captain, Angela Doohan. Pic Tom Callanan

Top left: Noel McGuire proudly displays the Nestor Cup following Sligo's Connacht Championship victory in 2007

Top right: Kieran Quinn, piano man and footballer extraordinaire. Pic *Sligo Champion*

Bottom left: Marty Duffy, All-Ireland Football Championship final referee 2009. Pic Eamonn McMunn

Bottom right: Former Sligo County Board Secretary Tommy Kilcoyne. Pic Eamonn McMunn

Top: The Tourlestrane team which won the County Senior Football Championship for the sixth year in a row in 2021. Pic Eamonn McMunn

Bottom left: Family affair: The Breheny brothers, Tommy (left) and Mark, with Tommy's son, Cian. Pic *Sligo Champion*

Bottom right: Loyal St Mary's club man John Kent. Pic *Sligo Champion*

Top: Sligo's Connacht Championship winning squad, 2007. Pic *Sligo Champion*

Middle: Sligo U-20 team celebrate their Connacht Championship victory in 2022. Pic Eamonn McMunn

Bottom: Sligo hurling squad, winners of the 2019 Rackard Cup. Pic Eamonn McMunn

Top: Sligo minor hurling team, winners of the Celtic Challenge Cup 2022. Pic Eamonn McMunn

Bottom left: Sligo captain, Kyle Davey, lifts the Tom Kilcoyne Cup after the 2021 Connacht final. Pic Eamonn McMunn

Bottom right: Keith Raymond with the Lory Meagher Cup after Sligo's victory in the 2018 final. Pic Eamonn McMunn

Barnes Murphy

A leader of men who remains tuned in

Barnes Murphy learned early about battling against the odds. Much of his extravagant success as a footballer – reflected in his selection as one of only four Sligo All Star winners – was marked by constant overturning of roadblocks and often railing against what he viewed as senseless authoritarian edicts. His single-minded determination infuriated as many as it inspired, but it was always driven by a near obsessive resolution not to be entrapped by what he regarded as the county's endemic inferiority complex.

Murphy always knew he was as good as the best. He just needed a chance to prove it. These traits can be traced back to a challenging childhood, where circumstances in rural Ireland of the 1950s were scarcely conducive to outlandish ambition.

For most of his early life, he was surrounded by darkness, not just in the grey complexion of the fields and mountains around Castleconnor in rural West Sligo, but in a family home which had not yet known the magical transformation of rural electrification.

His family was rocked by the death of his mother, Norah, in her forty-first year, just two weeks after the birth of her fourteenth child. At just 13 years of age, Murphy had seven younger siblings and did the best he could to assist his widowed father, Jim, eek a living from a small farm holding. Football, what little there was of it in the locality, was his life raft.

He declines to conclude that those are the circumstances which shaped his determined 'don't suffer fools gladly' personality, but there's plenty of evidence to suggest his early experiences moulded a man who always knew there was no short-cut to success.

"Nobody played football then," he recalls of his early days at Stokane National School. "We weren't even allowed to bring a ball to school."

But the organisational skills which would later see him lead Sligo to their first Connacht Senior Football Championship in 47 years and help him form two astonishingly successful GAA clubs in urban Sligo, were exercised when forming his own teams before he had reached his teens.

He began picking teams amongst his young pals. He remembers one seven-a-side team he put together for a sports day in Dromore West. The youngsters picked potatoes to earn a half-crown to pay a neighbour to drive them to the venue:

> There wouldn't be a half-crown spare at home, so you had to go out and earn it. That's the way it was. We thought nothing of it. If you wanted something, you got it for yourself. Nobody handed you anything.

The farm work was hard and time-consuming. There were cows to be fed, fields to be ploughed, potatoes to be sown and picked. School was but a few hours reprieve from tough, physical labour. And with no electricity in the home until 1958, much of the daily routine was shrouded in darkness.

> Football was a sort of escape from it all. I remember seeing big fellas playing an organised game in a field and I was absolutely flabbergasted. This is what I wanted. Later, I remember listening to an All-Ireland final, Dublin and Kerry I think, on an old radio. Michael O'Hehir was doing commentary, and it was like magic. I imagined one day being part of all that.

His mother's untimely death just as he was finishing national school briefly altered his education plans. He postponed boarding at St Nathy's College, Ballaghadereen for a year, opting instead for the technical school in nearby Corballa, although he recalls there was never much time for schoolwork as the chores at home grew ever more demanding.

He admits to being intensely unhappy during his years at St Nathy's, but not for the first time, football came to the rescue. A renowned football nursery, Nathy's always had a crop of some of the best players in Connacht, and Murphy at least felt at home on the football pitch. He won juvenile and junior Connacht titles and played in two senior finals.

After his Leaving Cert, he went to the Templemore Garda Training College, and enjoyed a 31-year career in the force, rising to the rank of inspector before his retirement in 1999.

Murphy made his senior debut for Sligo in 1967 and reached his first Connacht final four years later, when the county lost out to Galway. His All-Star recognition came in 1974, after a series of outstanding performances in League and Championship, particularly against Roscommon in both competitions, when he kept tabs on the multi-talented Dermot Early:

> Those were the games that got you noticed. Normally in those days, Sligo lads wouldn't draw much attention, but I had played well against Early, once at Croke Park, and I think if you did well there it gave you a better chance of catching somebody's eye.

The reward was a trip in April 1975 to San Francisco, Los Angeles and New York with the All Stars team. It was an eye-opener in more ways than one. He recalls:

> I got to know lads who I might have considered on another planet in terms of ability. But over the course of four games, it dawned on me I was as good as any of them. And I got to thinking about the really good players we had in Sligo who would also be as good as most of them. I got to know the great Dublin manager, Kevin Heffernan, and learned about preparation and how certain things needed to be in place. I came home really believing we had enough in Sligo to start seriously thinking about winning things.

The first round of the Connacht Championship was just a month away. Murphy was captain and coach and James Tiernan, for years associated with preparing Sligo Rovers' teams, was drafted in as trainer. Murphy sensed Sligo were ready this time. They had been in a Connacht final in 1971, had lost narrowly to Offaly in a League semi-final two years later, and the team was now backboned by the promising youngsters who had reached an All-Ireland minor final in 1968. And the maestro, Mickey Kearins, although no longer in the full flush of youth, was still capable of producing sufficient game-winning magic.

His confidence was validated by an impressive victory over Galway at Markievicz Park and he was equally enthused about the chances of an upset against Mayo in the final. The pendulum seemed against them, however, when Mayo took them back to Castlebar for a replay.

Murphy's recall of the historic day when Sligo bridged a 47-year gap is as clear as if it had happened yesterday:

> Mayo were convinced they had it won. They were always a bit sure of themselves. But we'd figured them out. Our goal was straight off the training ground. A great free kick by Tom Colleary found Mickey Kearins and he broke the ball into the path of Dessie Kerins, who buried it in the net. There was no way we were being beaten after that.

Given the 47-year famine without a trophy, Sligo were well entitled to celebrate the historic victory, and they did so abundantly, but with the mighty Kerry awaiting them in the All-Ireland semi-final a few weeks later, there were obvious problems looming on the horizon. Murphy recalls:

> It was our first Connacht title in 47 years, so, of course, there was a craziness about it. We spent a week carousing around the county. We brought the cup everywhere. Because we had to replay the Connacht final, our preparation time was cut by a couple of weeks anyway, and then we wasted a week celebrating. It was a pure roller-coaster.

The popular belief is that an ill-prepared Sligo were overawed by the occasion of a Croke Park semi-final and went in against Kerry like lambs to the slaughter, but Murphy's assessment is more informed:

> You hear talk that we were walking around before the game waving to the crowd like children on a school trip, but that wasn't the case. We had actually worked very hard in the two weeks before the game and we genuinely felt we had a good chance of beating Kerry. We missed an early penalty and a couple of other good chances, but we were still in the game with only five points between the teams going into the final quarter.
>
> Then some bright spark on the line decided to make a few changes, chiefly bringing John Brennan out to midfield from full-back. That was disastrous. We were all over the place and Kerry banged in three late goals. From my point of view, we put it up to Kerry as best we could and we were let down by people who should have had nothing to do with what was happening on the pitch. People forget that the Kerry team went on to hammer Dublin in the final. They didn't steamroll us until the late stages of the game, so I don't think we got enough credit for that performance.

A few months later, when Sligo re-grouped for league action, Murphy turned up for a game in Ballymote only to find there was a new captain at the helm. He had been stripped of the captaincy without being told and it left a sour taste. Although he would return as player-coach in his last inter-county season in 1981, the lure of playing for his county had been badly dented.

He concentrated on his club career, helping to bring about the amalgamation of Craobh Rua and Naomh Muire to form St Mary's in Sligo town. Enlisting the help of the legendary trainer Fr Cyril Haran, Murphy went on to captain St Mary's to an astonishing run of success, winning five senior county titles, five leagues, two Connacht club championships and reaching two All-Ireland club semi-finals.

Having briefly returned to his native club, Castleconnor, Murphy helped establish another town team, St John's, in 1986, winning a number of junior championship and league titles, before continuing his county career in an over-40s league. He was 43 years old when he last laced a pair of boots:

> I played as long as the body would allow me because I loved every minute of it. Along the way, I had a lot of success and a few disappointments. I probably made mistakes and might have done things a bit differently at times, but you have to be true to yourself. The GAA is still a huge part of my life, I love going to games, meeting old friends and making new ones. I still get excited by a good young player. That never leaves you.

Half a century on from the youngster enthralled by Michael O'Hehir's commentaries, Barnes Murphy is still tuned in.

EAMONN O'HARA

"I never thought I was anything special"

8 July 2007. It's 23 minutes into the Connacht Senior Football Final at Dr Hyde Park, Roscommon, and favourites Galway have just nudged ahead, building momentum in a tight game. Sligo's Michael McNamara wins an innocuous midfield tussle and dispatches a searching pass upfield. David Kelly, clever and nippy, springs out in front of his marker and deftly lays the ball into the path of the onrushing Eamonn O'Hara, who has charged forward from midfield. Six seconds later, the ball thunders into the roof of the Galway net, and Sligo are on their way to an historic title, their first for 32 years and only their third ever.

Pandemonium erupts. Sligo fans in the packed venue are delirious, barely able to believe the majesty of what they've just witnessed, almost afraid to entertain the notion of long-awaited glory. "Goal of the season", roars the RTE television commentator, as the occupants of the press box search for new superlatives.

The coolest man in the heaving stadium is the player whose left foot has just detonated the explosion of excitement. As he bears down on goal, bouncing once, soloing, bouncing again, ghosting beyond shell-shocked opponents, Eamonn O'Hara's mind flashes back to the little boy practicing this precise manoeuvre with his father in a back field near his family farm.

Every evening, when the homework and the milking chores were attended to, Jackie O'Hara took his youngest son out to the field near their home in the tiny village of Cloongoona, deep in the heart of rural south Sligo. There, he taught him the tricks he had learned himself as an accomplished player in the 1960s, before injury brought his playing days to a premature end. The youngster, who had won an All-Ireland silver medal in the under-8 80-metre sprint at the national Community Games in Mosney, was almost too fast for his own good.

"Slow down, take control, compose yourself before you shoot. Get it on target," the wise old man would tell him. "Now, do it again. And again. And again." And each time, the youngster would get better, realising the value of the knowledge being imparted. He soon mastered the technique, the same approach that was to lead to 'the goal of the season' in one of the most important games of his life. He recalls the lessons:

> We'd do it again and again, repeat, repeat, repeat, left foot, right foot, hit the target. That's all I did that day in Roscommon. Just found that one moment of composure when I needed it most. Forget the pressure, the crowd, the occasion, just concentrate on what I'd learned from my dad. At the moment the ball crashed into the net, I remembered those evenings with my dad. I was actually saying his words in my head as I ran towards the goal. That's what helped me. Nobody will ever tell me any different.

That golden goal embellished O'Hara's reputation as one of the best footballers of his or any other generation. The statistics scream of legendary achievement: one of only four Sligo All Stars, a Connacht Senior Football Championship, two National League medals (divisions three and four), representing his country in the International Rules Series, an All-Ireland B Colleges medal, a staggering eight Sligo Senior County Championship medals as a player and five more as manager.

Reared the youngest of five siblings on a small dairy farm, O'Hara was introduced to hard work from an early age. Lifting heavy creamery cans full of freshly produced milk and carrying 100kg bags of cattle feed pumped his young muscles long before he had ever heard of gym work. His father had served as treasurer and secretary of the local GAA club; his mother, Ann, was of Knockmore, Co. Mayo stock; and his uncle Fr Eamonn O'Hara was captain of the only St Nathy's College team ever to win an All-Ireland. There was football in the DNA. He admits:

> As a young lad, I loved all sport, particularly athletics. Gaelic football was always around. I can remember going to club matches quite early on, but I have no distinct memory of ever going to a Sligo game in those days. The thought of playing for Sligo wouldn't have occurred to me.

In the small local primary school, he was one of only two pupils in first class. By the time he reached sixth class, the number had grown to six, half the total number of students in the entire school. With barely enough numbers to field a team, heavy defeats were the order of the day. In his club, numbers were so short, lads would be asked to play three or four years above their age group. The defeats kept on coming. Maybe it was those early setbacks which instilled in O'Hara a facet of his character which dominated his career: a naked hatred of losing.

> For me, the hurt of losing is always greater than the warmth of winning. If we win, I'll celebrate as hard as anyone for maybe a day, but if we lose I'll be like an anti-Christ for three days, maybe longer. I just hate losing. I don't have the mentality to cope with it.

Success on the pitch soon became a habit, though. With a more structured approach to training and playing in Banada Abbey secondary school, O'Hara began to experience the winning feeling for the first time, and he liked it. Stylish and athletic, he began to stand out for both school and club. His school won an All-Ireland B title in 1992. People were beginning to take note. He was selected for county under-15 and under-16 development squads, on into the county minors and natural progression to the under-21s, where he captained the county in two Connacht finals.

It was a seamless transition into the senior team in 1994 under the joint management of Mick Laffey and the late Johnny Stenson, whose policy was dedicated to giving the emerging young talent its chance to progress. Although he was substituted in his Championship debut against Mayo – "I felt humiliated at the time" – it was the start of an unprecedented 19 years in the county colours.

Being called up to represent Ireland in the Compromise Rules series in 2001 and 2002 whetted his appetite for more success. Being around successful players from counties such as Galway, Dublin, Meath and Kildare, who were then riding high, opened his mind to what was needed for ultimate success.

> It was a massive learning curve. It was a huge honour to represent my country but the big thing for me was the exposure to a winning mentality. It drove me on to demand more of myself and to try to get the very best for our county. We had probably become too used to always losing out in Sligo. We needed to change that attitude.

For many observers, that change in attitude manifested itself in the 2002 Championship, when Sligo lost out narrowly in a quarter-final replay against Armagh, who went on to lift the All-Ireland title. He became only the third Sligoman at that point to be selected on the All Stars team. O'Hara agrees it was one of the better Sligo teams he played with but, on reflection, believes maybe there were unrealistic expectations.

> That period, 2001/2002, was definitely a bit special. We had a really athletic team, lads who were fully committed. With one or two extra players in key positions, who knows? Maybe we could have got over Armagh and gone all the way. It was certainly possible.
>
> But with my manager's hat on, I have to realistically wonder if we were good enough. Remember we hadn't won a Connacht title, and if you can't win Connacht can you really expect to win an All-Ireland? I don't think so. We had proven that we could live with All-Ireland champions, but when it came to the crunch, we just couldn't get over the line.

They did get over the line, in Connacht at least, in 2007, ending an agonising 32-year wait for provincial glory. O'Hara's famous goal still stirs the memory, but despite its magnificence, he's quick to downplay his role:

> People remember the goal, but they don't as easily recall that I had to go off injured fifteen minutes into the second half. The rest of the lads stood up to the challenge and got us through. Apart from the goal, my contribution that day was quite small.

The elation of the first Connacht title victory since 1975 is tainted somewhat, he says, by subsequent failure to capitalise on those foundations.

> Honestly, I think we suffered a bit from big head syndrome. Maybe we took our eye off the ball, thinking we were good enough to win without putting in the necessary work. There was definitely two and maybe three more Connacht titles that could have been won. We beat Mayo and Galway one year and then lost to Roscommon in the final. We had the beating of Mayo in another final and threw it away in the last few minutes. They built on that and have been in countless All-Ireland finals since. That could have been us. In a county like ours, we shouldn't be throwing away those opportunities. That's still a big annoyance for me.

At club level, however, Tourlestrane provided an abundance of riches, winning eight county titles between 1994 and 2013. Later, O'Hara and his lifelong friend and playing colleague Gerry McGowan would coach the team to five further titles. The measure of his delight in those success stories is unbridled.

> These things tend to come in cycles. Between 1982 and 1991, the club didn't win a single championship match. To go from such a stark place to become the best team in the county for a prolonged period was a fantastic achievement for everyone involved. To be part of it in your own community, to see lads travelling from all over the country for midweek training sessions, to see local people embrace the club and its players, to see volunteers rewarded for years of selfless service – all of that means so much. It simply can't be equaled.

Retired from the county scene since 2013, O'Hara's involvement in the game he has loved and graced is no less committed. He's helped out Dessie Sloyan with the history-making Sligo under-20 Connacht champions, he's managing Mohill in Leitrim, and he's using his analytical awareness to good effect as a highly regarded and outspoken RTE pundit. As he says:

> I have always called it the way I see it. I enjoy the punditry and I'm aware people won't always agree with me. But I'm not paid to make people happy. I do my research, give an honest opinion, and if people like it, fine. If they don't, well, they're entitled to their opinion.

Eamonn O'Hara wears his greatness lightly:

> I never thought I was anything special. I'm just a guy who used whatever ability I had as best I could, who demanded the best from myself and from those around me. I can't control what people think. I only know I always gave it my best shot.

GAA (Football)

Connacht Champions 1975

Boys of '75 set record straight

There's a touch of the Jekyll and Hyde about Sligo's historic 1975 Connacht Senior Football Championship title. It was the county's first JJ Nestor Cup in 47 years and only its second ever, and so is worthy of an exalted place in any roll of honour. Yet its lustre has always been unfairly tarnished by the team's subsequent annihilation by an emerging turbo-charged Kerry team in a notoriously one-sided All-Ireland semi-final at Croke Park.

The Sligo team which had so joyously ended the county's football famine when beating Mayo in a replayed Connacht final at McHale Park, Castlebar, on 20 July 1975, was itself devoured by a ravenous young Kerry team at Croke Park just three weeks later. It was as if they had emerged from unprecedented celebration and run headlong into the path of an unstoppable juggernaut.

Now, close to nearly 50 years after the events of that scorching summer, the breakthrough victory is hardly ever mentioned without the unwanted appendix of reference to the Kerry mauling. It is something the players who created their own piece of history have learned to accept. They've heard all the suggestions of how raucous celebrations in the wake of the Connacht success interfered with preparations for the All-Ireland semi-final; of naïve players waving to friends and family in the pre-match parade like distracted schoolchildren; of in-house disagreements and 'outside interference'. The legendary film director John Ford once famously said when you have to choose between history and legend, print the legend. He could have made a movie about the 1975 Sligo team.

But for those who fashioned that indelible page in Sligo GAA history, the vision from the rear-view mirror is one of undiluted satisfaction in the knowledge that they were part of something rare and beautiful.

"Nobody can ever take that away from us," insists Tourlestrane corner-back Paddy Henry, who was one of the stars of the campaign. "It was no fluke. We beat Galway and Mayo, the two giants of Connacht, and we beat Mayo in their own back yard. We got it across the line, where maybe better Sligo teams had failed for nearly half a century. It is something to be proud of."

A student at the time, Henry had planned to spend the summer in America, playing for the Chicago Wolf Tones, but a shock victory over Galway in the semi-final put his transatlantic adventure on hold. As he recalls:

> I didn't think we had a chance of beating Galway, so the flights were booked, accommodation and a job all sorted. I actually spent a week in New York visiting family, planning to head on to Chicago from there. I flew home a few days before the Galway match, and the rest is history.

To the utter surprise of most observers, Sligo hammered Galway 1–13 to 0–6 at Markievicz Park, setting up a home final meeting with Mayo, the first time the counties had met in the decider since 1928, which was the last time Sligo had won the Connacht title.

Under the disciplined guidance of player–manager Barnes Murphy, and with veteran Mickey Kearins playing in his fifteenth consecutive Connacht campaign, the Sligo team and its fanatical supporters could sense something special was on the horizon. The coveted title was tantalisingly close as Sligo led by six points early in the second half, but Mayo hit back with seven points without reply. In sweltering heat, a frantic climax saw both sides missing match-winning chances as the game ended 2–10 for Sligo against Mayo's 1–13.

"We rode our luck a little bit towards the end," concedes goalkeeper Tommy Cummins, who remembers one rasping shot from Mayo forward John P. Keane which nearly demolished the crossbar:

> He struck it so hard that when it hit the bar it rebounded nearly half the length of the pitch. I dived to try and stop it, but thank God I didn't get anything on it. Otherwise, it might have gone over the bar and that would have been the end of us.

Mayo were highly fancied for the replay in McHale Park on 20 July. In front of 20,000 spectators, the home side held the advantage at the break, but two crucial goals early in the second half swung the game in Sligo's favour.

Henry recalls:

> Mickey Kearins had a terrific game, having been quiet in the drawn game. He scored a penalty early in the second half and that settled us. Then he set up Des Kerins for our second goal, and although Mayo kept at it, we knew it was our day.

Coincidentally, Sligo clocked up the same score as in the drawn game, 2–10, but this time Mayo could only manage 0–15, and so the Nestor Cup headed back to the Yeats County for the first time since 1928. Cue spectacular celebrations.

"Of course, we celebrated," recalls rookie defender Tommie Carroll, who only found out he was in the team for the replay shortly before the game started. Aidan Caffrey felt unwell, and Carroll was given the nod by one of the selectors as he was about to settle in as a spectator. He reminisces:

> Some aul fella told me afterwards I was the luckiest so and so ever to win a Connacht medal. I didn't realise the magnitude of it at the time, but I know what he meant now. To be part of a team that is still one of only three to win Connacht was very special.

The team's powerful full-back, John Brennan, agrees it was inevitable there would be wild celebrations after waiting so long to enter the winner's enclosure, but he insists there was nothing 'over the top':

> The county went a bit mad, after waiting so long to win it. That was natural. People were entitled to celebrate but I don't think we went over the top. We trained really hard for the two weeks before the Kerry game.

Cummins reveals a more detailed account:

> Somebody decided we should do a tour of the constituency. Everybody wanted to see the cup, to join in the celebration. I was in parts of the county I'd never been in and I was certainly in pubs I'd never been in. But it wasn't as if we all went off on a bender. We got the celebrations out of the way and got back to work.

The contention that McHale Park celebration descended into Croke Park chaos remains undeniable, however. Nothing portrays the mayhem more profoundly than John Brennan's bizarre story about how he nearly missed the All-Ireland semi-final after falling asleep in the team hotel. The Mullinabreena man was the bedrock of the Sligo defence and rightly regarded as one of the best full-backs in the country, and yet his team arrived at Croke Park without him, and nobody seemed to notice. He relates the story:

> We had a pre-match meal about 12 noon and afterwards I went upstairs for a nap, as was my usual practice before a match. When I woke up, they'd all gone to Croke Park. I was on my own. I hadn't a clue how I'd get to the game. I was in an awful panic. There was no such thing as mobile phones or texts in those days so I had no way of contacting anyone.
>
> Thank God John Leydon, a big supporter of ours and a future county board chairman, walked into the hotel. He wasn't looking for me. He was shocked to see me. 'What the hell are you doing here?' is all he said before whisking me into his car and off to Croke Park.
>
> Once we got there, I had an awful time trying to persuade the security guys to let me in. They wouldn't believe I was one of the players. Eventually, we got word into the stadium somehow, and I arrived in the dressing room less than an hour before throw-in. I don't remember anyone asking where I was. To this day, I don't know how they left the hotel without recognising I wasn't with them. There was no bus, just a few cars, so I suppose fellas assumed I was in some other car.

Henry has a memory of a more prescient indicator of what was to come on that August afternoon in Croke Park:

> On the night before the match we all went to the cinema, the idea being we'd have a relaxing evening. We saw The Towering Inferno, with Steve McQueen and Paul Newman, and I often thought afterwards it was an apt metaphor for what was about to befall us, as our dreams of glory went up in smoke the following day.

All of the players insist, however, that for three-quarters of the game Sligo had kept Kerry within touching distance and that the late collapse was caused by ill-advised changes made from the sideline. Brennan was sent into midfield, Tom Colleary was moved into corner-back and Aidan Caffrey was switched to full-back. The unanimous view amongst the players is that the alterations led to disaster. As Brennan maintains:

> Within five minutes of those changes, John Egan had rattled in two goals for Kerry, and it was all over. The final scoreline looked like an annihilation but up to the final fifteen minutes we were still in it. It's such a pity that fifteen minutes of football took some of the gloss of what we had achieved in Connacht. It's a bit unfair.

Carroll, who was introduced as a late sub, recalls that he had more to do as an unofficial 'ball boy' than trying to subdue the Kerry onslaught.

"I must have been the first ball boy ever in Croke Park, picking the ball out of the net three times. That was about the height of my contribution," he wryly concedes.

The 3–13 to 0–5 defeat in front of over 32,000 spectators, the majority of whom were highly expectant Yeats County supporters, cast an ominous shadow over Sligo football, but it soon became obvious that their conquerors were something extra special. Kerry went on to wallop defending champions Dublin in the All-Ireland final and, powered by fledgling legends such as Pat Spillane, John Egan, Páidí Ó Sé, Ogie Moran and Mikey Sheehy amongst others, they would dominate football for the following decade.

There's no doubt the narrative around the 1975 campaign has attained almost mythical status. But none of the hyperbole which has festered over the decades should ever detract from the enormity of the achievement of that '75 panel in ending Sligo's lengthy quest for Connacht glory. To this day, that group remains one of only three Sligo teams ever to have done so. They are legends for all the right reasons.

For the record, the triumphant Sligo team which ended the 47-year wait for Connacht glory at McHale Park, Castlebar, on 20 July 1975, lined out as follows: T. Cummins, R. Lipsett, J. Brennan, T. Carroll; M. Brennan, B. Murphy, P. Henry; J. Stenson (0–1), T. Colleary; M. Laffey, M. Hoey (0–4), F. Henry; D. Kerins (1–1), M. Kearins (1–4), J. Kearins. Sub: B. Wilkinson for M. Laffey.

Breheny Brothers

Family at the core of GAA golden days

It was a typically scorching summer Sunday in New York. Irish emigrants dutifully observed the age-old ritual: morning Mass followed by a lavish helping of Gaelic football. The Mass was by way of adherence to tradition; the GAA was the religion.

Tommy Breheny, a native of Geevagh who had emigrated to the States in the 1950s, took his young son, Tommy Junior, to a local park in the Bronx, an expansive community facility that doubled as a corner of Ireland on sunny afternoons. Going to matches was as much a part of the family routine as the Sunday dinner. Tommy Senior worked tirelessly as a butcher all week. The weekend GAA activities gave him tangible connection with home.

On this day, he was uncharacteristically edgy, pacing along the field, transistor radio glued to his ear. And on it went until he unleashed an almighty roar of triumph. The broadest of smiles danced across his face.

"Sligo just won the Connacht Championship," he exclaimed, his body bursting with pride.

It was 20 July 1975, the day Sligo captured the coveted Nestor Cup for the first time since 1928.

The Sligo exiles in New York greeted the news with unbridled happiness.

As a misty-eyed Tommy Breheny Senior soaked up the sheer joy of it all he could hardly have imagined the next time Sligo would win a Connacht senior title his family would be at the very heart of the story, one son an inspirational manager, another a virtuoso forward.

By the time 2007 came around, with Sligo were still in vain pursuit of a return to the glory days, Tommy Breheny Senior had taken his wife, Mary, a proud Killarney woman, and their six children back to Ireland. They returned for a brief period in 1969 and made the move permanent in 1976. Their youngest son, Mark, was born in Sligo.

They settled in the Maugheraboy area of Sligo town and St Mary's GAA club became their second home. All the children were tidy footballers, but Tommy Junior and Mark were blessed with an extra sprinkle of stardust. There was thirteen years between them, but they shared a common passion for football.

Tommy was eight years old when the family returned to Ireland and readily admits Sligo was a bit of a culture shock. All that was familiar to him was Gaelic football. It afforded him a rite of passage. He was American by birth but Irish to the core. A sense of belonging, of pride of place was cultivated at St Mary's, a flourishing urban club with a prolific underage structure. His football skills were honed at St John's National School and given a semblance of maturity at Summerhill College where he was a star on the team which reached the All-Ireland Colleges final in 1985. He was a natural Gaelic footballer but his elevation to the senior county squad the following year was swifter than anticipated. He remembers:

> Sligo football was in the doldrums at the time. Then Mickey Moran became manager and there was an entirely different mood in the county. Talented young players like Eamonn O'Hara, David Durkin and Paul Taylor brought a new vibrancy. For the first time in years, Sligo seemed to be heading in the right direction.

Although Tommy missed Sligo's appearance in a Connacht final in 1997 through injury, he not only remained committed to the cause but was a highly influential personality in and around the squad.

His younger brother Mark was earning a bit of reputation in the underage grades at club and county level by then. The brothers moved in different social circles but football was an indestructible bond. It was as if destiny had ordained their football lives would forever be intertwined.

They were both exceptional footballers. They shared a burning passion for the game but had little else in common in the execution of their skills. Tommy was an inherently intelligent player, reliable and robust, a man-marker or defensive shield. Little got past him. In contrast, Mark was more creative, possessed of a cultured left foot and penetrating pace, the sort of player who could, and regularly did, change the course of a game with a flash of individual brilliance.

He played a record 55 senior championship games for Sligo and made a critical contribution in most. An early graduate of the fledgling Sligo School of Excellence, he played in an under-16 Manning Cup final as well as minor and under-21 Connacht finals before an inevitable call-up to the senior team for a championship opener against New York in 2001.

While Mark's playing career was in full flight, Tommy was finding his way in management, initially at St Mary's where he guided them to a senior championship title in 2001, and later with the Sligo senior team.

He was drafted in as emergency cover after Sligo parted ways with Dominic Corrigan in 2006. It was supposed to be a temporary arrangement, but the county board persuaded him to take the job permanently. He hesitated at first, then considered the untapped and heretofore underestimated potential within the squad and decided to give it a shot. He beefed up the panel – the returning pair of Kieran Quinn and Michael McNamara were key additions – and targeted the 2007 Connacht Championship. Most observers would have concluded it was an outrageous aspiration but Breheny was serious in his conviction that his players were good enough to land the coveted prize.

The launching pad for the adventure was New York. The GAA wheel of fortune had turned full circle for the Breheny family. As Tommy reasons:

> It was almost as if it had been written in the stars. It was a bit surreal, going back to the city where I was born, bringing a Sligo team to Gaelic Park, a venue where I spent so many happy childhood days, the place where my Mum and Dad first met as young Irish teenagers in a strange land far from home. And Mark, the only child in the family not born in New York, was part of the squad. It just seemed to square the circle. There were many memories and a lot of emotion wrapped up in all of it.

A perfectionist by nature, he was troubled by his lack of knowledge of the opposition. He got hold of New York's line-out the night before the game and immediately set about touching base with contacts back home. Some of them would have played with or against the New York boys over the years. Could they provide some useful information, anything at all?

> I was getting return calls in the middle of the night. It was all a bit crazy, but I wanted to be armed with as much information as possible on the New York team.

It all turned out perfectly in the end. Sligo won in a canter, spent a few days training and bonding in New York, and returned to Ireland chomping at the bit for a semi-final showdown with Roscommon at Dr Hyde Park.

They hadn't won a championship game at the venue since 1971 but they consigned that miserable record to history, producing a scintillating display of inventive football to thoroughly outclass their opponents.

Now the plan Tommy hatched within weeks of taking the Sligo job the previous season was about to come to fruition. And his younger brother would be a key component of the strategy.

But how did the two brothers adapt to the unusual scenario of one being manager and the other a player? Tommy insists:

> It was never a problem. Mark was always in the team on merit. If there was a better player in his position, I would have had no hesitation in leaving him out. He was an exceptional forward, so there was never a time when anybody had reason to question my judgement.

Likewise, it wasn't an issue which unduly bothered Mark:

> Tommy was my manager for a few years at club level, so it was something I was used to. If anything, the fact he was manager gave me added motivation to maintain my standards. I didn't want anybody to think I was in the team because my brother was the boss. I didn't detect any negativity about it, certainly not within the squad, but if there had been I would have ignored it.

The county was buzzing with anticipation in the build-up to the provincial final. Distancing the players from the understandable hype was key to Tommy's preparations, although he wanted them to feed off the emotion of the occasion. He recalls:

> We showed the lads a special motivational video the night before the final. They left the meeting absolutely fired up. I knew there was no way we'd be beaten.

It was back to Dr Hyde Park for the final. A sensational goal by Eamonn O'Hara illuminated a typically gripping showdown with Galway. In the end, Sligo had a point to spare. The victory owed as much to defensive resilience as it did to attacking flair. A multi-talented Galway team, which included such accomplished players as Nicky and Pádraic Joyce, Jarlath Fallon and Michael Meehan, lacked nothing in endeavour or quality but Breheny's defiant team refused to yield. When inspirational captain Noel McGuire proudly lifted the Nestor Cup, it ended a grim 32-year famine for the county.

"A lot of us had been through some tough days together, losing minor and under-21 finals," Mark reflects. "This was our moment of redemption. The fact that Tommy was the manager give it added significance for our family. It's a day that will live long in the memory."

At the final whistle, Tommy remembered the day in the Bronx in 1975 when his father was overcome with joy on hearing of his native county's Championship victory. Now Tommy Senior was here among his own people, witnessing two of his sons playing central roles on an occasion that would have an indelible place in the history of Sligo football.

"It was a very special day for our family but also for the whole county," says Tommy. "I was thrilled for the players too. They were a fantastic bunch of lads. When I took over as manager, I told them I believed they were good enough to win a Connacht title. They didn't let me down."

The brothers shared many memorable days at club level. Tommy was manager of the St Mary's teams which won senior county titles in 2001 and 2015, with Mark playing a starring role on both occasions. As a player, Tommy won two senior championship medals, in 1987 and 1996. He was captain of the 1987 team. The previous season, he had the distinction of playing in both the minor and senior county finals, claiming a winners' medal with the minors.

The Sligo squad which won the 2007 Connacht Championship: Philip Greene, Charlie Harrison, Noel McGuire, Ross Donavan, Paul McGovern, Michael McNamara, Jonathan Davey, Eamonn O'Hara, Kieran Quinn, Brian Curran, Brendan Egan, Seán Davey, David Kelly, Mark Breheny, John McPartland, Kenneth Sweeney, Adrian Marren, Pádraig Doohan, Brendan Phillips, Jason Farrell, Johnny Martyn, Patrick Naughton, Philip Gallagher, Gerry McGowan, Karol O'Neill, Barry Kivlehan, Fergus Horan, Conor McGowan, Darren Kearns, Dara McGarty, Paul Taylor, Kevin Byrne.

Angela Doohan

Third time lucky for ladies' legend

It was an occasion laced with novelty. Sligo and Leitrim, two counties accustomed to being peripheral bystanders on big days at Croke Park, were locked in an improbable showdown for one of the game's top prizes.

At stake was the All-Ireland Junior Ladies' Football Championship. It was 2006. Ladies' football was becoming big business. Once barely tolerated as an inconvenient sideshow with little or no public appeal, the game was flourishing.

Now the north-west rivals were going head-to-head in a battle for supremacy which had captured the imagination of supporters in the success-starved counties.

Angela Doohan made her debut for Sligo when she was 14 years old. The St Nathy's star never imagined she would end up sitting in the hallowed dressing rooms at Croke Park, ready to lead her county in an All-Ireland final. But here she was. The leader of a dedicated group of talented footballers, each prepared to leave everything on the pitch in pursuit of an elusive medal.

The girl from Doocastle, on a thin borderline between Sligo and Mayo, epitomised everything about Sligo's thirst for the big breakthrough. Mayo could have claimed her on geographical qualification – and she wouldn't have been out of place among their galaxy of exciting players – but she never remotely considered playing for any team other than her beloved Sligo. There were days when the relentless commitment might have seemed no more than a futile exercise in blind loyalty, but she never stopped believing.

She made it to Croke Park for the first time in 2004. It was magic but she and her Sligo teammates were caught in the headlights. They were imprisoned by the newness of it all. The hype, the pressure, the overwhelming thrill of just being there. They hadn't stocked up enough experience to cope. Kildare beat them without too much fuss.

They came back stronger the following year. Older and wiser. But they came up against an uncompromising Armagh team. Another day of unfulfilled promise. Back-to-back All-Ireland defeats. Only the most resilient recover from that sort of devastation. As Doonan reflects:

> The first year was the easier to take. At least we had the distinction of being the first Sligo ladies team to play at Croke Park. The occasion got the better of us but we had the consolation of knowing we made our own piece of history.

The players came to terms with the brutal reality that the Croke Park experience had suffocated them. It should have prepared them for all Armagh would throw at them in 2005. When they left the great stadium with nothing to show for their efforts, it was a demoralising blow.

"We were absolutely gutted," Doohan admits. "We had nothing to fall back on this time. We failed to deliver for a second year in a row and it was hard to take."

Kathleen Kane, then and now an iconic figure in ladies' football, masterminded the routes to the All-Ireland final in 2004 and 2005. The baton was passed on to Tourlestrane man Paddy Henry in 2006.

Sligo lost the Connacht final that year but the backdoor system offered a shot at redemption. They grabbed it with both hands. It brought them back to Croke Park for a third successive year.

It was impossible to avoid reference to the two previous defeats, but it remained an unspoken motivation among the players. The prosect of losing three All-Irelands in a row would have been too cruel to contemplate so positivity was the preferred creed. Doohan recalls:

> We had a meeting at the start of the year, and we resolved to give it everything we had. Too much time and effort had been invested to let it drift away without any reward. When we got back to Croke Park in 2006, the mood was upbeat. Deep down, we would have been thinking that a third All-Ireland defeat was out of the question. There was no fear factor within the squad. If anything, the bitter experience of the previous two years drove us on.

Leitrim and Sligo were frequent adversaries in those years. Many of the players went to college together, they shared the same social scene, they'd battled each other with fierce rivalry in league and championship games. There were no surprises on either side.

"We almost knew each other too well," reckons Doohan. "In the circumstances, it was hardly surprising that there was a lot of tension in the final. It was never going to be a free-flowing game, but we always had the upper hand."

Sligo goalkeeper Katrina Connolly, who later went on to represent Ireland at soccer, made a few crucial saves while at the other end of the pitch the Yeats County proved more incisive with Therese Marren contributing three vital points in a low-scoring decider.

At the call of time, Sligo were worthy winners on a 0–8 to 0–4 scoreline. The West County Cup was on its way to the Yeats County for the first time.

It meant Doohan had the distinction of becoming the first Sligo woman to lift a national trophy at Croke Park. She beams at the memory.

> It's a moment I'll never forget. Coming from a strong GAA background, it's the sort of stuff you dream of as a young girl but which you never imagine will come true. It was a great honour to captain my county but to climb those steps at Croke Park and lift an All-Ireland Cup was on a different level. Even now, all these years later, I still get goosebumps thinking about it.

The thrilling moment was appropriate reward for a player who had by then already registered thirteen years loyal service to the senior county team.

There was little or no structured ladies' football in Sligo when Doohan was growing up, but the lack of organised leagues wasn't going to deter the GAA-mad youngster from pursuing her ambitions.

Her later father, Paddy Joe, was one of the top players of his era, winning county senior championship medals with Curry in 1964 and 1972. After he married local girl Geraldine Watters, the couple set up home in Doocastle, just outside Bunninadden and their children – Myra, Martina, Pádraig and Angela – inherited their parents' love of Gaelic games.

Pádraig took the football pedigree from his father. He was on the Sligo panel which won the Connacht Championship in 2007 and scored the winning goal when Bunninadden won the senior county title in 2000, their first since 1891. He was Angela's hero.

She remembers:

> There was no organised football for girls, so I'd be out in the field with Pádraig. I was a bit of a tomboy. All I wanted to do was play football. Looking back now, it's great to see how our careers developed. He has a

> Connacht medal, and I captained an All-Ireland winning team. It's nice to have that in the family.

Ladies' football was established in Sligo in 1993, the same year Doohan made her debut for the senior county team. Marty Duffy and Mattie Hoey were the Sligo managers and others who were invaluable influences in her early career were Tom Keane, Liam McDonagh, Christina Johnson and the late Fr Paddy Kilcoyne.

At club level, Doohan won her first county medal with St Nathy's under-14s in 1993. It was the start of a spectacular adventure. By the time she retired, she had claimed 14 senior county championship medals with the club. Add in seven Connacht titles, one at schools level with Benada Abbey, three with St Nathy's and three with the county, and you get some idea of the colossal impact she has made on ladies' football, not just in Sligo but at provincial and national level.

It was all neatly capped off by an O'Connor Cup medal with Sligo IT, where she played alongside some of the leading personalities in ladies GAA, including Mayo's Christina Heffernan and Galway's Annette Clarke.

When ladies' football was introduced to Sligo in 1993, there were only eleven clubs affiliated to the county board and only two competitions, one at under-14 level and the other in the senior grade. Currently, over 2,000 players are registered at nineteen clubs with over 40 competitions in operation across the various age groups and at adult level.

There are many who have made substantial contributions to what is a compelling success story, but few match the extraordinary accomplishments of Doohan. She reflects:

> I enjoyed every minute of it. Football has been a massive part of my life and there were many challenges and a very high level of commitment along the way. But it was never a chore. I've played with some great players, made friends for life and picked up a few medals as well, including an All-Ireland with Sligo.

At administrative level, Sligo has played a prominent role in the promotion of ladies' football at regional and national level.

The national president of LGFA is Castleconnor native Mícheál Naughton. Kathleen Kane served two terms as Connacht president and is assistant secretary of the national association. Liam McDonagh was also president of the provincial council for two terms while others who have played key roles in ladies' football in the county include Marty Duffy, Tom Keane, Austin McTiernan,

Kathleen Marren, Christina Johnson, Raymond Carden, Olivia Flannery, Rita Brett, Ciara McAllister and Martin Seery.

Referees from the county have taken charge of several top ladies' games over the years. Marty Duffy refereed All-Ireland senior finals in 2001 and 2002; John Niland was in charge of the 2011, 2013 and 2015 senior finals, while Gus Chapman refereed the All-Ireland intermediate final in 2013.

On the field of play, Sligo has a recorded a number of notable achievements. As well as claiming the 2006 All-Ireland Championship, they won Division Three National League titles in 1995 and 2015.

The Sligo team which won the All-Ireland Junior Championship in 2006 was: K. Connolly, F. Maye, G. O'Gara, M. Keane; T. O'Hara, C. Kennedy, L. Harte; B. Byrne; S. McTiernan; E. Flanagan, S. O'Reilly, A. Doohan; H. Haran, N. Gormley, T. Marren. Subs: I. McNulty, L. Brett, L. Smyth, R. Goodwin, K. Maloney.

The Sligo minor team produced a timely reminder of the healthy state of ladies' football in the county when they won the Connacht B Championship in 2022, beating Roscommon in a dramatic shoot-out in the final.

The triumphant squad was: Macayla Burke, Orla Fleming, Ellie McDermott, Orla Delvin, Niamh Henry, Ruby Clark, Sarah Feeney, Caoimhe Connor, Tara Breheny, Chloe O'Beirne, Ellen Kelleher, Eimear Hunt, Maeve Casserly, Rianne Smith, Lauren Normanly, Amy Kennedy, Isabella Henry, Laura Foley, Cora Gilligan, Tara Casserly, Erin Deehan, Ruth Flanagan, Eabha Cawley, Jade Walsh, Emma O'Brien, Sarah Conheady, Hannah Willis, Aoife Cooke, Ciara Brennan, Lauren Durkan, Cianna Ruddy, Nisha McDonagh.

Marty Duffy

The best referees are rarely noticed

It was the night of the All-Ireland final in 2009. Kerry had beaten Cork in a novel decider and as rivalry transitioned to revelry, the victors and vanquished mingled merrily in the Clontarf Castle Hotel. Fans from both counties gathered around a TV set in the bar, anxious to hear what the *Sunday Game* pundits made of the day's action.

Blissfully detached from the noise and the cheerful banter, Sligoman Marty Duffy sipped a calming pint, happy now not to be the man in the middle. That afternoon, he had become the first man from his county to referee an All-Ireland final. Good referees are rarely noticed. They go about their business with quiet efficiency and the minimum of fuss. So perhaps it's a ringing endorsement of how well he performed his duties on the biggest stage of all in Irish sport that few in the crowded bar recognised him. He wouldn't have wanted it any other way.

Enjoying a quiet drink with his friend and fellow referee Joe McQuillan was the perfect end to one of the most memorable days in his career. He doesn't do tortured analysis or deep reflection. He's happy to let the professional experts take that role. They have their job to do; he has his. He rarely takes notice of what they say. His personal assessment is always thorough and honest and that's enough for him. As he admits:

> The Sunday Game was on the television but I didn't pass much heed of it. I was satisfied with how the day had gone. My job was done. Now the pundits were doing theirs. That's the way it works. It never bothers me what other people say as long as I'm happy with my own performance.

If that sounds as if the Enniscrone native regarded the All-Ireland final as just another day at the office, nothing could be further from the truth. He's immensely proud to have the honour on his CV and is keenly aware of what it means to his family, his club and his county.

All-Ireland referees receive a medal similar to the one presented to members of the winning team. It's a treasured possession – one that sets Duffy apart in the annals of Sligo GAA. No other person in the county has a senior men's All-Ireland medal.

From the moment he began refereeing, Marty was destined for the top. He has an impressive catalogue of big match assignments – two National League finals as well as Provincial deciders at inter-county and club level. Being selected as the man to take charge of the 2009 All-Ireland was the pinnacle, however. It's what every referee aspires to.

Pomp and ceremony surrounds the All-Ireland final and while referees accept this is all part of the big match ritual, nothing distracts them from the critical job they have to perform.

Once their appointment is confirmed, referees have discretion in selecting their own team of umpires. In Duffy's case, there was never any question of discarding the men who had soldiered with him from the start.

So, on the Saturday before the All-Ireland final, Duffy and his loyal crew – his brother, Michael, John Kilgannon from Enniscrone and the Easkey pair of Michael Kelly and Pat Cawley – made the journey from west Sligo to Dublin.

Among those included in the travelling party were Marty's mother, Anne, his wife, Geraldine, and his children, Amy, Aaron, Conal and Leah.

They stayed overnight at the Clontarf Castle Hotel and the following morning two buses were laid on to take them to Croke Park – one for the match officials, the other for family and friends.

The referee and his team arrived at the venue at about 12 noon, had a few casual meetings with Croke Park officials and then went off to watch the first half of the minor match. Then they made their way to the referees' dressing room, leaving themselves adequate time to change and do their warm-ups.

The President of the GAA, Christy Cooney, visited them briefly but there was no hard and fast ritual to be observed. Duffy recalls:

> Our focus was absolutely concentrated on the job we had to do. On the previous Thursday, we had a good meeting between ourselves, talked over all that was involved, how we would deal with everything. We had been together as a team for a few years and we had total trust in each other. We all had experience of doing big matches before and obviously an All-Ireland final is on a different level, but nothing was too much of a

> surprise. We were well prepared, and I don't think any of us were struggling with nerves or anything like that.

The referee isn't obliged to visit the competing teams' changing rooms before the game so the first contact Marty had with either the Kerry or Cork teams on the day was when the captains came to the centre of the pitch for the toss-up.

The atmosphere reaches fever-pitch just before throw-in but it's vital the match officials retain their composure.

"You have to distance yourself from the surroundings," Duffy explains. "A packed house at Croke Park is some spectacle and the atmosphere is electric but as the referee you can't take notice of any of that. You have to stay focused."

When Cork and Kerry meet there is always the potential for combustible encounters. The Sligo referee was in charge when the sides contested a Munster final in Killarney in 2007. The temperature was close to 30° and the heat of battle was only marginally less intense.

"They were in each other's faces from the start that day," remembers Duffy. "It was tough and competitive, as Munster finals usually are."

Curiously, the meeting of the great rivals in the All-Ireland final was short on acrimony, even if it was contested with vigorous passion by both sides.

> The teams gave it all they had but there were no major flashpoints. Of course, both sides wanted to win but they wanted to win it the right way which made my job a lot easier. As a game to referee, it was straight-forward. And it passed by quickly. My job was to referee it, minute by minute and I felt it went very well. At the end, the overriding emotion was one of relief. And there was a certain amount of satisfaction as well, knowing that we had done a good job.

The match officials were back in the tunnel by the time the Sam Maguire Cup was presented to Kerry captainDarren O'Sullivan.

Peripheral figures on the edge of history, they trooped back to their changing rooms, debriefed and were ferried back to their hotel where there was a special presentation dinner for the match officials and their families. The umpires were presented with commemorative trophies to mark the occasion. Duffy was presented with his All-Ireland medal at a special function later in the year.

On the Monday after the All-Ireland, the Sligoman was at home, settling in for an evening by the television when Geraldine persuaded him to call down to the Enniscrone pitch to take one of his regular coaching sessions with the under-12 team.

> I was drained, absolutely exhausted but I said I'd go down and do a bit with the young lads. When I got to the clubhouse, there were about 300 people there. The parish laid on a surprise function for me. We had a fantastic night. That's the nicest memory of all. It meant so much to me and my family.

Fifty-four-year-old Duffy retired from refereeing in 2018 and is now chairman of the Central Referees' Appointment Committee.

Tommy Kilcoyne

Lifetime of unconditional service to GAA

For 82 years the Kilcoyne family were at the core of GAA life in Sligo. Tom Kilcoyne served as secretary of the county board from 1924 until his death in 1968, and his son Tommy held the office from 1970 until he stepped down in 2007.

In a county more accustomed to adversity than achievement, there are many families who soldiered with distinction to ensure the national games retained respect and relevance, but few match the Kilcoynes' scale of unstinting service.

The family's unconditional loyalty to the GAA spread beyond county boundaries. Tom was secretary of the Connacht Council for 34 years and the trophy presented to the Connacht minor champions is named in his honour. When Sligo won the Championship in 2021 for the first time since 1968, the breakthrough victory carried added poignancy given the county's links with the famous trophy.

Another reminder of the family's deep-rooted devotion to the national games is illustrated by the naming of the Tubbercurry GAA grounds in memory of Mick Kilcoyne, Tom's brother, who was one of the greatest players of his era, starring on the Sligo team which won the Connacht Championship in 1928 and considered the first Sligoman to win a Sigerson Cup medal.

The family were farming stock from Oughram just outside Tubbercurry. Tommy remembers his grandfather Luke exporting eggs to England back in the day. If farming sustained them, they were nourished by their love of the GAA.

As a young boy, Tommy would help his father with some of the less demanding work associated with his role as county board secretary. Even if he couldn't have known it at the time, he was already preparing himself for a lifelong involvement in the administration of GAA affairs in the county and beyond. He recalls:

> Football was always part and parcel of our life. I remember going to games in Tuam and Castlebar with my father. Because of my father's role with the Connacht Council, he'd have to bring the day's takings to the bank that evening. I remember that clearly, especially in Tuam. The bank would open especially on the night of a big game and the Connacht Council officers would go in there and count the money. It was obviously for security reasons but as a young boy I was fascinated by it all.

Farming and teaching are important features of the Kilcoynes' story, but Gaelic football and the beguiling thrill of the big matches provided the soundtrack to their lives:

> My father would bring myself and my brother, Francis, to Croke Park, lifting us over the turnstiles on the way in. Afterwards, we'd be swept along in the crowds along Jones' Road. There were days our feet didn't touch the ground. But we were never scared. It was all part of the excitement.

When Tom passed away at the age of 71 in 1968, Pádraig Keane succeeded him as secretary of Sligo county board. Then, in 1970, Tommy took over the role.

> I watched and admired my father doing the job for over 40 years, so I knew exactly what I was letting myself in for in terms of workload and responsibility. It was a challenge I gladly accepted.

Brendan McAuley was elected chairman the same year. Joey Murphy became treasurer. All young men coming into office at a time of seismic change within the GAA. It wasn't long before they were confronted with one of the burning issues of the day, the campaign to remove the contentious rule forbidding members of the GAA from playing 'foreign' games.

Sligo was one of only two counties – Antrim was the other – which voted in favour of retaining Rule 27. At the annual Congress in Belfast, support in favour of scrapping the ban was so overwhelming that GAA President Pat Fanning decided a vote wasn't necessary. The controversial rule was consigned to history.

Ironically, Sligo was the first county to take advantage of the removal of the ban, selecting Sligo Rovers stalwarts Gerry Mitchell and David Pugh on their panel for the 1971 Championship campaign. The team reached the provincial final, losing narrowly to a talented Galway team in a replay.

Reflecting on an episode in the county's history which still, more than 50 years later, is the subject of deep contemplation, Tommy believes the removal of the ban was the correct course of action.

> I understand exactly why the rule was there in the first place, but it had lost its relevance by the 1970s. I think the time had come for its removal and the GAA did the right thing.
>
> Once the rule was removed, it was open to Sligo to select players from other sports and we brought in Gerry Mitchell and David Pugh. Not only were they exceptional footballers, but they were also very fine gentlemen. It was a pleasure to have them on board with the GAA team and everybody welcomed them with open arms.
>
> Even though Sligo was one of only two counties in favour of retaining the ban at the time, that was never thrown back in our faces. Everybody pulled together and there was never any animosity. Indeed, during my time involved with the GAA in Sligo, we enjoyed excellent relationships with all sports in the county. Sligo prides itself on the cooperation that exists between the various sporting organisations.

Tommy reckons the 1971 team was as close as Sligo ever had to winning an All-Ireland title.

> We were desperately unlucky to lose to Galway in Connacht and they went on to reach the All-Ireland final where they lost to Offaly. I genuinely believe we could have gone the whole way had we beaten Galway. That was our big chance to win the Sam Maguire.

Fortunately, his term in office included two historic Connacht titles for Sligo, in 1975 and 2007.

> They were very special victories for the county and for Sligo people everywhere. We were inundated with messages of congratulations from all over the world, which just proves the global reach of the GAA. We aren't one of the big counties, and we're always fighting against the

> power of Mayo and Galway in Connacht, but we're a very proud county. We've earned respect for the way we keep our shoulder to the wheel.

Another milestone event during Tommy's career was the opening up of Croke Park to soccer and rugby in 2005. Sligo put down the motion at annual Congress which led to the groundbreaking rule change.

Over the course of a lifelong of service to the GAA, Tommy also served on the Central Council, the National fixtures committee (CCCC) and Croke Park's planning and policy committee. He was also on the backroom team with the Irish International Rules squad on two occasions.

Although best known for his administrative skills, he also enjoyed an exciting playing career, giving 20 years' service to his local club, Mullinabreena.

He won a junior championship medal in 1968 and played in the 1970 senior county final. He played minor and under-21 football for Sligo and made a senior appearance for the county in the Hastings Cup competition in 1968. During his college days at St Pat's, he lined out in a league quarter-final match at Croke Park. He quips:

> It's nice to have a Croke Park outing on my CV. Mick Gleeson, the famous Kerry footballer, was on our team that day and Dublin stars Kevin Heffernan and Jimmy Keavney lined out for our opponents, St Vincents.

The Kilcoyne family also devoted years of distinguished service to the teaching profession.

Tommy was principal at St Lassara's National School, Ballincarrow, for many years; his father, Tom, was principal of Achonry National School; his brother, Francis, and sisters, Mary (RIP) and Kathleen, were vocational school teachers; and his daughters, Mary and Geraldine, are national school teachers.

Little wonder then that Tommy married a teacher, Rosaleen, a native of Cavan. The couple have four children, Mary, Geraldine, Tom Junior and Peter, and eight grandchildren.

Noel McGuire

"Captaining the 2007 team was the greatest moment of my career"

The rolling waves and challenging reef breaks off the coast of west Sligo attract some of the world's most adventurous surfers to the idyllic village of Easkey. The scenic seaside resort hosted the Pro/Am World Championships in 1979 and is regularly acclaimed as a top surfing destination in international magazines.

If the irresistible delights of the rugged coastline lure thrill-seeking tourists to Easkey every year, the windswept GAA field, perched on the very edge of the Atlantic Ocean, has always offered a more stimulating alternative for young locals.

The village features in an episode of the RTE programme *Reeling In The Years*. The storyline depicts a community ravaged by emigration; the local GAA team stripped of a generation of talented young players who were forced to abandon their home place in search of employment.

The club refused to succumb to adversity. Its place in the fabric of community life is too important to allow it to go under. In 2020, Easkey Juniors reached the All-Ireland final and it seemed as if the entire village decamped to Croke Park, such was the massive turn-out of fans cheering on the 'Sea Blues'. It was a graphic illustration of how much the GAA club means to the parish. It rhymes effortlessly with the ebb and flow of all that matters in the area.

Noel McGuire, the man who captained Sligo to only their third senior Connacht Championship triumph in 2007, is a product of Easkey's fervent GAA tradition. The day he lifted the Nestor Cup in Hyde Park was his crowning glory but the occasions he spent slogging it out in the cherished blue of Easkey are a treasured part of his story too.

As a player, he left it all on the pitch. There were days of unconfined joy and there were days of painful despair. He wasn't one for indulging in needless gloating on the good ones or in self-recrimination on the bad ones. It was all about giving it his best every time he pulled on the club or county jersey. That's what defined him as the perfect captain. A selfless leader who consistently contributed 100 per cent and demanded nothing less from those around him.

When Tommy Breheny was assembling a squad to launch a concerted bid for provincial glory in 2007, he was blessed with an abundance of outstanding footballers. By Sligo standards, it was something of a golden generation. There were many solid young men well qualified to assume the crucial role of captain. Breheny chose McGuire. It was as good a decision as he ever made.

The Easkey man, an uncompromising and fearless defender, led from the front. On and off the pitch he reflected Sligo's self-confidence, nothing flashy or arrogant, just a measured portrayal of the county's renewed sense of ambition. Sligo, so long the unconsidered outsiders, were overdue some respect. McGuire personified that defiance.

There had been better Sligo teams which crumbled under the weight of expectation but the 2007 squad was streetwise. They weren't seduced by the hype or exaggerated celebrity. They just got on with the job. And when the task was done, courtesy of a nailbiting one-point win over Galway in the decider at Hyde Park, McGuire emerged from the manic pitch celebrations to lift the coveted trophy.

He confirms:

> It's something I'll never take for granted. To captain the 2007 team was the greatest moment of my career. It meant so much to me personally, but it was also a very proud moment for my family, my club and the wider Easkey community. It was an unforgettable experience.

There was never a time when McGuire wasn't going to be a footballer. When he was a young boy, he would listen to stories of Easkey's greatest team, the side that won the senior county championship in 1966, thereby ending 25 barren seasons for the GAA-mad village. They reached two subsequent finals, losing to Coolooney/Ballisodare on both occasions, but those setbacks couldn't take the shine off the breakthrough achievement of the 1966 team.

McGuire's father, JP, lined out at centre-half back on the multi-talented team. His mother, Mary, had a brother on the team, PJ Sloyan, Dessie's father.

Mikey Kenny, a player of great renown with club and county, was another star. These are all household names in Easkey, revered to this day.

That was the rich football legacy McGuire inherited. It fired his imagination and fuelled his ambition.

He's the youngest of four brothers. Brian, the eldest, played regularly for the club but the other boys, Kenneth and Oliver, had no more than a passing interest.

McGuire was hooked from an early age, however. If the valiant deeds of his father's generation of footballers were the source of his initial fascination, he soon identified heroes of his own. Fintan Feeney, Declan and Dermot Kevany and Eamonn Sweeney were playing for the county team around the late 1980s and early 1990s. It was rare for Easkey to have so many lads on the county panel at the same time. It was an exciting time for the club.

He vividly remembers going to the county Intermediate final in 1990. It was the summer of Italia '90. All over the country, young kids were mesmerised by Jack's Army. The national party was in full swing. Back in Easkey, the super-stars were home-grown. McGuire remembers:

> The 1990 intermediate team were our heroes. It's my earliest memory of going to a match with my father. It was a huge day for the club. I was playing with the under-12s and the players on the intermediate team were my inspiration. That day sticks out in my memory. Even though I was still very young, I was already thinking in terms of following in those lads' footsteps.

He revelled in the busy schedule of underage football where Peter Brady, PJ Sloyan, John Lavelle, Paul O'Brien and Michael Kelly Senior were among the coaches who nurtured his fledgling talent. There was great fun too in the primary school competitions within the parish. He was beginning to become a stand-out player among his peers.

By the time he went to Jesus and Mary secondary school in Enniscrone, McGuire was already coming to the attention of the county selectors. The PRO at Easkey, the late Marty Duffy, was among those who spotted his potential.

"I remember Marty saying to me that I would play for Sligo one day. He was the first person to show that faith in me. It was a nice bit of encouragement which I probably needed at the time," says McGuire.

Leo Boland shared Duffy's appraisal of the young defender. He brought him into the county under-16 panel in 1994. An exciting crop of youngsters was coming through the system. Lads like Seán Davey, Philip Gallagher, Tommy Brennan, John McPartland, Eamonn Cawley, Seán Flannery and Kenneth

Morley were among McGuire's teammates when they won the Manning Cup. The following year, the same group of players ran Galway close in the Connacht Minor Championship.

It was a particularly productive era for underage football in the county, but the elusive Provincial title eluded them. McGuire was on an excellent minor team which lost to Mayo in a Connacht final in 1996 and the same group of players was beaten by Roscommon in an under-21 final three years later.

Those disappointments left a scar:

> We came so close at both minor and under-21 level but failed to make the breakthrough. It was hard to take. Looking back on it now, it probably gave us the motivation to succeed at senior level a few years later but it didn't feel like that at the time. It was heartbreaking.

There was some consolation when Sligo won the Hastings Cup in 1999. By then, the Easkey man had already sampled the demanding challenges of senior inter-county football.

He had just completed his Leaving Cert when he got the call from Mickey Moran. It was totally unexpected, not least because it was just weeks before the 1997 Connacht final. He was togged out on the day of the decider against Mayo at Dr Hyde Park but didn't see any action.

"To be honest, I was thrilled to be involved with the panel," he confesses. "We were beaten in the final, which took some of the shine off the occasion, but for a lad who was had just finished secondary school it was a big thing to be around the senior county squad."

He made his senior debut in a league match against Dublin the following autumn – a game that still retains a place in Sligo GAA folklore as a late Eamonn O'Hara goal gave the Yeats County an unlikely victory. McGuire remembers:

> It was some introduction to senior football. We felt we were at the start of something special. Mickey Moran changed the whole mindset of the county. We moved to a different level in terms of training and preparation, and it was a very exciting time to be involved with the county team.

He was a permanent fixture in the full-back line on the Sligo team which enjoyed a memorable run to the All-Ireland quarter-final in 2002, a thrilling campaign which ended with a controversial defeat to Armagh in a replay:

> We were definitely good enough to go at least one step further. Armagh went on to win the All-Ireland that year. We were that close. Who can say what might have happened if we'd beaten Armagh?

The agonising defeat to the Ulster side is one of many setbacks endured by the Easkey defender during years of loyal service to his native county. It comes with the territory when you play for Sligo. The upside is that the good days, though rare, are wonderfully invigorating.

The epic breakthrough in 2007 was the dividend from years of unyielding dedication.

"It took a while for it all to sink in," says McGuire.

> It seemed as if the whole of Sligo was on the pitch at the final whistle. Even making the victory speech was a bit surreal. I didn't have anything prepared so it was just a case of making it up as I went along.
>
> The next day, we did a tour of the county, and the high point was bringing the Cup to Easkey. I never thought I'd see the day. To be there with my club and my family and knowing that the whole county was behind us was so special.

McGuire was on the Sligo team which lost to Roscommon in the 2010 Connacht final and was on the bench when the Yeats County were beaten by Mayo in the provincial decider two years later. He played his last game for the county against New York in the 2012 campaign.

He's currently a selector with the senior county squad and is in his twenty-seventh year playing adult football for Easkey.

The football tradition is as strong as ever in the family. His niece Ellen plays for the Sligo senior ladies' team while her sister, Laura, is captain of the county under-14s.

He is married to Sineád and the couple live in Easkey with their two children, James and Emma, both of whom are already shaping up as future stars.

Kieran Quinn

Talented player who always knows the score

"Childhood dream comes true" is a common theme in the lives of most successful sportsmen and musicians. The story of the young lad fantasising about being a football star and then becoming one; or the garage band suddenly breaking out to world dominance. Kieran Quinn tears the script to shreds. He's scaled massive heights as a Gaelic footballer and as a professional musician – but he never dreamed of being either.

The Coolera man, one of a rare breed of Sligo footballers to own a Connacht Senior Championship winners' medal and to have played in Croke Park on six occasions, was nineteen years old before he engaged passionately with the game.

And Kieran Quinn the prolific pianist and composer, whose incredibly successful Theme Nights have transformed the face of Sligo's entertainment scene, only turned to music because he couldn't find exhilaration in any other career.

If both were life accidents waiting to happen, the consequences could scarcely be more fascinating. To excel in either discipline would be worthy of acclaim; to have mastered both in such spectacular fashion is worthy of a standing ovation.

On the face of it, there is little to connect what appear to be two completely divergent life paths, but Quinn sees a strong link between them:

> In both disciplines, the emphasis is always on the value of team work. As a footballer, a togetherness, a camaraderie, a belief in each other is essential. Precisely the same traits would be to the forefront of my

> career in music. I'd be nothing without the dedication and talent of the people I work with, and their willingness to work hard alongside me.

Although now better known as a top-class musician rather than a successful footballer – his sell-out Theme Nights have become a Sligo institution – he reflects that without his involvement in the GAA there might never have been a career in music.

Reconnecting with his parish club, which once represented little more for him than the opportunity for a childhood game of football, gave him a fresh awareness of belonging, a sense of identity, a foundation from which to build what has become a very tangible pride in his county. At a time when he faced an ambiguous future, Quinn's involvement in the GAA provided the illuminous signpost to a life he could have never imagined possible.

Born in Perth, Australia, where his father, Roddy, was a 'flying doctor', he moved to Sligo with his family as a young child. His first memory of Gaelic football is an under-9 tournament in which he lined out for his local club, Coolera/Strandhill, and he later played for them in an under-16 county final. For most of his teenage years, however, he hardly played any football, mainly because rugby was the prominent sport at his secondary school, Clongowes College. His brief claim to fame then was the fact that he managed to keep a certain Gordon D'Arcy out of the school's under-13 team.

It wasn't until he returned from a year in Australia, squeezed in between secondary school and the commencement of his Philosophy and Psychology degree at Trinity, that Quinn began to become enthralled with football. He reflects:

> After six years in boarding school and a year away in Australia, I had lost touch with my roots. Getting back on board with Coolera helped me bridge that gap. Friends I made on that team are still important people in my life. The club became a huge part of my life, not just in terms of winning trophies and helping me get on the county team, but in helping me settle down, connect with my community and my county. That's very important to me now, but I might not have discovered it at all had it not been for the GAA.

The Coolera team he joined on his return from Australia in 1999 was beginning to emerge from a barren century when mere survival rather than success was the big achievement. But reaching a county senior final in 2000, narrowly losing out to Bunninadden in a controversial climax, rejuvenated the club. They would contest four county finals in the following decade, finally reaching the Holy Grail in 2005, defeating Curry in a memorable decider. He explains:

> We'd been to a few county finals and semi-finals by that stage, and those defeats only increased our hunger to finally get a title. Winning in 2005, for the first time in 98 years, was so huge for all of us, the players, management, the entire community. Maybe we should have won a few more, but the relief of finally getting over the line that day is something I'll never forget.

By now, Quinn had established himself as a regular midfielder in a Sligo team that was beginning to cause minor shockwaves on the GAA scene. An astonishing victory over reigning Leinster champions, Kildare in the 2001 All-Ireland qualifiers, proved to be a crucial turning point. It was the county's first appearance at Croke Park for 26 years. Nobody was more surprised than Kieran Quinn to be part of such history.

> I never expected to be a county player, but I was tall and athletic, and even though my skill factor wouldn't have been huge, I suppose I brought a dimension to the team which it needed at that point. When I think of so many really talented guys who played for Sligo over the years and never got a chance to run out at Croke Park, I know how privileged I was. In a relatively short inter-county career, maybe six or seven years, I played at Croke Park six times. I was incredibly lucky.

The following year, Sligo went even further, reaching the quarter-finals where, after a thrilling drawn game against Armagh at Croke Park, they were narrowly beaten in a replay at Navan. Armagh would go on to clinch their first All-Ireland, leaving many observers to argue that this might have been Sligo's best ever chance at being the unlikely winners of the Sam Maguire. The hurt of the loss still resonates with Quinn, but the passage of time has allowed him to process it.

> At the time, Armagh and ourselves were seen as two new teams trying to do something really special. Armagh had won three of the four previous Ulster titles and would go on to win an All-Ireland and four more Ulsters, so they weren't quite the rookies we were. We were going into that game on the back of very little, and it's very difficult to suddenly reach that standard.
>
> We missed so many chances over both games and we should have had a penalty towards the end of the replay. In that sense, we were unlucky. But our prospects of winning an All-Ireland even if we'd beaten Armagh were always remote. We would have had to face Dublin at Croke Park in

the semi-final. Maybe we were good enough to beat one of those teams on any given day, but not two in succession.

Perhaps if we'd had a fully-firing Paul Taylor in the forward line it might have been a factor. Paul was one of the best players the county ever had, but he was rattled with injury that year. At his fittest, he might have made a difference.

What I take away from that year is that it should have been the start of a process. We should have been able to build on it and maybe become a realistic contender, but it didn't happen.

Nonetheless, under the shrewd management of Tommy Breheny, Sligo had recovered sufficiently to finally win a Connacht title in 2007, bridging a 28-year gap in a final victory against highly-fancied Galway.

The secret of that team was the togetherness of the group. We'd started the championship with a trip to New York. There was plenty of craic, but a lot of work, too. We felt we had a chance, and our self-belief grew to a degree of utter confidence once Eamonn O'Hara scored that wonder goal in the final. In the end, we just about fell over the line, but after such a long wait for a Connacht title, the entire county just breathed a huge sigh of relief.

Having been part of title-winning club and county teams in the space of two years, how does he compare the two?

I couldn't rate one above the other. For five years, the club had been such a huge part of my personal life, let alone the football side of things, so to finally get a county title for Coolera was exceptionally special. The county success was on a much bigger scale, a different type of buzz, bigger crowds, live television coverage, bonfires blazing on the road home. Totally different. But at the heart of it, the emotions were similar.

It was about this time that Quinn's musical career began to gather momentum. A few years earlier, he'd done a course in professional music training in Dublin and was now beginning to play gigs around local pubs. The prospect of making a living from something he had once regarded only as a fulfilling hobby began to take shape.

> Becoming a professional musician would have been a real left-field choice for somebody with my background. Both my parents are in the medical profession. I had a degree in psychology and philosophy. But I didn't want to be a doctor. I didn't know what I wanted to be but I knew what I didn't want to be. I couldn't find anything to excite me. I looked everywhere for inspiration but could not find it anywhere, until I saw an advertisement for a professional musician course in Dublin. And it just clicked. For the first time I had found something which gave me the same buzz as I'd experienced from football. I wanted more of it.

During regular gigs at the local Source club, he would invite guest musicians to sing a song or two, which proved to be the genesis of the famous Theme Nights. The idea originated with Dervish singer Cathy Jordan, who, in 2011, suggested a Christmas get-together of the various guests, and it grew from there.

What began as an informal gathering of like-minded friends and musicians has become a musical phenomenon in Sligo and further afield. When the merry troupe headed to the iconic Dublin venue Vicar Street in 2018, they played to a sold-out audience. With such a wealth of local talent to call upon, Quinn is never stuck for participants, but alongside the cream of the county's professional ranks, he always makes a point of having at least one newcomer for each show. He also hosts Teenage Theme Nights, where gifted youngsters are given their shot in the limelight. He confides:

> It's a bit like being a football manager when it comes to the Theme Nights. I choose the theme, the songs, the singers, the orchestra. It has to be a collaborative effort, just as football teams are, but I'm the one making the final choices. With the teenage theme nights, it's like being in charge of the county minors and hoping some of them will make the senior team. It's all about that feeling of being part of a team and achieving something together.

Between writing and recording albums, hosting a popular podcast, his piano teaching, a weekly newspaper column, and two or three theme nights each year, it's hard to figure where the affable musician would find time for many leisure pursuits. But a couple of hours each week are sacrosanct. That's when you'll find him down at the Coolera/Strandhill GAA pitch, coaching the under-12s. The roots will always need tending to.

Local GAA Clubs

Heartbeat of community life

There are twenty-five GAA clubs in Sligo. The rivalry can be claustrophobic and sometimes robust in a relatively small county but there's an upside, too. The tight network of clubs generates an alliance that is uniquely intimate, leading to tribal confrontations on the pitch and a supportive and empathetic coalition off it.

In times of triumph or tragedy, the club is a beacon of communal solidarity, the source of joyous celebration on the glory days or a sanctuary of heartfelt kindness on occasions of pain and heartbreak. In essence, it is the heartbeat of the community, the glue that holds everything together.

In the last few years, Curry GAA club has had cause to illustrate its compassionate soul on more occasions that any organisation should have to.

"It's in times of despair that the real strength of the GAA at club level is seen at its best," declares Curry's long-serving footballer Kevin Giblin. "The club is there to offer whatever support it can in difficult times. There's much more to a GAA club than just winning football matches."

Inclusivity is another laudable feature of grassroots football, according to Giblin.

> Nobody is left out. People are drawn to football for different reasons. It isn't always about the medals. For many, it will be the ambition of having a great career, for others it will be just to feel involved. The club provides that focal point.

A principal at Moylough National School, Giblin made his senior club debut in 1986 and played his last game in the 2015 county championship final against

St Mary's. His wife, Naoimh, served as Curry club secretary for a few years, strengthening the family's bond with the club.

"It's part of our lives. It's the way it is for a lot of families. The GAA means so much," he says.

Gaelic football DNA runs deep in the Kent family in Sligo town. St Mary's club named their splendid home venue at Ballydoogan in honour of founding member Dick Kent, whose sons, John and Jim, were revered footballers for more than three decades with the club. The boys' mother, Theresa, doubled as club secretary and laundry lady for several years.

"Our family is steeped in the history of St Mary's, right back to when the club was founded in the 1970s", John Kent points out.

A quintessential club man, he made his senior debut in 1976 and went on to win nine senior championship medals with St Mary's. Between times, he went on a soccer scholarship to the University of Florida, played for Sligo Rovers, with whom he won a runners-up medal in the League Cup in 1975, and had a pre-season trial with Glasgow Celtic.

"They let me go and kept Kenny Dalglish, so I suppose they knew what they were doing," jokes Kent.

A gifted forward, he was the star of the Sligo county team for many years but playing for St Mary's was more fulfilling.

> I won my first Championship medal in 1977 and the last of nine in 2001. I also won three Connacht club medals with the club and played on the losing side in three other provincial finals. It was great to be involved in some of the club's greatest days, especially playing alongside my brother, Jim. Given our family's strong association with the club, those victories meant everything to us.

A knee injury prevented him from prolonging his stay in Florida and curtailed any ambitions of a career in professional soccer. He often wonders how things might have worked out had he completed the scholarship in America or if he had an extended run in the League of Ireland with Rovers.

Instead, he had a sort of homecoming at St Mary's, displaying unconditional loyalty to the club his father helped to create.

> Playing for St Mary's involved a lot of commitment, but it was never a burden. We enjoyed the craic, even meeting our parents for a few drinks and a chat after the games was great fun. We took the football seriously too. Everybody in the county was delighted when we won our first title, because we were new on the scene, but I think they got a bit fed up with

> us when we started winning so many championships. It generated a fair bit of intense rivalry, but it was all part and parcel of the club scene and I absolutely loved it.

The McPartland family from Strandhill share a unique story which illustrates the limitless appeal of Gaelic games. John Senior and his sons, John Junior and Adrian, manage three different clubs in the county, each obsessively committed to the cause.

Coolera/Strandhill manager Adrian McPartland admits:

> It's crazy to have three managers from the same family. Our father, a proud Fermanagh man, has been involved in the GAA all his life. He's managed clubs in four different counties, Sligo, Fermanagh, Leitrim and Donegal, and he passed on his passion for the game to his sons.

John Senior is manager of intermediate side Ballymote, while John Junior is in charge at junior outfit Owenmore Gaels.

"GAA is the topic of conversation when we get together, and dad is always willing to pass on the odd word of advice. It's great craic in some ways but very serious at the same time," Adrian asserts.

He made his senior debut for Coolera/Strandhill in 2002 and only hung up his boots when he was appointed manager in 2020:

> I loved every minute of it. I played alongside my brother, John, for many years and my father was manager and selector at different stages over the years. It was part and parcel of family life. It was great to represent the community, playing with friends you'd have known since you started off in national school. The sense that we were all in it together meant everything.

The standout moment was the club's success in the senior championship in 2005. Adrian was one of the youngest members of the team and his brother, John, won the man-of-the-match award.

Tourlestrane's Shane Dunne holds the record for most senior championship medals in Sligo. He's won a magical total of ten during a career which started with his debut in a county final as a sixteen-year-old forward in 1997.

He scored the winning goal in the 2009 final and was captain when Tourlestrane won the title in 2013. He played in his last final in 2018 before a nagging back injury brought his 21-year senior career to an end. He says:

> I live five minutes down the road from the club, so the GAA was always a huge part of my life. The friends you make, the memories of the great days, the social aspect of it all. That's what the club is all about. Now that I'm retired, I miss the matches and the training but most of all I miss the interaction with everybody. Playing for the club was a great way of getting out and meeting people, of just being involved in the community and being part of something that meant so much to everybody.

The Carden brothers, JP, Kevin, Keith and Raymond, were mainstays of the Enniscrone team for over three decades. Their careers didn't run concurrently but they all played together on the intermediate team which endured agonising defeats in successive semi-finals in 2004 and 2005.

"We looked out for each other, drove each other on," insists JP. "The family has always had a strong association with the club and long may that continue."

JP made his senior debut in 1995 and turned out for the club for the last time in 2020.

"I played 25 years in the league and 23 in the championship and I still haven't announced my retirement," he jokes. "Most of those seasons were spent in the intermediate grade, always battling against the odds trying to win promotion to the senior ranks."

Emigration and academic pursuits make it difficult for rural clubs to maintain playing resources and Enniscrone has felt the pinch in recent years. As JP reveals:

> Some years you could have as much as 40 per cent of players living away from home. It makes it difficult to field strong teams, but the club keeps going. That's the way of things for a rural club. There will always be a few barren years, but you take that in your stride and move on.

JP was involved in the management team of the county minor squad which won the Connacht Minor Championship in 2021 and is currently managing the Enniscrone intermediate team.

> As long as I'm enjoying it, I'll keep going. I've been involved in the GAA all my life. At club level, it's all about enjoyment, making friends, getting involved in the social side of things. Nearly everything in the parish revolves around the club. It's the heartbeat of the community.

Most clubs in the county field two teams in league and championship competitions, meaning that the level of GAA activity in the county is as dynamic and competitive as anywhere in the country. It's estimated that up to 1,500 participants, including players, managers, mentors and back-up volunteers are engaged in adult club games on weekends from April to October every year.

It's a gigantic operation and offers graphic affirmation that club football in Sligo is not only relevant but is an essential component of the sporting fabric of a county proudly committed to the national games.

Sligo Rising

Youngsters driving a football revolution

It was over. But it didn't feel like the end.

As Dessie Sloyan surveyed a disconsolate dressing room at Kingspan Breffni Park after his gallant under-20 team had been beaten by Kildare in the All-Ireland semi-final in 2022, his gut instinct told him this could be the start of an exciting new era for Sligo football rather than a bitter conclusion to a one-off adventure.

Sure, there would be hurt and a sense of a missed opportunity. There would be painstaking analysis of the 'what-if' moments, the small margins that tipped the balance. It would all be in the mix, the carcass of another unfulfilled day for Sligo laid bare for an unforgiving bone-picking ritual.

But none of that could diminish the historic breakthrough engineered by Sloyan's exhilarating young squad – the first Sligo team to win a Connacht under-20 title (previously contested at under-21 level).

Nobody would ever forget the emotion and unrestrained joy of a dramatic evening at Markievicz Park when Sligo threw off the shackles to fashion a pulsating win over Mayo in the Connacht final. It wasn't just the result that hammered out a defiant statement of intent. The team's courageous performance in the face of adversity – they were a man down and five points in arrears on the home stretch – revealed a new breed of Sligo footballer: stubborn, fearless and totally absorbed in the doctrine of self-belief.

With the game in the melting pot and a precious title there to be won, it was the Yeats County who found a way to deliver the fatal blow. And when Jack Lavin's speculative last-ditch effort somehow traced a thunderous route to the back of the net, it was at once glorious affirmation of Sligo's arrival as a serious force and a launching pad for a prosperous future.

Even if the pursuit of an All-Ireland title came unstuck against a marginally superior Kildare team in the semi-final, it doesn't require a major excavation exercise to unearth genuine reasons for optimism in the county.

"We would have loved to have taken the journey at least one step further but the mood in the county is still fairly positive", reports Sloyan.

> When I took over as under-20 manager in 2019, my plan was to develop a conveyor belt of good footballers and to create an environment where we wouldn't lose players during the transition period from minor to under 20s to senior. We've done well in that regard and won a coveted Connacht title along the way. The big positive from it all is that Sligo players can now stand toe-to-toe with any other county and know they are as good as them in terms of confidence, ability and preparation. That is the dividend from what the under-20 team achieved.

The breakthrough success also unveiled a stirring unity of purpose in the county. When the players threatened to boycott the Connacht final in a row over the venue, the county board weighed in with their full support. The provincial council wanted to stage the final at the Connacht headquarters in Bekan in Mayo but Sligo were entitled to home advantage on a long-established home and away arrangement. The Yeats County dug their heels in and the authorities relented. The game went ahead at Markievicz Park.

"It was no idle threat from the players; they wouldn't have played the game in Mayo", confirms Sloyan. "Full credit to the Connacht Council, they took on board Sligo's position and made the right decision. It was a moral victory."

The controversy served only to fire the passion of Sligo supporters. Markievicz Park was bouncing on the day of the final. Rarely had a home crowd being so vocal in support of their team.

"The atmosphere was incredible," agrees Sligo captain Jack Lavin. "We never experienced anything like it. There's no doubt the crowd carried us over the line."

Lavin's late goal, following on quickly from Eoin Smith's goal a few minutes earlier, was crucial in swinging the game in Sligo's favour. He insists:

> People can talk about luck all they like but I firmly believe you make your own luck in football. Whatever bit of good fortune we got, we fully earned it.

Following on from the breakthrough success of the Sligo minor team in 2021 which won the provincial crown for the first time since 1968, the achievement of the under-20 squad offers compelling evidence that the colossal work invested in underage football in the county is at last reaping tangible reward.

Here's the context. Over the course of 72 barren years, from 1949 to 2021, Sligo claimed just one underage title of note, the minor win in 1968. It amounted to a grim record in a province with just five competing counties. Now they've captured back-to-back minor and under-20 Connacht championships in successive seasons.

The underage famine was ended by the 2021 minors, itself an inspiring story four years in the making.

Zoom meetings, quiz nights, ice-bucket challenges, sessions of trick-shots and all sorts of random offbeat forms of entertainment would not be a typical schedule of preparation for promising young footballers but minor manager Paul Henry had to think outside the box during a global pandemic. Covid restrictions severely impacted the squad's plans and necessitated a somewhat novel approach. As the manager explains:

> It was bizarre in some ways but, at the same time, it helped create a tight bond between the players. The nucleus of the group had been together since the under-14 grade so they grew up together in a football sense. When Covid hit, they were determined it wouldn't derail all the progress we made up to that point. We had to do things in a different way, and they bought into it. Indeed, a lot of the novel stuff came from the players themselves. It created a special dynamic within the squad and the players brought that into match situations.

No generation of footballers had ever had to contend with the strange, soulless environment unleashed by the Covid outbreak. Here were young men who should have been enjoying the thrills and spills of teenage liberation. Instead, they were trapped in a miserable cycle of constraints, denied even the routine formalities associated with their fledgling football careers. Henry elaborates:

> We couldn't travel to matches together on a team coach. The players' parents had to drive them to the games. We even had to tog out in the stands for the Connacht semi-final and final. It was surreal. It says a lot about the character of the players that they were able to deal with all that and still emerge as worthy champions.

A confident win over Leitrim in the semi-final set up a showdown with Roscommon in the decider at Hyde Park. The weight of history was against them, but Henry was anxious not to dwell on the past.

> There was a lot of talk about the fact that Sligo hadn't won a minor championship since 1968 and we didn't want that to become an issue for the players. It was never referenced within our own bubble. Our lads were young, carefree and excited about the prospect of playing in a final. They just wanted to go out and play football. There was no point in burdening them with any historical stuff.

As it turned out, the team created their own history, producing a title-winning performance deserving of a treasured place in the folklore of Sligo football.

A few days later, Henry and one of his selectors, Colm McGee, visited Colm Mullarkey in Tubbercurry with the Tom Kilcoyne Cup. Mullarkey was the manager of the Sligo team which won the championship in 1968. He was overjoyed that the gap had been bridged. As Henry says:

> That was a lovely moment. It was then that the enormity of what we achieved hit home. Hopefully, we won't have to wait as long again before the next title. The aim must be to get to a situation where Sligo winning Connacht championships at any level is the norm rather than the exception. I believe that's a realistic target.

Two underage titles in two years are encouraging but nobody is losing the run of themselves.

"It might have the appearance of an overnight success," says county board chariman Seán Carroll, "but nothing could be further from the truth. It's the result of relentless work at county board and club level over a long number of years."

The appointment of Liam Óg Gormley as games manager was the catalyst. His fingerprints are all over the development of the game in schools, colleges and clubs throughout the county. There's invaluable input too from the county's four full-time coaches, Stephen Henry, Pat Kilcoyne, Cian O'Connor and Aaron McGowan, and the county board's coaching and games development officer, Peadar Niland, is a progressive and innovative administrator. The recruitment of athletic performance coaches was crucial too. The network of volunteers spreads far and wide. There are thriving nurseries at every club in the county. The nerve centre is the recently developed centre of excellence at Scarden, where further investment in coaching and development infrastructure is in the pipeline.

"We're on the right track but we're not kidding ourselves. We know there's still a massive amount of work to do," concedes Carroll.

> In terms of developing players, we're casting the net wider than ever. Eleven of the starting fifteen on the under-20 team for the Connacht final were not with senior clubs. And three of the players in the under-20 squad did not make the minor panel when they were younger. It proves that we're not leaving anybody behind. Ultimately, it's all about bringing through quality footballers for the senior team. In that regard, winning minor and under-20 titles is hugely significant, in terms of morale and confidence. It's also a reward for the loyal support the GAA receives within the county, not just in attendance at matches but in relation to our various fund-raising efforts. We're always looking at ways to improve numbers in those areas as well.

The chairman is convinced Sligo should be competing for Connacht titles and doing well in the higher regions of the National League on a consistent basis.

"We've fallen behind counties of similar size and we need to address that," he concedes.

> Our minors and under-20s have proven that we can make progress. The under-20 team was the first ever to win a Connacht title on Sligo soil. That was so special and the joy and emotion it generated throughout the county was wonderful to see. Now we've got to move on to the next level. That's the challenge and we're up for it.

If 2022 will forever have an indelible place in Sligo's roll of honour, it will also be remembered for a more sombre reason, the sad passing of Red Óg Murphy, one of the county's most gifted young footballers.

Members of the under-20 team formed a guard of honour at Red Óg's funeral, and team captain Jack Lavin dedicated the championship win to the former player and his family.

Sligo minor team which beat Roscommon in the Connacht Championship final at Hyde Park, 2021: K. Davey, R. O'Hehir, C. Johnston, R. O'Kellly-Lynch; D. Walsh, D. McLoughlin, J. Donlon; R. Doherty, C. Sheridan; M. McDaniel, R. Niland, S. Rogan; L. Marren, J. Flynn, B. Duffy. Subs: J. McGovern, S. Donoghue, C. McMorrow.

Sligo under-20 team which beat Mayo in the Connacht final at Markievicz Park, 2022: K. Davey, S. Molloy, M. McGowan, F. O'Donnell; J. Donlon, J. Lavin, C. Johnston; C. Mulligan, J. Keaney; M. Henry, E. Smith, D. Walsh; L. Marren, L. Deignan, J. Davitt. Subs: O. Flynn, G. Duffy, L. Casserly, B. Byrne, O. Gorman.

GAA (Handball)

Paddy Walsh

The man from the Angelus

Which Sligo sportsperson has appeared on television most often? It's a head-scratcher with an unlikely answer.

On at least one evening every week, just before the main *Six One News* on RTE television, Paddy Walsh is featured on the *Angelus*, a 60-second feature which attracts an average audience of more than 300,000 viewers. He can be seen deep in prayer at Sligo's Tobarnalt Holy Well, where he has worked as a volunteer caretaker for several years.

But what most viewers probably don't realise is that the man from the *Angelus* is one of Sligo's most outstanding sportsmen, having won an astonishing 30 All-Ireland handball titles as well as half a dozen county football titles. At 82 years young, he still plays handball twice a week and remains as competitive as he was when winning his first medals as far back as 1958.

"I'd still be fierce disappointed if I lost a game," he confirms, revealing his ambition to continue playing until he's at least 90 years old. "I'm in great shape, so after playing for 65 years, I don't see the point in stopping now."

Regarded as the county's greatest ever handball player, the Collooney native has swept all before him in singles and doubles championships at county, provincial and national level and crowned a remarkable career when winning his last Masters title at the age of 73 in 2013.

His passion for the game he has graced over six decades was sparked as a young man pounding a ball against the walls of an open alley near his home in Collooney. One of Ireland's oldest games, handball was a popular pastime in a 1950s Ireland which offered little else in terms of recreational pursuits. He recalls:

> Literally, there was nothing else to do. There was no television and very little money, so you spent your evenings at the ball alley. We'd play until it got dark, and the more you played the better you got. You were picking up skills without even realising it.

With the game thriving in the county, there were ball alleys in even the most remote locations. Walsh recalls epic games at alleys in Ballymote, Lissadell, Aughamore, Banada and Ballisodare, where huge crowds would assemble to pass long summer nights.

> Not many people owned cars and even bicycles were scarce enough. We used to hitch lifts the eight miles from Collooney to Ballymote for a game, and very often you'd have to walk there and back. But you thought nothing of it. It kept you fit.

His passionate commitment was rewarded with his first handball medals in 1958, when he won both the singles and doubles county championship, in the same year as he won a minor championship football medal with Ballinacarrow. Going on to win several Connacht minor and junior titles, Paddy's breakthrough at national level came when he won his first All-Ireland in 1974, a doubles championship with the late Eamon Hannon from Ballymote.

Although he had to wait until 1982 for his next national title, a Masters A championship medal, the following two decades proved to be a spectacular rollercoaster of success for the Collooney man as he clocked up a remarkable 27 All-Ireland titles in both singles and doubles. In one twelve-month period, he won four separate national titles.

> It was non-stop, but I suppose the more you win, the more you want. Playing at Croke Park in top class courts and facilities and against players regarded as the best in the country gave you an appetite for it. It was the love of the game rather than winning which kept me going, but the titles and awards along the way were always a lovely bonus.

What made his achievements ever more remarkable was the fact that he had two hip replacements at the height of his career and later battled back from two separate cancers.

> Despite all those health problems, I'd say I only rested for six months. Sometimes, you'd take a painkiller before a match and away you went. Between the handball and the football, I was always active so the

> thought of giving into an injury or illness would never have crossed my mind.

Twice named as Handballer of the Year and a recipient of a Special Achievement Award at the GAA Handball All Stars in 2009, Paddy's devotion to the game has also included many years as a coach of underage players at his local club, many of whom have gone on to become Connacht champions at various grades.

He also played a key role in the upgrading of the Collooney Handball Club, where his illustrious career began in the early 1950s. A state-of-the art 40x20 court has been built in recent years at a cost of €270,000, almost all of which had to be raised locally. Paddy's skills as a bingo organiser came in useful. He points out:

> We got a fair bit of funding, but it was still a daunting task to raise hundreds of thousands of euro in our own community. It's amazing to think two of the oldest pastimes in the country, bingo and handball, went hand-in-hand to help us raise so much money.

It was his battles with bowel and prostate cancer in 2015 which eventually brought him to his cherished role as caretaker at the Tobernalt Holy Well, not far from his home. The holy well, an ancient Christian religious shrine set in scenic woodland on the shores of Lough Gill, is especially associated with the early eighteenth century Penal times when Mass was secretly celebrated. Over the years, generations of Sligo people, of all faiths and none, have flocked to this place of secluded tranquility, where candles constantly twinkle as a representation of people's hopes and prayers.

The handball maestro found solace there during his own difficult times, so when the opportunity arose to become a voluntary caretaker, he was only too delighted to oblige, spending hours there every day making sure used candles are replaced and that the grounds are always spick and span.

When RTE revamped the daily broadcast of the *Angelus* in 2009, Tobernalt was chosen as one of a number of different locations for the one-minute feature produced by Kairos Communications. Paddy is among those featured prominently in the clip. As he admits:

> I got a bit of a shock when I first saw myself on screen. It took several hours to film the one-minute piece, but I didn't realise it would be shown so often. A lot of people recognise me from it, and of course, I get the occasional smart remark.

> But it's a very special place. I genuinely believe the prayers said there helped in my own recovery, and I have met several people who told me they were cured of some serious illnesses through their devotion to Our Lady at the Well.

Retired from his post as manager of the local FAS community workshop - he had previously been transport manager at the GWI factory in Collooney - Paddy and his wife, Theresa, are involved in a number of community organisations, but no matter how busy his schedule, time must always be found for handball.

"I'd be lost without it," confirms the man whose record of 30 All-Irelands is unlikely ever to be equalled in any Sligo sport.

GAA (Hurling)

Heroic Hurlers

National titles point way forward

Three national titles and a steady rise through the league rankings hardly qualifies as a quiet revolution. Yet Sligo's spectacular hurling revival has gone largely under the radar.

Not so long ago, the hurling landscape in the county was so barren there was no opportunity for children to play the game, no structured club or inter-county underage competitions and only a handful of senior clubs dotted around the county. Most of those promoting or playing the game were from traditional hurling bases, residing in Sligo and battling against the odds to transplant the love of the game from their home clubs to their adopted county.

Back then, Sligo was an infertile hurling outpost, scarce on resources and interest. The gulf between it and the more active counties, even those operating in the lower tiers, was so great it was impossible to imagine it would ever be bridged.

Now Sligo's stock has risen so dramatically that other counties are following their template.

"We are perceived as one of the most progressive developing counties," explains Sligo Hurling Board Chairman Seán Reynolds. "There's no magic formula. It's down to hard work at grassroots level and a supportive buy-in from the county board."

To appreciate the vast scale of the improbable transformation over the last two decades, one only has to survey the informative statistics which paint a glowing picture of unprecedented progress, not just in the numbers playing the game at school, club and county level but also in the impressive haul of silverware captured by the county's hurlers.

Where once there were no juvenile or underage outlets for the game, there are now 36 primary schools actively engaged in organised coaching, five secondary schools involved in similar programmes and eight clubs fielding underage teams. At senior level, six clubs contest a highly competitive county championship.

Another telling indication of the explosion of interest in the ancient game is the fact that the county's two most recent triumphs on the national stage, the Lory Meagher Cup in 2018 and the Nicky Rackard Cup the following year, were fashioned by teams almost exclusively made up of home-grown players.

A pivotal achievement came in 2008 when Sligo won the Rackard Cup for the first time, defeating Louth by nine points in the final at Croke Park. Managed by the late Michael Galvin and bolstered by such accomplished hurlers as Mark Burke, Ronan Cox, Liam Reidy, Michael Gilmartin, Keith Raymond and Paul Severs, the talented team broke the mould.

Although there would be some disappointments in the years that followed, the boys of 2008 proved the days of humiliation and despair were consigned to history.

Daithí Hand, a teacher at the local Mercy College, joined forces with Darragh Cox to guide the county to national glory again in the Lory Meagher Cup in 2018 and he was at the helm when the hurlers made it back-to-back Croke Park victories by claiming the Nicky Rackard Cup for a second time the following year.

Sligo also won successive promotions in the League during those years, taking the Division 3 B and Division 3 A titles in a particularly productive era for the county.

Hurling Promotion Officer Darragh Cox is a key figure in the success story, ensuring that hurling is accessible to a new generation of aspiring young players. He enthuses:

> There are thousands of primary school children actively engaged in hurling. They're getting a taste for the game in the schools and that develops at their clubs. We have Go Games from under 7s up to under 11s and club championships for under 13s, under 15s and under 17s. The county is buzzing.

Previous promotion officers Johnny Mullins and Benny Kenny did incredible work in local schools and now those solid foundations are bearing fruit.

At senior level, there have been four different county champions in recent years – Coolera, Easkey, Calry and Naomh Eoin – a healthy change from the days when the roll of honour was the exclusive domain of Calry and Tubbercurry.

Calry embellished the standard of club hurling by winning four Connacht junior titles, another significant achievement on Sligo's increasingly impressive CV.

It's also noteworthy that a growing number of talented footballers are now opting for hurling as their preferred game.

"These lads have a choice now," explains Cox. "That wasn't always the case"

Now in his 25th year playing with his local club, Calry, Cox is supremely optimistic for the future of Sligo hurling:

> We can't afford to be complacent or take our eye off the ball, but the rate of progress has been so impressive at every level of the game within the county over the last decade.

Among those putting their shoulder to the wheel to keep hurling alive in the county during less prosperous times was Mick Burke, a native of Clonmel, Co. Tipperary, who came to Sligo through his job with Coillte in 1965.

A talented hurler with his local club, Moyle Rovers, he was anxious to transfer some of his passion for the game to his new neighbours and friends in Tubbercurry.

He became a member of Sligo Hurling Board, serving as secretary for 30 years, and was involved in management and coaching teams at club and inter-county level.

Along with Jarlath McDonagh, a teacher at Tubbercurry Vocational School, he did the heavy lifting in reviving interest in the south Sligo town.

At county level, there were also encouraging signs of improvement. Among the foot soldiers in the battle to spread the appeal of hurling were men like Michael McTighe, Mick Severs, Joe Cawley, Arthur Kinsella, Joe Keane, Ray Mullen, Pat Maguire, Tom Brenan and David McVeigh.

In 1968, the Sligo junior team reached the All-Ireland junior final and there was a steady increase in the number of clubs getting involved in juvenile hurling.

"The introduction of Féile Na Gael in 1971 was a major breakthrough," according to Burke. "That was the starting point for bringing young lads through the system."

It all led to a glorious day in Croke Park in 1986 when Sligo minors won the All-Ireland B Championship, defeating Tyrone 1–9 to 1–5 in a thrilling final.

While Craobh Rua and Tubbercurry were the main players at club level for several seasons, the emergence of Tourlestrane, Western Gaels, Calry/St Joseph's, Coolera and Naomh Eoin at different periods over more recent years reflects the spread of the game. Easkey/St Farnan's, with Mickey Gordon a driving force, have planted flourishing seeds in the west of the county.

Burke believes the catalyst for Sligo's improvement was a restructuring of provincial and national competitions and the introduction of the Nicky Rackard, Christy Ring and Lory Meagher Cups.

Another loyal servant to club and county, Henry Cox, has witnessed Sligo's resurgence at first hand.

A native of Roscommon, he moved to Sligo when he secured a job with AnCo in 1977. A few years later he joined Craobh Rua and became a regular on the county team.

He was one of the founding members of the progressive Calry/St Joseph's club. They literally took the county by storm, winning several county and Connacht titles. He reports:

> There was no tradition of hurling in the club but once we introduced the game it was amazing how quickly we progressed. We started training for young lads and we didn't think it would last a month. But those first sessions were the building blocks for a very successful senior team in later years.

Cox was a selector with the triumphant Nicky Rackard squad in 2008 and took great satisfaction from the fact that so many of the winning team had come up through the underage grades at clubs around the county. Calry had ten representatives on the team.

Throughout the county, there are dedicated hurling men and women devoting endless hours to the promotion of the game. Ronan Waters, Aidan O'Reilly, Jimmy O'Brien, Declan O'Brien, John Doyle, Brian White, Edwin Mullane, Bill O'Kelly-Lynch, Brian McCann, Michael Gordon, Tom Evans, MJ Crean, Frances Howley, John Hughes and Stephen Whelan are among those working beyond the call of duty to carry on the county's rich hurling tradition. The late Donie Kirby was another prominent personality in Sligo hurling.

Under the astute leadership of Hurling Board Chairman Reynolds, Sligo continued to make impressive strides in 2022, winning the Under-17 All-Ireland Celtic Challenge Cup title for the second time in four years. An exciting campaign, which highlighted the tremendous progress at underage level in the county, reached a thrilling climax when Sligo defeated Mayo 1–11 to 2–7 in the final at Markievicz Park. The team was superbly managed by Martin Feeney and his backroom team of Stephen Whelan, Tony Quigley, Brian White and Declan O'Brien.

The Sligo team which beat Louth in the 2008 Nicky Rackard Cup final at Croke Park: C. Brennan, F. Coyne, W. Gill, R. Cox; D. Clarke, M. Burke, L. Reidy; J. Mullins, D. Collery; M. Gilmartin, D. Burke, P. Severs; J. Bannerton, K. Raymond, L. Cadden. Subs: C. Herrity, M. Shelley, C. O'Mahoney.

The Sligo team which beat Lancashire in the 2018 Lory Meagher Cup final at Croke Park: D. Reidy, J. Weir, C. O'Mahoney, T. Brennan; D. Collery, K. Raymond, N. Feehily; R. Cox, G. Cadden; J. MHugh, E. Comerford, F. Banks, G. O'Kelly-Lynch, K. Gilmartin, L. Cadden. Subs: T. O'Kelly-Lynch, N. McDermott, K. Prior, M. Davey, M. Burke.

The Sligo team which beat Armagh in the 2019 Nicky Rackard Cup final at Croke Park: M. Burke, J. Weir, N. Feehily, F. O'Kennedy; K. Banks, L. Reidy, R. McHugh; R. Cox, J. Starr; G. O'Kelly-Lynch, C. Griffin, K. Gilmartin; T. O'Kelly-Lynch, K. Raymond, G. Cadden. Subs: S. Crowley, M. Gordon, K. Prior.

The Sligo Under-17 team which won the Celtic Challenge Cup in 2022: T. Hargadon, C. O'Dowd, C. White, E. Durkan; D. Dunleavy, N. Kelly, M. Costigan; M. Carroll, C. Lang; P. Walsh, R. O'Kelly-Lynch, J. Feeney; A. Rolston, C. Keenan, D. O'Brien. Other members of the panel were T. Sheridan, O. Hennessey, J. McCaughey, M. Percy, C. Hughes, O. Whelan, M. Gray, S. O'Loughlin, C. Vereker, J. McDaniel, R. Connellan, H. Cawley, S. McDonagh, D. Tiernan, A. Kearns, T. Doggett, T. Kinnane.

Keith Raymond

Sparkling gem in hurling's backwaters

Keith Raymond's story is slightly unusual. If he was a native of Kilkenny or Cork or Tipperary, it would fit neatly into a pattern of routine achievement. What distinguishes his extraordinary journey on the long and winding road to hurling success is that it starts and finishes in Sligo.

His accolades include three All-Ireland medals – two Nicky Rackards and one Lory Meagher – three Railway Cup final appearances and five Champion 15 awards (the equivalent of the All Stars in football and top tier hurling). He's also represented Ireland in the annual shinty matches against Scotland.

It's an impressive catalogue of accomplishment yet there is a lingering sense it falls short of appropriate reward for a supremely talented hurler who made his senior club debut with Calry/St Joseph's at just thirteen years of age and his senior inter-county debut two years later.

He devoted seventeen seasons to Sligo's cause, many of them in the unfulfilling obscurity of the lower regions of the national league. Far from the glitz and glamour of big-ticket theatres, his unique talent illuminated the barren environs of the backwaters. Defying the conventional notion that so-called weaker counties can't produce quality hurlers, Raymond was a compelling beacon of hope, not just for Sligo but for all the lower-ranked counties dreaming of a big breakthrough.

There were days he pondered if he belonged in the relatively limited confines of Sligo hurling. In a searingly honest reflection of his career he says:

> At times, I felt trapped. I knew I was good enough to play at a higher level. I'd watch Tipperary or Kilkenny and I'd say to myself that I was every bit as good a hurler as any of those lads. I'd often wonder what

> I might have achieved had I been from one of the traditional hurling counties. That played on my mind for a few years, but I got my head around it and knuckled down.

A teacher at Coola post-primary school, Raymond's commitment to Sligo never wavered. He loved playing for the county. He wouldn't have put his life on hold for nearly two decades if he hadn't been passionate about pulling on the black and white jersey.

Even if he was occasionally seduced by the prospect of playing for more prosperous counties, the bond with Sligo was ultimately unbreakable.

It's not hard to trace his hurling DNA. The family roots branch out from Killenaule in Co. Tipperary. Fanatical hurling country. His father, Richard, a dentist, died when he was two years old. His mother, Margaret, moved the family to Sligo to be close to her sister, Sheelagh Hanly, a former mayor of the town. Her children, Yvette and Keith, merged into the ebb and flow of life in their new home without any fuss.

Growing up in the heartland of Calry/St Joseph's GAA club, Raymond attended St. Edward's national school, where one of the teachers, Bernard Mulhern, a former Sligo county footballer, encouraged his love of Gaelic games.

He wasn't instantly attracted to the joys of hurling, however. Twice, he rejected his mother's suggestion to join the local club.

"She brought me out the third day and more or less said it was my last chance," he recalls. "So, I reluctantly got out of the car and never looked back."

Joe Keane and Henry Cox were building a strong senior hurling team at the club which would go on to claim multiple county titles and it wasn't long before Raymond's flourishing talent caught their eye.

He was fourteen years old when he played in his first county senior final in 2002. The record books reveal Tubbercurry won the match. Raymond remembers little else.

"All that sticks in my memory is that I was frozen to the bone. There wasn't a pick on me. I had no strength at all", he muses.

In the years that followed he bulked up and was obsessed with improving his game.

He became so proficient he could play in any position. And he did, in goals, in the backs, at midfield and in the forwards. It didn't matter where he lined out, he was a merciless scoring machine. He contributed 1–8 on the sublime day Sligo beat Louth in the final of the Nicky Rackard Cup at Croke Park in 2008.

It represented an historic breakthrough for the county and a dream come true for their top marksman. He beams at the memory.

> Just to run out on Croke Park was pure magic. I said to my mother before the game that if I score a point in the final, I will be happy to retire there and then. As it happened, I got our first score, and I was thinking that no matter what happens I can always say I scored a point at Croke Park. I was buzzing.

The following year he was selected on the Connacht Railway Cup squad – the only player outside Galway to make the panel. He felt like a fish out of water:

> I went down to the first training session and I was looking around at all these household names in the dressing room and I was gobsmacked. Lads like Ollie and Joe Canning were legends to me and here I was from Sligo mixing in with them.

He was starstruck too on a trip to Dubai for an exhibition game between Connacht and Leinster. He could hardly believe he was in the same company as Henry Shefflin and Tommy Walsh, players he admired from afar. Now he was competing against them. This was big-time hurling, and he was part of it. The child inside him was chuffed.

"I was on cloud nine," he laughs. "It was as if all my dreams had come true."

He made the Railway Cup teams again in 2012 and 2014 and was the talisman for Sligo when they won the Lory Meagher Cup in 2018 and the Nicky Rackard Cup for a second time the following year.

He was captain in 2018 and reckons he played some of the best hurling of his career in the Rackard Cup campaign the next season. But what he remembers most about both those years is the poignant visits he made to the grave of his boyhood friend Gary Dillon, who died in 2014 after a brave battle with cystic fibrosis.

The year he was captain he got a commemorative sliothar at a press day in the build-up to the final. On the Saturday before the match, he laid it on Gary's grave at Scarden cemetery.

"I whispered a little prayer and asked Gary to send one over the bar for me at Croke Park," remembers Raymond.

> I did the same thing the following year on the day before the Nicky Rackard Cup final. Just one point Gary, I prayed. And we won both finals by a single point. I'm convinced they were Gary's scores.

As a further tribute to his dear friend, Raymond had Gary's nickname, "Dilzy", tattooed on his left arm before the Lory Meagher Cup final. There's an iconic photograph of the Sligo captain lifting the trophy after the game and there for all to see on Raymond's extended arm is the name of the little boy with whom he shared so many carefree childhood days.

> Gary was my hero. Every time I look at that photograph of me lifting the cup at Croke Park, I see his name on my arm. It means more than anything.

Sligo's success in the 2019 Rackard Cup elevated them to the Christy Ring tier the following season. They were drawn against Offaly, once one of the superpowers of the game and now throwing serious shapes at getting back to the top table again.

It was a tantalising prospect for Sligo hurlers.

"I don't think anybody envisaged a scenario where Sligo and Offaly would be sharing the same pitch in an All-Ireland Championship match, but it was about to happen and I just couldn't wait," is how Raymond recalls the excitement generated by the draw.

After years toiling in the lower tiers, here was Sligo's chance to showcase all the hard-earned progress of recent years on the big stage.

There were times when Raymond's family flirted with the possibility of moving back to Tipperary. His uncles in Killenaule were sure he'd make the Tipperary team if he relocated to the county. It would have given him the platform his prodigious talent deserved. It never happened and now Raymond was content the Christy Ring Cup would satisfy his thirst for a taste of the big time.

His preparations were all-consuming. He even hired a personal nutritionist and strength and conditioning coach at his own expense. For eight grueling months, he pushed himself to the limit of endurance, all so that he would have what he terms "an outrageous year of hurling" in 2020.

Then the world changed. In the blink of an eye, the devastating impact of Covid-19 wiped out everything, including the GAA's scheduled programme of fixtures. He fumes:

> All I put myself through was all for nothing. At first, the expectation was that it would be a short break, but it just dragged on and on. The uncertainty was killing me. I became very disillusioned.

Years earlier, he had purchased a racing bike, initially as a way of sharpening up his fitness levels. Now in desperation he turned to the thrills and spills of race riding to fill the void caused by the absence of hurling in his life.

He wondered if it would give him the same fulfilment he experienced in the heat of battle on a hurling field. It did. And he was good at it. He won the Connacht A4 Championship in Loughrea in August 2020.

"I have to be involved in a competitive sport at a high level," he stresses. "I lost that in hurling, but I rediscovered it on the bike."

He was 32 years old when he played his last match for Sligo. He never officially retired but it's unlikely he'll return to the fold.

He misses the buzz of matchdays and the camaraderie of the dressing room, but he's happy to leave it all behind, content in the knowledge he contributed more than most to the hurling revival in the county.

Golf

Cecil Ewing

One of the greatest amateur golfers of all time

Two months after her father's untimely death in 1973, grief still raw and even happy memories laced with pain, Ann Bradshaw received an uplifting letter at her home in Cleveragh, Sligo, bearing an American postmark. It proved a fitting epitaph to one of Sligo's greatest ever sportsmen, Cecil Ewing, whose towering legacy still resonates over Irish amateur golf nearly 50 years after his death.

Perhaps the pinnacle of his glittering career came at the 1938 British Amateur Championship at Troon, where as a 40/1 outsider, Ewing surpassed all expectations to reach the final, causing a frenzy of excitement throughout Ireland and particularly in his local County Sligo Golf Club, where he was regarded as its greatest ambassador. Although there was to be no fairytale ending, as American Charlie Yates took the honours, the feat was still regarded as one of the greatest performances by an Irish golfer of any generation.

Then, 35 years after their epic match, the man who had deprived Ewing of what would have been his greatest golfing honour wrote in affectionate admiration of his old adversary. The letter from Atlanta, Georgia, was not merely an expression of sympathy from a life-long friend, but a glowing testimony to one of the game's greatest ever exponents.

Ann Bradshaw treasures that letter from Charlie Yates, regarding the spirit in which it was written as a permanent reminder of her father's indelible legacy.

"Cecil was a wonderful person, full of life and always a pleasure to be with," Yates had written. The extraordinary events at Troon in 1938 suddenly became more than a distant memory. Yates' generous token of admiration had illustrated the greatness of Ewing not only as a supreme golfer but as a loyal friend and respected opponent, the very essence of a remarkable sportsperson. As Ann Bradshaw says:

> It was such a lovely surprise to receive that letter after all those years. For such a distinguished golfer, who had achieved so much in his own career, to remember my father in that way was very special. It remains a treasured possession.

A company representative for Guinness, initially based in Ballina, Ewing returned to Sligo after his marriage to Cecilia Noone, whose family owned a pub in O'Connell Street. Interestingly, Cecilia was always called Cecil, so the pair were known as Big Cecil (he was more than six foot tall) and Little Cecil.

During the war years, when petrol was rationed and, therefore, the use of cars was withdrawn from company reps, he would take the bus to major towns in the region and then cycle around that particular district meeting clients. It was a convenient, if unusual, way of keeping fit.

Ann remembers her father as a shy, reserved man who could be full of fun and boisterous good humour away from the course, but a deadly serious competitor on it. She recalls fondly:

> As a young girl, I went everywhere I could to see him play. My brother, Tom, and I loved being around golf. I just thought dad was the greatest thing. It was never a case of him being a star or anything like that. I suppose we lived in a golf bubble in that sense, and maybe didn't view him as others did, but we knew he was a special golfer. To us, he was a special dad.

If his demeanour on a golf course could be dour and fiercely competitive as he strode impassively through the fairways, Ewing was a tender, kind and considerate man in his private life. Only his close friends and family were aware of the depth of his devotion and care to his wife, who predeceased him after a long and difficult illness. Ann recalls:

> My mother was diagnosed with MS in her early 40s and slowly and steadily over the following years she became more disabled. I have vivid memories of dad helping her use her wheelchair and carrying her upstairs to bed. He was really great with her. Very few people who admired him as a golfer got to see that side of him.

Reginald Cecil Ewing was born on 11 July 1910, the son of Rosses Point hotelier Tom Ewing. The hotel, now known as the Yeats County, had been used by golfers at Rosses Point as their clubhouse before their own facilities were built. Indeed, Ewing's father had been a founder member of the County Sligo club.

Although proficient at rugby, cricket and water-polo, golf was Ewing's undisputed domain. As a schoolboy he was already winning high-profile club competitions and announced his arrival as a serious contender when reaching the final of the West of Ireland Championship in 1928 while still only 17 years old. That performance was to characterise Ewing's enormous impact on amateur golf, as he became one of the game's finest match players. His national prominence was confirmed when he won the West in 1930, the first of ten victories in the famous competition. In 1934, he set a new course record of 70 for Rosses Point when winning the Coombe Cup.

In his first appearance in the Home Internationals he won all three singles, setting a standard which he lived up to and sometimes exceeded in subsequent tournaments. In all, he played sixteen times in the Home Internationals, a number surpassed only by the legendary Joe Carr. But for the years lost during the Second World War it's likely the Sligoman would have secured that particular record.

His first selection to the Walker Cup team was in 1936 and two years later came the historic first victory over the US, in which he played such a major role. It was just a week after his defeat at the British Amateur Championship at Troon, and it was to be one of the most memorable battles in the rich history of the event.

Ewing did not play in the opening day's foursomes but was drafted in for the singles, where he faced a 24-year-old native of Wisconsen by the name of Ray Billows, the reigning New York state champion. It turned out to be one of the closest matches of the day, with the Sligo man edging it by a single hole. Ewing's victory clinched an historic 7–4 win for the home side and brought 10,000 wildly excited spectators breaking through barriers and rushing across the hallowed St Andrews turf to acclaim their heroes. It was the first British and Irish win in the Walker Cup since the series was launched in 1922, and the Sligoman had played a key role.

He later played in post-war Walker Cup matches at St Andrews 1947, Winged Foot New York in 1949 and Royal Birkdale in 1951.

In 1952, a spell of poor health seemed to mark the end of his playing career and he was appointed a Walker Cup selector. However, making a better than expected recovery, he had the unique distinction of having to opt out of being a selector as he was chosen for the team for the 1955 Walker Cup at St Andrews.

Match play was his forte, and he built up a formidable record. He won the West of Ireland ten times over a twenty-year period and was also runner-up on eight occasions. He won the Irish Amateur Open Championship in 1948 and 1951, and was runner-up on three other occasions. In the Irish Close

Championship, he was runner-up in 1946 and winner in 1948 and 1958. He was still playing for Connacht in the Inter Provincials in 1963, at the age of 53.

Ewing is one of only four players to have won the Irish Close and Open Amateur Championships in the same year, achieving the feat in 1948, 1950 and 1958.

Once his playing career ended, he still had more to achieve, making a valued contribution as Irish international selector, Walker Cup selector and member of the Committee of the R&A from 1959 to 1962. He was captain of the Irish team for ten years from 1960 onwards and guided them to notable successes in the European Team Golf Championships in Sandwich in 1965 and Turin in 1967.

This remarkable lifetime of golf was rounded off with victory at Lahinch in the inaugural Irish Seniors Amateur Open Championship in 1970, at the age of 60, when he won the trophy he himself had presented! That year he served as president of the Golfing Union of Ireland.

His death in 1973 at the young age of 63 marked the end of an era, as Cecil Ewing had been a commanding presence at County Sligo Golf Club and in the national and international golfing community for more than 45 years.

In an obituary in *Country Life*, distinguished golf writer Pat Ward Thomas described Ewing as "an outstanding golfer in a rare company, unlikely to be matched in the forseeable future."

His family donated his treasure-trove of trophies to the County Sligo Golf Club, where they are displayed alongside a wealth of other items of importance from his career in a specially dedicated Cecil Ewing Room. Sometimes, Ann Bradshaw takes a moment there to remember the good times:

> It's lovely that he's remembered in this way at a club which he truly loved. Other than his family and work, his whole life was consumed by golf. Having this room, similar to those honouring other golfers at famous clubs in other parts of the world, also brings a certain amount of gravitas to our local club. He'd like that.

**With the kind permission of the publishers, extracts are used in this article from the County Sligo Golf Club Centenary book by Dermot Gilleece; and from* Get to the Point *by Steven Reid.*

TJ Ford and Alan Gaynor

Rosses Point golfers breaking new ground

It's Easter so perhaps it is with an appropriate sense of timing that Rory McIlroy chose this as the moment to announce his arrival as the new Messiah of the golfing world. The wise men among the assembled journalists feverishly search out the boy wonder, like midwives in the delivery ward proudly proclaiming they were there at the birth.

At fifteen years of age, McIlroy has become the youngest ever winner of the fabled West of Ireland Championship at Rosses Point. Lost in the euphoria of it all and swamped by a raucous army of well-wishers and hardened hacks, the teenager from Hollywood, County Down, could hardly have imagined this would be the launching pad for a stellar career which would captivate and enthral millions of golf fans worldwide.

The year is 2005. TJ Ford, destined to become the first Sligo-born winner of the prestigious South of Ireland Open Amateur Championship, is still a few months short of his eighth birthday. His heroes don't wear capes, they launch golf balls with devastating precision, land them on the green with unerring accuracy and then roll them into a hole with such carefree abandon they might as well be out for a leisurely stroll on a sun-drenched beach.

Now he's about to get up close and personal with his idol. The young boy waits for the mayhem to dissipate, then nervously approaches the newly crowned champion. He offers McIlroy a towel – it's what passes as an autograph book for young golf fans – and the champ duly signs. Wow. It gets better. Just as he's about to be driven away, McIlroy opens the car door, signs one of his golf balls and hands it to the young Sligo fan. It's wonderful end to a magical day.

Top: The Sligo 1971 team which reached the Connacht final – Back row (l-r): David Pugh, Seán Davey, Barnes Murphy, PJ Brennan, Jim Colleary, Hugh Quinn, Aidan Caffrey, Tom Colleary; Front row (l-r): Liam Caffrey, John Brennan, Gerry Mitchell, Tommy Cummins, Mickey Kearins, Paddy Henry, Mattie Brennan. Pic *Sligo Champion*

Bottom left: Cecil Ewing with the Irish Close Championship trophy, the Irish Open Championship trophy, and the West of Ireland Championship trophy, a unique treble which he won in the 1948/49 season. Pic courtesy Anne Bradshaw

Bottom right: World kickboxing champion Jonathan Sweeney with Mayor Seán McManus. Pic courtesy *Sligo Champion*

Top: TJ Ford (left) winner of the South of Ireland Open Amateur Championship at Lahinch Golf Club, pictured with Johnny Flynn, captain, Lahinch GC, and Alan Fahy, runner-up. Pic courtesy Lahinch GC

Bottom left: Multiple All-Ireland handball champion Paddy Walsh. Pic *Sligo Champion*

Bottom right: Barry Anderson, winner of the West of Ireland Open Amateur Championship 2017. Pic *Sligo Champion*

Top: Sligo's Irish hockey international Elayne McDermott

Bottom: Multiple Irish senior singles and doubles badminton champion Jonathan Dolan

Left: Darragh Keenan on Goddess of Fire at Doncaster in 2020. Pic Nigel Kirby photography

Right: Kilcoleman led into the winners' enclosure at Cheltenham by Michael McElhone. Provincial Press Agency, Southport. (Pics courtesy Paul Clarke)

Top left: Sligo's Aisling Blake, one of the world's top squash players. Pic Professional Squash Association

Top right: Keith Moran pictured with the Irish Masters National Championship trophy which he won in 2020

Bottom: Derek Fox and his mother Jacqueline pictured after the 2017 Aintree Grand National

Top left: Dual rugby and basketball star Aoife McDermott pictured at her mural in Riverstown. Pic Susie Carr

Top right: Junior soccer supremo Noel Kennedy. Pic *Sligo Champion*

Bottom: Carbury FC celebrate League and Cup double 2022. Pic Carl Brennan

Top left: Sligo's much travelled rugby star Conán O'Donnell, pictured with his parents, Cathal and Collette

Top right: Mary Forte, daughter of the late Alex MacArthur, pictured with the MacArthur Cup. Pic Darren Carr

Bottom: FAI referees observer Sligoman Paul Deering officiating at the Sligo Rovers v Everton friendly game at the Showgrounds in 2010 with respective captains Seamus Coleman (Everton) and Danny Ventre (Sligo Rovers). Pic *Sligo Champion*

Top: One of the legendary teams of the MacArthur Cup, Denny's FC, pictured in the 1960s. Pic *Sligo Champion*

Bottom: The Hannaway's MacArthur Cup-winning team of 1968

It would be stretching the point to suggest the occasion planted in Ford an obsessive desire to become a top-class golfer, but it left a lasting impression.

"Maybe I'm biased because of McIlroy's association with Co. Sligo and because I witnessed him growing into the superstar he became but, for me, he's the greatest golfer there's ever been," reasons Ford.

Even if he hadn't been caught in the charismatic whirlwind of the McIlroy phenomenon, it's likely the Rosses Point native would have found the appeal of golf too hard to resist. His grandfather Tom Ford was captain and president of Galway Golf Club, where his grandmother Dympna was also a prominent member. His uncle Darragh Ford was assistant professional at Galway Bay GC in Oranmore. His father, Tom Ford, is an accomplished player. Ford remembers:

> There was always golf around the family. Growing up in Rosses Point, the West of Ireland Championship was the mecca. As kids, we looked forward to it every Easter and it coincided with the Masters on television, so it was golf, golf and more golf, and we were totally immersed in it.

Ford's earliest memory of playing golf is his participation in the "Wee Wonders" tournament, an event put on every summer for young boys and girls as part of County Sligo's excellent juvenile programme.

Although he made the Irish under-14 panel, Ford was seduced by the irresistible appeal of rugby once he went to Sligo Grammar School. He was good enough to make the Connacht schoolboys' squad. A demanding training schedule meant golf was put on the back burner.

"The more rugby I played, the more my golf went into decline," he admits.

He might well have turned his back on golf altogether but for a bizarre set of circumstances surrounding his selection for the Connacht under-19 rugby panel. An e-mail informing him of his call-up went astray and Ford, disappointed at the apparent snub, decided to commit permanently to golf. It was only later he discovered he had made the provincial rugby squad.

The defining point in his career was his decision to go to Maynooth University, where he studied marketing and finance. Everything about the college was tailor-made to improve his game – the coaching, facilities, access to nutritionists, strength and conditioning regimes and sports psychologists, even the more favourable weather conditions in the east of the country. He joined Carton House and was playing with and learning from the best young players in the country. Although he wasn't a member of the National Golf Academy, he was in and around elite golfers.

> Maynooth was the making of me as a golfer. Seán Flanagan, a lifelong friend and fellow student, was a great help, introducing me to all the top players there. Playing in that company improved my game.

His breakthrough season was 2021 when a series of impressive achievements confirmed his status as one of the top amateurs in the country.

It all began with a stunning performance at the South of Ireland Championship in Lahinch, an historic victory which owed as much to physical endurance as golfing supremacy. Throughout the tournament, the Sligoman was crippled with severely blistered feet, a curse which might well have scuppered the chances of players of less resolve. Ford modestly recollects his storming march to the final:

> I had a little luck along the way. In the semi-final my opponent had a double bogey on the seventeenth, which let me off the hook. The match could easily have gone the other way.

If there was a hint of good fortune in the earlier rounds, there was no denying the Sligo player's stunning performance in the final. He recorded a staggering seven birdies, including three in succession to round off a facile 5 and 4 victory over Dún Laoghaire's Alan Fahy.

"That was the best I've ever played," he confirms. "It was just one of those days when everything went right. Even the weather was scorching, a perfect setting to record such a fantastic win."

The fact he became the first Sligo player to take the coveted title added extra significance to the achievement.

A couple of weeks later, Ford came agonisingly close to clocking up what would have been a sensational double when he lost by just one shot to Jake Whelan (Grange) in the final of the Mullingar Scratch Cup.

The year finished on an appropriately high note when he marked his first cap for Ireland by helping his country to a thrilling victory in the Home Nations Championship at Hankley Common, Surrey. A 3 and 1 win over Haider Hussain in the singles in the final day's pulsating match with England a particular highlight of an impressive international debut.

With the South of Ireland Championship already proudly etched on his CV, Ford would love to add a coveted "West" title to his list of achievements. He says:

> I was asked once which I'd like to achieve most – score the winning try for Ireland in a World Cup final or win the West of Ireland. It's a no brainer. Winning the West would be greatest thing I could ever achieve.

***

A unique addition to Sligo's pantheon of golfing greats is Rosses Point native Alan Gaynor, who was a member of the four-strong Irish team which won the European Team Championship for golfers with a disability in Belgium in June 2022.

The first Irish team ever to compete at the event consisted of Gaynor, Ballinasloe's Aidan Grehan, Brendan Lawlor from Dundalk, and Carton House member Conor Stone. They won the title by a massive 25 shots.

Reared just 100 yards from County Sligo Golf Club, Alan has been playing his favourite sport since he was only four years old. But his story is one of inspirational fortitude as he was born missing the wrist on his left hand. As an infant, he underwent revolutionary toe-to-hand transfer surgery where a toe from each foot was transferred to his left hand.

With an improved quality of life, he enjoyed the full spectrum of sporting activity, including football and tennis, but he found he had a particular proficiency in golf.

Disability golf is a relatively new concept, but its growth has allowed Alan to make the most of his undoubted talent. He has always been competitive at amateur tournaments, being a regular player at the West of Ireland Championship, but is now regarded as one of the better players on the European Disabled Golf Association (EDGA) circuit.

The emergence of the EDGA has opened up new pathways and ambitions for disabled golfers across Ireland and Europe, and 27-year-old Alan is set to take full advantage.

The 'West'

Launchpad for global superstars

Embedded in the sporting soul of Sligo for almost 100 years, the West of Ireland Open Amateur Championship has generated an abundance of compelling stories.

From the valiant exploits of Sligo's Cecil Ewing and Sutton's Joe Carr, who between them claimed a combined total of twenty-two titles over four all-conquering decades, to the fledgling victories of future global stars Pádraig Harrington, Rory McIlroy and Shane Lowry, the 'West' has engaged and enthralled generations of local sports fans.

Synonymous with the Easter holiday in Sligo, the Championship is followed with almost Biblical passion, maintaining a glorious tradition which dates back to the inaugural tournament in 1923, when LP Verdon gained the distinction of becoming the first winner, defeating BH Cook 3 and 2 in the final.

A glittering roll of honour boasts some of the most iconic names in world golf, yet nothing stirs the emotions as much as a local triumph. The legendary Ewing obliged with devasting regularity, capturing ten wins, including a three-in-a-row sequence, between 1930 and 1950, but, amazingly, it was 67 years before another Sligo golfer prevailed.

Many supremely talented players tried in vain to end the barren years, but it wasn't until Barry Anderson finally made the breakthrough in 2017 that the drought was at last consigned to history.

Hurling was Anderson's sport of choice when he was growing up in Leixlip, County Kildare, but he succumbed to the irresistible delights of golf when the family moved to Sligo, his father's home county.

He was sixteen years old and his peripheral interest in golf up to that time was more of a concession to the enthusiastic mentoring of his uncle Aiden than any burning ambition to forge a career in the sport.

But once his parents, Roy and Eithne, relocated to Sligo with Barry and his sister, Amy, there was only one sport that captured his imagination. He reveals:

> It was close to an obsession. My uncle Aiden was the driving force. He'd spend hours with me at County Sligo Golf Club or at Bertie's Pitch and Putt course, teaching me the basics, encouraging me to improve every aspect of my game.

Within a few years, Anderson was good enough to earn selection on the Irish Boys' team. He had the distinction of producing the winning putt against England in the Home Internationals in Royal County Down in 2008.

"That's a special memory," he confirms. "It's always nice to get one over on the auld enemy and to have the distinction of clinching the winning putt was a real thrill."

It was a particularly productive time for Co. Sligo, with a host of exciting young hopefuls coming through. Tommy McGowan, David Brady, Stefan O'Hara and the more experienced Gary McDermott were among a strong group of golfers entitled to harbour realistic ambitions of securing the elusive 'West' title.

Anderson's debut in the Championship as a raw teenager in 2008 offered little hint of what was to come.

"My first tee shot caught a ferocious gale and ended up out of bounds on the road," he recounts. "I can joke about it now, but it was no laughing matter at the time. It was so embarrassing."

A couple of quarter-final appearances in the years that followed underlined his potential but still there was little fuss or fanfare when he lined up for the 2017 Championship, representing Royal Dublin.

He was in good form leading up to the tournament and was hopeful rather than confident of a concerted bid for ultimate glory.

He came from three down after four holes to beat Newland's Jake Whelan in the semi-final and produced a whirlwind performance in the decider against Jack Pierce (Portmarnock). He was three up after four and maintained the edge throughout a gripping encounter, eventually clinching a 3 and 2 victory on the sixteenth. He reasons:

> Making a solid start was vital. Once I built up a three-hole lead, it was all about keeping the distance between us. Thankfully, I was able to maintain my focus and see it out.

His unexpected victory sparked off scenes of wild jubilation.

> My family and friends were thrilled. It was a wonderful occasion; one I'll never forget.
>
> The Championship was a stepping-stone to super stardom for the likes of Harrington, McIlroy and Lowry, but for me it was like reaching the top of the mountain. It was more than I ever hoped for.
>
> I look at some of the names who have won the 'West' and I'm proud to be among such illustrious company.

There had been a few notable victories for golfers with links to Co. Sligo before Anderson made his historic breakthrough.

Derbyshire-born Jimmy Feeney, son of Rosses Point native Leo, won the title in 1985, playing out of Chapel en Le Frith, while Ken Kearney, later to become a member of the host club, was champion in 1992, representing County Roscommon GC.

The 2001 winner, Michael McDermott (Stackstown) is a son of Riverstown native Noel.

Rory McNamara, whose mother, Geraldine, and grandparents, the late Tom and Dell Rogers, were from Sligo, won the title in 2013. The Headfort GC member was born in Sligo and lived in the county until he was three years old, when the family moved to Kells in County Meath.

Long established as one of the country's elite amateur championships, the 'West' was the launching pad for the stellar careers of three of Ireland's most celebrated professional golfers - Harrington, McIlroy and Lowry - all of whom frequently acknowledge the invaluable role played by the County Sligo Golf Club in paving the way for their global success.

Harrington, representing Stackstown, claimed the 1994 title, dashing the hopes Co. Sligo's Ken Kearney in the final.

He subsequently became one of the country's most cherished sporting personalities, winning back-to-back British Open championships. He was the first Irishman in 60 years to capture the coveted Claret Jug when he defeated Sergio Garcia in a four-hole play-off at Carnoustie in 2007. He successfully defended his title the following year at Royal Birkdale, thereby becoming the first European to retain the Championship since 1906.

Harrington won a third major, the PGA Championship, in 2008 and played on six successive Ryder Cup teams from 1999 to 2010.

McIlroy, rightly acclaimed as one of the greatest golfers the world has ever seen, announced his awesome potential at Co. Sligo, winning successive 'West' titles in 2005 and 2006.

He was a few weeks short of his sixteenth birthday when he won the Championship for the first time, thrilling a captivated audience as he battled his way to a 2 and 1 victory over Mallow's David Finn in the decider. The Hollywood youngster made it two-in-a-row the following year, this time accounting for Paul O'Hanlon (Curragh) 3 and 1 in the final.

By now, the County Down teenager was already being hailed as a potential superstar and crowds flocked to Rosses Point to witness his bid for a hat-trick of 'West' titles in 2007. He made it all the way to the semi-final before losing out to Paul Cutler. The Portstewart man lost the final that year but came back to win the trophy in 2011. He will probably be best remembered, however, as the last man to defeat McIlroy in the 'West'.

Within months of his farewell outing at Co. Sligo, McIlroy joined the professional ranks, setting off on a breathtaking odyssey which would confirm his status as one of the all-time greats.

By the age of 25, he was a four-time Major champion, claiming the US Open in 2011, the PGA Championship in 2012 and 2014 and the British Open in 2014. He played on four triumphant European Ryder Cup teams, 2010, 2012, 2014 and 2018.

Lowry unveiled his blossoming talent at Rosses Point in 2008, battling his way to an impressive 2 and 1 win over Mullingar's Desmond Morgan in the final. He came agonisingly close to claiming successive titles when he lost to David Crosby from Royal Lytham on the nineteenth in the 2009 decider.

Only a few months later, the Esker Hills golfer made worldwide headlines when he claimed a sensational victory in the Irish Open at County Louth Golf Club while still an amateur.

It was a tantalising foretaste of what was to come from the popular County Offaly golfer, who counts a memorable victory in the 2009 British Open at Royal Portrush among a list of outstanding achievements.

Harrington, McIlroy and Lowry have become global superstars, loved and admired throughout Ireland and around the world, and have claimed the greatest prizes golf has to offer. And it all began at County Sligo Golf Club, the majestic links course where legends are born.

Hockey

Elayne McDermott

Hockey international broke new boundaries

She's Sligo's only senior Irish hockey international, and yet even her close family barely know the details. Elayne McDermott, capped 35 times for Ireland at a time when selection for the senior international team rarely extended beyond Dublin or Belfast, left it all behind at just 24 years of age, and hasn't regretted a single minute.

Now the driving force behind the Connacht Hockey Academy, which she established in 2020, McDermott is fairly nonchalant about the premature end to an astonishingly successful career which had the potential to produce even greater bounties had she chosen to continue playing.

Early retirements are not uncommon in top class sport, of course. Björn Borg famously packed in his glorious tennis career at 26 and Georgie Best was just a year older when the appeal of a less disciplined lifestyle scuppered his football genius. But McDermott's severance from a sport in which she constantly broke new boundaries seems to have been far less traumatic or dramatic.

"I just felt as though I'd done enough," she nods, almost dismissing the enormity of her achievement in representing her country at schoolgirl, under-21 and senior level, as well as countless inter-pros and inter-varsity successes.

At the time, Ireland had narrowly failed to qualify for what would have been the country's first hockey entry at the Olympics, in Barcelona 1992, having missed out on goal difference in a qualifying tournament in New Zealand. A 1–1 draw with China proved insufficient, so her last cap against Argentina proved to be merely academic. Surprisingly, she doesn't believe the disappointment of missing out on the Olympics played any major factor in her decision.

> I don't remember being particularly gutted. I just decided that was that. Even though I was only 24, I'd played an awful lot. From a young age, I'd played on every team it was possible to play for, and I'd given it everything I had. I just felt a bit of a change would be good for me, and I knew when to let go. I didn't miss it for a single second.

So early was her retirement that her husband, the award-winning cabinet-maker Fergal Spain, has never seen her play hockey and her grown-up children, Eoghan and Maedhbh, are only recently discovering their mum's glorious sporting past.

"They're into sport, so they'd have a bit of a clue about their mum being a former international sports person, but it's no big deal. Never has been," she confirms.

The Rosses Point native comes from a family steeped in sport. Her late father, PJ, played minor football for Mayo and remained an avid follower of his native county all his life. He had also turned out for Donegal, when stationed in Buncrana as a Garda officer, and her brothers, John and David, were both accomplished soccer players.

Indeed, the first hint of the future hockey international's aptitude for sport was as a talented young soccer player. She won an All-Ireland Community Games football medal as part of a Rosses Point team coached by her father and was so good that, in her early teens, she had the opportunity of a soccer scholarship in Sweden. By then, however, hockey was the dominant sport in her life.

She began playing hockey as a first-year student at the Ursuline College, using the natural instincts of structure and formation she'd learned on the soccer fields as early tools to help her adapt to her new sport:

> Although the skill sets are vastly different, stuff like structure and formation would be similar, and I'd learned that in soccer. Otherwise, I hadn't a notion about hockey when I started. It just seemed to come naturally.

By third year, she was on the Connacht inter-pros team, and a whole new world opened up when she was later selected for the Irish schools team, which would have been highly unusual for a player beyond the hockey pale.

For the Sligo teenager, it's clear the experience was both exhilarating and challenging in equal measure:

> At the time, most of the players would have been from Dublin or Northern Ireland, maybe a few from Munster. At seventeen years, I was

> far younger than most of them. I used to get the train up from Sligo for training sessions in Dublin and stay with host families. It was a complete eye-opener, mixing with girls from leafy south County Dublin. On the pitch, I was grand, as good as any of them, but it took me a while to settle off the pitch. Initially, I felt like I was being viewed a bit like this country bumpkin who didn't belong. It was challenging, but it was a breakthrough not just as a hockey player, but as a person, too. To this day, we're all still great pals.

At Jordanstown College, University of Ulster, she captained the college to an inter-varsity title in 1987, as her game improved by virtue of highly competitive weekly games in a collegiate league which boasted some of the best players in the country. Her international career blossomed as captain of the under-21 team for three years, winning a bronze medal at a European championship in Scotland, and her first senior cap arrived when she was just 18 years old.

Typically, the milestone seems to have been taken in her stride:

> I'm sure my dad, being a sports fanatic, must have been tickled pink about me playing for Ireland, but I honestly don't recall any great excitement about it. It was an honour, of course, but maybe its significance seems more important now than it did at the time.

What followed was a hugely successful career, bringing McDermott to all corners of the world representing her country. A particular highlight, she reports, was a six-week World Cup qualifying tournament in India in 1989 and the Olympics qualifiers in New Zealand two years later.

In recent years, she's dusted off the hockey shoes to play for Ireland in a Masters Tournament in Holland, alongside her lifelong pal Clodagh McMoreland-Lynch, who captained the team with distinction. Although immensely enjoyable, the experience merely confirmed her resolve to make her retirement permanent.

"It was great craic meeting up with the girls again, but it's hard on the body. That's definitely it, I'm working on my golf handicap now," she pledges.

But it's not just the golf. A much more exotic pursuit is her enjoyment of rock-climbing, which she and husband, Fergal, have been tackling for a long number of years. Although she claims they look for much easier challenges these days, their endeavours have included scaling the awesome peaks of Wadi Rum in the deserts of southern Jordan, as well as in Spain, Italy and France, seeking out the less travelled mountainous routes.

A PE teacher at Sligo Grammar School, where she coaches the successful hockey teams, McDermott is passionate about providing pathways for talented young players to follow their dreams of one day emulating her achievements. She recently set up the Connacht Hockey Academy, an initiative aimed at nurturing young talent and developing a pool of players capable of playing at inter-provincial and national level. She and a team of top-level coaches run regular training sessions throughout Connacht, catering for girls aged 11 to 16. The idea is to produce not just talented players but new coaches to help develop the game in the province.

She is acutely aware of studies which prove teenage girls drop out of sport far earlier than their male counterparts, and believes intervention is needed to reverse that worrying trend:

> I see it in my own school. The lads would play sport all day if you let them, but mostly the girls are happy just to sit and watch. We have to change that.
>
> It's great that girls now have role models such as Katie Taylor, Kellie Harrington and Rachael Blackmore. It shows that women can be high achievers in sport, and we've got to build on that.
>
> When I was playing, people were barely looking outside Dublin, so even very talented girls from the provinces hardly got a chance. I would love to change that. In Sligo, for instance, we've got 1,000 girls in secondary schools, and we need to tap into that, whether it's hockey or other sports. We've got to provide the pathways, particularly in places like Sligo.
>
> I've got so much from sport in my life, and I love the idea of giving something back, and for me, that entails providing encouragement for women in sport but also promoting physical activity in general.

Thirty years after her early retirement, Elayne McDermott carries the distinction of being Sligo's only senior hockey international with considerable ease and grace, and she continues to make a valuable contribution to her sport.

**Other Sligo hockey legends who have worked tirelessly to promote the game in Sligo as players, coaches and administrators over the years include Emer Concannon, Aisling Lupton, Brenda Burns-McCallion, Katie Cadden-Maher, Clodagh McMoreland-Lynch, Zandra Howley, Hazel Sweetnam, Conor Fraser, and Ailish Downes.*

Martial Arts

Martial Arts

Getting their kicks at top of the world

The thriving martial arts community in Sligo has provided the county with more world and European champions than any other sport.

For nearly fifty years, thousands of local competitors from clubs throughout the town and county have amassed a mouth-watering haul of gold, silver and bronze medals across various disciplines and age groups, principally in karate and kickboxing.

Early pioneers Michael McDermott and John Sweeney, and, more recently, top-class coaches such as Áine Conlon and Des Leonard, have nurtured generations of skilled athletes, many of whom have become outstanding world champions in their chosen discipline.

Martial arts was indelibly woven into the civic and sporting history of Sligo in 2000 when the town's highest civic honour, the Freedom of the Borough, was bestowed on WKO Karate World Champion Jonathan Sweeney, a member of the Green Dragon club which his father, John, had established some twenty years earlier.

Now a Garda sergeant based in Buncrana, Co. Donegal, Sweeney was 21 years old when he upset the form book to topple Italy's highly rated Marco Caridi to win Ireland's first ever world title. He successfully defended his title the following year. His sister, Breege, had been a European champion and his brother, Michael, a national champion, so his world titles consolidated his family's place as one of the county's top sporting achievers. Sweeney confirms:

> My dad had been running the club since the early 80s. There were literally hundreds of talented karate and kickboxing enthusiasts training with him every week. I'd been there since I was four years old, so to

> become the country's first ever WKO world champion with my dad as coach was really special for all of us.
>
> The highlight, of course, was being made a Freeman of the Borough. To be given such an honour in my home town and to join such a prestigious list of famous recipients was something I could never have imagined. My mum and dad, who had shared my journey from childhood, were so proud. I'll never forget it.

Although he retired from the sport nine years later, having added national and European titles to his trophy cabinet, Sweeney returned briefly in 2013 to take a silver in the World Police Games.

> My wife, Marcella, had never seen me compete. And, of course, my young children, Freya, Remy and Saul, only knew about my achievements from listening to stories from my mum. So at least now they know I wasn't making it all up.

While the civic honour gave Sweeney's achievement more prominence, a huge litany of national, European and world title holders have emerged from the Green Dragon Club over the years. Naomi Nibbs won her first world title as a 13-year-old competing in the WTKA championships in Florida and added ten Europeans and twelve more worlds before retiring in 2010. Fighters such as Geraldine Gorman, Kayleigh O'Donnell, Hannah Kelly, Sarah McInerney, Kevin McKenna, Mark McGee and Shelly Langan have all featured on the winners' podium. In 2013, Ballygawley's Liam Codd was a treble gold medalist at the WTKA world championships, a highlight of a golden career which saw him scoop more than 60 medals at various championships.

Another massively successful local club is the Sligo Mugendo Club, based in St Joseph's Church Hall in Ballytivnan, and established in 1985 by Manorhamilton native Michael McDermott, a Brown Belt in karate and Black Belt in Mugendo.

Among the club's early successes was a European ladies' full contact title won by Mercedes Taaffe in 1988. Mercedes later won gold in light contact and bronze in full contact at the AKAI world championships in 1994. At the European Junior Championships in Italy in 2004, Lorraine McDermott, Orla Healy, Kathleen Kerrigan, Roisin Mitchell, Louise Conlon, Laura Goonan, Aoife Dolan and Niall McDermott were among the medals. In addition, Lorraine McDermott won European and world bronze in points fighting.

More glory followed in 2008 when Enya Clarke won gold in world light contact and Aisling McDermott won gold in the European Championships. Niall McDermott won two European Cups and Cathal O'Dowd won gold in the World Junior Championships in 2012 as the club continued to thrive. More recently, Nora Walsh won a silver medal at the European Championships in 2019.

Club founder Michael McDermott has been national president of AKAI for the past twelve years and is currently its director of coaching. With kickboxing now a recognised Olympics sport, he sees a bright future for the sport locally:

> Olympic recognition places the sport on the podium with the best in the world, and adds a whole new meaning to Mugendo being the 'unlimited way'. We will continue to lay down our floor mats at St Joseph's Church Hall every week, and, who knows, we may well be nurturing Olympic stars of the future.

In recent years, sisters Ruth and Lucy Conlon-Oates from Ballisodare have brought European and world medals to Sligo. Members of the Collooney Kickboxing Club, where their mum, Áine, is a senior instructor, Ruth won a European title in 2015, having won a world bronze a year earlier, while Lucy was a world silver medalist in 2018 before winning the European title a year later.

The Collooney club was founded in 2002 by chief instructor Des Leonard, who returned from America to establish the club in the local parish hall. He had previously trained in Sligo and Dublin to fourth degree black belt grade under renowned coaches George Canning and Michael McDermott. Shortly after, Áine Conlon, a fellow black belt and now senior instructor, joined the coaching team as both coach and fighter. The club caters for adults and children from Collooney and the surrounding areas and has over 120 members from all diversities and community backgrounds.

The club continues to travel to various international 'open' tournaments where their fighters compete against the best in the world for international recognition and prestige. It already has an impressive list of achievements.

Dessie Leonard has been world champion on five occasions and has attained a similar number of European titles. Áine Leonard won the world championship in 2012 and 2014, adding European titles in 2011 and 2013.

Jordan O' Boyle became world champion in 2012, before the Conlon-Oates sisters took up the mantle in recent years. The club has also gathered a host of silver and bronze medals over the years.

Although often unheralded, there's no doubt the selfless dedication of coaches, volunteers and fighters at a range of clubs throughout the county have propelled Sligo to the forefront of martial arts competition, adding great honour and distinction to the local sporting landscape.

Motor Sport

Art McCarrick

Driving force in Motorsport Ireland

Sligo's proud history in motor sport, dating back to the 1940s, was further enhanced by the appointment in 2022 of Cloonacool native Art McCarrick to the important role of sporting manager with Motorsport Ireland.

Thirty-four-year-old McCarrick, who has been employed with the national governing body since 2015, has responsibility for the development of motor sport in several key areas.

One of only five professional staff with Motorsport Ireland, he is the point of contact between the national association and the world governing body, the FIA, and Sport Ireland.

A keen motor sport fan all his life, the Sligoman says it is a privilege to have such a crucial role in the shaping of the future of the sport in Ireland.

"I'm very passionate about motor sport," he confirms. "There are a lot of challenges and changes in plotting the way forward and I'm excited by the task of creating a vision for the future of the sport."

Motorsport Ireland is responsible for over 150 events across 12 different disciplines every year and McCarrick is in the engine room, liaising with the various commissions and clubs and ensuring the smooth running of all aspects of the sport.

A qualified secondary school teacher, McCarrick joined Motorsport Ireland as sporting development officer in 2015. He explains:

> It was something of a dream job. As a motor sport fanatic and an active competitor, I always had an ambition to work in the administrative side of things. I've enjoyed the sport from both sides so that gives me invaluable experience in carrying out my duties as sporting manager.

Growing up in Cloonacool, McCarrick was attracted to the thrill of motor sport from an early age, attending many rallies all over Ireland and was particularly enthused by the Sligo Stages Rally.

He was 27 when he took part in his first competition, a rally in Enniskillen. Driving a Honda Civic, he won his class at the Irish Tarmac Championships in 2017, an event he describes as "the longest and most expensive birthday present ever". He took part in the Sligo Stages Rally in 2019 before competing in his last event, an endurance trial at Lucan, the following year.

He had some hair-raising experiences along the way, most alarmingly when he crashed out of the Ulster Rally in Derry in 2017.

> I took out a telegraph pole at 80 mph. It was a frightening incident, but I walked away injury-free and was back at work within a few days. The safety measures in the cars are impeccable, which dilutes the fear-factor. Indeed, Motorsport Ireland prides itself on its safety record, which is acknowledged by the FIA.

McCarrick is proud of his links with the local Connacht Motor Club, one of the most respected in the country.

Its history stretches back to 1947. Two years later, the club was registered as a limited company with about fifty members. Among the early competitions organised by the club was the Circuit of Connacht rally.

The Sligo Stages Rally was held for the first time in 1980 in conjunction with Ballina Motor Club. The event was hosted exclusively by the Connacht Motor Club the following year and has established a cherished place in the local sporting calendar ever since. Autocross, Night Navigation events and Autotests have become popular competitions in the club's schedule in recent years.

Interest in motor sport in Sligo reached new heights when rounds of the World Rally Championship were staged in the county in 2007 and 2009. Connacht Motor Club members were heavily involved in the massive operation to ensure the efficient running of these iconic events.

The WRC rallies attracted thousands of spectators to Sligo and generated a massive boost for the local economy. It's estimated that the championships, which covered routes in Sligo and throughout the northwest region, were watched by a worldwide TV audience in excess of 120 million and were worth in the region of 100 million euro in tourism revenue.

Club members have also excelled in competitions at home and abroad over the years. In 2021, Niall Burns recorded a particularly noteworthy achievement, navigating his way to four championship titles in one season. He navigated

Scotland's Garry Pearson to success in the Scottish rally championship, the BTRDA Gold Star event, the British Rally Championship national cup and the Welsh national title.

It was the high point of Burns' exciting career, which included participation at prestige championships in Europe, the Middle East, South Africa and America.

Sligo's Paul Kiely navigated Wexford man Tim McNulty to a national and tarmac championship double, while Dominic McLoughlin has been a prolific championship winner over the course of a distinguished career. Navigators Emer Mahon and Áine Phelan have also been to the fore in many local and national rallies.

Among the dedicated officials who have played prominent roles in the promotion of motor sport in the region are Joe Gilligan, Joe Corcoran, Padraic Boylan, Rosemary Walsh, Robert Lyttle and Jarlath Barry.

Racing

Derek Fox

How a Sligoman won the greatest race in the world

Grand National, Aintree racecourse, 8 April 2017

It was a day borrowed from high summer, unseasonably warm for the second Saturday in April. Grand National day at Aintree racecourse is theatrical by nature and tradition and when the sun shines the whole occasion is elevated to an enthralling spectacle unrivalled in global sport.

Twenty-three-year-old Sligo-born jockey Derek Fox walked the iconic course mid-morning, a ritual designed to relax and inform in equal measure. If the benign weather hadn't dried out the ground too much, he was hopeful of a good ride aboard One for Arthur in the world's most famous steeplechase. It was his first ride in the race. The child in him remembered a boyhood fascination with the event. But the demanding challenge which lay ahead left no room for sentiment.

Trained by Lucinda Russell at Kinross, 20 miles northwest of Edinburgh, the eight-year-old One for Arthur was bidding to become the first Scottish horse to win the National since Rubstic in 1979. Encouraging early season form had earned a growing number of admirers, but few held the horse in such high regard as his pilot.

Fox reveals:

> From the first time I sat on the horse, I felt he was something special. He had all the attributes of a typical National horse, a brilliant jumper, a big heart and plenty of staying power. I genuinely felt we had a real good

> chance, certainly to be in the mix and, with a bit of luck, maybe even better.

To fully appreciate the kindred partnership between horse and jockey, it is helpful to turn the clock back to an autumnal day at Kelso on 22 October 2016. One for Arthur's regular rider, Peter Buchanan, had recently retired and Fox was entrusted with the job of steering the improving chaser.

The chemistry was instant. The Sligo jockey recalls:

> We won by five lengths. He was so impressive. He wasn't overly quick but his ability to jump a fence was something else and he was relentless, kept galloping on and on.

One for Arthur finished an impressive fifth in the Beecher Chase over the National fences at Aintree in November 2016. Even more informative was a spectacular runaway win in the Classic Chase at Warwick the following January. Connections began to think seriously about a crack at the Aintree showpiece.

A jockey's life is never that simple, however. Just a month before the National, Fox sustained a broken wrist and a dislocated collar bone in a fall. It meant negotiating a tough recovery regime at Jack Berry House to be fit to partner One for Arthur at Liverpool. He won the race against time. It was a good omen.

He had a ride on the undercard on the day of the big race. He wasn't overworked, however, as his mount, Ruben Cotter, a 33/1 shot trained by fellow Sligoman Mark McNiff, downed tools before the twelfth fence in a three-mile handicap.

By mid-afternoon Aintree was buzzing in anticipation of the big race. Fox recalls:

> The atmosphere was electric. I said a quick hello to the owners of One for Arthur, Debs Thompson and Belinda McClung, and had a word with Peter Scudamore, the trainer's assistant. I wasn't tied down to any specific tactics. Peter basically said to get the horse settled early and get into a nice rhythm.

In keeping with the well-established ritual of the race, there was a cavalry charge to the first. One for Arthur started well and was close to the front as they cleared the first but soon dropped towards the rear. Fox was happy with that.

"The horse routinely starts slowly and then warms to the task as the race unfolds so I wasn't at all concerned when we dropped back after jumping the first. In fact, that was ideal for us," the rider explains.

By the notorious Becher's Brook on the first circuit, Rogue Angel and Franc De Roi were cutting out the running and the chasing pack were keeping them honest. But One for Arthur was nowhere to be seen. As they headed out on the second circuit, Fox's mount had only four or five horses behind him, but the Sligo rider saw no reason to press the panic button.

> One for Arthur was foot perfect all the way round. We were a long way back, but I knew the horse would stay and it really was a question of keeping out of trouble and let the race unfold ahead of us. There was a strong pace, but I was quietly confident we could pick them off.

Soon the stragglers were adrift and the weary horses either pulled up or had fallen victim to the unforgiving obstacles. Only the truly tenacious remained standing as the pursuit of the most coveted prize in racing developed into an intriguing battle for survival.

All the while, the calculating Fox was cajoling One for Arthur into a challenging position, filling the horse with confidence as one by one he left a trailing field in his wake. The jockey's swashbuckling ride was a textbook illustration of the art of race riding.

Crossing the Melling Road with two jumps to negotiate ahead of a lung-bursting drive to the winning post, the jockey sensed this was it, the greatest race in the world was there to be won. There were still six or seven horses in front him, among them Blaklion, under the brilliant Noel Fehily, who was making a gallant bid to stretch his pursuers, and Cause of Causes, the Gordon Elliott trained horse.

One for Arthur had been so far back for most of the marathon trip that not even the TV commentators had flagged him but now the horse was in full flight, gaining momentum with every stride. His jockey, motionless early on, now bore the determination of a man on a once-in-a-lifetime mission. Fox remembers:

> The jockeys ahead of me were sending out the distress signals. They were slapping and kicking, very animated. All the while, my fellow was cruising. There were still two fences to jump but once we crossed the Melling Road I knew we were there with every chance. Even so far from home, I began to believe we were going to win.

There was a brief moment of anxiety at the second last when One for Arthur appeared to jump into the back of Blaklion but Fox, the masterful horseman, quickly regained his mount's balance. What could have been a disastrous incident in the hands of a less accomplished rider, passed off with the minimum of fuss.

Now it was down to the last with Blaklion, Cause of Causes and the spring-heeled One for Arthur battling for supremacy. A colossal leap propelled the Scottish horse to the front for the first time. Displaying boundless energy and astonishing courage, One for Arthur stayed on past the elbow and all the way to the line, rarely looking in the remotest danger of being caught on the run-in. The winning distance was officially recorded as four-and-a-half lengths, but the victory was more comprehensive than that. Fox admits:

> There was one brief moment when I felt the winning line would never come. But that was just in the heat of battle. The reality was that once he got in front, he was never going to be beaten.

As he passed the finishing post, right hand aloft in triumph, and lost in the euphoria of it all, Fox's first thought was that his mother Jacqueline was in the stand watching history unfold.

> I felt for my mother in that situation because I knew she would have been anxious and nervous watching the race. For me, I was in control of the situation, the master of my own destiny, but she was watching from the stands and there was nothing she could do to alter anything. It must be harder to watch a race than ride in one.

The enormity of what he had achieved quickly sunk in. He beams at the memory:

> Yeah, I was aware of what it all meant. I remember as a child watching the Grand National on television and wondering what it would be like to ride in it, never mind winning it. And then you think of the many top jockeys who go through their whole career without winning it – Peter Scudamore was champion jockey eight times but never won the National. So, I realised I was a very lucky man. It was an incredible feeling, hard to put into words. It felt as if I was walking on air.

The winning jockey was denied the triumphant return to the winner's enclosure, however. Even in the greatest moment of his career, the welfare of his horse was uppermost in his mind.

"I could tell the horse was very tired. It was an extremely hot day and he was feeling it. So almost as soon as we passed the winning post, I dismounted and unsaddled the horse", he relates.

After the obligatory TV and radio interviews, the rider was ushered into a press conference where he met his mother for the first time since the race. He remembers that moment vividly.

There were extravagant celebrations in Liverpool that evening and the party extended to Scotland in the days and weeks that followed.

"There seemed to be a One for Arthur party every night for weeks, if not months", reports the Sligoman. "It was relentless but understandable because it was such a wonderful occasion for everybody associated with the horse."

Fox rarely watches re-runs of the greatest day in his career and has never spoken to anybody in detail about the occasion until now.

> That's the way this industry works. You can't look back; you're looking for the next winner. You can't stay stuck in the past. Winning the Grand National was a very special day, probably the best I'll ever experience but I've got to focus on my career going forward. That's just the way it is.

One for Arthur is happily retired, something that is a source of great satisfaction for his former partner.

> I'm delighted he retired safe and well. He's such a good-natured horse, a real pet. Everybody loves him and it's easy to see why. He won the National in 2017 and went back again two years later and finished sixth. By any standards, that's a proud record.

The Sligo jockey had his first Cheltenham Festival win in 2022, producing a text-book ride on 10/1 shot Corach Rambler in the Ultima Handicap Chase. He registered another noteworthy victory aboard the highly rated Ahoy Senor at the Aintree festival the following month.

Fox is the second Sligo jockey to have won the Aintree Grand National. The first was Leo McMorrow from Mount Shannon who rode 66/1 outsider Russian Hero to victory in 1949. McMorrow began his racing career with Mr Jack Farrell in Mullingar, for whom he rode many winners. His younger brother, Vincent, was also a successful jockey in the 1940s and 1950s.

Another successful Sligo jockey was Declan Gillespie. A native of Knocknarea, Coolera, he won the Irish Oaks on Give Thanks, trained by Jim Bolger, in 1983. He was stable jockey to Mr Bolger for a number of years before moving to England where he was attached to the powerful John Dunlop yard.

Darragh Keenan

Ballymote jockey on fast track to the top

It's a bleak, grey day, locked in the sour grip of early spring.

There's only one flat race meeting in Britain on 8 February 2022, in Southwell in the East Midlands.

The alarm screams at 4 a.m. Darragh Keenan kicks off the duvet, slides out of bed, showers and gets dressed. He's off to work at an hour when many young people of his age would be on their way home after a boisterous night on the town. It will be 18 hours before his head hits the pillow again.

His working day involves a lot of lonely time in the car, driving first to Robyn Brisland's yard about two hours from his rented home in Newmarket. He rides out there, finishing around noon, and then drives on to Southwell. He has one ride. He's booked to take the mount on Silver Dollar for Robert Eddery in the second last race.

Following his trainer's instructions, Keenan keeps the horse tucked in behind the leaders, then produces a late surge but the 6/5 favourite, Won Love, has bolted for home and holds on for a three-quarter length victory. Beaten into second place in a tight finish is scant consolation for the 22-year-old Sligo rider at the end of a long, arduous day. On the drive home, he replays the race over and over in his mind, wondering if he could have done anything differently tactically. Would it have changed the outcome if he had? Was there anything that would have turned a narrow defeat into a thrilling victory? He concludes it would have been better to finish tailed off last. Such harsh contemplation only adds to his sense of frustration. It's gone 10 p.m. when he gets back to Newmarket. Shattered and disappointed, he seeks the comfort of a warm bed. Tomorrow is another day.

This is the life the young Irishman has chosen; the life he loves. The adrenalin rush of zipping past the post ahead of a trailing field, the heartbreak of narrow failure, the never-ending pursuit of greatness. It defines him. He's a professional jockey. He never wanted it any other way.

He was just 15 years old when he said goodbye to a happy family life in Ardnaglass, a few miles outside the neat rural town of Ballymote in County Sligo, leaving behind his parents, Gavin and Eileen, and his siblings, Diarmuid and Tommy.

He was chasing his dream, but it was uncharted territory. This wasn't a young man from a racing dynasty following a long family tradition; this was a quiet boy who used to split timber and sell it door to door around the housing estates in Ballymote to earn enough money to pay for riding lessons. If he was to eke out a living in the rough and tumble of the unforgiving horse racing industry, he would have to do it the hard way.

Although there's no racing heritage in his family, his dad, a butcher by trade, kept a few ponies and Keenan reckons that's where the love affair with racing began. He was five years old when he had his first riding lessons. He would go to McGarry's riding centre in Carrowmore or to Markree Castle and when he got a bit older, he went to Paddy Kerins' stables in Tubberbride. There he got some serious tuition, not just in the art of riding but about horses, how to handle them, the quirky ones, the lively ones, the sulky ones. Just all about being around horses, how to look after them, how to look after yourself. He'd go hunting with the Sligo Foxhunters and the Mayo Harriers. The thrill of jumping ditches and hedges was sensational. He would do some showjumping on the local and regional circuit as well.

By now, he was thinking seriously about becoming a jockey, so he went to Mark McNiff's yard in Culleenamore to further his riding education. It was an invaluable experience. One of the jockeys there took him under his wing, offered priceless advice and honed his riding style. His mentor was Derek Fox.

Keenan remembers shooting the breeze with the older jockey one day. He asked him if he thought he'd ever win the Grand National. "Sure every jockey would love to win that race," replied Fox.

In 2017, Fox rode One For Arthur to a spectacular success in the Aintree National. Watching on television, Keenan recalled the random conversation between the two Sligomen years before and a cheeky smile skipped across his face.

During his time at McNiff's, Keenan was doing well on the pony racing circuit and was beginning to attract some attention from shrewd judges of the game. Then out of the blue, he got a call from Kieran Egan, father of established jockey John Egan, enquiring if he would like to try his luck in England. There was an opening at John Butler's yard in Newmarket.

It was the opportunity he'd been waiting for. He recalls:

> I went over to Butler's yard on a Thursday, came back the following day to ride in a pony race at Ramelton in Donegal and rushed back to Newmarket on Saturday. I've been here since.

Hundreds of young boys and girls embark on similar journeys, hoping to make the grade in one of the most competitive sports on the planet and it really is a case of the survival of the fittest. The Ballymote boy was keenly aware he'd have to grow up quickly if he wanted to make an impact.

A short stint with Gavin Slater in Perth, Australia, proved enormously beneficial. There he learned a lot about pace and timing and the nuts and bolts of his craft. Shortly after returning to England, he switched to Robert Eddery's yard and soon had his first ride in public aboard Dance with Kate at Chelmsford. He admits:

> I was a bit cocky. I thought I was on a certainty, couldn't be beaten. Finished eighth or ninth. My confidence was blown out of the water. It was a harsh lesson.

The scar didn't take long to heal. About a week later, on 22 October 2017, he rode his first winner on Piazon, a 13/2 shot, in a 5-furlong race at Southwell. His delight was enhanced by the fact the trainer was John Butler, the man who had given him his first opportunity in England. Keenan says:

> When I first went over, I thought I would be lucky to have five rides in a year, never mind a few winners. But things went very well right from the start, far better than I could have hoped for.

He rode lots of winners for Eddery and picked up plenty of rides for outside stables, always an encouraging sign.

He worked his way through the apprenticeship allowances with impressive momentum, losing his claim and becoming a fully-fledged professional jockey after clocking up 95 winners.

He reached the golden landmark on an emotional night at Newcastle in April 2021. He rode a double for trainer David Evans on Martha's Boy and Almost An Angel. The brother of his sponsor had recently lost his wife to cancer. Her name was Martha so there was a poignant touch to the success of Martha's Boy.

Entering the professional ranks is a double-edged sword. Trainers like to use claiming apprentices because it means their horses will have less weight to carry, hence the greater chance of winning. But once a rider loses his or her claim, it can be more difficult to persuade trainers to consider them.

Keenan cautions:

> It can be a perilous situation. So many promising young jockeys just get washed up after they lose their claim. Thankfully, plenty of trainers kept faith in me and I continued to clock up the winners.

Getting to the top is tough; staying there is tougher. That's the conventional notion and Keenan subscribes to it.

> I was a bit of a slow learner when I came to England. But once the penny dropped, I went full throttle, no half-measures. It can be a case of every man for himself at times but some of the experienced lads – Adam Kirby, Tom Queally and Leitrim man Shane Kelly – were very good to me when I was starting out. There are good days and bad days. You take it all in your stride. When you're in the wrong, you accept it. When you're right, you stand your ground.

The fluctuating fortunes in the life of a jockey were encapsulated in a dramatic week for Keenen early in 2022. He was booked to ride a horse for John Ryan in Bahrain – a pleasant prospect in any working week. But it all turned sour when the jockey tested positive for Covid. A lonely week of isolation in a flat in Bahrain was soul-destroying, especially as he felt fit as a fiddle. Once the isolation period ended, he picked up three unplaced rides before returning to the UK.

On his first day back, he rode a winner at Lingfield. Bang. The good times rolled again.

A freelancer based in Newmarket, the nerve centre of the racing game in Britain, the Sligo rider enjoys an excellent relationship with several trainers. Recently, the powerful Mick Channon yard has been giving him plenty of rides. Every winner increases his profile, keeps him in the shop window.

Down the line, he'd love to land a job at one of the high-profile yards, ride a group winner or two and put his name up in lights at the big festival meetings. Whatever transpires, he'll continue to invest all he has in his chosen profession.

"I rarely have a day off and I don't know what to do with myself when I have some spare time", he confesses. "Everything revolves around racing".

Considered tall for a flat jockey, Keenan's average racing weight would be around 8st, 12lb. A diet of lettuce leaves and scraps of chicken helps to stave off the danger of adding unwanted weight but he's not one for torturous hours in the sauna. There's always the option of a career in the National Hunt code should his weight ever become a problem, but that's not on the radar now.

He would like to ride at Sligo Races one day - it's something he'd like to mark up on the CV. His growing army of local followers would love that too.

Kilcoleman

Horse with heart of a lion defied all the odds

It could have been lifted straight from the script of a Hollywood movie. The day a humble racing yard in a remote seaside village in the west of Ireland conquered Cheltenham. It's a heartwarming story of a small-time trainer and a local cattle dealer combining to capture one of racing's most cherished prizes with a horse purchased only a year before for a modest fee.

When Paul Clarke, a live cattle trader from Beltra, purchased Kilcoleman for little over 3,000 guineas, he could hardly have anticipated the horse would turn out to be a serial winner, clocking up an impressive list of high-class victories, including the coveted County Hurdle at the Cheltenham Festival.

Trained at Rosses Point by Billy Boyers, Kilcoleman defied form and logic to land the big prize on an unforgettable St Patrick's Day in 1977.

The captivating tale of how the Sligomen plotted their assault on Cheltenham began when Co. Clare man James Conheady, a friend of Clarke's through the cattle trade, alerted them to the potential of a young horse. The horse was entered in a point-to-point meeting at Sligo and Clarke determined he would purchase the animal if it won the race. Kilcoleman duly obliged and the deal was done.

Boyers brought the horse to his stables at Rosses Point. A training regime, which included gallops and schooling at the third beach at the popular seaside resort and swims off Oyster Island, proved ideal preparation for a demanding career in the unforgiving National Hunt code.

Kilcoleman's first run under rules was at Dundalk in May 1976. He won at odds of 25/1 and followed with impressive victories over hurdles at Sligo, Limerick and Ballinrobe.

Clarke and Boyers were convinced they had a potential superstar on their hands but because they were not one of the big operations in the sport, few outside their own circle passed much heed. And so Kilcoleman was largely ignored by punters when he lined up for the County Hurdle at Cheltenham on the final day of the 1977 festival.

The build-up to the race wasn't uppermost in Clarke's list of priorities. His wife, Terry, gave birth to the couple's fifth child at Mount Carmel hospital in Dublin a few days before the Cheltenham meeting. So, Clarke left it late into the week before catching an overnight ferry to Liverpool and then driving to Cheltenham on the day of Kilcoleman's race.

Ireland didn't dominate Cheltenham in those days but that particular week was relatively successful. By the time the last race of the festival came around, Irish punters had plenty of cash to splash and weighed in heavily on the favourite, the John Bryce-Smith trained Mwanadike.

"We quietly fancied Kilcoleman to run a big race," says Clarke. "We backed it on the tote, small enough bets but we got a good price."

The horse was backed in from 33/1 to 14/1.

"I'd say there was a fair bit of Sligo money riding on him," remarks Boyers. "I didn't have a bet myself but there were a few lads who weren't shy about having a good punt."

With Tommy Kinane on his back and a sprig of shamrock in his bridle, Kilcoleman gradually picked his way through a big field after a less than inspiring start.

Watching from the stands, Boyers was momentarily perplexed at the way the race unfolded. He says:

> When I saw him at the back of the field, I was wondering was I an awful eejit to send him over. Was I mad entering this horse in a big race at Cheltenham? Who did I think I was?

However, his apprehension was misplaced as Kilcoleman's eye-catching momentum took him to the front as they jumped the last hurdle.

Clarke viewed the horse's storming victory as a fitting reward for a carefully planned campaign.

> We'd run him in a few maiden hurdles so he was well educated. Tommy Kinane gave him a patient ride. He was nearer last than first for most of the race but he came with a great run and just got in front as he jumped the last. The jockey drove him up the hill on the far rail and he got home by about three-quarters of a length.

There was great jubilation among the Sligo contingent as Michael McElhone led the horse back to the winners' enclosure. Boyers admits:

> I was stunned. I started off training with two or three horses in 1968 and little could I have imagined I would have a winner at Cheltenham. It took a while for it all to sink in.

In stark contrast to the wild celebrations which greet an Irish winner at Cheltenham these days, there was no extravagant party to acclaim Kilcoleman's historic feat.

"We had to rush back to Liverpool to get the boat to Dublin so there wasn't time to celebrate. I had a few quiet drinks in the bar on the boat and that was it," remembers Boyers.

Among the lucky punters who put their faith in Kilcoleman was Sligo dentist Paddy McNamara. He had been called to Boyers' yard in the weeks leading up to Cheltenham to extract one of the horse's teeth.

When he went to collect his winnings, the bookie was curious as to why he had backed an unconsidered outsider. The dentist revealed the horse, its trainer and its owner were all clients. According to Boyers, the bookie didn't know whether to laugh or cry as he paid out on the bet.

Arriving back in Dublin, Clarke dashed to Mount Carmel hospital to collect his wife and new-born baby, Paul Junior. The journey to Sligo included a stop-off at Longford for a GAA game. His three passions – family, horse racing and GAA – all contributed to a glorious weekend.

Kilcoleman, meanwhile, went on to enjoy a lucrative career, claiming high-profile races such as the Eadestown Chase at Punchestown, the Connacht National at Sligo, the Sean Graham Cup at Leopardstown, the Easter Chase at Fairyhouse and the Munster National at Limerick.

A further indication of his all-conquering prowess was a particularly courageous double at Sligo, winning on successive days at the August meeting in 1979, carrying 12-7 on the first evening and 12-10 the following afternoon.

Clarke boasts:

> He was a wonderful horse. Indeed, we were confident he would win at Cheltenham again in 1978. He was a stronger and better horse and we fancied his chances. However, the meeting was abandoned due to a heavy snowfall. We brought him to Newbury for a big race that year too but the course was waterlogged and the race didn't go ahead. Maybe we weren't meant to win another big prize with him in England. In any event,

> he won some of the most coveted prizes in racing and probably never got the credit he deserved.

Boyers, who celebrated his ninety-first birthday this year and is as enthusiastic about the racing game now as when he started out as a stable boy with Charlie Rogers in the mid-1940s, rates Kilcoleman as one of the best he's ever trained. He explains:

> He won eight chases, seven hurdle races, a bumper and a point-to-point race. He was a lazy horse at home; he did absolutely nothing. But once you put a saddle and a bridle on him, he was transformed. He loved a walk in the water and a roll on the beach. Once he got to the track, he tried his heart out every time. He was a lovely horse.

Clarke honoured the stable's star by donating a special cup to Sligo Races. The Kilcoleman Cup became one of the most competitive races at his local track for many years. Indeed, Kilcoleman, typical of his warrior-like personality, actually won the cup named in his honour at Sligo's summer meeting in 1979.

"We had memorable days at Cheltenham and all the prestige tracks in Ireland but having a winner at Sligo always meant a lot to us," according to Clarke.

Tragically, Kilcoleman was killed when he fell during the Sweeps Hurdle at Leopardstown in December 1980. He was just eight years old.

Although a horse of Kilcoleman's quality only comes along once in a lifetime, the Boyers–Clarke partnership continued to enjoy some magnificent days at courses all over the country. Sir Barry won the Galway Plate in 1980 and classy horses Artistic Prince, Glenvale Prince and High Diver were other multiple winners from their Rosses Point base.

Given their relatively modest operation and the powerful opposition they faced in the racing industry, the Sligomen achieved phenomenal success. Clarke was the leading National Hunt owner in 1980 and Boyers was fifth in the trainers' list the same year. Boyers remarks:

> I never had more than fourteen horses in the yard at any one time, but I managed to train 140 winners during my career, which was very satisfying. I started out of necessity. We had a shop in Rosses Point village but we were bypassed by a new road and promenade and then the supermarkets came along and we were nearly wiped out. If I hadn't taken up training horses, I might have ended up in the workhouse. Local contractor Eoin Carty sent me a few horses and it all took off from there.

> I was lucky to enjoy a great partnership with Paul Clarke. He bought some nice horses and was happy to leave them with me rather than selling them on. That was a big part of my success.

Clarke is immensely proud of what the partnership achieved in one of the most competitive sports in the country, asserting:

> We were a bit remote in the West of Ireland but that didn't deter us. Billy was a brilliant trainer and we were fortunate to have some top-class horses. We put Sligo on the map in the racing world.

Away from racing, Clarke was deeply involved in GAA activities. He was manager of his local club, St Patrick's, Dromard, guiding them to successive county football championship titles in 1988 and 1989, and was in charge of the Sligo senior county team for a number of years in the 1990s.

In his business life, he had the distinction of being the first exporter to send a shipment of cattle to Europe after Ireland joined the EEC in 1973.

***

Sligo has a long and proud tradition in National Hunt racing. One of the most famous horses from the county was the prolific Ballinode, the winner of the second running of the Cheltenham Gold Cup in 1925. Owned by Christopher Bentley of Kevinsfort House, it was trained by Frank Morgan and ridden by champion jockey of the day Ted Leader. Ballinode also won the Grand Sefton Steeplechase at Aintree and the Nottingham Steeplechase.

The first Irish-trained winner of the Aintree Grand National, in 1847, was a horse called Matthew. It was bred in County Sligo by Col. C.J. Westerna, one of the leading owner/breeders at the time. The 2005 National winner, Hedgehunter, was bred in Sligo by Mary Lang and J. Anthony Keough.

Racketball Sports

Game, Set and Match

Racket sports stars court success

Aisling Blake has always relished a challenge. If reaching number 21 in the world rankings was the pinnacle of an outstanding career, she looks back with equal satisfaction on the countless triumphs she recorded on an epic journey which took her from Sligo Tennis Club to the elite level of professional squash.

Now one of America's leading coaches, the 41-year-old former Irish champion traces her uncompromising competitive streak back to the sibling rivalry with her three older brothers during a gloriously happy childhood.

Growing up in Carraroe on the outskirts of Sligo town, Aisling and her brothers, Cian, Fintan and Garrett, were mad into sport. Their parents, Ed and Bríd, played tennis recreationally. They took out family membership at Sligo Tennis Club and observed with pride the impressive progress of their four children.

The boys won Connacht titles and represented Ireland. Their younger sister didn't have to look beyond the family home for inspiring role models.

"My brothers were very talented at tennis and squash", recalls Aisling. "As the youngest in the family, I had a bit of catching up to do. That's where I got my competitive edge."

She was eight years old when she first stepped on the courts at the local tennis club. Hand-eye coordination came naturally to her.

She explains:

> I wouldn't have been too comfortable with a ball at my feet – soccer or GAA certainly wouldn't have been for me – but once I had a racket and ball in my hand, I was flying. I loved it.

She absorbed the advice, encouragement and expertise of the volunteer coaches at the club. Bernadette and Les Parker, John Kielty and David Taylor were great mentors. She settled on squash as her number one game, and it soon became clear she was a bit special.

The training was relentless. She sacrificed a lot of the things her peers took for granted. It got harder as she grew into a teenager. The devotion to her sporting career demanded unconditional discipline.

"There were times when it was tough," she admits, "but the payback was being able to compete successfully at tournaments all around the country and beyond."

She won national championships at all the junior grades, from under 12s right up to under 19s. She was only fourteen years old when she was selected on Irish teams for European and World Championships. She competed at the Belgian Junior Open Championship and made the semi-finals of the under-19 British Open. The World Junior Championships in Brazil in 1996 was another crucial landmark on an increasingly noteworthy CV.

One of Blake's most memorable achievements in those years was ending the reign of the outstanding Madeline Perry as Ireland's national senior champion.

> Madeline was an icon in Irish squash; somebody I'd always admired. I'd been ranked number two for a few years and desperately wanted to win the national championship. So, to beat Madeline in the final was a standout moment in my career. Psychologically, it was crucially important because it gave me the belief that I really was among the best players in the country. It validated everything I'd put into the sport from when I was a young girl.

After graduating from Trinity College with a degree in Business Studies, Blake made the brave decision to pursue a career in professional squash.

The seeds for the momentous move were planted during summer stints in Australia during her last two years at college. She was based at the Victorian Institute of Sport and participated in several high-class tournaments.

She subsequently teamed up with renowned coach Liz Irving, and moved to Amsterdam to begin her pro career in 2004. She trained alongside the legendary Nicol David, multiple world champion, and her game improved rapidly.

> Turning professional was a massive learning curve. It was like going back and learning a lot of basic stuff. In terms of technique, I had a lot of work

> to do but I adapted quite quickly and before too long I was ticking a lot of the boxes which were required to achieve results at the elite level of the sport.

She was unyielding in her determination to succeed, constantly pushing the boundaries to test herself against the world's best players. In one tournament in China, she beat the world number 10, Camille Serme. The result fired her ambition. She dared to dream of breaking into the top 20 in the world.

In 2010, Blake peaked at number 21. It was a colossal achievement for a girl who started out from a modest club in the west of Ireland.

> I just missed out on making the top 20 and that was frustrating at the time. I look back on it now with immense pride, however. It represented a major breakthrough. It would have been beyond my wildest dreams when I was playing squash just for the fun of it as a carefree young girl in Sligo.

After competing in tournaments all over the world and representing her country with distinction, she finally succumbed to a troublesome lower back injury which sidelined her for nine months. She called it a day in 2016 but bowed out in the knowledge she had given everything she had in pursuit of her dream.

"I squeezed all the juice from the orange," she jokes. "I knew when enough was enough and was happy with my decision. I retired with no regrets."

She's now settled in San Francisco where she's director of operations at the Squash Zone club.

> It reminds me of Sligo Tennis Club. There's a real community feel to it, and it's wonderful to have the opportunity to pass on my expertise and knowledge of the game to a new generation of players.

Blake is also assistant coach to the USA under-19 squash team, which reached the last 16 of the World Championships in France in 2022.

Whatever the future holds, Sligo will forever be close to her heart.

"Nothing compares to a sunny day in Strandhill", she insists. "Sligo will always be home for me."

***

Another highly decorated Sligo squash star is Keith Moran, who has been playing the sport, man and boy, for nearly 35 years. He has represented Ireland on almost 50 occasions across all grades, has been national champion at every level from underage to masters, and continued his remarkable longevity in the game by competing in the World Masters Championships in Poland in 2022.

His interest stirred by watching his father, Michael, play in local tournaments on one of Sligo's early squash courts at St Mary's GAA club, Keith confirms he became "addicted" to the game fairly quickly.

> As soon as dad would leave down his racket, I'd pick it up and start slamming a few shots. It felt good almost immediately, the realisation that I was handy at it came quite quickly. I was hooked from about 10 years old.
>
> Squash was massive in Sligo back then. I'd say we had the strongest squash contingent in the country. Dave Taylor, a teacher at Summerhill College, was the main instigator. He put a structure in place and organised training on three nights a week. Without his commitment, and the help of a few other parents, it would never have happened.

Within a year of taking up the game, Moran was under-12 national champion. It was the start of an incredible run of success at junior level as he captured national titles at under-14, under-16 and under-19 grades. He also represented Ireland at every age level in the junior ranks.

In 2009, he became one of only three Connacht players ever to represent Ireland at senior level when he made his debut at the European Championships in Denmark. A good indicator of his quality at that stage is the fact that the other players on the four-man team were full-time professionals.

As the years ticked by, Moran's enthusiasm for the game remained intact, as he became one of the top players on the Masters Circuit. A significant milestone was achieved in 2014 when he was part of the first Irish Masters team ever to defeat England in the Home Internationals series. As he recalls:

> The match was tied at 2–2 and I had to play the last game, which I managed to win and get us over the line. It was a big deal, a bit of history.

Moran won the Irish Open over-35 championship on three occasions and the over-40s title twice, and in 2020 became one of only a handful of players to win both the open and closed championships in the same year. Crowning his successful run of recent years, Moran won the over-40 Danish Open Masters Championship in June 2022.

At masters level, he has represented Ireland 30 times, which, added to his fifteen junior caps and three senior caps, makes him one of Sligo's leading international sportsmen.

A successful businessman, Moran is CEO of SL Controls, the software integration company he co-founded in 2002 and which currently employs 140 people with offices throughout Ireland and the U.S. He contends his involvement in squash has helped enormously in his business life. He explains:

> A lot of my strengths in my work life are linked to squash, which is a very competitive and individual sport. You have to be very driven to succeed at it, and I've found the commitment and determination I've invested in squash over the years is precisely the sort of quality which has served me well in the business world.
>
> It's also a great respite from my work life. No matter where I'm working in the country I will find a squash court, a place to play or train. It's a great way to unwind, and although the body is starting to ask a few tough questions these days, squash keeps me fit and active and ticking over. It's a huge help.

***

Sligo also boasts a high achiever in badminton. Jonathan Dolan from Calry is a multiple singles and doubles champion at national and international level and is considered one of the top exponents of the game in the country. He has represented Ireland at tournaments throughout the world on numerous occasions.

His passion for the sport was nurtured by his uncle, John, a badminton coach at Sligo Tennis Club. Initially, his interest was no more than casual but it gradually got a grip on him.

> I played a lot of team sports, but badminton gave me added stimulation. The idea of being involved in an individual sport where I controlled my own destiny appealed to me. I was surprised at how quickly I adapted to the game. It all just came naturally to me. Soon, it became an obsession. I was playing before school, after school, at weekends. It got to the stage where I was phoning my uncle and some of the adult players at the club and literally pleading with them to play against me. I was only a young boy, but I couldn't get enough badminton. I was totally absorbed by the sport.

After a string of impressive victories in the underage grades, Dolan had something of a breakthrough year in 2012, winning the Belgian Junior Open and the Irish Junior Championship. He reached the last sixteen of the World Junior Championships, losing out to the current world number one, Viktor Axelsen from Denmark. His eye-catching exploits elevated him to a ranking of number 8 in the world junior ratings.

> It wasn't a big deal at the time. I was playing so well that I expected to be in contention at the big tournaments in Ireland and abroad. Looking back at those achievements now, I realise it was quite something for a young lad from Sligo, where there is no great tradition of badminton, to accomplish so much at such a young age.

The following year he won the men's singles and doubles senior Irish championships before taking the Irish Open National Championship doubles title with his partner, Sam Magee, in 2014.

He has since added two further national senior titles, 2019 and 2022, as well as a second doubles national senior crown to his stunning CV.

On the international circuit, the Calry man clocked up major wins in tournaments in the Czech Republic and Cyprus, both achieved within a whirlwind seven days in 2019.

He considers those two victories and his national title the same year as his most satisfying accomplishments to date

> I hadn't played much badminton in the previous two years so to come back and win those tournaments was very special. It proved that I had the desire and the ability to be up there with the best players in Ireland and further afield.

The 27-year-old Sligo player spent three years at the Badminton European Academy in Denmark and is now based at the Badminton Ireland High Performance Centre at the Irish Sports Council's headquarters in Blanchardstown.

He commenced a course in Community and Youth Development at the Technical University Dublin in 2022, and continues to participate in national and international tournaments.

> I've had some setbacks during the course of my career, but I rediscovered my best form in the last few years. I'm looking forward to the future with renewed confidence.

Rugby

Dear Kevin,
Enjoy the book!

Aoife McDermott

Elite international – on the double

An extraordinary journey from shy schoolgirl to top international athlete in two different sports - that's the inspiring story of Aoife McDermott, the current Irish rugby star who has also represented her country in a success-laden basketball career.

It all began in her native Riverstown, a typical rural village ten miles south of Sligo town where sport is the heartbeat of community life. Local heroes abound. Frank Henry was on the Sligo GAA team which won the Connacht Championship in 1975, Johnny Kenny won an FAI Cup medal with Sligo Rovers in 1994, his son, Johnny Junior, is forging a career at Celtic, Ann Kelly is the spine of a vibrant Community Games movement in the county. In the hypnotic years when Sligo Rovers seemed to win all before them, most of their players resided in the village. It became known as 'Roverstown'.

This is the sports-crazy environment which shaped the future dual international.

McDermott's parents, Seán and Cora, ran a pub and shop in the village. Locals would pop in for a loaf of bread or a pint. The cheerful banter always came back to sport. The children loved it, eavesdropping on the adult analysis, picking up the odd nugget of priceless wisdom. It filled their heads with impossible dreams.

McDermott remembers working behind the bar and listening to the animated re-telling of the big games. It was like their own personal *Sunday Game* studio. Everybody had an opinion. She lapped it all up. Her siblings, Brian and Sonia, were enthralled to. The addiction to sport took root there.

There was great excitement when she came home from the national finals of Community Games with a silver medal in shot put of all things. She was handy at soccer and Gaelic football, dabbled a bit in rounders and handball but shot put? It was almost as foreign to her as basketball and rugby, two sports to which she showed no inclination.

She was a student at Coola post-primary school before she encountered any form of serious basketball. She was 12 years old, nearly six foot tall and a natural athlete. A ready-made basketball player. She was encouraged to give it a go, but the game didn't steal her heart. Fair to say, the romance was a slow burner. Her first training session with Sligo All-Stars nearly derailed the relationship, as she confesses:

> I was self-conscious and awkward. I found it hard to mix. I didn't want to go back a second time. My mother and the coach at the club, Shane O'Meara, eventually persuaded me to stick with it.

The reluctant convert was soon a stand-out star. On one memorable occasion, she won two league titles with the All-Stars on the same day, one with the under-14 team and one with the under-16s. Her father frequently reminds her of that special feat. He considers it her most remarkable achievement.

She was still playing in the under-14 leagues when she was called up to the under-16 international squad. Despite what she describes as a calamitous trial, when she fell on her backside a few times, she quickly established herself as a regular with the national team.

The highlight was the European Under-16 Championships in Italy in 2007. From there came the inevitable progression to the senior squad. She was on the Irish team which reached the final of the 'Small Countries' European tournament in Gibraltar in 2016. They were beaten by Malta in the decider. The pain still hurts.

By way of compensation, McDermott had a sparkling career in domestic basketball to sustain her. She won a national league title with Sligo All-Stars before switching to University of Limerick's multi-talented team, UL Huskies.

It was a spectacularly productive period in her career. The Huskies were invincible, at one stage clocking up a staggering 45-match unbeaten run. During her four years with the club, McDermott won three national Super League titles and two National Cups.

Her exciting college career also included stints with DCU Mercy, with whom she won a Super League title, and the Meteors. She won an Inter-Varsities medal with Trinity College.

She invested everything in basketball until she had nothing left to give. And it got to the stage where the sport didn't have much to offer in return. As she concedes:

> Walking away from basketball was difficult but the sport had little left to excite me. I had a special bond with the girls at UL. We had been through so much together, winning all before us. It would have been impossible to replicate it anywhere else.

The search for alternative stimulation led her to rugby. It was a chance meeting with Irish international Jenny Murphy which opened the door. They met while they were both involved with the Sky Sports *Living for Sport* programme. McDermott spent three years as an ambassador with Sky, undertaking motivational work with schoolchildren all around Ireland. It gave her a broader perspective on the value of sport. When Murphy suggested changing codes, she took the bait.

The transition was embraced with typical passion and commitment. Initially, it was Sevens Rugby but eventually she teamed up with Sandymount-based club Railway Union. It was her first exposure to the sport at competitive level, but she was a quick learner. Almost immediately, she became a regular starter, playing a key role in the club's impressive haul of silverware, and attracting the attention of the international and inter-provincial selectors.

She made her debut for Ireland against Wales in the 2018 Six Nations Championship. It's an occasion which still radiates immense pride and joy.

"I remember not being able to take the smile off my face," McDermott recalls. "There's no feeling like it; it was a high I never experienced before or since."

Even the formalities of the build-up to the game left a lasting impression for the dual international.

It was all new to her. The intensive preparations, the thrill of the Captain's Run, the formal presentation of her jersey on the night before the game. She was so lost in the giddy excitement of it all she barely recognised former Irish hero Luke Fitzgerald as he performed the ceremonial duties. It was a struggle to keep her emotions in check.

"When I was presented with my jersey, everybody in the room stood up and gave me a standing ovation. I'd no idea this was part of the routine. I swear to God, I was bawling," she admits.

It was only on the morning of the game she learned she would be in the starting fifteen after Nichola Fryday dropped out due to illness. Her recollection is that she 'freaked out' when coach Adam Griggs gave her the welcome news as the squad was preparing to leave their hotel.

"The other girls said I went white in the face," she laughs. "I was stunned. It suddenly dawned on me I would be starting a Six Nations game. It took a while to sink in."

Her brother, Brian, had flown home from Abu Dhabi for the game. Her parents were there too.

She vividly remembers the sheer joy of walking out on the pitch as a fully-fledged international. The 31-year-old lock forward recalls:

> It was very moving, hearing the anthem, standing shoulder to shoulder with my teammates, looking for my family in the stands. The memories of those special moments will stay with me forever.

McDermott has played in five Six Nations tournaments and represented Leinster in the inter-provincials on many occasions. She's won two National League titles and a National Cup with Railway Union.

There have been a few setbacks along the way, the most devastating of which was Ireland's failure to qualify for the 2022 World Cup in New Zealand. They underperformed spectacularly in a qualification campaign in Italy, where a victory over the hosts wasn't enough to compensate for shock defeats to Scotland and Spain.

"That wound will take a long time to heal", she agrees. "It was the lowest point in my rugby career."

McDermott's exceptional sporting exploits are celebrated in a beautiful mural on the wall of the local playground in her home village. It was commissioned by IRFU sponsors Aer Lingus, as part of their Home Advantage initiative in 2020. It's one of only five in the country and is designed to highlight the growth of rugby in areas not traditionally associated with the sport.

> I love it. If the local kids see me as a role model, I'm fine with that. I've been very lucky to have enjoyed so much success in my career and if that inspires more girls to get involved in sport that would be brilliant.

There's another precious memento of her glittering career in Riverstown. Her Irish international cap, which represents all the appearances she's made for her country, has pride of place in the family home.

In the real world, McDermott is playing a hugely important role as well. She's working on heart failure research as part of her employment with the Heartbeat Trust charity based at St Michael's Hospital, Dun Laoghaire. She has a BA in Nursing (Intellectual Disabilities) from the University of Limerick and a Masters from Trinity College.

Conán O'Donnell

Globetrotting rugby player 'living the dream'

He's played professional rugby in Japan, South Africa, Australia, Argentina and New Zealand, sharing pitches with some of the world's greatest players along the way. No wonder Sligo's globetrotting star, Conán O'Donnell, gleefully declares he's 'living the dream'.

It's all a far cry from the muddy rain-soaked fields where he honed his talents as a young hopeful in the obscurity of schoolboy rugby back home but at 26 years of age, he's confident his best years are still ahead of him.

He explains:

> The ambition would be to land a full-time contract with one of the top clubs in Europe or back in Ireland but, for the moment, it's a case of taking each challenge as it comes.

Based in Whangarei in the Northland region of New Zealand's North Island, the talented prop has been involved with several top clubs in both the Super Rugby League and the National Provincial Championships. He's lived in Pukekohe, Christchurch, Mount Maunganui and Dunedin and lists Counties Manukau, Crusaders, Highlanders and current club Northland among the teams he's represented in New Zealand. He entuses:

> It's been an unreal experience. I've been fortunate to have lived in some great cities, met wonderful people, and played rugby at the very highest level with and against many of the top players in the world. It really is the stuff of dreams and something I could never have imagined when I was a young rugby-mad kid growing up in Sligo.

The travel bug hit him after he was released by Connacht at the end of the 2019 season. It was a bitter blow but former Connacht Academy coach Corey Brown remained convinced of the Sligo player's potential and offered him an opportunity to play for Japanese team Sunwolves for the last five weeks of the Super League season. He beams at the memory.

> It was a once-in-a-lifetime opportunity. Little did I know it would be the start of an incredible adventure which would take me to some of the most stunning locations in the world.

O'Donnell made his Sunwolves debut against the Brumbies at the iconic GIO Stadium in Canberra and went on to play for the team in Japan, Cape Town and Buenos Aires. It paved the way for a move to New Zealand where he teamed up with Counties Manukau, based in South Auckland.

"I played the best rugby of my career there, although we had a disappointing season and were relegated," he relates.

O'Donnell went on to secure what are known as 'medical joker' contracts with a number of clubs; basically, short-term deals covering for injured players.

> Ideally, it would be great to pin down a long-term contract but it's the way it works in New Zealand. It means I've had the opportunity to sample life in different regions and cities and that's been a wonderful experience.

O'Donnell has had to be resourceful and flexible in his attitude to life as a professional rugby player. He explains:

> Literally, it means turning your hand to everything and anything to keep going between professional contracts. I've worked as a painter and a landscaper and just doing odd jobs.

Among the clubs he's represented is Crusaders, a cover team for absent All-Blacks players. "It was a humbling experience to play there," he insists. "It was a case of learning from the best."

His love of rugby was nurtured in his primary school days in Sligo town. Coming from a well-known sporting family – his father, Cathal, won several county and Connacht championship medals with St Mary's GAA club – O'Donnell displayed a natural talent for the game from a very young age. His earliest memory of playing the sport is as a six-year-old in the mini-rugby programme at Sligo Rugby Club. He jokes:

> It was the only sport I had any talent for. Over the years, I played soccer, hurling, Gaelic football and even table tennis but the plain truth is that I wasn't any good at any of them.

He was already totally absorbed in the game by the time he went to secondary school at Summerhill College. On his first day in the college, O'Donnell noticed international jerseys hanging on the wall. They belonged to past pupils Aaron Spring and Billy Leahy, who had represented Ireland in rugby at schoolboy level.

"That was all the motivation I needed," he says. "I saw these lads as trail-blazers and I was determined to follow in their footsteps."

Meanwhile, Sligo Rugby Club was thriving at underage level, enjoying some thrilling campaigns in Connacht.

O'Donnell was part of the under-17 squad which made it all the way to the All-Ireland final in 2013. A multi-talented squad recorded a League and Cup double in Connacht and had a pulsating win over Clonakilty in the All-Ireland semi-finals. However, the thrilling adventure ended in heartbreak when they lost narrowly to Navan in the decider.

The Sligo player's unsparing commitment was rewarded with selection for the Irish schools' team and he enthusiastically embraced the challenges of life as an international player. He explains:

> I put the hammer down in training. I would go for regular runs in the local Mitchell Curley Park, do extra gym work many times during the week and go training with the seniors at Sligo Rugby Club. I felt I had to put in extra effort to keep pace with players from the traditional rugby schools.

He was part of the Irish schools' team which enjoyed a great run in the European Championships in Poland, losing to England in the final. He subsequently played for the Connacht and Irish under-20s, making his debut for the national team against Italy in 2015 Six Nations. He played in all five games and was selected for the World Cup in Italy later that year. He laughs:

> That was a fantastic experience and a great excuse for the family to have a nice holiday. We played against some of the top teams in the world, including the "Baby Blacks", a terrific team which went on to win the tournament.

The Sligoman made his senior Connacht debut at the age of 19 and was the youngest player on the squad which won the Pro 12 in 2015–2016 alongside household names Robbie Henshaw, Bundee Aki, John Muldoon, Andrew Brown and Roman Loughney.

In his last season with Connacht, he featured in seven games under new coach Andy Friend, and was on the Connacht development team which travelled to Boston to play MLR team New England Freejacks.

Since then, he's tasted the highs and lows of professional rugby on a pulsating odyssey which scarcely seemed possible during his schoolboy days. Pulling on the green jersey for his country still ranks among his proudest moments and it's something he'd love to do at senior level.

"That's the ultimate aim," he confesses.

***

Founded in 1890, Sligo Rugby Football club is one of the oldest sporting institutions in Sligo, and there wouldn't be too many older in the entire country. The club played its first Connacht Senior Cup game in 1896, winning the title in 1914, 2017 and completing a remarkable Cup and League double in 2018. As a junior side, Sligo won the Connacht Junior Cup for the first time in 1925 and has repeated the feat on six further occasions since.

Currently one of the fastest growing rugby clubs in Connacht, Sligo boasts a thriving underage section, fielding seventeen teams from under-7s to under-18s, many of whom have achieved national and provincial titles. In 2005, under coaches Brendan Leahy and Joe Walsh, the under-18s won an All-Ireland League title for the first time. In 2022, all three youth girls' teams reached their cup finals, with the under-18 girls winning the Connacht Girls Cup for the first time. The under-17 and under-15 boys, meanwhile, won the Cup and League double. The under-15 captain, William Draper, is a great-grandson of one of the club's legendary figures, Bob Hamilton, in whose honour the club's home ground at Strandhill is named.

Several club officers have also given solid service to the game at provincial level. Club president Joe Burgess was elected president of the Connacht Branch IRFU in 1994, and Michael O'Hehir will assume the same office in the 2023–2024 season. In 2012, Clare Storey was the first woman to become president of a senior club in Ireland.

Sligo RFC has a long list of representative honours at national and interprovincial level in men's, women's and underage grades. Notable alumni include Cathal Sheridan, who is director of rugby with the Munster Academy; Niall Kenneally, captain of Cork Con and Ireland Club team; David McGowan, the club's first professional player in 2007; and current professionals Seán Henry, Stephen Kerins, Cillian Gallagher and Conan O'Donnell; Anne O'Toole and Therese Cosgrove have won international caps; Pat Curran, one of the longest serving club members, has been inducted into the local Sports Hall of Fame; and Vinnie O'Brien is one of the longest serving stalwarts on the Connacht Branch IRFU. Ross Mannion, who has served as club senior coach and youth development officer, is currently the Connacht Women's head coach.

Soccer (Junior)

Junior Soccer

A ritual endures on football's factory floor

Every weekend every year, from autumn to spring, nearly 400 amateur footballers take to pitches the length and breadth of County Sligo, bolstered by a significant army of coaches, bag-carriers, supporters and well-meaning hangers-on. The head count on any given Sunday could tip the 1,000 mark. This is junior soccer, a ritual with roots traceable over more than 100 years, and one which has become almost a rite of passage for any footballer worth his salt.

It is a remarkable history fashioned by remarkable people. It's a story of farmers' fields plastered with cow-dung masquerading as football pitches; it's about togging out under wind-swept bushes or in derelict sheds; cornflake boxes stuffed into mismatched socks so as to resemble shin-guards; pints before, occasionally during, and after games; epic tussles won and lost, friendships forged and rivalries fierce but soon forgotten. More recently, it's about posh all-weather playing surfaces and beaming floodlights. In Sligo football circles, it's part of who we are, the factory floor of the giant football conglomerate.

But what is the alluring attraction of this football mainstay? How has it captivated generations of Sligonians in every pocket of the county, and why is its popularity thriving in an age of so many other distractions?

Peter Walsh from Gurteen should know. He's in his fourth decade playing junior soccer in Sligo, and at 51 years young the notion of retirement is a foreign concept.

Having played for a number of years as a goalkeeper with the county GAA team, under astute managers such as Mickey Moran and Peter Ford, and winning an impressive six county titles with Eastern Harps, Walsh might have been forgiven an early abandonment of his soccer activities, but that was never an option. He recalls:

> I think the craic and the banter was a bit better with the soccer. The GAA was a bit more serious, which was understandable if you were chasing county titles or playing for Sligo in big championship games. At times like that, we weren't supposed to have anything to do with soccer, which we mostly complied with, although we'd sneak in a game if we could.

Starting 36 years ago as a free-scoring striker with Gara Celtic, the forerunner to his current club, Gurteen Celtic, he now lines out as a goalkeeper, mostly in emergency situations these days, but still capable of rolling back the years.

Delighted with the tremendous advances in terms of facilities and perfectly manicured pitches dotted around the county, he nonetheless enjoys the nostalgia of times when junior soccer offered a far less salubrious picture.

> We played in fields rather than pitches. We'd tog out in cars or under bushes or on the cold steps of Gurteen Health Centre. The pitches were rented from a local farmer and we'd often have to shovel away the cow dung and fill in the patches with buckets of sand before the referee arrived. Often, we'd leave our clothes in bags at the side of the pitch and they'd be drenched with rain after the game. No showers, home for a bath if you were lucky. And yet we couldn't wait for the next game.

Francie 'Horse' Candon, who's been playing for the Ballinafad-based club Aughanagh Celtic for the past 30 years, is still enticed by the lure of Sunday morning football.

He made his debut in the junior ranks as a timid 15-year-old and still lines out whenever the need arises, though the call for his services is less frequent these days.

"I go to every game and I always bring my gear just in case," he says. "I get the occasional game as a sub. That keeps me ticking over."

Junior football, he relates, has been his life. A regular with his local GAA club, Eastern Harps, for many years, it is the golden memories of his soccer career with his village club which clearly bring him most joy:

> I loved the GAA. There were some weekends when I'd play for the intermediates on a Saturday evening, then the soccer on a Sunday morning and the senior GAA team on a Sunday afternoon. Some people might call

> that commitment, but I never saw it that way. To me it was fun, a way of life, and I loved it.

Their Wembley Stadium was Creggs Field, elevated high on a hill overlooking the village, where epic games were fought and friendships forged. Candon fondly recalls:

> We'd tog out in an old tool shed, stuffing bits of cornflake boxes down our socks to look like shin guards. Not too many people had cars in those days, and there was certainly no such thing as a team bus. We had two cars for away matches, the manager and five players in one and six more of us crammed into the second. That was our team bonding.

Junior football's ancestral home is the Forthill area of Sligo town, where Glenview Stars are the current flag bearers of a tradition that stretches back more than 100 years. In that time, it's highly likely that every house in the tight-knit working class community has produced at least one gifted footballer.

Local councillor and former mayor of Sligo Gino O'Boyle represents all that is good and glorious about the football tradition of the area known as 'The Hill', regularly digging deep into his own pockets to keep the club afloat in challenging times.

"For us, junior football is everything," proclaims the 38-year-old, who has scored goals in Glenview's colours in each of four decades, since making his debut as a raw 13-year-old in 1999.

His late father, Seamie, in whose honour the local community park is named, taught him the ropes and he finds it's an inescapable inheritance. O'Boyle explains:

> From a very young age I was conscious of my dad's massive devotion to football. He was the manager, the chairman, whatever needed to be done. He lined pitches, drove all over the county to matches, dragged fellas out of bed on a Sunday morning. My mother washed the shirts. That's where the inspiration comes from.

While the veterans inch ever closer to retirement, a fresh generation of young players is willingly carrying the mantle, intent on injecting youthful exuberance into the circle of Sligo life which is junior football.

NUIG student Cian Basquille is typical of a new generation of younger players graduating from the youth leagues to the junior ranks. A goalkeeper for Strand Celtic, one of the league's most progressive clubs which has just celebrated the fiftieth anniversary of its foundation, the 21-year-old is adapting well to new challenges. Having won six league titles playing for the club's underage teams, Cian made his debut in the junior league as a nervous 16-year-old. He enthuses:

> Playing football has taught me life lessons, greatly improved my social involvement and I have made lifelong friends who I get to play alongside every week. Even at my age, I'm aware this won't last forever, so I embrace it now as a really important part of my life. We are so blessed to have those opportunities.

Of course, those opportunities only exist because of a meticulously oiled Sligo–Leitrim and District League organisation, where Noel Kennedy has been running the operation with dedicated professionalism for over 40 years. At local, regional and national level he's filled a vast array of administrative roles, successfully transforming the local leagues into one of the most impressive in the country.

In 1991, he masterminded the transformation of a near derelict site at Cranmore Road into one of the country's top junior soccer venues. The magnificent headquarters, Ray MacSharry Complex, was built at a cost of €300,000 and 30 years later another €400,00 was invested in a sparkling new state-of-the art AstroTurf playing surface, which is a hive of activity for all age groups seven days a week.

The land at Cranmore had been acquired from the Sisters of Mercy in the early 1970s by a visionary Sligo–Leitrim FA, under the stewardship of Gerry McMorrow, Christy Kennedy, Leo Gray Senior and Tony McGee. Their good work had been built upon by men like Michael Green and Cyril Moran before Noel Kennedy took matters to a new level.

"Do it right or don't do it at all," is Noel's motto, and his ambition is undeterred by a challenging financial position. He contends:

> We operate on a shoestring. Truthfully, we get very little financial support outside our own clubs and local backers. We have loans to repay and big running costs to meet, but the effort is well worthwhile.
>
> We have about 800 registered players, and when you add in coaches, volunteers, supporters, you're talking about thousands of people involved every weekend. Our league is in a very healthy condition, and everybody owns that success. There are a lot of moving parts, but the important thing is we move in the same direction. People talk a lot about

> the future of football in this country. Junior soccer must be part of that discussion.

Football at any level could not be played without referees, and Sligo is fortunate to have had a long history of top-class officials whose expertise and enthusiasm enhance the game at youth, schoolboy and junior level.

The standards set by revered characters such as Willie Bradley, Bertie McGowan and Kevin 'Neighbour' Fallon in previous generations are carried today by two local branches of the Irish Soccer Referees Society, with up to thirty referees in action each weekend, sometimes taking charge of two or three games in the space of a few days.

FAI referees observer Paul Deering has been involved in local refereeing for over three decades. The only local referee to have officiated at a European Champions League game, he has also been an assistant referee at an FAI Cup final, an honour he shares with another Sligoman, Noel Foley. Both men also served on the League of Ireland panel along with current Sligo Rovers chairman, Tommie Higgins, and Paul Hynes and Kieran O'Dowd. Currently, Keenan Deering and Darren Corcoran are on the referees' elite panel. Deering reports:

> Both branches of the Irish Soccer Referees Society have a great relationship with the league and the clubs locally. It's a huge commitment these days with so much football being played, from the local youth and junior leagues right up to the League of Ireland underage games. When you consider lads would also have full-time jobs, it takes massive dedication. Luckily, both in terms of numbers and standard, Sligo is very well served by referees these days, and it's encouraging that a long tradition is being upheld every weekend.

From any viewpoint, it's clear that junior soccer's legacy is in good hands. It has had a storied past, is enjoying a thriving present and is assured of a bright future. Long may it continue.

MacArthur Cup

History and mystery rhyme in iconic tournament

Although it hasn't been contested for more than 45 years, having disappeared in circumstances which would have stretched Agatha Christie's convoluted imagination, the MacArthur Cup continues to retain an almost mythical place in Sligo's soccer history.

An inter-firms competition played annually on long hot summer evenings dating back to 1927 and enjoying a prosperous revival between the 1950s and 1970s, the MacArthur Cup is famous not only for a legion of local football legends but also because it illuminates an era of Sligo's prosperous industrial growth.

The names of long-forgotten businesses and the town's traditional football families punctuate the history of the competition. Young men – and indeed not-so-young – who availed of plentiful employment in a burgeoning list of factories and hardware stores would finish their day's work playing their hearts out for those firms in epic games at Abbeyville Park.

Massive crowds, men and women yet to know the distraction of television or fancy cabaret lounges, flocked to the sidelines of the Abbeyquarter venue. There, they would cheer lustily in uniquely Sligo banter, a humorous concoction of extravagant admiration and mild abuse.

The protagonists, often an engaging mixture of spotty-faced youths and barrel-bellied veterans, emitted an intoxicating odour of muscle lubricant, hair oil and a faint whiff of post-work beer. They took immense pride in representing their various workplaces, their enthusiastic efforts producing memorable games of football which have deservedly become part of Sligo folklore. In

Sligo, a MacArthur Cup winners' medal was as precious as an All-Ireland in Kerry. The intensity of the games mirrored the importance of the silverware.

The competition was first played in 1927, pre-dating even the formation of Sligo Rovers, making it one of the oldest tournaments in the country. It was contested throughout the 1920s and 30s, and intermittently in the 40s, before being revived in the early 1950s by a cash-strapped local junior football committee who hoped it would provide a badly needed financial boost. Between sponsorship, entry fees and big 'gates' – a nightly take of a handsome ten shillings wasn't uncommon – it was an instant and enduring success.

The sponsor was a local bakery. MacArthur's Bakery can be traced back to 1870, when it was one of a remarkable total of 27 confectionary businesses operating in the town. For all of its 93 years history it operated out of the same premises on a street then known as Knox Street, now the town's main thoroughfare of O'Connell Street. It was based in the buildings which currently house the street frontage of the Tesco Arcade.

It's likely that the bakery's link-up with the football association came about through its employee, Alderman John Fallon, an early local soccer administrator whose influence spread well beyond the confines of sport. He served as a member of both Sligo Corporation and Sligo County Council for an unbroken record of 46 years and was one of the founding members of Sligo Rovers football club. If the junior football committee, of which he served as chairman, was seeking an impressive trophy for its new competition, Alderman Fallon's influence with his bosses at MacArthur's would have been invaluable.

The sponsors regularly entered their own team in the competition, winning it at the fourth attempt in 1962, ironically the year before the bakery closed.

Sadly, almost all of the firms in the competition's roll of honour have also long since disappeared. Workplaces such as Denny's, Meldrum's, Foley's Brewery, Woods, McMenamin's, The Foundry, The Spinning Factory, Filler & Fiebeg's, Sligo Models, Hanson's, Avena, Gowna and Hannaway's were not only leading lights in the MacArthur Cup but provided the bedrock wages of a then-booming local economy.

Employment numbers at most of these firms were sufficient to field full teams, sometimes a second selection, from their own resources. Smaller firms, meanwhile, were permitted to amalgamate in order to reach the required number of players. Thus, teams such as Painters/Grocers or Printers/Post Office or Hannaway/Meat Company were regular participants. Teams were also allowed one guest player from outside the particular workplace, which often led to controversy as the town's best players were courted by a queue of admirers. It was a regular practice that summer jobs would be allocated on the basis of an applicant's propensity for a tough tackle or a goal-poacher's instinct.

One such player was a teenage Gerry Conway, now the owner of Eason's bookstore in the centre of town. An accomplished GAA footballer, who represented the county at minor, under-21, junior and senior levels, Gerry didn't care much for soccer until he landed a summer job at Hannaway's Food Company in 1968. Gerry recalls:

> I wasn't really into soccer at all, but they knew in Hannaway's that I played Gaelic football and that I was strong and fit, so they put me in at centre-half. Everything in the air was mine and I was tough in the tackle, but my touch was way off.

He must have been a quick learner, though, because not only did Hannaway's go on to win the MacArthur Cup that year, but a year later Gerry was playing Colllingwood Cup football for UCG and won an Irish Universities cap. He enthuses at the memories:

> I'll never forget the craic we had in the MacArthur Cup. Most teams had a few quality players and the games were always tough. Denny's always seemed to be the team to beat. They had terrific forwards like Bob Munds and Francie Dunleavy, and they regularly won the trophy. I think it was a bit of a shock when we beat them in the final, but we were well organised by the late Michael McGowan, who was a terrific player. Speedie Heraughty, Andrew Lang, Jackie Keenan and Charlie Scanlon were other guys who gave us an extra edge.
>
> The thing I remember most was the huge crowds. It was such a thrill as a young fella to play in front of so many people, and the banter from the sidelines was often hilarious.
>
> Most of us took it quite seriously, but at the same time it wasn't unusual to see a few lads having a bottle of stout or a couple of ciggies at half time or fellas arguing and refusing to leave the field when they were substituted. It was that sort of competition. It had a bit of everything.

The last MacArthur Cup final was played in 1975, featuring CIE/Henderson's and newcomers Snia, a giant Italian nylon manufacturing company which had just established headquarters in Hazelwood, creating hundreds of badly needed jobs.

As a parting shot, the final could scarcely have been more dramatic, a dizzy combination of mischief, mystery and mayhem. By now, Abbbeyville Park had become a building site so the final was played on a perfectly manicured pitch at Summerhill College. The match proved to be a thriller, ending in a 2–2 draw. The replay was even better. This time, six goals were evenly shared, and the stage was set for an enthralling second replay.

But a tournament which had been fuelled by high drama ever since its inception was about to deliver a gripping twist. CIE/Henderson's failed to turn up, claiming a glut of injuries had depleted their ranks beyond repair and alleging that Snia had broken regulations in their team selection. They demanded the final be postponed until all issues were resolved, but the organisers stood firm, and Snia were awarded the cup.

Chris Benson from Ballisodare was in the Snia team that night. As he remembers it, their striker, John 'Tramp' Brennan, tipped off and then ran from the halfway line of a deserted pitch to rattle the ball into an empty net, thus scoring the most unlikely winner in the history of the competition. As Chris maintains:

> It was an awful way to win it, but what were we to do? It wasn't our fault there was no opposition. We would have been quite happy to play. It was such a thrill to win the MacArthur Cup, but I would have preferred to win it after playing a game.

By that stage, Chris was a MacArthur Cup veteran, having made his debut years earlier as a 16-year-old summer worker with W&GT Pollexfin Ltd, the flour mill in his native village, whose team was known as Avena. He sums up precisely what the MacArthur Cup meant to him and to so many local players:

> I was working for the summer, sweeping floors in the flour mill. Clocking out one day, I saw the team for that night's game against the Builders posted on the wall, and there was my name. I couldn't believe it. Seeing my name on that team sheet was like being picked for the England team in the 1966 World Cup Final. It was that exciting. I remember it to this day.

But what became of the MacArthur Cup trophy? Amidst the chaotic celebrations following the final that never was, the famous old cup went missing. With no bloodhound to locate it, as happened when the Jules Remit trophy disappeared before the 1966 World Cup, the whereabouts of the silver cup remained an unsolved mystery, never to be played for again.

Until one dark night many years later, an unknown man knocked on a door at the home of Johnny MacArthur in Rosses Point and handed back the trophy, of which there had been no sight or knowledge for more than forty years.

Johnny's late father, Alex, was the last owner of the bakery before it closed in 1963. He doesn't know the identity of the man who returned the cup, nor where it had been in the intervening years, but the family is delighted to have it back.

Amazingly, the famous trophy is still contested each year - but not on a football pitch as was its traditional use. Mary Forte, Alex MacArthur's daughter, is a rowing enthusiast, so each year at the annual Lough Gill regatta, the MacArthur Cup is one of a large range of prizes on offer. There is one important stipulation: the winning team must have a MacArthur family member in their boat.

"That way, we can always trace the trophy," Mary explains. "It means it will never go missing again".

And so, the mystery is solved, the future of one of the town's most iconic trophies is safeguarded, and, each summer, as has been the case for close to a century, somebody is still celebrating winning the MacArthur Cup.

MacArthur Cup Final Teams

1951: Hanley's 3, CIE 1
Hanley's: B. Callaghan, F. Brannigan, J. Marshall, J. Glynn, K. Mitchell, P. Rooney, M. Hynes, M. Scanlon, J. Wynne, L. Houze, E. Devaney.
CIE: J. Feeney, J. McHale, P. Keville, C. Gurrie, J. Moran, W. Stewart, P. Cox, R. Farrell, L. Deignan, M. Neilan.

1952: Denny's 3, Foley's Brewery 1
Denny's: T. Oates, R. Lynch, J. Tiernan, P. Moran, F. Munds, T. Watson, F. Quigley, S. McDonagh, W. Monaghan, A. Kelly, V. Meldrum.
Foley's Brewery: V. Flannery, B. Keighron, J. Hynes, P. Cawley, M. Sweeney, C. Howley, B. McKenna, S. Melly, T. Mooney, P. Rooney, B. Dolan.

1954: Foley's 5, Meldrum's 2.
Foley's: P. McGarry, W. Hudson, J. Hynes, S. Maughan, M. Sweeney, P. Cawley, R. Rooney, S. Melly, B. Keighron, C. Howley, M. Hallinan.
Meldrum's: M. Devaney, P. Brennan, J. Doogan, M. Doyle, W. Bradley, L. Dykes, L. Chapman, J. Cooper, S. Dykes, O. Marshall, M. Langan.

1955: Foley's 3, Woods 1 (Teams unavailable)

1956: MacArthur's/Post Office 1, McMenamin's 0
MacArthur's/Post Office: F. Mulligan, J. McHugh, M. Gilmartin, J. Doherty, E. Monaghan, F. Loftus, A. Lynch, J. Farry, T. McDonagh, F. Conlon, M. Maughan.
McMenamin's: P. Gilmartin, M. McLoughlin, P. O'Brien, S. Maughan, M. Ward, P. Lynch, A. Gray, M. Scanlon, E. Elliott, S. McDonagh, M. Monaghan.

1957: Foundry 2, Denny's 0
Foundry: J. Hynes, J. Crystal, T. Monds, A. Langan, B. Carroll, K. Flynn, E. Cox, B. O'Connell, J. Hannon, (team incomplete)
Denny's: T. Oates, N. Walsh, J. Tiernan, J. McGarry, J. Kelly, F. Johnston, M. Conway, M. Feeney, V. Meldrum, A. Hamill, W. Conlon.

1958: Denny's 4, Spinners 3.
Denny's: T. Watson, M. Feeney, J. Kelly, P. Moran, W. Bradley, A. Kelly, A. Hamill, S. McDonagh, V. Meldrum, W. Conlon J. McTiernan.
Spinners: P. Byrne, E. Kelleher, E. Scanlon, J. Doherty, N. Monds, K. McDonagh, C. McDonagh, C. Mashall, J. Burnside, M. Monaghan.

1959: Spinners 3, MacArthur's 1
Spinners: Lynch, Henderson, Scanlon, Mitchell, Chatten, McDonagh, Marshall, Reddy, Dolan, Henry (team incomplete)
MacArthur's: Mulligan, McDonagh, Monaghan, Monds, Farry, Gallagher, Finan, Gorevan, McLynn, Melly, Maughan.

1960: Spinners 'A' 4, MacArthur's/Meat Factory 0
Spinners 'A': J. Callaghan, M. McMorrow, E. Scanlon, G. Mitchell, A. Lynch, K. McDonagh, S. Higgins, K. McDonagh, C. Marshall, J. Henry, B. Dolan.
MacArthur's/Meat Factory: R. Mulligan, N. Elliott, J. Gallagher, R. Cawley, A. Reilly, T. McDonagh, R. Gorevan, J. Keenaghan, J. Farry, E. Monaghan, P. Melly.

1962: Denny's/MacArthur's 4, Foley's/GWI 3. (Teams unavailable)

1963: Denny's 4, Foley's/GWI 2
Denny's: E. Lynch, P. Tiernan, J. Kelly, M. Scanlon, M. Coen, J. Stanford, M. Feeney, F. Dunleavy, B. Monds, D. Currid, M. Gallagher.
Foley's/GWI: M. Mannion, S. Melly, S. Reilly, B. Byrne, R. Lynch, F. Hopper, V. Middleton, C. Howley, P. McDaniel, M. Sweeney, J. Armstrong.

1964: Denny's 3, Post Office 2
Denny's: E. Lynch, P. Tiernan, J. Kelly, B. Monds, D. Pugh, M. Coen, F Dunleavy, M. Downes, A. Lynch, J. Burnside, C. Currid.
Post Office: F. Conlon, C. Hynes, B. Burnside, A. Henry, N. Higgins, C. Coyle, C. Scanlon, V. Dolan, M. Rooney, P. Costello.

1965: Post Office 3, Filler & Fiebeg/Sligo Models 2
Post Office: M. McMenamin, A. Henry, J. Callaghan, G. Mitchell, M. Keane, N. Higgins, V. Dolan, M. Rooney, N. Reddy, C. Coyle, P. Costello.
Filler & Fiebeg/Sligo Models: B. Conway, P. Ward, J. Scanlon, J. Curran, K. McDonagh, C. Grandison, T. Culkin, K. Winkler, H. Demmel, M. Dunbar.

1966: Denny's 2, Hansons/Meldrums 1
Denny's: P. Smith, M. Coen, J. Kelly, P. Tiernan, G. Lynch, J. Keenan, J. Burnside, F. Dunleavy, M. Scanlon, M. McLoughlin.
Hanson's/Meldrum's: J. Callaghan, W. Craig, C. McGowan, B. Jones, J. Henry, L. Dykes, J. McManus, P. McDonagh, J. Kielty, D. Gallagher, M. Monaghan.

1967: Hanson's 2, Avena (Ballisodare) 1
(Teams unavailable)

1968: Hannaway's Meat Co. 3, Denny's 1
Hannaway's/Meat Co: B. Cadden, E. Foley, G. Mahon, M. McGowan, G. Conway, T. Herrity, M. McGarry, C. Scanlon, D. Kennedy, J. Keenan, A. Lang.
Denny's: P. Smith, M. Scanlon, T. Tiernan, B. Monds, G. Lynch, J. Kelly, D. Henry, F. Dunleavy, B. Frazer, A. Tiernan, D. Currid.

1969: Gowna 3, Meldrum's/Hannaway's 2
Gowna: McLoughlin, Mullen, Scanlon Doherty, Reilly, Foley, Walsh, Brennan, Leonard, Armstrong, Burke.
Meldrum's/Hannaway's: Beckett,Conlon, Langan, Craig, Jones, Dykes, McNasser, Meldrum, Lang, J. McNasser, Callaghan.

1970: Grocers 3, Denny's 1
Grocers: C. Branley, L. Quinn, M. Oates, K. Murphy, S. Fox, R. Hanney, D. McLynn, J. McNasser, M. Flynn.
Denny's: P. Smith, P. Tiernan, L. McGowan, A. Tiernan, B. Monds, J. Kelly, P.J. Devanney, F. Dunleavy, G. Lynch, K. Monaghan, D. Henry; 12th man: M. Scanlon for Devanney.

1971: Brooks Hanley 3, Post Office 0
Brooks Hanley: Wynne, Conlon, T. McLoughlin, Finan, Kelly, Watters, O'Malley, Hannahan, Dunleavy, M. McLoughlin, Horgan; 12th man: Shannon.
Post Office: Kelly, Moore, Sexton, Rooney, Devanney, McManus, Nealon, Mulligan, McGowan, Burns, Smyth; 12th man: Gaffney for Mulligan.

1972: Post Office 6, Brooks Hanley 0
Post Office: A. Mahon, F. Sexton, D. Moore, J. Devanney, P. McManus, T. Rooney, J. Henry, M. Hannon, E. McGowan, J. Nealon, E. Mongey.
Brooks Hanley: G. Wynne, W. Marshall, M. Conlon, G. Finan, F. Kelly, E. Watters, J. O'Malley, V. Dunleavy, T. McLoughlin, M. McLoughlin, R. Gordon.

1973: Brooks Hanley 5, Electrical Traders/Painters 2
Brooks Hanley: Wynne, Conlon, Marshall, Finan, Kelly, M. McLoughlin, Dunleavy, Watters, Adams, McGee.
Electrical Traders/Painters: Brett, Langan, Conlon, Mahon, Finan, Burrows, Greene, Monaghan, Scanlon, D. Monaghan, Higgins; 12th man: Melly.

1975: CIE/Henderson's 2, Snia 2
REPLAY: CIE/Henderson's 3, Snia 3.
CIE/Henderson's: G. Finan, C. Davey, J. Hanney, T. Flynn, T. Burns, M. Monaghan, F. Hargadon, M. Gilmartin, M. McCrann, S. Carr (E. McGarrigle replaced Burns in replay).
Snia: F. Rainey, J. Marshall, L. Keeney, B. Ryan, F. Kelly, J. McDonnell, C. Benson, J. Brennan, B. Devanney, T. Kennedy, S. Kilfeather (W. Rutherford played in replay).

** CIE failed to turn up for second replay, claiming Snia had breached regulations in earlier rounds. Snia were awarded the famous old cup, which in the ensuing red-hot controversy mysteriously went missing for over 40 years.

Soccer (Ladies)

Women's Soccer

From a windswept hill to the national league

On a windswept bumpy green rectangle elevated on the edge of Sligo harbour, a raggle-taggle bunch of 12-year-old girls chase a football with careless abandon. It's nominally known as a 'blitz day' and about thirty youngsters have turned up to kill an hour on an empty Saturday afternoon. It's the furthest scene imaginable from the glitz and fanfare of an historic League of Ireland debut for a Sligo Rovers senior women's team. But this is it. This is where it started.

It's 1997 and Finola Monaghan's playing days are beginning to run out of steam. For the past five years she's played in the Sligo Ladies League with the appropriately named Oddsorts team, one of only a half-dozen in the county. But life is moving on for these pioneers of women's football. Limbs are beginning to tire, there are weddings to be planned, families to rear. Football is beginning to take a back seat.

But Strandhill's Finola is a football nut. Along with her football soulmates, Gurteen's Stephen McCoy and Noel O'Donnell from North Sligo, she realises the future is best served by encouraging young girls to take up the baton. But there is no formal structure, no leagues, no committee, zero facilities. First step, organise a blitz, invite existing clubs to send in a few girls, see what happens.

And from that initial blitz, a mini-league is formed, with six clubs fielding under-12 teams. For the first time, young Sligo girls are playing weekly in a structured format. Monaghan recalls:

> The initial motivation was to get young girls playing football so that there would be a supply-line for the women's league. But as it happened, the

> older age league just faded away and the underage set-up took on a life of its own. We knew it would. There was never a single doubt in our minds that young girls would enjoy playing football just as much as boys would.

Expected early challenges were outweighed by the infectious enthusiasm of the young participants.

"At that stage, we were very much on our own," recalls Monaghan, who is now secretary of the Sligo-Leitrim Schoolboy and Girls League.

> We weren't affiliated to the Sligo-Leitrim Youth League, we had to do it all ourselves. We had problems getting pitches, arranging fixtures, getting referees. But the kids were really into it, the coaches started to develop, and we had a very dedicated committee who were determined to keep going. It was that kind of vibe, something very special.

Early enthusiasts included Regina Feeney from Cliffoney, Tina Beirne from Charlestown, Ballymote's Michael McMorrow, and Manorhamilton's Bernie Cleary, who were assisted by the WSAI regional development officer, Moya Parke from Ballymote. Niall Harrison from Cliffoney, a gifted footballer in his days with Sligo Rovers and now the head of the FAI's Emerging Talent Programme, was an influential friend who helped forged the amalgamation of the girls' and boys' leagues under the umbrella of the Sligo-Leitrim Boys and Girls District League in 2005.

Hugh Cunningham is another remarkable football man, whose pedigree includes playing for Celtic and Fulham, as well as working as a PE teacher, youth worker and soccer coach in London for 25 years. Since arriving in Sligo from his native Scotland nearly 40 years ago, he's been involved in youth football as coach, talent scout and at least a dozen other roles.

A member of the inaugural Sligo Rovers women's set-up, Hugh believes young girls, for the first time, now have real opportunities to achieve their football ambitions. Cunningham insists:

> I have witnessed first-hand the coaching and dedication of volunteers who've grown girls' football here over the years. In our own club, Kilglass-Enniscrone in the west of the county, we have seen a young girl progress through the Sligo-Leitrim Emerging Talent Programme to play for Ireland and onto Sligo Rovers underage teams and potentially to the League of Ireland team. That would have been unimaginable only a few short years ago.

> The pathway is now open and young girls can dream of playing for their local club, their country and, who knows, possibly have a professional career in a European League. They can dream of achieving what boys and men have taken for granted for many years.

Brian Chambers has been involved in underage girls' football for nearly 20 years, having initially been pressed into action as an emergency manager of his daughter's under-10 team at Yeats United. He's since played a pivotal role in the growth of the game in roles ranging from coach and treasurer at his own club, coaching in the league's Emerging Talent Programme, and scouting for the FAI. If all that sounds very grand, one of his main jobs remains "lining the pitch". As he explains:

> In my early years of involvement, there were leagues catering for under-12, -14 and -16 girls, and some of the leagues might have had only four teams. It meant girls finished playing once they reached 16, so the important challenge in those days was to get an under-18 league up and running to keep the girls engaged.

The pathway is now clearly sign-posted from a very young age. There's an opportunity for players of sufficient quality to go all the way to League of Ireland football. In successive seasons, a total of 11 girls from the youth league's Gaynor Cup representative team have signed for Rovers under-17 side. "The system is working," Chambers observes. "The hard work invested by clubs at underage level throughout the county is paying dividends."

The point is not lost on the man sitting atop the girls' football pyramid in Sligo. Steve Feeney is manager of the first Sligo Rovers Senior Women's Team now cutting its teeth in the National Women's League.

With an impressive pedigree which includes a 20-year playing career with Sligo Rovers and Ballinamallard, and a coaching CV topped by a hard-earned UEFA A licence, Feeney is acutely aware of the importance of underage girls' football. He's convinced the League of Ireland women's team will have a positive effect on the growth of the game at grassroots level:

> Growing up playing football in the local leagues, my dream was always to play for Sligo Rovers. Now young girls can have that same dream. Having a local national league team gives the youngsters a team to support and to aspire playing for. That has to be good for all of the clubs in the county. It creates interest, awareness and an incentive.

> So many people have been volunteering and coaching in girls' football under the radar for years. Now people are talking about women's football, people are coming to games. The unseen work of so many over a long number of years is now visible.

But will the transition from underage football to national league grade be attainable? Feeney concedes:

> It's a huge jump. But I believe the structures are now in place in Sligo to provide that pathway. Rovers have under-17 and under-19 teams in place, excellently coached by Aaron O'Connor and Darragh Healy respectively, as well as the senior team, so the club would have about 50 local girls on its books. That's a huge achievement in a relatively short space of time.
>
> Of my senior squad, seven are Sligo girls which, for a first ever senior team, is a healthy number. I would expect it to grow as our teams develop.

Having spent most of his career around men's teams as player and coach, he has some very interesting observations about the comparisons between male and female footballers.

> Firstly, I would say football is football, no matter what the gender, insofar as it throws up the same problems and similar solutions. But what I have found is that girls are that bit quicker to learn, to take in what they're told, to pick up on things. Luckily, I've always been around good groups of players, so I'm not complaining about any of the lads I've worked with over the years, but I have found girls to be more receptive. Maybe it's an attitude, I don't know, but it's definitely there.

As for Rovers' debut season in the National League, the coach is under no illusions about the magnitude of the task.

> We'll need patience and support, but Sligo Rovers has always had those qualities in abundance. I'm sure it will be the same with the women;s team. We'll have good days and bad, but we'll do our work with the sort of pride which this club and town deserves. That's all we can promise.

As the senior ladies' team fashion a new chapter in Sligo Rovers' fabled history, there are currently eleven hundred young girls playing for nearly fifty teams in nineteen clubs in every village and parish throughout the Sligo-Leitrim youth leagues. They are all part of a remarkable voyage which began in inauspicious circumstances all those years ago on a lonely clifftop pitch overlooking Sligo harbour. Like all voyages, it has led to some unexpected and many exciting places. And, unquestionably, there are a multitude of thrilling adventures ahead.

Emma Hansberry and Catherine Hyndman

Tomboys became international stars

A pair of tomboys tearing up street football. Teasing the boys with their outrageous skill. Little girls with big ideas, defying established norms, daring to break the mould.

"They said I played like a boy", Catherine 'Dizzy' Hyndman recounts.

"They'd come knocking on our front door, not for my brothers, but for me", Emma Hansberry affirms.

"Please, Mrs Hansberry, can Emma come out to play."

The football urchins, young girls invading a boys' world, would grow up to become top international players, gracing European Championships, World Cups and Champions League. They were the original of the species, female players ploughing an often awkward furrow, making their mark, clearing a path for others to follow.

Initially excelling in boys' company simply because there were no other girls to play with or against, they would become the brightest stars in a fledgling women's soccer movement. By any standards, the heights scaled by Hansberry and Hyndman have been phenomenal.

They grew up hundreds of miles and some years apart – the older Hyndman in a small town on the outskirts of Belfast; Hansberry in the heart of Sligo town. But the story of their formative years is remarkably similar. Both honed their natural skills on the streets around their homes and they each nurtured that remarkable ability in the formal structures of the Sligo–Leitrim Youth Leagues.

Effortlessly, they were the best players on their street by a country mile. Both slender-framed, they possessed an incongruous mix of the balance of a ballerina and the nerve of an assassin, at once all slinky George Best and ruthless Roy Keane.

They were natural and, paradoxically, slightly unnatural. Most girls didn't play football in those days. At least, they didn't play football like this pair.

The conventional wisdom once upon a time was that boys wore cowboy suits and football boots, not always separately, and girls pushed their tattered dolls in grotty prams. Guys flicked through the pages of *Shoot* and their female peers swooned over pop stars in *Jackie*. That was it. Lines neatly drawn and rarely questioned. But these girls were of a new generation. They were changing the narrative.

Emma's Story

Emma Hansberry is Sligo's most decorated football player. She's won three National Women's League titles, two FAI Cups, has played in a World Cup and the Champions League, represented her country at underage and senior level, all crowned by winning the coveted FAI Player of the Year award. To have reached such remarkable heights by the age of 27 is an astounding achievement.

Born within a corner kick of the Showgrounds, she learned her football on the other side of town, on streets around Cartron Estate where she was looked after by her aunt Bernie after happy school days in St Edward's national school. Bernie is married to Sligo Rovers League and FAI Cup winner Chris Rutherford.

> Because Chris was so well known as a Rovers legend, I suppose he must have been a sort of silent influence, but it was Bernie who took me out on the streets kicking ball. None of it would ever have happened without her.
>
> My brothers, Stephen and Brian, played as well, but I suppose it was when the other lads starting calling to the house for me and not them to join in the games that I realised I might be a bit of a player.

Most seven-year-old girls look forward to their First Holy Communion Day with the gleeful anticipation of that glamourous white dress and lucrative bounty-hunting. A princess for a day. Not Emma.

"I fought with my mother to let me wear a white tracksuit. I begged her. As soon as the Mass was over, I flung the dress to one side and put on the Celtic tracksuit," she boldly recalls.

She was eight years old when she finally got to play in a girls' team, playing four years above her age in the Merville under-12 team under the guidance of Ann Fox, an early influence she still treasures.

Soon it was on to the more challenging environment of Strand Celtic, eventually making it to the Connacht Gaynor Cup team and, as a transition year student at Ursuline College, on to the Irish under-16 team, her first experience of international football.

She earned her first under-17 cap in the 2010 World Cup in Trinidad and Tobago, a trip which included a month-long acclimatisation period in Miami. An unforgettable trip, made even better because her parents, Tony and Sandra, and her brothers flew out for their own holiday of a lifetime.

Emma made her Women's National League debut with Castlebar Celtic in 2012, memorably reaching the FAI Cup final at the Aviva stadium, where the Mayo side were narrowly beaten by red-hot favourites Raheny.

A technically gifted midfield player, her success with the Irish under-19 team was crowned by being appointed captain and named International Player of the Year.

Later, with Wexford Youths, she would play in three FAI Cup finals at the Aviva, winning two, and amass three League of Ireland titles. She also became the only Sligo player ever to feature in the Champions League.

She's also played twice in the World Student games, in Russia and South Korea, the world's biggest sporting event outside of the Olympics.

After moving to Newcastle to pursue a three-year physiotherapy degree, Emma took a sabbatical from the game which had been her life since childhood. The perfectly timed formation of the Sligo Rovers' senior team and its entry into the National Women's League enticed her out of retirement.

> As a young girl, the notion of playing in the League of Ireland for Sligo Rovers would not have even been on the radar because that possibility didn't exist then. All I wanted to do was play for Ireland.
>
> But here I am, back in senior football, playing for my hometown team. Having travelled all over the country and indeed the world to follow my football dream, it's such a joy to have it on my own doorstep.

Dizzy's Story

Catherine 'Dizzy' Hyndman, capped a dozen times at senior level by Northern Ireland, has always had a steely determination propelling her to push doors and demolish obstacles whenever the occasion demanded. As she recounts:

> Being the only girl playing football on our streets in a small village outside Belfast, I quickly learned the meaning of grit and perseverance,

> qualities which would stand to me in later life. There were no age limits, no goalposts, no rules. You get kicked, you get back up again, otherwise you're eating tarmac.

Her first organised football was with her brother's under-8 team at Comber Rec FC. Her coaches would tell her 'she played like a boy', which she took as a compliment.

She wasn't to play in a girls' team until her family moved to Grange in North Sligo when she was ten years old. Under the guidance of coach Regina Feeney, the Cliffoney/Grange team won numerous local league titles and, more significantly, conquered the best the country had to offer when winning the under-15 Community Games National Title. In that campaign, Dizzy scored a phenomenal 36 goals out of the team's total of 42.

Instinctively, she knew she was capable of playing at a higher standard. So, at 15 years old, she rather cheekily wrote to Arsenal Ladies Academy, seeking a trial.

Shortly afterwards, during a transition year business class at the Ursuline College, her computer buzzed, and an email bearing the famous Gunners' cannon gun logo delivered the exciting news. Three months later, accompanied by her mum, Bernadette, and bursting with nervous anticipation, she was on her way to London for a two-day trial, held at the renowned Arsenal training ground at London Colney.

> I was fed up banging my head on closed doors in Ireland, so I felt I'd take the next step myself. I'd been an Arsenal fan all my life, so arriving there, training on the same campus as the senior team players, was a little surreal and yet there was this terrific sense of adventure.

She officially signed for Arsenal on her sixteenth birthday, spending a year at the Academy, going to college by day and training with a host of other starry-eyed hopefuls each evening. She admits:

> It was fairly regimental, breakfast together, college together, training together, dinner together, and, naturally, it was a fairly competitive environment. Looking back, I'm not sure if I ever really came to grips with the change of lifestyle.

Moving on to Watford, where she played first team games every week, Dizzy's ambitions now encompassed representing her country.

> I contacted the Northern Ireland manager, Alfie Wylie, who brought me straight into the under-19 squad for the European qualifiers and then I got my first senior cap at just 17 years old against Belarus. Proud of my Belfast roots, this was a really big honour for me.

Back home and recovered from a torn cruciate ligament she suffered while playing for Colchester United, she played for two seasons with Castlebar Celtic in the National Women's League before moving to Strabane-based Sion Swifts in the Northern Ireland Women's Premier League, where she currently plays.

Mum to two-year-old son Mason, the Strabane link-up fits in perfectly with her domestic arrangements. She explains:

> Strabane's an hour-and-a-half drive from Sligo, so I travel to train on a Monday, play a game on Wednesday, do my own workouts at home on Friday, and have the weekend free with my family. My partner, Alan Henry, is on the coaching staff at Finn Harps, so we each have a full understanding of each other's commitments and how all of that works.

At 32 years of age and creeping towards 'veteran' status, Dizzy still lives her life by a rather inspiring motto. It perfectly sums up her own career and applies equally to the journey followed by Emma Hansberry. In fact, it makes sense in any walk of life: "Know your worth and don't stop until everyone else knows it too."

Soccer (Sligo Rovers)

League Champions 2012

Stopwatch on day the famine ended

13 October 2012

2 p.m.

A blazing sun betrays the creeping incursion of late autumn. Joe Scanlon swings open the main gates at Sligo Showgrounds. A colosseum pounding with reverberations of a storied past awaits the arrival of the gladiators.

Already, hundreds of fans have gathered along Church Hill and on the road which sweeps down from Ballydoogan. An expectant army on the march, weaponised by memories and dreams and tales of long departed warriors.

This is the improbable theatre where Dixie Dean professed to have experienced the happiest days of his spectacularly decorated career, where fabled heroes such as Seán Fallon, Mickey Sweeney, Jimmy Burnsides, David Pugh, Gerry Mitchell, Tony Fagan, Harry McLoughlin, Paul McGee, Raff Cretaro and Seamus Coleman gracefully sprinkled their stardust, where despair and triumph tantalised the emotions of generations of hard-core disciples.

Now a new glorious chapter beckons. Ninety minutes of football is all that separates Sligo Rovers from their first League of Ireland title since 1977.

The friendly turnstile operators, Noel Scott, Kevin Colreavy, Seán McLoughlin and Loman Gallagher, are the sentries on duty, providing orderly access to the immaculately prepared stadium.

Michael Doddy, a devotee since the heady days of Lawrie Sanchez's title chasing team in the mid-1990s, is among the early arrivals.

He's made the 60-mile round trip from his home in Gurteen for every home match for nearly three decades but today's date with destiny stirs the blood like never before.

He's accompanied by his wife, Gertie, who in a matter of weeks will deliver the couple's first child, and his brother, Fintan.

Michael recalls:

> We arrived about two hours before kick-off. As we made our way to the ground, the atmosphere was electric. I'd never witnessed anything like it.

John McDwyer has followed Rovers through thick and thin all his life but missed the League-winning game in 1977 as he was in hospital. There's no way he's missing this one.

His grown-up sons, Joe and Donal, who inherited their father's passion for the Bit O'Red, make up the travelling party from Carrick on Shannon. John remembers:

> We got to the ground early and the first people I met were two old friends from Ballymote. I'd say they weren't in the Showgrounds since the days of Straka and Johnny Armstrong. But that's the kind of occasion it was, everybody wanted to be part of it. There was a wave of optimism in the ground, which I found a bit strange. It's not the Sligo Rovers way. We usually expect the worst.

2.30 p.m.

The team bus pulls into the ground. Rovers' beguiling striker, Mark Quigley, has the swagger of a man out for a casual stroll as he skips off the coach. A crowd of giddy young fans burst into spontaneous song. "He's Mark Quigley, he can do what he wants." The party is getting into full swing.

3.30 p.m.

The stadium announcer, Graham Monaghan, is whipping the crowd into a frenzy with a succession of popular Rovers songs. With kick- off fast approaching, it's time to air the clarion call of one of the club's most revered servants, Johnny Chadda. A native of India, the late Mr Chadda, who arrived in Sligo in 1953 and fell hopelessly in love with the local soccer club, composed a poem in tribute to his beloved team. Just before the start of every home game, a recording of his recitation is played as a motivational boost for the players and fans. On this very special day, his words carry added poignancy.

> Even if the sun ceases to rise
> Even if the wind stops to blow
> The name of Sligo Rovers will shine and shine forever
> Like a morning glittering star in the sky

Seated in the main stand, George Chadda is fighting back tears as his father's inspiring message booms from the PA system. He recalls:

> My father put his shoulder to wheel for Rovers for more than fifty years, serving as chairman, treasurer and many other roles. For most of that time, it was a struggle to keep the club alive. He ran bingo nights and sold golden goal tickets in pubs. When we were growing up, our entire family routine, even down to the timing of our Sunday dinner, was organised around Sligo Rovers. Every time I hear his voice and that lovely poem, it's very emotional. And on that day in 2012, with Rovers on the cusp of winning the League, it was especially moving.

As Rovers and their nearest rivals in the title race, St Patrick's Athletic, emerge from the dressing rooms, there's an explosion of noise, so intense it seems to shake the very foundations of Benbulben, itself a towering backdrop of majestic splendour adding an appropriate sense of theatre to an occasion already soaked in nailbiting tension.

In the Treacy Avenue stand, Mary McGowan is taking it all in with nervous anticipation. Her late father, Packie, an unsparing volunteer at Rovers for most of his life, brought her to the Showgrounds for the first time back in the 1960s. Her love affair with the team included 23 years on the club's management committee, sixteen of them as secretary. Today, she's a passionate fan:

> Sligo Rovers have been a constant part of my family's life from when I was a very young girl so I was very much aware of the emotional roller-coaster we were all going through.

4.06 p.m.

Raffaele Cretaro, the 'Tubbercurry Tornado' with an Italian bloodline and feet of Roman wizardry, dances through the Pat's defence to give Rovers the lead.

In the chaos in the stands, John McDwyer retains sufficient calm to appreciate the sheer magnificence of Cretaro's effort. "It was a sensational goal, so typical of Raff, a born magician," he observes.

4.09 p.m.

Cretaro strikes again, this time escaping the cover of the Pat's defence to smuggle the ball home at the back post. The Showgrounds is rocking.

"I couldn't believe we were two nil up. The title was in touching distance. It was almost too good to be true," beams Michael Doddy.

John McDwyer recalls the mood was close to disbelief among some the more senior supporters:

> It was going better than we dared hope. Some fans were already beginning to celebrate as if we had won the league. Those who had experienced a lot of heartbreak over the years were in a bit of shock that it was going so well.

Mary McGowan feels the job is nearly done and takes delight in the fact that a local hero is emerging as one of the stars of the day.

"I was thrilled for Raff. One of our own scoring two goals to take us to the League title. That was the way I was thinking after the second goal went in," she points out.

5.05 p.m.

A ghostly stillness envelope the Showgrounds. St Pat's, still in with a chance of snatching the title from under Rovers' nose, have clawed their way back to equality thanks to goals from Christy Fagan and Chris Forrester.

In the Volkswagen Stand at the Railway End, Gerard O'Connor is fearing the worst. He's been a fanatical supporter since his late father, Kevin, brought him to his first game when he was just eight years of age. He's never stopped following his dream of seeing his beloved team winning the League. Now he's petrified it will all be snatched away.

"I really thought we blew it", he admits. "It was a dreadful feeling. I was convinced it was about to go horribly wrong."

John McDwyer was also fearful:

> Oh, here we go again. You get used to hard luck stories following Rovers but this was just so hard to take. There was still time to turn things around, but I was worried how our players would react. What would be going through their heads? Would they throw it all away?

5.34 p.m.

A pulsating encounter of epic proportions produces one last moment of drama. John Russell's corner sparks off a manic scramble in St Pat's goalmouth; the ball canons off a defender and the referee, Damien Hancock, alerted to an infringement by his assistant, immediately points to the spot. A penalty to Rovers. Thirty-five barren years of toil and heartbreak comes down to this – one kick of a ball.

"I couldn't watch", recalls Gerard O'Connor. "Everybody around me was going mental but I had to turn my back to the action. The tension was unbearable."

Michael Doddy put his hands across his eyes and peers through shaking fingers.

"I was breathless", he admits. "It was as if time stood still. It seemed like ages before the penalty was taken."

As Mark Quigley steps forward to take the kick, John McDwyer digs deep into his memory bank, recalling the injustice of a penalty award against Rovers which decided the 1978 FAI Cup final in favour of arch-rivals Shamrock Rovers.

"The penalty was a close call," he confesses. "I think it was the linesman who gave it. For me, it was payback for the injustice of 1978. I knew Quigley would put it away."

Not everybody shares John's confidence. The terraces and stands fall silent as Quigley and Pat's keeper, Barry Murphy, square up to each other, like gunfighters in the old Hollywood movies, a deadly showdown in which the winner takes all.

With ice in his veins and magic in his boots, Quigley is casual in his approach but lethal in his execution, dispatching a shot of unwavering precision to the keeper's right. The net dances. Let the carnival begin.

Mary McGowan is overcome by the emotion of it all.

> I was thinking of my mum and dad and how Rovers were at the very core of our family life. I was hugging everybody around me. Then I ran on to the pitch and the first person I met was Rovers midfielder Danny Ventre. We just looked at each other. Neither of us could find the words. We didn't need to. We both knew what this moment meant. Tears were streaming down my face, but I didn't care. I was so happy.

Gerard O'Connor, who skipped a cousin's wedding to attend the match, resists the temptation to join in the celebrations on the pitch.

> I was with my friends in the Volkswagen Stand and I just wanted to stay with them for a while; to soak it all in. We used to go to all the matches home and away, have a few pints and enjoy the craic as best we could whether Rovers won or lost. Now here we were together on the day Rovers won the League. Maybe a day none of us really believed we would ever see. So, I just wanted to be with my mates, sharing the moment together. When everything settled down, we went across to Mooney's pub and the party was in full swing. I don't think I ever saw as many happy people under the same roof. Hard to put into words really but just so wonderful.

The Doddy brothers, Michael and Fintan, race on to the pitch.

> It was great to be out on the pitch with the hard-core Rovers fans. They're the lads who stick by the club through thick and thin, follow them all over the country and keep the show on the road. I was thrilled for them as much as for myself. In all the years I'd been going to the Showgrounds I never thought I'd see Rovers winning the League. Now here I was in the middle of all the celebrations, and I wanted to enjoy the atmosphere as much as I could.

> A few weeks later, Gertie gave birth to our beautiful baby girl, Clodagh. Now Clodagh and her younger sister, Grace, are regulars at the Showgrounds. We make a family night out of it. I always tell Clodagh she was there the day Rovers won the League. That's what I love about following Rovers. It's a real community team, and the pride passes from one generation to the next.

In the delirious mayhem, John McDwyer reflects on his father, Joe, and his unconditional romance with Sligo Rovers. A native of Glenties in County Donegal, he was a garda sergeant based in Ballintogher, a rural village about ten miles from Sligo town. As John jokes:

> What he loved about soccer was that games always started on time. In those days, a GAA match would be scheduled for 3 p.m. on a Sunday afternoon but it could be after 5 p.m. before it started. My father couldn't be bothered with that. So, he took to going to the Showgrounds and he'd bring me with him. We established a deep passion for Rovers and it's a love that never ends.

> It was very special for me to be there with my two sons on the day Rovers won the League. There was a sense of quiet satisfaction among the three of us. A lot of memories flooded through my mind, but most of all I thought about my father.

George Chadda and his sons, Arvin and Ranan, are swamped by a sea of well-wishers. Everybody appreciates this is a particularly nostalgic day for them. George says:

> It's lovely that the people of Sligo have such affection for my father. It ensures his legacy will live on. As I left the ground that evening, I knew he would have been so proud of Rovers. Naturally, my thoughts were with him and all the volunteers he had soldiered with through the barren years, men like Eddie and Dermot McCullough and Packie McGowan and many others.

8 p.m.

The darkening clouds close in, pilfering the light but not the shine from a momentous day. Deserted now, the Showgrounds is a tranquil oasis, contrasting starkly with the raucous excitement of a manic afternoon. Joe Scanlon slams shut the old gates to the echoes of history and the last feeble wail from the famine ghosts.

Sligo Rovers are League champions.

Top: Sligo Rovers ladies team, 2022.
Pic James Fallon

Bottom left: Catherine Hyndman, pictured in action for Northern Ireland. Pic courtesy Ivor Dallinger

Bottom right: Sligo Rovers and Republic of Ireland star Emma Hansberry. Pic James Fallon

Top: History makers: The Sligo Rovers 1983 squad who won the FAI Cup for the first time in the club's history. Back row (l-r): Paul Fielding (player–manager), Gus Gilligan, Graham Fox, Chris Rutherford, Colin Oakley, Tony Stenson, Mick Graham, Paul Moylan (RIP), Pádraig McManus. Front row (l-r): Mick Ferry, Harry McLoughlin, Andy Elliott, Tony Fagan, John Skeffington, Mick Savage, Martin McDonnell. Pic *Sligo Champion*

Bottom: Sligo Rovers' League-winning manager, Ian Baraclough. Pic Sportsfile (Courtesy Sligo Rovers FC)

Top: Sligo Rovers' Cup-winning captains, Gavin Dykes (1994) and Conor O'Grady (2010).
Pic *Sligo Champion*

Bottom: Raff Cretaro celebrates with his dad, Raffaele, and nephew, Carlo, after the 2011 Cup final.
Pic Tom Callanan

Top: The all-conquering Sligo Rovers 1994 squad. Pic *Sligo Champion*

Bottom: Sligo Rovers 1977: The first Sligo Rovers team ever to compete in European competition, against Red Star Belgrade, September 1977. Back row: Paul Fielding, Tony Stenson, Alan Paterson, Chris Rutherford, Kevin McCool, Padraig McManus. Front row: Billy Sinclair, Marty Kelly, Graham Fox, Mick Leonard, Tony Fagan, Paul McGee. Pic *Sligo Champion*

Top: Sligo Rovers manager Paul Cook with the FAI Cup in 2011. Pic Sportsfile. (Courtesy Sligo Rovers FC)

Bottom left: Sligo soccer legend Seán Fallon pictured with lifelong friend Sir Alex Ferguson. Pic courtesy Seán Cunningham

Bottom right: Seamus Coleman showing his support for Sligo Rovers, with Sligo Rovers scarf. Pic Carl Brennan

Top: Local soccer legends Tony Fagan and Paul McGee. Pic *Sligo Champion*

Middle: A triumphant Willie McStay after the 1994 FAI Cup final. Pic Sportsfile. (Courtesy Sligo Rovers FC)

Bottom: Sligo Rovers 2010 and 2011 Cup final hero Ciarán Kelly. Pic Carl Brennan

Top: Barry Cogan in action for Milwall against Manchester United in the 2004 FA Cup final

Bottom left: David Pugh in action against Pele

Bottom right: David Pugh with his Irish U23 cap

Top left: Sligo surfer Gearóid McDaid riding the waves all over the world. Pic *Sligo Champion*

Top right: Ian Rossiter, who won an U16 European Championship medal with the famous Brian Kerr's kids. Pic *Sligo Champion*

Bottom: Rovers fans in full voice at Fir Park, Motherwell. Pic James Fallon, courtesy Sligo Rovers

Ian Baraclough

Mastermind of a golden era

Ian Baraclough took the scenic route to Sligo.

Two appearances at Wembley, one as a player with Notts County and the other as assistant head coach with Scunthorpe United, were spine-tingling adventures along the way, but other stop-off points were less exotic. A nomadic playing career, totalling over 600 appearances, included service at eight clubs, most of them in the obscure backwaters of the English league. He was well-travelled but had never been to Ireland. He was a keen student of the game but had never heard of Sligo Rovers.

By the time he left the Bit O'Red after just over two years in charge, he had rewritten the club's history book, bringing a League of Ireland title to the Showgrounds for the first time in 35 years. During his whirlwind reign, he also guided Rovers to FAI Cup and Setanta Cup glory, confirming his status as one of the club's most successful managers.

It all came to a sour end when he was surprisingly relieved of his duties just weeks after claiming the Setanta Cup – a decision he readily admits still evokes a mixture of bewilderment and hurt. But when he reflects on his time in Sligo, he's happy to accentuate the positive, finding contentment in the scale of his achievement.

Taking the job was a gamble, he maintains. He had no idea what he was letting himself in for when he accepted an offer of an interview for the Showgrounds vacancy in February 2012. He was 41 years old, with a young family and no job, having been sacked by Scunthorpe the previous March. He explains:

> I knew nothing about Irish football or Sligo Rovers. It was a step into the unknown which could easily have backfired. But I was unemployed, apart

> from some scouting work with Watford, and I desperately wanted to get back in the game.
>
> There were statistics at the time which revealed a very high percentage of first-time managers never got a second chance. That was in the back of my mind. I didn't want to end up on the scrapheap like so many other young managers. The Sligo job was a risk worth taking.

He was recommended for the position by former Rovers' boss Steve Cotterrill, a casual acquaintance with whom he had crossed swords on the managerial circuit in England.

The chance to manage again excited him, especially as his new club was already on an upward curve, having won the FAI Cup in 2010 and 2011 and had a Europa League campaign to look forward to.

It was at once tantalising and daunting. But Baraclough had a sense of perspective not always shared by his comrades in the unforgiving profession of football management.

He was just eight years old when he lost his mother, Shirley, to cancer. The youngest of four boys, he was fast-tracked out of necessity to the realities of an adult world, helping his father, Roy, on his rounds as a debt collector. His father worked a second job just to keep food on the table. Their mother's passing hit hard but it served to strengthen the bond between the bereaved husband and his four boys.

One of Baraclough's most vivid memories of the day Sligo Rovers won the League of Ireland Championship in 2012 is the loving embrace he shared with his father minutes after the full-time whistle. He admits:

> That was quite emotional. Of course, I understood how much it meant to the people of Sligo, and I was proud to have played such an important role in the story. There was a personal side to it as well. Having my father there to share that special day was, and is, a memory I will cherish forever.

Baraclough was raised in Wigston, a small village on the outskirts of Leicester. Football was pretty much all he was bothered about. It was a big deal for the family when he was taken on by Leicester City. None of his older brothers made it that far.

He was left-footed, excelled at left-back in his days with City's youth team and would later switch to left-side midfield and then to an orthodox winger. He even had a spell as a striker. His versatility stood to him. He didn't make the first team at Leicester but fulfilled his ambition of becoming a full-time professional footballer, enjoying spells at Wigan, Grimsby Town, Lincoln City, Mansfield Town, Notts County (twice), QPR and Scunthorpe.

When his playing career came to an end, he was appointed first team head coach at Scunthorpe and was promoted to manager when Nigel Adkins left for Southampton in September 2010. Six months later, he was out of a job, ruthlessly dismissed after a home defeat to Preston plunged Scunthorpe into the drop zone in the Championship. It was the start of a dismal downward slide for the club, culminating in the indignity of relegation to the Conference League in 2022.

Scunthorpe's loss was Sligo's gain. Taking over from the charismatic Paul Cook just a few days before the start of the 2012 season was far from ideal but Baraclough, forever the optimist, wasted no time in stamping his personality on the squad.

Less exuberant than his predecessor and certainly not as animated on match nights, Baraclough was more pragmatic, coaxing the best out of his players, finding ways to win borderline matches, gradually persuading the unconvinced among the fan base that he was the man to deliver the long-awaited League title.

Man management was one of his virtues. Players like Jeff Henderson, Jason McGuinness, Ross Gaynor, Pascal Millien, Lee Lynch and Seamus Conneely played the best football of their careers during that hypnotic season.

And then there was Mark Quigley. He was sent off in Baraclough's first game in charge, a riveting 1–1 draw away to Shels, failed to travel for a Europa League game mid-season and finally emerged as Sligo's own captivating version of 'the Prodigal Son' when he claimed the winning goal with virtually the last kick of the match in the League clincher against St Pat's. Baraclough agrees:

> Mark was a big part of the story alright. At one stage, it looked as if he was on his way out the door. He didn't show up for the team's trip to Slovakia for a Europa League match. He wanted to move back to Dublin and the club was reluctant to let him leave. I had several conversations with him, trying to persuade him he would be better off staying in Sligo. It took a lot of hard work but, fortunately, he agreed to see out his contract. And then he comes up with the winning penalty in the game that decided the League. He was a terrific player.

Baraclough inherited a richly talented squad. There are those who credit the team's success in 2012 to his predecessor, Paul Cook. But that theory does a disservice to Baraclough. He came into the job at short notice, with no experience of Irish football, no knowledge of his own players or of the other teams in the league, and no time to oversee a proper pre-season schedule. Yet he navigated his way through a demanding campaign, learning on the hoof, and shaping a team good enough to storm its way to an historic League triumph. In ten short months, he achieved what had eluded Sligo Rovers' managers for 35 years. Even the scripts for the *Roy of the Rovers* comic books weren't as far-fetched. Baraclough reflects:

> It was incredible. The Dublin clubs dominated the League for many years and then we upset the pattern by taking the title. I don't believe we got the credit we deserved, certainly not from the national media.
>
> The day we beat St Pat's to clinch the League is etched in my memory. I had to maintain a calm exterior but I was quite emotional. My father and brothers came over from England for the game and that meant a lot. The atmosphere was electric and what pleased me most was the way the players handled that side of things. They played with a lot of passion and belief and proved themselves worthy champions.

The rollercoaster ride thundered on for two more seasons. Baraclough was the only English-born manager in the Champions League in 2013. Later that year, Rovers won the FAI Cup, defeating Drogheda United in a five-goal thriller in the final, and their relentless pursuit of silverware continued when they captured the Setanta Cup the following season.

Baraclough looks back on the big calls and is satisfied he got most of them right. The hardest one was picking Anthony Elding ahead of Danny North for the 2013 Cup final. It was a story with a happy ending. North was sprung from the bench, grabbed two typically instinctive goals and set up a sensational winner for Elding.

The Sentanta Cup decider against Dundalk at a rain-soaked Tallaght Stadium weaved a novel story too. Two men who would go on to manage the Republic of Ireland and Northern Ireland were in opposing dug-outs, Baraclough with Rovers, Stephen Kenny in charge of Dundalk. Rovers scraped a 1-0 win, meaning their manager had secured three of the major trophies on offer in domestic soccer.

The magnitude of that substantial record of achievement was matched only by the club's shock decision to dismiss the manager in June 2014. Baraclough confirms:

> It was a bombshell, a complete and utter shock. I got a call out of the blue informing me of the club's decision to fire me. It was during the summer break and I was at home in Leicester. I didn't see it coming. I pleaded my case, reminded them of the success we had, and told them I felt they were making a big mistake. But they had their minds made up. I didn't understand it. To me, it made no sense. The three seasons I was there were the best in the club's history. I felt it was so unfair. Of course, it left a sour taste.

If the parting of the ways was painful, the former manager's glorious legacy remains intact. He's still a revered figure among the club's fan base. He smiles:

> That pleases me greatly. I went back to Sligo with Motherwell a few years ago and I was given a wonderful reception. It was gratifying to know the club's supporters appreciated and acknowledged all the success I had during my time there. I like to think I helped create some special days for the club. It worked both ways. I have a lot of very fond memories of Sligo, too.

After leaving Sligo, Baraclough managed Motherwell and was assistant manager at Oldham before becoming manager of the Northern Ireland under-21 team. He was subsequently promoted to manager of the senior squad.

It's a long way from the rough and tumble of the League of Ireland but there's a corner in the Englishman's heart which will always have a Sligo beat.

Rovers League Championship winning squad 2012: Gary Rogers, Alan Keane, Gavin Peers, Jason McGuinness, Ross Gaynor, Danny Ventre, John Dillon, Romauld Boco, Joseph Ndo, Mark Quigley, Danny North, Lee Lynch, Iarfhlaith Davoren, Raffaele Cretaro, David Cawley, Mark McGoldrick, Martin Owens, Pascal Millien, Jake Dykes, Seamus Conneely, Liam Buchanan, Jeff Henderson, Ryan Connolly, Richard Brush, Liam Martin.

Rovers FAI Cup winning team 2013: Gary Rogers, Alan Keane, Gavin Peers, Jeff Henderson, Iarfhlaith Davoren, Raffaele Cretaro, Joseph Ndo, Danny Ventre, Kieran Djilali, Aaron Greene, Anthony Elding. Subs: Evan McMillan, Danny North, Ross Gaynor.

Rovers Setanta Cup winning team 2014: Gary Rogers, Seamus Conneely, Jeff Henderson, Evan McMillan, Ross Gaynor, John Russell, Joseph Ndo, David Cawley, Paul O'Connor, Aaron Greene, Danny North. Sub: Danny Ledwith.

Seamus Coleman

"Sligo will always be massive in my life"

> Without a shadow of a doubt what Sligo Rovers did for me and my family gave me some of the best years of my life. That period, and the people I met there, will always be a massive part of my journey.

Seamus Coleman luxuriates in reminiscing about his breakthrough as a teenage full-back with Sligo Rovers, a prodigious two years which provided the springboard to a spectacularly successful career as captain of Ireland and Everton.

It might not have happened, however. If Finn Harps had tried a bit harder. If the lure of the Donegal GAA minor team had been a shade stronger. If a meaningless pre-season friendly had been arranged elsewhere. If Rob McDonald had stayed longer than a few months in charge of Sligo Rovers.

Coleman doesn't like using the word 'luck' – "you have to earn what you get", he reasons. But he acknowledges there have been some uncanny twists along his remarkable journey from the shy teenager raised in a council estate in the fishing port of Killybegs to the assured, consummate professional who has matured into one of the greatest footballers of his generation.

His remarkable story has its genesis in an innocuous friendly match in 2006 between his Donegal League team, St Catherine's FC, and Sligo Rovers, who had travelled the 54-kilometre journey on a crisp February Saturday afternoon to help with their preparations for the opening of the League of Ireland season a month later. For the Donegal club, it was an exciting chance to pit their wits against a senior club but it was also a tad intrusive, as they had an important League game of their own the following day as they chased down the Donegal League championship.

One of their players, 17-year-old Seamus Coleman from the nearby St Cummins Hill housing estate, had a lot on his mind too. The following day's game was far more important, for one. There was also the prospect of lining out with the Donegal GAA minor team, who were on a bit of a roll towards provincial and maybe All-Ireland honours. And just the night before, another tantalising opportunity had opened up when Donegal's only League of Ireland team, Finn Harps, had initiated a courtship. Somewhere in that cluttered young mind, the prospect of a looming Leaving Cert was also fighting for space.

Coleman played for just over an hour against Rovers, his manager sparing him the extra exertion in anticipation of the tougher League game which awaited on the Sunday. He felt he'd played quite well, and though he had not set out to impress anyone other than his own coaches, he quickly discovered he had caught the attention of Rovers' manager, Seán Connor. Coleman reports:

> It all happened very quickly. The night before the game, I had gone to Ballybofey with my parents to meet representatives of Finn Harps, and there was talk about signing for them. Nothing was concluded and maybe there would have been further talks if Sligo hadn't made an offer the following day. The difference was they were offering me a full-time contract, a chance to play football for a living.

The decision, surprisingly, was not straightforward, as he explains:

> The choice I had to make was between Rovers and the county minor team. The GAA had always been a big part of my life. I played for the local club; my uncle Dessie Farrell was winning All-Irelands with Dublin; other uncles had played at a decent level; so for me to have the opportunity of playing with a very good Donegal minor team was a really big deal. Believe it or not, it was a tough decision.

Joining Rovers the following July under the care of Seán Connor, Coleman was making slow but steady progress in the professional ranks before a sudden change of manager almost derailed his career before it had even begun. Connor was tempted away by Bohemians and Rovers recruited Rob McDonald, an Englishman who had played for Hull City and Newcastle United and whose managerial career had been honed in Dutch football.

The new manager's attempt to offload Coleman is well documented. McDonald decided early that Coleman had had his chips. Years later, when the Donegal man had emerged as one of the best defenders in European football,

McDonald conceded his mistake, but stood by his assertion that Coleman at that time was too shy for the harsh realities of professional football.

Coleman's insight into that period differs significantly:

> I was a 17-year-old boy in a man's world. I was playing alongside seasoned professionals, men who had families to feed, who depended on their career for a living. I had not experienced anything like that before. In addition, the standard of football was far higher than anything I'd been used to, and although I was working hard, I was struggling a bit in the first few months. Naturally, I was quiet in that environment, but I was not overly shy. I held nothing back in training or in matches. I don't buy Rob's assessment on that score.

His memory of the night his football career almost collapsed is still crystal clear, but typically, he holds no grudges.

> I was called to a meeting with the manager in November and my dad drove me up from Killybegs. It was a short meeting. Rob said I didn't feature in his plans and there was talk of a loan move, perhaps to Finn Harps. I knew I had a year left on my contract, so my attitude was that I would keep my head down, work harder than ever, and see what happened. There was something in me telling me I would find my way, that I would make this work.
>
> It wasn't an easy time, but I made no fuss about it. I didn't even tell my dad on the way home to Killybegs. I knew how much he enjoyed coming to Sligo for the games, so I saw no point in upsetting him. I kept it to myself and just stayed focused on making the most of it. Luckily for me, Rob didn't stay around too long.
>
> I bear no grudges whatsoever. These things happen in football. There's loads of cases where managers come in and don't fancy a player or feel he won't suit their style of play. Rob didn't think I'd make it. I knew I would. And that's the end of it as far as I'm concerned.

Caretaker managers Leo Tierney, the club's goalkeeping coach, and Dessie Cawley, a local football man who was in charge of the under-18s, took an immediate shine to Coleman, giving him an extended run of games in the first team, so that by the time Paul Cook's revolution began, Coleman was an integral part of the club.

He hasn't forgotten the importance of the role those people played in his development:

> There's no doubt Leo and Dessie resurrected my career, and I would never forget that. Then Paul Cook came, and it was a game-changer, both for the club and for myself. I always had great belief in myself and a determination that I could make it. Now I had a manager who was telling me I was the best full-back in the League and that there were no limits. I can't underestimate how important Paul Cook was to my development as a footballer and a person.

It wasn't long before the young full-back with a penchant for storming into fruitful attacking positions began attracting the attention of bigger clubs. Short trials with Burnley and Celtic proved unproductive, but Coleman could sense he was on the cusp of a life-changing breakthrough. He recalls:

> There were little bits appearing in newspapers and RTE came down to do a special piece about me. I was selected for the Ireland under-21 team, so there was a sense that something different was happening. Then, I was told Everton wanted me, and the attraction was that there was no trial involved. I could sign straight away. That was a massive moment.

From a close-knit family, making the move to live in Liverpool presented obvious difficulties, but Coleman was determined to make the most of the opportunity. He concedes:

> Homesickness was a problem at first. Leaving home for the first time, away from my parents and brothers, my girlfriend, none of that was easy, but I looked upon it as just another obstacle to be overcome. Luckily, I hadn't any distractions away from football. I would stay at training as long as they'd allow me, and I'm ok in my own company. I can cope quite easily with boredom.

The rest, as they say, is history. Coleman has gone on to make more than 300 Premier League appearances, has captained Ireland at European Championships, and has won over 60 caps for his country. Remarkably, he remains totally unaffected by the fame and celebrity which pervades his industry, steadfast in the core beliefs instilled in him as a child.

> It becomes a bit embarrassing when people talk about how it hasn't changed me. Why should I change, just because I get paid for kicking a ball around a field? I like to think that no matter what I had done in life I would be the same person. Football has given me a great life, it has changed my life but it has not changed me as a person. My parents brought me up to be mannerly and respectful, and I never deviated from that. That's why it's never a big deal for me to sign an autograph or pose for a photograph. If that makes me a good role model then I'm quite happy with that.

Although he played just 56 games for Rovers over a two-and-a-half year period, Coleman reflects on his time with the club as one of the most important and enjoyable of his life. It's obvious from his cheerful reminiscing that Sligo will always loom large in his story.

"Sligo will always be a massive part of my life," he confirms. "It's an important part of my family's life, too. Mum and Dad and my brothers, Francis and Stevie, used to drive up to all the matches, and they loved it. We still talk about it. They miss those nights out in Sligo."

He's determined that the next generation will appreciate the indelible place Sligo has in their history:

> After a holiday in Donegal last year, we were flying back to Liverpool from Knock. I pulled into Sligo on the way, headed up to the Showgrounds, and gave my wife, Rachel, and young daughters, Ellie and Lilly, the grand tour. I showed them the pitch, the outdoor museum and took them into the dressing rooms. I wanted them to see where it all started. Our son, Blake, was only an infant then, but as soon as he's old enough, I'll have him up there. That's how important Sligo and Sligo Rovers is to my family.

Sligo took Seamie Coleman to its heart as soon as he pulled on the famous Bit O'Red. It's abundantly clear the feeling remains mutual.

Paul Cook

Sligo still pulls at the heartstrings

Chris Cook's life revolved around his family and Liverpool Football Club. A season-ticket holder at Anfield for 55 years, he rarely missed a game. As is often the case when a devoted fan passes away, his coffin was draped in the famous red scarf of his beloved team during his funeral Mass at St Peter and Paul's Church, Kirkby, Merseyside, in September 2021. In their mourning, compounded by Covid restrictions which curtailed the numbers who could share their grief, his family found comfort in that tangible connection with a team who'd brought him so much joy in his well-lived life.

But there was one other soccer scarf placed neatly on his coffin, also red and white, reflecting Chris's love affair with a different football club, a beguiling lover whose late entry into his life had brought him new and unexpected delight. A Sligo Rovers scarf was folded side by side with the Liverpool one, deliberately afforded equality of esteem.

Paul Cook, one of the most outstanding managers in Sligo Rovers' long and occasionally successful history, is Chris Cook's son. He listened intently as his brother, Ian, in a beautiful eulogy, thanked Paul for opening the door to Sligo for their father, informing mourners that little meant more to Chris in the last twenty years of his life than becoming a Sligo Rovers supporter.

A funeral on a bleak September day in a small church six miles from Liverpool had served to graphically underline not only the indelible mark Paul Cook's colossal success had left on Sligo Rovers but also how the club and the town had embraced his parents, an English couple who hadn't even known the town existed. The small number of Sligo people who had travelled to console their former manager were amazed at the central place their club had been given in the obsequies.

Cook says his dad, his best friend, would have been "chuffed" by the Sligo attendance and "so proud" to have the scarves of his two favourite clubs resting side by side:

> Sligo will always be an important part of my life, wherever my career takes me, but the nicest part for me was the way my dad embraced it. He just fell in love with the town, the club and its people. In some places, particularly the pubs, he and my mum, Eileen, will be more fondly remembered than I am!
>
> He'd come over regularly on the plane from Liverpool to Knock, it was so accessible. He'd stay for the weekend of the match, and then maybe a quick decision to stay an extra day or two. They absolutely loved Sligo.
>
> It's strange. In my career as player and manager, I must have had 20 clubs, and while he would have always followed my progress, he never had the affection for any of them that he had for Sligo. And he made so many friends. I can't be sure if Sligo ever really took me to its heart – though I like to think there is a mutual affection – but they definitely took Dad on board and vice versa. That'll do for me.

Cook grew up in Kirkby, one of Merseyside's largest satellite towns with a population about twice the size of Sligo. It was tough and uncompromising, and football offered a way out. It was a well-travelled route. Many of the town's young men carved out professional careers: Denis Mortimer captained Aston Villa to the European Cup in 1982; Terry McDermott became a legend of Liverpool and Newcastle; Phil Thompson played for Liverpool and England before becoming an insightful TV pundit. Most astounding of all, John Coleman would follow his townsman into the manager's hot seat at Sligo Rovers.

Cook was a distinguished journeyman footballer, probably disappointed that his excursion through eight professional clubs over 23 years didn't include a stop-over at his beloved Liverpool. Still, he amassed a very impressive 643 appearances in top-flight football, including 37 in the Premier League for Coventry City.

Ten years after the dizzy heights of the Premier League, however, he was out of work, and management seemed the only option. He'd worked with good football men in his career, soaked in their knowledge, had a few innovative ideas of his own, and was ready to take the first tentative steps in what he suspected would be a cut-throat, shark-filled environment.

So, Southport in the Conference League seemed a good place to start. It wasn't. Sacked after six months, he was back on the scrapheap.

Then came a phone call that was to change not only his life but the fortunes of a struggling football club on the other side of the Irish Sea. Cookie, with his distinctive, gravel-throated Scouse accent, and his revolutionary football plan, was about to bring the Mersey beat to Sligo.

The original phone call came from Enniskillen-based football scout Gerry Cassidy, whose bulging contact book and intimate knowledge of England's lower leagues had rescued Rovers many times in the past. Cook's interest was sufficiently piqued. He travelled over to watch a rather shambolic Rovers team being slaughtered by St Patrick's Athletic at the Showgrounds. He remembers:

> The team wasn't very good, but everything else was appealing. The facilities weren't great, but they were okay and there was ambition to improve on and off the field. There was a multi-national squad - Polish, Australian, Hungarian lads, and a few locals - but the budget was there to help me build something. People were honest with me so I knew where I stood. It was a bit of a chance, coming over and leaving my family and friends, but it turned out to be the best decision I ever made.

As has often been the case, recruitment of players proved difficult, but Cook was always one step ahead. His trick was to bring over potential signings whenever there was a big game at the Showgrounds, knowing the special atmosphere would hook them. As he confides:

> On a big night in the Showgrounds, be it in the League, Cup or Europe, the atmosphere is electric. The place would be bouncing. So, I'd bring lads over, get them seated in the most boisterous part of the stand, and let them experience it for themselves. There was never a problem getting them to sign after that.

Two years after his arrival, Cook had steered Rovers to their first FAI Cup final in fifteen years, where they were surprisingly beaten by Sporting Final, who scored two late goals at Tallaght Stadium. But the cunning Cook had caught the Cup bug which had been infecting Sligo soccer followers for generations. He vowed the team would be back the following season.

And so, to the first ever Cup final at Dublin's magnificent Aviva Stadium on 14 November 2010, where Cook's men faced arch-rivals Shamrock Rovers, who were bidding to complete a League and Cup double. It turned out to be an epic game which caught the imagination of the soccer public as seldom before, with over 36,000 fans, the biggest attendance in more than 40 years, turning up to watch the gripping drama unfold.

Ninety minutes of fiercely competitive action and thirty more in extra time could not separate the teams, so the dreaded penalty shoot-out was required to decide the outcome. Thanks to the heroics of Sligo goalkeeper Ciarán Kelly, who saved four of the opponent's spot-kicks, the Rovers from Sligo lifted the trophy on a 2–0 scoreline, sparking deliriously wild celebrations.

But the man who had masterminded it all was nowhere to be seen. He had not watched a single second of the excruciatingly tense conclusion.

Where was he? Outside the stadium, praying like a Trappist monk, and squinting through a window where a helpful steward kept him updated with an improvised code of thumbs up, thumbs down.

Cook explains this novel turn of events:

> It wasn't that I couldn't take the tension. It's just that as a manager in a penalty shoot-out you've done all you can. It's in the lap of the gods, and it's now down to the players on the pitch. Before I left the arena, I gathered them around, told them to focus on the pain of the previous year and not to allow themselves even contemplate going through that again. My final words to them were "we're bringing home the Cup" and then I walked down the tunnel, onto a concourse area outside the stadium.
>
> I was pacing up and down, reciting any prayer I could remember, must have been about twenty, and peeking in this small window, where a steward would give me a thumbs up if we scored or they missed. We'd practiced penalties all week, and I knew we had the best penalty stopper in the League so I was genuinely confident we'd do it.

Remarkably, a quite similar train of events unfolded the following year, as Rovers faced Shelbourne in the 2011 final. Again, 120 minutes of football had failed to break the stalemate, and penalties were once more required.

No racing towards the exit door this time, though. Now, the manager had a big call to make. Ciarán Kelly, the penalty-saving hero of twelve months earlier, was on the bench. Brendan Clarke, the regular keeper, had played well in the course of the game. Cook took the courageous, if potentially disastrous, decision to change his keepers for the shoot-out. Almost to script, Kelly saved two penalties and Rovers retained the Cup. Cook declares:

> It was a no-brainer. We had a proven penalty-stopper so it made perfect sense to use him. There was a psychological element at play, too, because I knew the Shelbourne players would be thinking "this is the guy who saved four last year". That would have unnerved them.
>
> It was tough on Brendan Clarke and he was understandably upset, but a manager is paid to make big calls and I got that one right.

Since leaving Rovers, Cook has had considerable managerial success in England. He's won the League Two championship twice, with Chesterfield and Portsmouth, and the League One title with Wigan Athletic. His one setback came when he was sacked by Ipswich Town after nine months in charge, but he remains optimistic about future opportunities in the game.

When we met, he was 'helping out' at Chesterfield, one of his old clubs, but he remained adamant he still had much to offer at a higher level. In any event, he will forever be grateful to Sligo Rovers for taking a chance on a rookie manager and providing a platform for an eventful career.

> Sligo will always be a huge part of my story. The passion for football there is unreal; the town is the club's best friend. Not too many clubs, even some big ones, can say that. I made life-long friends there, both players and administrators, and I have memories to last a lifetime.

It's more than eleven years since Cook won his last trophy with the club, yet he is still spoken of with great affection by Sligo soccer followers. He has carved a place in the history of the club and of the county. His dad would be proud.

Raffaele Cretaro

Rovers' red-hot scoring machine

The Italian influence is striking. It's easy to detect in the way he played, a maestro of bewildering brilliance, delivering performances of outrageous beauty to the ecstatic delight of a captivated audience.

Meet Raffaele Cretaro, veteran of 393 appearances for Sligo Rovers, the holder of two FAI Cup medals and one League Championship medal, the scorer of critical League-winning goals and a Cup-winning penalty. A red-hot scoring machine who clocked up a staggering 79 goals for his local club over the course of a superlative career.

He's known to the Sligo Rovers faithful as 'Raff', itself a sort of coronation. Only football royalty is referred to by first name only. The media hang headlines of a more fanciful moniker, 'the Tubbercurry Tornado', in venerable recognition of the devastating carnage his scoring exploits visited upon opposing teams down through the years.

The son of an Italian emigrant who came to Ireland in search of a more prosperous life in the early 1970s, he inherited a passion for football from his father and the desire to play it so delightfully from the rich tradition of Italian artistry.

Raffaele Cretaro Senior and his brothers, Franco and Lorettico, arrived in Ireland in the summer of 1972. Their local village, Macchia, Casalattico in southern Italy, offered little by way of employment or prospects so they sought out family associates and friends in Ireland and headed off for pastures green.

Franco settled in Dublin, Lorettico got a place in Boyle, County Roscommon, and Raffaele made his way to Gurteen in east Sligo. They operated fish-and-chip shops. The business in Gurteen went well for Raffaele but the opportunity of moving to a larger premises in Tubbercurry, a town with a greater population, proved too strong to resist. He married Loretta Gorman from Ballina and the couple quickly immersed themselves in the community life of their adopted town.

Raffaele Junior was their first born. Maurizio, Fabio and Nicole came later. The family name was curiously exotic by rural Sligo standards, but they were warmly welcomed in the town. Cretaro reflects:

> We had a shop in Humbert Street, a great place to live. My mother was a great one for the big welcome. She had a word for everybody. There were two old lads who were regular customers. Mum got to know them so well that instead of serving them fish and chips, she'd bring them into the kitchen and give them a full dinner. We had a very open house.

Most summers, Raffaele Senior would bring his kids back to his home place. There they sampled the Italian way of life, met their relations, tasted the exotic food, soaked up the sun. And played football. Lots of football.

Far from the madness of Italia 90 in Ireland, the Cretaro kids experienced the real thing, up close and personal. Cretaro beams at the memory:

> It was the best summer ever. We were in Italy for the whole tournament and Dad brought us to a few matches. I was ten years old. It was magical. That's when I first fell in love with football.

His earliest memory of playing organised soccer was with the Real Tubber under-11 team. They beat Strand Celtic in a final that went all the way to a penalty shoot-out. He scored one of the penalties.

After starring for the Sligo-Leitrim which team won the Inter-League Cup, he made the progression to Sligo Rovers. He scored on his debut off the bench against Monaghan United at Gortakeegan in 2000. It was the start of a glorious adventure.

He had spells away at Galway United and Bohemians, but home was always where the heart was.

This was crystalised during an injury-interrupted season at Bohs in 2010. He had been Rovers' leading scorer the previous season, helping them to reach the FAI Cup final where they lost to Sporting Fingal, but was tempted by a generous offer from the Dublin club. He admits:

> At the time, I felt the move was right for me. I was offered a contract the likes of which I'd never seen before. It was impossible to turn down. But

> I soon learned that the grass isn't always greener on the other side. The whole culture of professional football in Dublin was something I wasn't used to. I missed living at home. The whole experience was a bit of an eye-opener.

Cretaro's spell at Bohs meant he missed out on Rovers' epic Cup final win over Shamrock Rovers at a packed Aviva Stadium in 2010, so he was determined to make up for lost time when he returned to his hometown club:

> I was delighted to come back. I'd played the best football of my career under Paul Cook at Rovers in 2009 and I was thrilled to team up with him again. He had man management off to an art. He was always telling me I was the best striker in Ireland. Just go out and prove me right, he'd say. Even if I had a bad game, he would stand by me.

Rovers battled their way to the final again in 2011. Once more the decider, this time against Shels, then a first division outfit, went right down to a dreaded penalty shoot-out.

Alan Keane, who had missed a penalty in the 2010 final, was eager for redemption.

"Far from being haunted by my miss the previous year, I was buzzing to take one of the penalties. It was a chance to set the record straight. I was confident I'd score", says Keane.

In contrast, the club's top marksman was reluctant to get involved in the spot-kick lottery. It was a surprising display of unease from a man habitually acquainted with the art of goalscoring.

"I didn't want to take one", reveals Cretaro, "but I couldn't talk my way out of it. I'd scored a lot of goals during my career, but I was never the most confident penalty taker."

Eoin Doyle, Richie Ryan and Keane slotted home their penalties for Rovers. Super-hero Ciarán Kelly saved two of Shelbourne's efforts, which meant the destination of the most coveted trophy in Irish soccer came down to Cretaro's kick.

As he made the long, agonising walk from the centre circle to the penalty spot, the Tubbercurry man glanced around at the packed stands, knowing his family and his childhood sweetheart, Joanne Henry, were there, gripped with nerves and probably deep in prayer. He knew he had to detach himself from the emotion of it all.

"My instinct was to block everything out, to somehow focus on taking the penalty and nothing else," he recalls.

Then a strange thing happened. The Rihanna song 'Cheers' infiltrated his thought process. He recounts:

> It was mental. I don't know why but I just started singing the song.
>
> "Takin' shots in here, you want one?
> "Yeah-e-yeah, yeah-e-yeah."
>
> And on it went. I'm going up to take what could be a Cup-winning penalty and I'm singing this random song to myself. Absolutely nuts.

By the time he got to the penalty spot, he'd made up his mind to shoot to the keeper's left. As he expected, Shels' keeper, Dean Delaney, gambled on diving to his right, meaning the Sligo player's crisply struck shot ripped into the unguarded side of the net.

The Rovers' fans crammed into the South Stand burst into spontaneous acclaim. "There's only one Raff Cretaro", they boomed.

The following day, Rovers took a detour on their homecoming lap of honour, bringing the famous trophy to Tubbercurry for the first time. There was a carnival atmosphere in the town. They came from all over south Sligo to pay homage to their local hero. Cretaro recalls:

> That was special. Coming back to my home place with the Cup. Back to where it all began. The people of Tubbercurry were always so supportive during my career. I played soccer and GAA for the local clubs, and they were with me every step of the way. Now we were all celebrating together in the square in the town. My family was there, decked out in their red-and-white colours. The place was packed with schoolchildren too. It seemed as if the whole of south Sligo had turned out to join in the celebrations. It's a day I'll never forget.

Destined to become part of Sligo's soccer folklore, the prolific striker was a highly influential figure when Rovers won the League of Ireland Championship in 2012. The title was clinched in a titanic showdown with St Patrick's Athletic at the Showgrounds. The 'Tubbercurry Tornado' scored two exquisite goals in an unforgettable 3–2 victory.

The first was a breathtaking solo effort, the product of quick feet, a typically cheeky nutmeg, and a flawless finish. It was a goal minted from Italian flamboyance. The second revealed more streetwise qualities, the instinct of a merciless marksman, escaping the security men in a packed defence to deliver the fatal blow from close range.

It was entirely appropriate that the momentous occasion was adorned with the irresistible craftsmanship of one of the county's most revered footballers.

When the dust settled, the striker snatched a moment of quiet reflection. He remembered the first match to which his father brought him. It was a European Cup Winners' Cup game against FC Brugge at the Showgrounds. The Belgians had the arrogant swagger of aristocrats; Rovers were working-class heroes. Brugge smuggled a rather fortunate 2–1 win, but the result didn't matter all that much to the Tubbercurry boy. He fell hopelessly in love with Sligo Rovers. He was a dreamer then. Later, he'd be the maker of dreams.

Cretaro won a second FAI Cup medal with the Bit O'Red in 2013 and played his last game for Rovers against Motherwell in the Irn Bru Cup in October 2018.

The Tubbercurry man brought the curtain down on his decorated playing career at Finn Harps.

He's married to local girl Joanne, and the couple live in south Sligo with their two children, Matteo and Milana.

The Rovers team which won the FAI Cup in 2011: Brendan Clarke, Alan Keane, Gavin Peers, Jason McGuinness, Iarfhlaith Davoren, John Dillon, Richie Ryan, Danny Ventre, Aaron Greene, John Russell, Eoin Doyle. Subs: Matthew Blinkhorn, Raffaele Cretaro, Ciarán Kelly.

Gavin Dykes and Conor O'Grady

Tales from the captain's table

Given Sligo's near obsessive craving for the FAI Cup, having waited 55 years to win it, how entirely appropriate is the fact that the first three winning captains were natives of the town. Gavin Dykes in 1994 and Conor O'Grady in 2010 followed the hallowed footsteps of Tony Fagan, who was the first Sligoman to hoist the famous trophy in 1983.

All fairy tales seem to have unlikely genesis. For Gavin Dykes, League of Ireland legend as player, manager and coach, it began in a pub!

A promising youth player who'd spent a year at Swindon Town learning the nuts and bolts of the professional game under former Manchester United star Lou Macari, Dykes was back in junior football, enjoying the freedom and craic with his mates at Strand Celtic. After a Sunday morning game in October 1987, they'd retreated for the usual lunch-time pints to Sonny Bree's nearby hostelry. Just about to sip into his second drink, the youngster's happy diversion was interrupted by a phone call from his father, Kevin: "Gerry Mitchell's been on, they're stuck, they need you in the Showgrounds."

Drinks abandoned, the 20-year-old rushed the six miles into town. Kick-off and his Sligo Rovers' debut was less than two hours away. He laughs handsomely at the memory, recalling:

> It happened so quickly. I'd always dreamed of playing for Rovers, but I never imagined it would happen like this. We were up against Cork City, who were flying at the time. I was marking Patsy Freyne, who was one of the best wingers in the League, and I remember after about 25 minutes

> saying to him, I was wrecked 'cos I had had a few pints. He told me he had a few the night before, too, and we had a laugh about it.

It was the first of more than 250 appearances for the club in a spectacularly successful career which yielded a League Championship and FAI Cup medal, First Division Championship and Shield medals, European football and a junior international cap.

But nothing compares to 1993–1994 when Sligo Rovers, a club whose trophy cabinet had known more dust than silverware, remarkably captured three major titles in one season, with Dykes as the inspirational skipper.

First Division Championship and Shield had already been tucked away by Willie McStay's swashbuckling young team when they faced Premier League side Derry City, in the final of the FAI Cup at Lansdowne Road, on 15 May 1994, in pursuit of an unprecedented treble.

On the morning of the match, Dykes looked out from his hotel bedroom window and was delighted to see the rain bucketing down from grey Dublin skies. He recalls:

> I immediately thought of the 1983 final and Fago lifting the cup on the wettest day of the year. I had been there as a young fella and got soaked to the skin. When I saw it was a similar day for us, I felt it was as a good omen.

Another good luck charm was even more unlikely. Francie Middleton's tiny mini-bus had ferried Rovers throughout the country during that all-conquering season, but had been dispensed with in favour of more luxurious transport to the cup final. As captain, Dykes insisted the team should travel to the game with Francie.

> We travelled to Dublin in a posh coach on the day before the match. But I wanted us to go from our hotel to the ground in Francie's bus because we'd been everywhere with Francie, and he was great craic, an integral part of the group. It was about keeping to a ritual we were used to, treating it like any other game, and it worked. We arrived at the ground without any fanfare, hardly anyone noticed us. It was like a regular game and that helped settle us.

Gerry Carr's winner meant Dykes would become only the second Sligoman to lift the famous old trophy. Aware of his place in history, he knew instantly it was a big deal. Being mobbed by both friends and strangers in floods of tears at the end of the match confirmed the feeling:

> Going up the steps to collect the cup, I remember seeking out my wife, Siobhán, and saying to her things will never be the same again. I knew it was a place in history, something we could always be proud of.

The occasion was rendered even more special by the fact that his father, Kevin, was chairman of the club that year, although the unique situation was not without its problems.

> When he became chairman and I was captain, I might have thought this is not good. I was aware some people would be on about nepotism and the usual stuff about me only being captain because my dad was chairman. But I honestly couldn't care less about that. He had his job and I had mine, and, thankfully, we both did quite well. What people wouldn't know was that as captain I was the one who had to fight with him over bonuses and things like that. And, believe me, they were arguments I rarely won.

Dykes would play in two further FAI Cup finals for Finn Harps and Derry City and would go on to coach, manage and assistant manage a host of League clubs, as well as being an early mentor in Rovers' fledgling academy system. He's still involved at the top level, as assistant manager to Ollie Horgan at Finn Harps, but nothing will ever beat 15 May 1994.

> To win the Cup for your hometown club, to see the absolute joy it brought to so many people, to be part of such a brilliant team, many of whom I'd still regard as very special friends – nothing could ever beat that.

***

Like the children in *The Chronicles of Narnia*, who were transported to a fantasy realm through a wardrobe, Conor O'Grady hopped over his granny's back wall to find his own magical world. Her house backed onto the Showgrounds, home of Sligo Rovers, and as a youngster O'Grady liked nothing better than to nip over the boundary wall to watch his floodlit heroes.

> Floodlights were still a novelty when I was young, and I remember they'd light up Granny's whole house. It was sort of magical, and as a young fella you just instinctively knew something special was going on.

He became part of the magic in 1998. As had been the case with Dykes, his transition from junior football to the League of Ireland happened very quickly and seamlessly. That year, he was a supporter in the fabled 'Shed' watching Rovers play Home Farm in the semi-final of the League Cup. By the time the final came around, he was in the team, winning a senior medal under Nicky Reid while still a raw novice.

In 2010, aged 30 and nearing the end of a distinguished career – he'd been a professional at Cork City and Derry City before returning to Rovers – he became the third Sligo native to captain Rovers to FAI Cup glory, as the Bit O'Red overcame Shamrock Rovers in a dramatic penalty shoot-out at the Aviva Stadium.

As that youngster sneaking into matches from the Treacy Avenue gardens, he would surely have dreamed of one day skippering Rovers in a big cup final, maybe even of scoring a match-winning penalty. The prospect of missing a crucial spot kick in front of 36,000 fans in what was his last game for the club would have been the stuff of nightmares.

But that's how it turned out. From the distance of twelve years, O'Grady is philosophical about an isolated moment from an otherwise flawless career. He confides:

> I'll never forget it, but it doesn't haunt me in any way. If we'd lost the match it would have been torture, I would have wanted the ground to open up and swallow me, but I had great confidence in the other players, particularly goalkeeper Ciarán Kelly, who saved four penalties. It might seem strange, but I knew in my heart we'd win that game, so the penalty miss never really mattered. The only annoying thing about it now is that my young son, Harry, has watched it and he gives me a bit of a ribbing.

A late substitute on the day, as club captain, O'Grady got to lift the cup along with Danny Ventre and Richie Ryan, thus following in the footsteps of Tony Fagan and Gavin Dykes. He says:

> It's great company to be in. I was at the '94 final as a young teenager, delighted to see Gavin lifting the cup, and it's moments like that which inspire you in so many ways. To achieve it myself was such an unbelievable feeling, but the emotions that day were mainly for my parents and

> my brothers. I knew how proud they'd be, and that meant more than anything.

Now the club's academy director, with overall responsibility for more than 120 players and 20 coaches across six boys' and girls' teams, O'Grady has great hopes for the future of the club:

> The club has a history of bringing in players from outside the region, stretching back to its origins, but the future has to be about producing our own players. That's the aim of the academy. Maybe, these boys and girls won't all play for us in the League of Ireland, but we'll give all of them the grounding necessary to become professional players at senior level, and hopefully we'll help them become better people as well. Our philosophy is built on three H's – hard work, humility and honesty. They're qualities which will help youngsters in any walk of life.

Legends in their own rights, both Dykes and O'Grady are now at the 'giving back' stage. Soccer stars of the future will owe them a huge debt.

Tony Fagan

Legend known only as Fago

It was the gifted Kerry sportswriter the late Con Houlihan, writing in his *Irish Press* column in the 1980s, who memorably drew attention to the physical comparison between the image of Christ and that of the Sligo Rovers footballer Tony Fagan. With his shoulder-length jet-black hair, a full sprout of meticulously shaped facial hair, sunken blue eyes and high cheekbones, Fago could well have been an artist's model for a Biblical figure. Houlihan's eloquent description would not have been considered even remotely blasphemous in Sligo, where the long-held belief in soccer circles is that Fago is, indeed, something of a football Messiah.

Interestingly, there's a real-life miracle documented in Fagan's family. In the late 1960s, his uncle John Fagan, a Glasgow dock worker, was on his death bed, having given up a long, painful fight against pancreatic cancer, when his wife, in a last desperate search for redemption, placed a relic of the Scottish martyr John Ogilvie under his pillow. To the astonishment of his doctors, the grievously ill man woke up the next morning in fine fettle, all trace of his cancerous tumours disappeared. Science could not explain the startling transformation, and the Catholic Church, after exhaustive investigations, declared the recovery a miracle. Ogilvie became a revered saint and John Fagan lived for another 26 years, having survived two further cancer battles.

There must be something in the Fagan blood, because the Sligo Rovers Fago has performed countless miraculous football deeds in a fabled career which stretched over three decades. To this day, nearly 35 years after he last kicked a ball in the Showgrounds, his image still adorns banners hoisted in reverence by young fans nowhere near old enough to have seen him play. Countless soccer heroes have come and gone, before and since Fagan's heyday, but his legendary status endures. Everybody loves Fago. As with Paul Hewson, who will only ever be known as Bono, so it is with Tony Fagan's immortal identity as Fago.

In a 20-year playing career with the club, encompassing a record 590 appearances, Fago epitomised the heart and soul of Sligo Rovers. His playing days were practically a microcosm of the club's history, more bad days than good, constantly battling against the odds, revelling in the role of perpetual underdog. The fact that for many of those years he was the constant local connection in various teams of full-time professionals served only to consolidate his reputation.

Although he played at a time when the club's trophy cabinet was as bare as a student's wallet at the end of Rag Week, he still managed to win both a League and FAI Cup medal and to play in the European Cup. Very often, he was the one leading the charge to these rare bounties. The fact that the famous Cup win in 1983 was the club's first ever in a competition over which supporters had obsessed for half a century, and that it came after he had suffered the ignominy of defeat in three previous finals, embellished the legend.

Reared in the working-class St Brigid's Place on the Mail Coach Road area of the town, where street football offered the only form of recreation, the slightly built youngster was a nippy GAA footballer, good enough for the county minors, but his heart was in soccer. Nurturing his natural ability with the local St Joseph's club, run by Charlie Devaneny, and later with the Boys' Club, under the tuition of Fr Gerry Donnelly and Frank Ballantyne, he was soon on the radar of Sligo Rovers. A lot of the lads he played with in those teams might have been good enough for the League of Ireland, maybe some even better than himself, but Fago's fire burned more fiercely than most.

As a seventeen-year-old, he made a goal-scoring debut against Shamrock Rovers in 1967. The memory of that momentous day has never faded:

> As a young fella, you dream of playing for your hometown club. To finally get the chance, against a Shamrock Rovers team packed with international players, the glamour club of Ireland at the time, was unbelievable. We were 2–0 down, and then myself and Dessie Gallagher scored to earn a 2–2 draw. Dessie grew up just down the road, a neighbour, and for the two of us to score in that game was like something from a comic book.

Three years later, he was part of a Rovers team playing in an FAI Cup final for the first time in 30 years. The town went mad as the final turned into a boisterous three-game marathon, with Bohemians eventually breaking Sligo hearts in the second replay.

However, in 1977, years of despair were transformed into unprecedented delight when Rovers won the League of Ireland title for the first time in 40 years, and only their second ever. What's rare is beautiful, and Fago liked being a winner at last, and he has no doubt where the laurels should rest.

"Billy Sinclair transformed everything," he insists.

> For most of my time, teams had been made up of lads coming in on match days from Dublin or Derry. Sinky changed that. He brought in full-timers from England, ambitious young lads, and we all trained together. We had a small panel, and a lot of us played through injuries, but Sinky had us all believing we could do something special.

It was certainly special, but even the enormity of that thrilling breakthrough was eclipsed six years later when Rovers finally won the FAI Cup for the first time, beating Bohemians 2–1 on an unforgettable rain-sodden April day at Dalymount Park. Fago became the first Sligoman to lift the Blue Riband trophy of Irish football

'The Cup', as it's only ever labelled in Sligo, has represented the holy grail for local supporters ever since the club was formed in 1928. The legendary Dixie Dean played for Rovers in their first Cup final in 1939 but ended up on the losing side. Further final defeats followed in 1940, 1970, 1978, and 1981. Fago had a losers' medal from three of those finals. So, it meant more to him than anyone.

His first memory of Cup football is as a teenager working in a local factory, when he borrowed the price of a train fare from his boss so he could travel to Dublin to watch Rovers play in the 1966 semi-final.

"They were hammered 3–0 by Limerick at Tolka Park. A bag of chips and back on the train home. Another miserable night," is his recollection. Little could he have imagined then how significant the FAI Cup would become in his life.

By the time the 1983 decider came along he was beginning to wonder if the elusive medal would ever become reality. He reasons:

> I guessed it might be my last chance. Rovers had never won the Cup, but I sensed it was bound to happen sooner or later. If they had won it after I retired, I would probably have felt a little cheated, given all I'd been through with them. So, I suppose more than ever, I was determined not to let this one slip.

There was little evidence to support any optimism in the 1983 team. Working off a limited panel of no more than fifteen players at any one time under rookie player-manager Paul Fielding, the team had managed just four League wins all season.

But the transformation was sparked by a first-ever Cup win against old rivals Shamrock Rovers, with Fagan scoring a late winner. Next up was what proved to be an epic four-game semi-final tussle with non-league Cobh Ramblers.

Fago was more surprised than anyone by the strength of Cobh's resistance. He explains:

> I was suspended for a League game so Paul Fielding sent me to Richmond Park to watch Cobh. They were terrible on the day and I reported back that we'd have no problem beating them. We had nothing to worry about. Needless to say, that was the end of my scouting career.

In the event, it took four gripping games to separate the teams. Rovers eventually needed two goals from Chris Rutherford and a winner from Gus Gilligan to come from two goals down to win 3–2 in extra time of a Showgrounds thriller.

Becoming the first Sligo man to lift the FAI Cup, Fagan has little memory of the detail of that famous day, though he still marvels at the brilliance of the crucial goals scored by Tony Stenson and Harry McLoughlin. He reflects:

> Maybe two of the best goals we have ever scored, and they came in a Cup final. Couldn't make it up. What I remember most was the joy on people's faces. As a player, win, lose or draw, you get something out of it, but all there is for supporters is winning. And our supporters hadn't had that for so long. It was their day more than it was ours.

Like a warrior captain still defending his players, he gets annoyed by any suggestion that better Rovers teams would have been more deserving of a place in history. He contends:

> I played in four Cup finals, and any one of those teams would have been worthy winners. Listen, we were poor in the League, but the Cobh games made us. Any team with the likes of Chris Rutherford, Paul Fielding, Tony Stenson, Bomber Savage, Harry McLoughlin, Martin McDonnell, Mick Ferry or Gus Gilligan in it is a good team. It annoys me when they don't get the recognition they deserve.

Four years later, his Rovers career ended as it had begun – against Shamrock Rovers, fittingly in an FAI Cup semi-final – this time perhaps in keeping with a more familiar script. Over two legs, the teams were still tied, with the Hoops eventually going through with a ninety-second-minute winner in the replay. Fago was saddened by the manner of his departure, a sordid dispute over a paltry sum of money:

> They thought I was finished, although I'd just played a full season. I asked for a pay rise and they never even asked how much I wanted. I don't hurt easily, but I was hurt by the way it ended. But it's water under the bridge now.

He played on for a further season with Finn Harps, under Patsy McGowan, one of the men he admires most from his career, and later returned to Rovers to manage the reserves and help out in the backroom team of Willie McStay's all-conquering 1994 squad.

These days, for every home game, he strolls the 100 yards from his front door to the Showgrounds to take the same seats in the Treacy Avenue stand alongside his son-in-law and four grandchildren. Locals need no introduction; often visiting fans or past players will greet him like long a lost pal – "Fago, how's the craic?" He enjoys the recognition and the banter, but he's not sure about the 'legend' stuff:

> I played nearly 600 games, so people got used to seeing me, I suppose. The way I see it, if you give everything you have in every game you play, people will respect you for that. I can't control what was written about me, or what people said about me, good or bad. If people think what I did was worth something, then I'm happy. I'm just a guy who got to do something he loved.

Other heroes from the historic 1983 FAI Cup winning squad included: Paul Fielding (player-manager), Colin Oakley, Mick Ferry, Tony Stenson, Chris Rutherford, Graham Fox, Harry McLaughlin, Michael Savage, Martin McDonnell, Andy Elliott, Gus Gilligan, Mick Graham, John Skeffington, Keith Parkinson, Paul Moylan (RIP).

Seán Fallon

Iron Man's love of all things Sligo

Deep in untamed woodlands nestling high above Sligo's sacred Tobernalt Holy Well, camouflaged amongst a thicket of tangled briers and sharp-thorned brambles, rests a 10-inch plaque bearing the name of Seán Fallon. The only person who knows its location and its significance is the man who put it there, Fallon's only son, Seán T.

In a gesture graphically illustrating his late father's indelible connection with his birthplace, Fallon Junior brought the plaque, which had been used as a temporary monument on his father's grave in Glasgow, to the place he knew his dad would most like to be remembered.

As a child, he was brought to this holy place by his father every summer. Far from the fame of Glasgow Celtic's "Iron Man" status, Seán Fallon would come here with his young family, unknown and unfettered, to touch base with a tradition he'd learned as a young boy growing up in St Anne's Terrace on the banks of the Garavogue River.

Now, months after his death in 2013, his son was back on familiar turf. He climbed slippery rocks, battled his way through thick, prickly shrubs and gorse, found an isolated patch and, with hands torn and scratched from the effort, placed the nameplate in its new home.

"For me, it's his homecoming. I just wanted to signify his love of Sligo and of the Holy Well in particular," Fallon Junior explains.

It's but one of many engrossing stories which illuminate the larger-than-life character of a genuine Sligo legend – a man from a humble working-class background who went on to become an iconic figure at Glasgow Celtic Football Club; who discovered, nurtured and constructed the immortal Lisbon Lions, a team named after the city in which Celtic became the first British team to win the European Cup in 1967; whose unerring eye for raw potential unearthed further generations of international footballers; who travelled the world as a football ambassador, uniquely playing for both the Republic of Ireland and a Northern Ireland representative team; who counted luminaries such as Alex Ferguson and Sean Connery as close personal friends; but who was never more at home than playing a round of golf at Rosses Point or kneeling in prayer at the Holy Well.

Seán Fallon's astonishing football exploits are well-documented. He is revered in his adopted city of Glasgow, even amongst the hard-lined Rangers supporters, and he is honoured with two separate football pitches named after him in his native town, the county-council-owned pitch at Cranmore and the Sligo Rovers AstroTurf facility at the Showgrounds, which fittingly serves as the home venue and training facility for the club's academy teams.

But the gregarious, magnanimous man behind the legend is in many ways even more impressive. His innate kindness suited his role as a father figure to so many aspiring footballers, many of whom owe their extravagant careers to his early down-to-earth guidance and advice.

Legendary Irish goalkeeper Packie Bonner, the hero of Italia 90, is one of those whom Fallon took under his wing, and he has never forgotten the Sligo man's early influences.

Signed by Fallon in 1977 when he was just 17 years old, Bonner was surprised and a little disappointed to learn the Sligoman had left the club by the time he arrived in Glasgow a few months later. But he needn't have worried. Although fortunate to live with his aunt in the Simshill district of Glasgow – many of his contemporaries would have been in 'digs' with families they didn't know – Bonner was nonetheless naturally homesick. He had left a close-knit family in the small fishing village of Burtonport, Co. Donegal, and was particularly missing the company of his twin brother, Denis. When he most needed a comforting, reassuring arm around his shoulders, Seán Fallon provided it. Bonner confides:

> He was still looking out for me. He'd regularly invite me to his house for Sunday lunch, and I got to know his family really well. We had a great relationship.
>
> I never knew him as a coach or a manager, but I knew him as a man, a really good man. He was a real Irish man, and you could see those Irish qualities, particularly when it came to his family, who he adored. He was always the one who seemed to be picking me up and dropping me off wherever I was going.

> He knew my dad had died at a relatively young age and that there were six of us at home, so he was always asking after my mum. I remember when his own daughter, a doctor, went abroad to work for a short while, Seán was devastated because she was the first to go and he missed her so much. There were tears in his eyes. He could identify with that, and I suppose that's why he looked out for all the young lads away from home at Celtic.

Bonner also witnessed Fallon's immortal devotion to his hometown. He reveals:

> God, he never stopped talking about Sligo. The late Celtic manager Tommy Burns told me once how they had gone to play Finn Harps in a friendly match in Ballybofey, and Seán insisted they stop off at Rosses Point for a round of golf on the way home. Tommy said he was like a little boy showing off a new toy, he was so proud to show them the beauty of his home county.

Seán T. Fallon would be familiar with that trait in his late father, who gathered his young family into a packed people carrier every summer, sailing from Stranraer to Larne or Liverpool to Dublin, and then driving on to Sligo. He recalls:

> That was our summer holiday every year. We took a house from Johnny McGonigle in Rosses Point, we'd go swimming in the sea, play golf, visit our grandparents in St Anne's and, always, the Holy Well. Dad could have taken us abroad for holidays, but he never wanted to be anywhere but Sligo, and he instilled that in all of us. Myself and my five sisters still come back as often as we can.

Being the only son of a famous football man had other benefits, too, of course, as Seán T explains:

> I'd sometimes be allowed on the team bus, that was great fun. I remember once Lou Macari, who my dad had signed for Celtic, coming to our house and giving me a pair of boots he'd just worn in a testimonial game between Celtic and Manchester United.
>
> On another occasion, I was at a pro-am golf tournament with dad when Sean Connery, 007 himself, came over for a chat. Later, he wrote Dad a lovely letter on specially headed notepaper, and I sneaked it out and

> copied down the phone number. I went into school next day boasting that I had James Bond's personal number!

Another of Fallon's life-long friends was Sir Alex Ferguson. The pair had met when Fallon was at his peak, assistant manager to Jock Stien in charge of an all-conquering Celtic team, and Ferguson was a rookie boss, cutting his managerial teeth. Fallon, perhaps seeing something of himself in the ambitious, working-class young man from Glasgow's tough Govan area, became a willing and valuable mentor. More than thirty years later, Ferguson, then a global football legend, travelled to Sligo as guest speaker at a function to honour Fallon's career. When Fallon died in January 2013, Ferguson broke away from a Manchester United trip abroad to deliver a touching eulogy at his friend's funeral.

Former RTE northern editor and Sligoman Tommie Gorman, who was the last journalist to interview Fallon for an RTE *Nationwide* programme only days before his sudden death, had a first-hand view of the strong friendship between the two football greats.

In 2012, Ferguson was in Belfast at an event honouring United's Munich air disaster survivor Harry Gregg, and the strict official line was that there would be no press interviews. When Gorman got word through that his request was for a tribute to Fallon, the access policy changed and Ferguson readily made himself available to talk about his old friend.

A few months later, on the day of Fallon's funeral, Ferguson sought Gorman out. Gorman recalls:

> He quietly called me aside because he knew I had been involved in what was Seán's final interview. We sat in his car, and we chatted about Seán Fallon, the family man, the football man. Ferguson was keen to know what sort of form his friend had been in during those last days of his life. He really cared about him. You could sense the depth of their friendship.

Seán Fallon played as a full-back and centre-forward for Celtic from 1950 to 1958, making a total of 254 appearances, winning a Scottish League and two Scottish Cup medals, and earning eight caps for the Republic of Ireland. During one game, at a time before substitutes were allowed, he went off injured only to return and complete the game with his arm in a sling, thus earning him the immortal 'Iron Man' nickname.

Those who knew him as a youngster in Sligo would not have been surprised by such athleticism, as he had been a keen swimmer, boxer, Gaelic footballer and soccer player in his youth. He famously scored two goals for Sligo against

Kerry in a 1948 National League game, one of the few GAA matches ever to be staged in the Showgrounds. A baker by profession, he played locally for MacArthur's and Distillery and always retained a fondness for those formative years.

He played for Longford Town, Sligo Rovers and Glenavon before making the move to full-time football with Celtic, where he soon became a firm favourite, initially as a fearless player and later as coach, assistant manager and chief scout.

More than half of Celtic's European Cup winning team had been recruited by Fallon. Lisbon Lions such as Bertie Auld, Ronnie Simpson, Tommie Gemmill, John Craig, and Bobby Murdoch had all been unearthed and tutored by the Sligoman. Later, a new generation of Celtic greats, players of the calibre of David Hay, Danny McGrain, Lou Macari, Kenny Dalglish, Paul McStay and Packie Bonner came through the Fallon production line. Two players with lasting links to the history of Sligo Rovers, Willie McStay and the late Pat McCluskey, were others signed for Celtic by Fallon.

Honoured as a Freeman of his native Sligo in 2002, Fallon's last public act for his beloved Celtic was to unfurl the league winners' flag at Parkhead during the club's 125th anniversary season in 2012. He died a much-loved man in January 2013, survived by his wife, Myra, five daughters and a son.

His old pal Alex Ferguson summed him up perfectly in his eulogy at his funeral Mass in the Church of Christ the King, King's Park, Glasgow: "It's very difficult for people who are successful to remain humble. It's a touch of greatness. Seán always had that greatness."

***

Three other Sligomen have been capped at senior level by the Republic of Ireland:

John Joe Dykes: Represented Ireland at the 1924 Olympics, playing in a 1–0 win over Bulgaria and a 2–1 defeat to Holland. The team also beat Estonia in Paris after they were eliminated from the tournament, a game in which Dykes captained his country. Later that year, he played in a friendly game against the USA. In 1999, FIFA ruled that all Olympic Games football matches were to be regarded as full internationals. Therefore, Dykes is officially recognised as a full Irish international player. His domestic career included winning the FAI Cup with Athlone Town in 1924.

Paddy 'Monty' Monaghan: Played for the Irish Free State against Switzerland and Germany in 1935. He has the distinction of being the only player capped for Ireland while playing for Sligo Rovers. He won Leinster Senior

League, Metropolitan Cup and FAI Intermediate Cup medals with Rovers before they joined the League of Ireland. He was on the Rovers team which won the League of Ireland for the first time in 1937 and two years later played for Rovers alongside Dixie Dean in the club's first FAI Cup final, losing to Shelbourne after a replay. He played a total of 165 times for the Bit O'Red, scoring 57 goals in senior football.

Paul 'Ski' McGee: Profiled on pages 250–254.

Ciarán Kelly

Hidden trauma behind glorious triumph

To Sligo Rovers fans, and League of Ireland supporters generally, Ciarán Kelly's amazing feats in the FAI cup finals of 2010 and 2011, saving an aggregate of six penalty kicks, elevated him to the status of a modern-day superhero, blessed with powers beyond the reach of mere mortals. His name is indelibly etched in football folklore.

But behind the astonishing triumphs, played out in front of packed stands at the Aviva Stadium and a watching television audience of multiples of thousands, lurks the cataclysmic tale of a broken man, grappling in a dark pit of mental illness, searching for a way to make sense of a menacing cloud which had enveloped his heretofore seemingly perfect life.

Unknown to anyone beyond family and a close circle of friends, Ciarán Kelly spent several months between the Sligo Rovers' Cup finals of 2009 and 2010 in mental turmoil. His self-confidence shattered by events in the 2009 defeat to unfancied Sporting Fingal, he allowed an unwarranted burden of blame to infiltrate his then fragile mind, leading to long bouts of negative thoughts on a frightening and lonely journey.

At a time when mental health issues had not yet become a comfortable topic of discussion, he found it impossible to confide in his peers or to seek help or advice from football colleagues. Eventually, when the weight of his troubles became too onerous, he reached out for professional help.

By the time the 2010 Cup final rolled around, with the meeting of Sligo Rovers and Shamrock Rovers igniting a new lease of life for domestic football, nobody was more up for the fight than Ciarán Kelly. He had been given his chance in the team only because the number one choice goalkeeper, Richard

Brush, was sidelined with a wrist injury. It was time to exorcise some unwanted ghosts. He reveals:

> After the 2009 final I fell into a very bad place mentally. Only my family and a few close friends knew the situation. Because we were playing a team from a lower division, Sporting Fingal, in that final, we felt it was a huge opportunity to win the Cup, and I knew how much that meant to the club and its supporters. I had convinced myself it was going to be a glorious day.
>
> We were a goal up going into the final ten minutes and all set for a famous victory. Then I gave away a stupid penalty and conceded another goal in the last minute. In the blink of an eye, what appeared to be certain victory was snatched from us.
>
> I took a lot of that burden on my own shoulders. I couldn't get rid of this feeling of total regret. My self-confidence was shattered. I felt I'd let down the club, my colleagues and my family. I allowed that mentality to become a burden. Looking back now, from a position of full recovery, I realise how stupid that seems, but back then I couldn't get my head around it.
>
> It took me a long time to deal with it. Mental health was not something spoken about back then. I would never have spoken about it. I didn't fully understand what was happening. During those months, there were moments of real depression, negative thoughts, feeling the world was against me. I couldn't talk about it. I felt I would have been mocked or frowned upon. I thought if I'd tried to have that conversation with my peers I'd be told to cop on, to grow up or to man up. I didn't understand that it was ok not to be ok, as people say now. In those days, nobody talked about mental health or how to cope with it or deal with it.
>
> Thankfully, with professional help I got to understand it a lot better. It gave me the tools to use negatives and turn them into positives. So, I was much stronger as a person going into the 2010 final.

Kelly retains a photographic memory as well as a detailed analysis of events before, during and after the incredible penalty shoot-out which was to catapult him into headlines all over the world. His crystal-clear recall provides a fascinating insight into perhaps the most famous ten minutes in the history of Sligo Rovers.

> At the end of extra time, the game was still scoreless; everyone knew it was now down to the penalties. History in the making and all that. I left the pitch and went to the changing rooms, where I said a quick thank you to whoever, maybe God or deceased relatives, for this opportunity to make up for what happened the previous year. I didn't want to engage in conversation with the other players. I wanted to escape from that environment, just for a few minutes, to compose myself, to zone out, regain the focus I had at the start of the match.
>
> When I came back up the tunnel towards the pitch, Cookie, our manager, was heading in the opposite direction, charging out of the stadium to say his own prayers. He might have tried to say something to me as we passed, but I didn't want to engage with him. I wanted to remain calm, and I remember using breathing techniques to help me.
>
> Eoin Doyle scored first for us, and then Gary Twigg was first up for them. He was a very good goal-scorer, a clever player, but I knew he was tired. He'd just played 120 minutes at the end of a long, hard season, and I knew by his body shape he was feeling sluggish. Every player has a technique they revert to under pressure, something they would feel comfortable with. I knew what Twigg's comfort kick was, he would open his left foot up and try to steer the ball into the bottom corner. I dived low to my right-hand side and luckily that's where he went. Save number one.
>
> At this stage I wasn't watching our penalties at all. I didn't want to become emotionally involved. I needed just to concentrate on my own job. Next up for Shamrock Rovers was Pat Flynn, I think maybe he had come on as a sub. I could tell he wasn't confident. He was easy enough to read. I went to my left this time, and it was as if he'd passed the ball to me. I managed to scramble it away.
>
> Their next one was interesting. As soon as I saw Chris Turner stepping forward, I remembered he'd scored a penalty against me the previous year while playing for Dundalk at Oriel Park. I had gone early to my right and he'd drilled the ball straight down the middle into the roof of the net. So, I decided I would stand as long as I could in the middle of the goal,

> and sure enough that's where he aimed with a really hard shot. I almost lost my balance, but managed just to stretch upwards and shove the ball away.
>
> By the time their fourth penalty came up, Gary McCabe had scored our second. Now I realised if I could save this one, we would win the Cup. I was very confident by now. I was so certain, in fact, that I was already thinking about how we would celebrate. I hope that doesn't sound arrogant, but that's how clear my thoughts were. I had my mind made up that Paddy Kavanagh was going to my left-hand side, and I actually dived so early I think I might have been on the ground when the ball hit me.
>
> The relief was extraordinary. I wasn't thinking I'd done anything spectacular. It was just this feeling of "wow, we've won the Cup". I was really conscious of how much that would mean to the people of Sligo. It wasn't until the media attention started building up over the next few days that I fully realised the magnitude of saving four penalties in a Cup final. It was really exciting and great for my family, particularly because they knew what I had gone through to get to this position.

But, of course, there was to be a dramatic sequel. Exactly twelve months later, Rovers and Shelbourne could not be separated in normal and extra time in the 2011 Cup final. Kelly had not started the game, as he was now the second-choice goalkeeper behind regular Brendan Clarke. But as the minutes ticked towards another penalty shoot-out, he was told to warm up, he'd be going on as substitute. Kelly recalls:

> I felt a bit sorry for Brendan. He'd had a great season and this wasn't nice for him, but there's not much sentiment when you're trying to win a Cup final. They were sending me on to win it, it was as clear-cut as that.
>
> I remember warming up on the sideline and Tony O'Donoghue from RTE asked me "is it happening again?" I went down a corridor in the stadium, started throwing a ball against a wall, just to get in that zone again.
>
> When I came back out for the penalties, I looked up at the big screen in the stadium and there I was, in full technicolour. Our fans erupted. I knew then this was for real.

Disappointed not to save Shelbourne's first penalty, the Mayo man realised there was still plenty of time. He saved the next penalty, and with Rovers notching all of theirs, the scene was set for an uncanny conclusion to the unfolding drama.

The man who had broken Kelly's heart by converting a crucial penalty for Sporting Fingal in the 2009 final – an event which triggered his mental health issues – was Collie James. Now, the same player was standing before him again, this time in the Shelbourne colours. Redemption beckoned.

> Collie had scored into the top corner against me in 2009, so as he was about to step up, I pointed to that same corner. I was trying to get inside his head, and he confessed afterwards that I had spooked him a bit and that he had changed his mind about where he was going to place it. That's always fatal for a penalty-taker. He went low to my right, and I got across to save it. Raff Cretaro scored our fourth penalty, and we'd won the Cup again. It was as if all the troubles and bad memories associated with 2009 had finally been put to bed.

Now based in Qatar with his Sligo-born wife, Orla McGowan, Kelly works as a technical director and coach with the Lusail Sports Club, a second-division team with a massive academy of talented young players. He used the Covid pandemic as a time of reflection and re-connection with some of his former Rovers' colleagues. He now allows himself, he says, a feeling of "immense pride" at what he achieved on those grey November days in the Aviva Stadium over ten years ago.

His contentment is palpable:

> I'm in a good place, physically and mentally. I'm enjoying life, I've come to terms with the bad things which happened me along the way, and I've learned to feel good about the many great things in my life.
>
> There will always be that special connection with Sligo Rovers. Here I am, 7,500 kilometres away and I'm as excited as if I was sitting in the Showgrounds. Hopefully, I'll be back in Sligo to live with our new family at some stage in the near future.

Paul McGee

Still buzzing after all these years

Paul McGee, arguably the greatest footballer Sligo has ever produced, works as a busy driving instructor in Galway. Most of his young students wouldn't have a clue that they're sitting beside a former Irish international, one of the League of Ireland's all-time top goal-scorers, a man who has played in all of the major European competitions. They wouldn't recognise him as 'Ski', as he's always been known in his native Sligo, or as 'Magoo', his dressing-room nickname amongst his colleagues in the English leagues. To them, he's just the friendly, smiling instructor who will do everything he can to help them succeed. That's his nature.

But a strange thing happened one day last summer. The father of a student who'd just passed his driving test sent McGee a photograph as a thank you. The image shows him taking a corner kick in a packed Showgrounds, probably captured late in his career during his last stint with Sligo Rovers.

"Scroll along towards the goalposts," the father instructed. "That young lad looking at you with such excitement is the man you've just helped pass his driving test. He was eight years old at the time."

Turns out the proud father is a native of Manorhamilton, who never missed a game at the Showgrounds in those halcyon days. He was Ski's biggest fan.

"I love that," McGee beams, and you can tell he means it. "Such a lovely thing. To still be remembered in that way."

There's a lot to remember. In his home in Barna, McGee keeps five massive boxes packed with treasured memorabilia – Ireland caps, League winners' medals from Rovers and Burnley, an FAI Cup medal, dozens of match programmes and photographs, and a collection of assorted shirts he's swapped with opponents, notably those worn by Diego Maradona and Argentinian World

Cup captain Daniel Paseralla. His entire career in five boxes. The past is always present.

Having wandered nomadically through fourteen different clubs – some of them more than once – taking in Ireland, England and the Netherlands, the perception is that McGee might have been a mercenary journeyman. He robustly insists this is not the case, although his preferred title for a book he hopes to write someday soon might hint otherwise: *Have Boots, Will Travel*. He contends:

> On paper, it looks like I was a bit of a wanderer, but the statistics aren't always correct, and even when they are, they don't tell the full story. There were times when clubs didn't honour contracts, or where they ran out of money and simply couldn't pay wages. I was a professional footballer, so I had to move to earn a living.
>
> On top of all that, it's always the case in football where certain managers won't like you, where you might not suit their style of play, where they want to move you on for reasons of their own. I experienced quite a bit of that unfortunately. The moves weren't always my decision.

In any event, it made for a varied, exciting and very fulfilling career for the player who, as a fourteen-year-old kid, cycled into the Showgrounds, boots slung across his shoulders, and demanded that the Rovers boss, Ken Turner, grant him an audience.

A year earlier, in common with the rest of Sligo's soccer-mad citizens, he'd been enthralled by Turner's team's march to the 1970 FAI Cup final, the club's first in 30 years.

"I remember all the excitement, going off to Dublin on the train for the final and the replays. My ambition was fired by that", he recalls.

Two of the prominent players in that Rovers' team, Johnny Brookes and Kevin Fallon, coached McGee's Summerhill College team, with whom he won two All-Ireland titles, and they urged him to contact Turner. Thus, he made his League of Ireland debut as a fifteen-year-old winger, and a legend was born.

Wanderlust soon manifested itself, however, as he drifted away to join English non-leaguers Kidderminster Harriers, prompting the editorial writer in the Rovers' match-day programme to conclude, perhaps harshly, that McGee had "folded his tent like an Arab in the night". It proved the forerunner to an often-fractious relationship between player and club, as McGee re-joined and departed on no fewer than six occasions throughout his career.

By far his most joyous spell with his hometown club came under Billy Sinclair between 1975 and 1977, when his scintillating displays and wonderous goals fired Rovers to their first League of Ireland title in 40 years. The campaign still holds a special place amongst his treasure trove of memories:

> Nothing meant more to me than winning the League with Rovers. Sinclair was one of the best managers I ever played for, thoroughly professional. He put together a young team and gave us the belief we could be successful. I had never trained as hard in my life. I loved every minute of it. I've always been a very proud Sligoman, so that year was truly special.

His magical form soon earned him a dream move to Queens Park Rangers, who had just finished second in the English First Division, the top tier in pre-Premier League days. Brimming with self-confidence, he was not in the least over-awed in the company of a star-studded team, playing at stadia he had dreamed of as a boy. After scoring a hat-trick for the reserve side during a week-long trial, he negotiated his own deal into the big time. Agents had not yet infiltrated the football world.

"The only agent I ever knew was James Bond," he quips. "I did all my own haggling with the directors, got myself a three-year contract at 350 quid a week plus bonuses. I was flying", he says.

Widespread fame came after a fairytale appearance on ITV's flagship soccer programme, *The Big Match*. The cameras were at Loftus Road to capture QPR against League leaders Ipswich Town. McGee came on as a sub to score a wonder goal, racing almost the entire length of the pitch, leaving bewildered defenders in his wake, before nonchalanty sliding the ball into the net. Legendary commentator Brian Moore was dumbfounded. "Goal of the season," he proclaimed, as McGee charmed him in an engaging after-match interview. The young Sligoman, who only months earlier had been doing an AnCO course in television repairs, was now a television star. As McGee confirms:

> That goal and the interview changed everything. The fans, newspapers, TV – all wanted to know me after that. I loved the attention, thrived on it. This was what I'd always wanted.

The illusion of grandeur was shattered two seasons later, however, with the arrival of one Tommy Docherty, former manager of Manchester United, as the new master at QPR. Legend has it that the two never saw eye-to-eye and that the player's departure was hastened by a bust-up.

McGee's version is totally different.

> I've heard all the nonsense, that I'd told Docherty to feck off and he threw me out. None of that is true. To this day, I don't understand why he didn't take to me, but the truth is he treated me badly. He practically ignored me at his first pre-season photo-call and then left me out of the first two games of a pre-season tour in Denmark. When I asked why, he promised me I'd play the next game. An hour before kick-off he named the team and I wasn't even on the bench. That's the way he was.

Ironically, after McGee had moved to Preston North End and enjoyed a great run of goal-scoring form, Docherty appeared again like an unwanted ghost, once more throwing the Sligoman's career into turmoil. McGee recalls:

> I knew as soon as he was appointed that it would mean trouble. I was banished to the reserves without explanation. The only option was to keep my head down, work hard and hope a move would materialise.

A move to Burnley proved fortuitous. In a young team containing emerging players such as Trevor Steven, Lee Dixon, Brian Laws and Mickey Phelan, all of whom would become full internationals, Burnley won the third division title with McGee as their top scorer.

"It was one of the happiest times of my career in England, a really good team, great fans, and a fantastic club. I got a League winners' medal at Burnley and Docherty got the sack at Preston. Sometimes things work out," McGee says, with just a hint of well-preserved satisfaction.

At international level, the Sligoman made sixteen appearances under Johnny Giles, alongside luminaries such as Liam Brady, Dave O'Leary, Frank Stapleton, Steve Heighway, Gerry Daly and Don Givens. The first Sligoman to earn a senior cap in more than 30 years and one of only four ever to pull on the green shirt, he earned a man-of-the-match nomination from no less than Kevin Keegan after a game against England at Lansdowne Road. The abrupt ending of his international career still rankles, however.

Although his club form was impressive, Giles' replacement as Ireland manager, Eoin Hand, was not convinced. He gave the striker a ten-minute run as substitute in his first game, but never selected him again. It hurt. McGee admits:

> I was down in the dumps for months. I was proud to play for my country, but it all ended without an explanation, without a handshake, a letter, nothing. I'd look at the Irish squads when they were announced, hoping to see my name, but it never happened. I don't know how I got through

> it. Luckily, the good times at Burnley cheered me up. The former Irish goalkeeper Alan Kelly Senior was a coach there and he looked after me. I honestly believe I had more years left as an international. I'd love to have had the chance to play in that famous Euro '88 team.

Although he'll never see 60 on a birthday card again, he resolutely dismisses any talk of ageing – "I don't believe in that concept" – and there are still glimpses of the old magic when he lines out every Tuesday night in the over-40s Galway Astro League. He's also a regular visitor to a golf club just minutes from his Barna home, where he plays off an impressive handicap of 11.

Happily reflecting on a 25-year career which included a successful season with Dutch club FC Haarlem, as well as spells at eight League of Ireland clubs, McGee doesn't tolerate any notion of wasted years, believing instead he made the most of his natural talents. He asserts:

> There were good days and bad. I think most footballers would say the same. Overall, though, I'm very happy with how it worked out. To win a League with your hometown club, to play for your country, score nearly 200 goals, play in all the major European competitions, it's a pretty good return. A few regrets along the way, maybe, but I'm still the smiling Irishman Brian Moore described. I'm still buzzing.

Under the inspirational management of Billy Sinclair, the Rovers squad who won the League of Ireland Championship for the first time in 40 years in 1977 included: Alan Paterson, Paul Fielding, Graham Fox, Tony Stenson, Chris Rutherford, Tony Fagan, Michael Betts, Mick Leonard, Gary Hulmes, Paul McGee, Padraig McManus, Shane Walker, Ernie Bailey, Charlie Ferry, Andy Stewart, David Pugh, Gerry Harrigan, Michael Angelotti, Art Roderick.

Willie McStay

Once, twice, three times a winner

It was the football equivalent of the old bus story. You wait ages for one to come along and then three arrive together. At the start of the 1993–1994 season, Sligo Rovers had just been relegated to the League of Ireland First Division, hadn't been within a sniff of silverware for eleven bleak years, and were teetering precariously on the brink of what had become a perennial struggle for survival.

In the most unlikely transformation in the club's long history of fairytale resuscitations, they finished the season with three major trophies: the League of Ireland Shield, First Division Championship and FAI Cup. As rags to riches stories go, the astounding metamorphosis has had few equals.

Willie McStay, whose family is steeped in the glorious history of Glasgow Celtic, had won Scottish League and Cup medals with the Scottish giants, and he had captained his country at schoolboy level. But he was no stranger to Sligo. He'd been signed for Celtic by Seán Fallon, a Sligo native who'd carved legendary status in the East End of Glasgow. He had visited the county in 1989 with his old pal, Ireland's legendary goalkeeper Packie Bonner, for the opening of the Brother Walfrid Community Park in Ballymote. Brother Walfrid Kerins was the Sligo-born Marist Brother who had founded Celtic in 1888. And, best of all as it turned out, he had married Mary Brady, whose mother hailed from Carney in north Sligo, and who had numerous family members still living there.

It was as if the stars suddenly aligned on the day Willie McStay, then nearing the end of his playing career with Kilmarnock, was told representatives from Sligo Rovers had been making enquiries about his availability.

His first phone call was to his old mentor, Seán Fallon. As McStay recalls:

> I knew Seán had a great affinity with Sligo, and would have a feel for the football community there. His words of advice always remained with me. He told me, "your football knowledge will carry you, but you will have to work hard every day and be one of the people, become part of their community", and that's what I strived to do from day one.

The team was already doomed to relegation when he took over, but influenced by the positivity and ambition of the management committee, he began formulating a plan to transform the fortunes of the club:

> The first big decision was to go full-time and have the team based in the town. When I arrived, we had lads from Dublin who I would see only on match days. I once went to a training session in Dublin, only to find some of them hadn't even turned up. So, that had to change.

Recruitment was crucial. Using contacts he had built up in the Scottish game, and with the help of an old friend, football scout Gerry Cassidy, talented young professionals from across the UK were drafted in. Soon, promising youngsters like David Reid, Eddie Annand, Mark McLean, Pádraig Moran, Will Hastie, Gerry Kelly, and Declan Boyle were teaming up with locals Gavin Dykes, Johnny Kenny, Martin McDonnell and Ian Lynch and others to form the nucleus of an exciting new squad. The old ad-hoc arrangement of veteran part-time footballers merely fulfilling a contractual obligation was replaced by a dynamic set of young players with a ravenous appetite for success.

But any exaggerated notions any of them might have had about hitting the big time were soon dispelled by an unusual intrusion on the Showgrounds playing surface.

McStay takes up the story:

> I was sitting in my little prefab office in a small corner of the ground one day when the door burst open and there was my wife, Mary, in a state of panic. "Willie", she yells, "come quick, a load of sheep has broken on to the pitch. They'll destroy it." Actually, I knew the sheep were grazing there, because we'd been told they were better than any lawnmower at keeping the grass down, and that their droppings would nourish the roots. I was told we'd have the best pitch in Ireland. So, very often, when the players arrived for training they would have to negotiate their way around a field of sheep. That's the sort of stuff we had to put up with in the early days.

But when it came to steady progress, nobody was pulling the wool over McStay's eyes. For his first game in charge during the relegation year, the 'gate' receipts amounted to a paltry IR£500. The crippling lack of finance was a daily worry, and he realised they needed to increase attendances. Although results had improved, the soccer public had yet to be convinced. Working in tandem with an ambitious committee led by Kevin Dykes, Ray Gallagher, Kevin Colreavey and Mary McGowan, they managed to complete the installation of floodlights at the Showgrounds. As McStay recounts:

> It was literally as if someone had flicked a switch. We were able to change our games from Sunday afternoon to Saturday night. Suddenly, the Showgrounds was the place to be, there was a bit of magic about. Every game was now a big game. The whole town benefitted, because people were coming to our games then heading off for a few pints or a meal in local pubs and restaurants. The team became the centre of a huge lift-off. It was amazing.

It was the classic case of 'build it and they will come', as curious fans flocked from every corner of the county to sample this new phenomenon of floodlit football. It helped that the team suddenly started winning. The first floodlit game, on 26 November 1993, resulted in a celebratory 4–1 win against Home Farm, and Rovers would remain unbeaten at the Showgrounds for the rest of the season. They had clinched promotion back to the top tier by the following March and the first division title itself ten days later. By that stage, they'd already won the League of Ireland Shield, beating Waterford in a two-legged final.

And so, it was on to the final of the FAI Cup on 15 May 1994. This was a competition which had long been an obsession for Sligo soccer supporters, but which had only ever been won once before, in 1983. With the team back in the final for the first time in eleven years, against highly fancied Derry City, and bidding for an unprecedented treble of trophies, the entire county was engulfed in an unexpected football frenzy.

A three-week delay in staging the game, as authorities awaited the availability of the old Lansdowne Road, proved an awkward distraction, but McStay made good use of the time. He reports:

> We took the lads away to the National Training Centre in Scotland for a few days, fantastic facilities, brilliant playing surfaces. We had gelled well as a group by then, but this was an important bonding exercise aimed specifically at preparing for the final. We went to a Celtic match, just to

> give the boys a taste of a big crowd in a big stadium. We left no stone unturned.

As it happened, one of the drills they had perfected during those days of intense preparation proved decisive on the big day. McStay explains:

> We'd put a lot of work into set-pieces. We knew, for example, that from corner-kicks, the likes of Declan O'Boyle and Gavin Dykes would be tightly marked, so we devised a way in which they would distract opposing players and Gerry Carr would sneak free to the near post. That's exactly what happened for our winning goal, with Gerry just getting enough of a glance on a corner to guide the ball into the net.

A rapturous homecoming awaited the treble heroes as they made their way back to Sligo the following evening, the scale of which took the manager and his players by surprise. McStay declares:

> We expected a big turn out because we knew what it meant to our supporters and the county generally. But nothing could have prepared us for the massive crowds and the deafening noise and singing and dancing everywhere we went. I particularly remember bonfires blazing in Riverstown, the home of our winger, Johnny Kenny. I thought we'd never get out of there. Then, at the town hall, there was just a massive sea of red and white. It was truly amazing.
>
> Listen, I've won Scottish leagues and cups, but you don't get that type of community outpouring in Glasgow because the city is divided in a football sense, and there would never be such a united celebration. So, for all I'd achieved at a higher level, this was totally new to me. I was blown away by it.

Flushed with such unprecedent success, McStay had already begun planning for the new season, Rovers first back in the top division, when an unexpected phone call changed the course of his life. McStay admits:

> Out of the blue, then Celtic manager, the late Tommy Burns, phoned me up and offered me a job as Celtic youth coach. He'd been over at the Cup final and said he was really impressed with how I'd developed a successful young team. That's what they were looking for. It was a very

> difficult decision, but it was very hard to say no to a club of that size and a club that had been in my blood from the day I was born.

Unknown to anyone outside his family, there was another poignant dimension to his decision. Mary's sister, Bernie, was extremely ill with cancer at home in Glasgow. Away from the public perception of a happy couple enjoying lavish sporting success, Willie and Mary had been quietly visiting the Marian Shrine at Knock, praying for Bernie's recovery. Now, Mary knew her beloved sister had not long to live and she wanted to be with her. McStay explains:

> Maybe, there was the sense we'd never forgive ourselves if we hadn't been there for Bernie's final months. Mary had given up a lot to come over to Sligo with me and to bring our two young boys away from their familiar environment. Now, she wanted to go home to be with her sister. The opportunity presented by the Celtic job allowed us to do so. That was never part of any public explanation, but privately it was a big factor for us as a family.

Bernie Brady passed away on New Year's Day 1995.

In the notoriously fickle world of professional football, so many managers and players have come and gone from Sligo Rovers over the generations. Some leave their mark; others disappear never to be heard of again. Because of the unrivalled success he brought to the club and his deep personal relationship with the county, Willie McStay is destined to always be an important part of the Rovers story, and it's a two-way street. He confirms:

> I can vividly recall almost every single day I spent at Sligo, naturally the good ones, but also a few difficult times. Those memories will stay with me for life – the great friendships we made, the players we helped develop, the fun we had, the trophies, the likes of Chris Rutherford and Tony Fagan coming on board with all their experience to help the young lads along, Francie Middleton's little bus and big trumpet. I could go on forever.
>
> I've played for one of the biggest clubs in Europe, I've scored against Rangers, which for a Celtic boy is a really big deal, I've managed clubs in Europe, I've unearthed a few future stars. I've done a lot in my career which I'm proud of. But looking back, I can honestly say, above all of that, Sligo really was a bit special. It always will be.

Under McStay's guidance both as player and manager, the historic treble-winning squad included Mark McLean, Declan Boyle, Johnny Kenny, Gavin Dykes, Eddie Annand, Gerry Carr, Will Hastie, Martin McDonnell, David Reid, Gerry Kelly, Pádraig Moran, Ian Lynch, Ger Houlahan, Riccardo Gabbiadini, Pierce Devaney, Trevor Scanlon, Ray Rooney, Tony Blake.

David Pugh

Snapshot of a glorious career

Who's that guy with David Pugh? It's a 58-year-old photograph, one of those monochrome shots which has the ability to speak a thousand words. A moment in time. Two footballers glued to each other and to their task. One is a strong, fair-haired Sligoman; the other is the unmistakable figure of the best footballer on the planet. But, in the vein of mock admiration patented by Sligonians, those who see it still ignore the familiar poise of Edson Arantes do Nascimento and ask instead: who's the guy with Pughie? It's funny, but like a lot of comedy, it hits the spot. In Sligo, David Pugh stands taller than Pelé.

It is perhaps one of the most iconic photographs of any Sligo sports star, but typical of a man whose genius is matched only by a complete lack of ego, Pugh has no idea where it is.

"It's probably around the house somewhere," he reports dismissively. "Maybe one of my daughters has it." Maybe it's as well he missed out on swapping jerseys with the Brazilian legend. The world's most famous number ten shirt would more than likely be discarded in the pit of a long-forgotten laundry basket.

That's the thing about Pugh – nobody takes his massive achievements less seriously than himself. A modesty fuelled by adolescent shyness colours his outlook, but he's never been anybody's fool either. As a young man, he nonchalantly dismissed tantalising offers of a professional career with both Chelsea and Celtic because "it wasn't for me", and he fell out with a Sligo Rovers manager who had the audacity to question his professional integrity.

If Pugh is a mass of contradictions, the one constant is his unequalled brilliance across a vast range of sports.

Before Sligo Rovers acquired the palatable habit of regularly winning FAI Cups, he was one of the few locals to pocket a coveted winners' medal. When the GAA finally kicked to touch their infamous ban on 'foreign' sports, he was among the first soccer players in the country to play in a provincial football final. He captained an Irish under-23 international team where most of the players were cross-channel professionals. He drove a lightning-fast car at breakneck speeds at motor rallies all over the country. He played in three West of Ireland golf championships off an eye-watering three handicap. He won a Sigerson Cup and played basketball for Ireland.

His love of sport manifested early and he was always a dual player: "We weren't allowed play soccer in school, so it was Gaelic football in St John's and soccer in the nun's field", he recalls.

Later in life, those fields of dreams would become the Showgrounds and Croke Park and countless other sports arenas, but the odd thing about a lad with such awesome ability was that his natural gifts were never matched by extravagant ambition. On the pitch, he was an unbeatable goliath, but outside the sidelines there reigned a shy and introverted youngster.

He vividly recalls "shaking like a leaf" in his early days in the Rovers dressing rooms. On one occasion the club's wily trainer, James Tiernan, offered him a plastic bag into which he could spill his nerves and told him he'd be ok once the game started. He was right. The young centre-half had a blinder.

Perhaps it was that inherent shyness which influenced his decision not to join Celtic as a teenager and, some years later, to reject Chelsea's advances. But there are no regrets.

The Celtic offer came after a month-long trial arranged by Seán Fallon when Pugh was a fourth-year student at Summerhill College. Chelsea's approach came following a successful season with Boston Beacons in 1968.

> At Celtic, I was just a kid. I looked around at the great players they had, people like Billy McNeill and Paddy Crerand, and I decided I didn't belong there. I asked myself "what am I doing here?" They asked me to sign and without hesitation I said no. Looking back, it was probably a lack of self-belief.
>
> With Chelsea, it was a more mature decision. I was a grown man with plenty of experience behind me. It was at the end of the season with Boston Beacons, and the manager, Jack Mansell, told me he could lift the phone and have me at Chelsea in the morning. I told him "I don't think so." He was flabbergasted, but it just wasn't for me. I didn't want that lifestyle.

Instead, his Boston roommate, Paddy Mulligan, signed for Chelsea and enjoyed a prolonged career in the English First Division and with Ireland.

All Pugh ever wanted was to play for Sligo Rovers. His uncle Ray Foley had brought him to the Showgrounds every Sunday and soon he was caught up in the frenzy which envelopes almost every Sligo town child who ever kicked a ball. As a teenager, he played for Collegians in the junior league and was good enough to win an Irish cap. It was only a matter of time before the senior club came calling, but it was an inauspicious start.

Rovers had just returned to senior football in 1963 after a year's absence and their 'new' team was a mixture of Dublin-based veterans and untried locals, but the Sligo lads were very often at the back of the queue when it came to selection. Pugh recalls:

> I was all set for my debut, togged out in the dressing room, nervous but excited. My dad, uncles, brothers all there to see me play for Rovers, a big day for the family. Then, shortly before kick-off, the manager arrives in with a few Dublin lads off the train. "You won't be needed today", he tells me. I was absolutely devastated, heartbroken, but that's the way it was in those days. Locals would get one game and never be heard of again once there were enough Dubs to fill the shirts. I was determined from very early on that it wouldn't happen to me, and once I got my chance, I made sure they couldn't shift me.

Regularly picked for inter-league teams in the following years, his stock rose significantly when he was selected to captain a star-studded under-23 international team against France at Dalymount Park in 1966.

However, Pugh's Rovers' career suffered an unsavoury interruption the following year when Tony Bartley, an English journeyman player, was recruited as the club's first full-time professional manager. Before long, the pair fell out and Pugh was on his way to Shamrock Rovers.

"He accused me of not trying hard enough, which was the ultimate insult. I'd given years of everything I had to the club, and for anyone to suggest otherwise was something I couldn't tolerate", is how Pugh recalls the tumultuous events.

He joined a Shamrock Rovers team laden with talent, and he slotted in comfortably alongside some of the greatest players ever to grace the League under the expert management of the legendary Liam Tuohy. A memorable season with the Hoops was capped by the club's record-breaking sixth successive FAI Cup victory, with Pugh becoming only the second Sligoman ever to win a cup medal.

The following season he was back with his hometown club and back in an FAI Cup final, as Rovers reached the decider for the first time in 30 years. A three-game marathon was eventually won by Bohemians. In the second replay, following a collision with fellow defender Kevin Fallon, Pugh finished the game concussed and confused. It would be two hours after the game before he realised the result.

> Apparently, I was walking the wrong way off the pitch and somebody had to get me by the arm and lead me in the right direction. I was totally out of it, and it was about two hours before I came around. I remember a doctor asking how I'd been allowed to stay on the pitch. All I wanted to know was the score. I couldn't believe it when I heard we'd lost.

One of the better days, however, was when he got the chance to share a field with the fabulous Pelé, winner of three World Cup medals and acknowledged as the best player in the world. Pugh was midway through a one-year contract with Boston Beacons, when they faced Pelé's club, Santos, in an exhibition game. It still feels slightly surreal:

> I was casually told "you pick up Pelé", and I thought "yeah, no problem." Just to be on the same pitch was such a thrill. All of the Santos players were Brazilian internationals, fabulous players. I would have paid in to see them and here I was on the same pitch, trying to keep Pelé quiet. I actually won a few headers from him, but even to get close to him was hard enough.
>
> The one regret is that I didn't get his shirt. Our manager ran on after the match and grabbed it. I've never forgiven him for that.

When the GAA voted to abolish the ban on foreign games – ironically Sligo was one of only two counties who objected – another intriguing chapter opened up for Pugh. A talented if under-utilised Gaelic footballer, he had won a Sigerson Cup with St Joseph's College, Belfast, where he was doing his PE teacher training, scoring a spectacular goal in the final at Croke Park. Sligo manager Brendan McCauley invited Pugh and his Rovers pal Gerry Mitchell to join the county panel in 1971. They reached the Connacht final, losing out to Galway after a replay, in which Pugh scored a goal with a bullet-like shot from a 14-yard free.

"It was unusual being the first soccer players to play Gaelic football after the removal of the ban, but I loved it," he confirms. "We were unlucky not to win Connacht. To get an opportunity to play alongside fellas like Mickey Kearins and Barnes Murphy was a great experience."

He continued to play Gaelic football, even when himself and Mitchell took over as Rovers joint managers in 1972. He managed the team again in 1988 and was assistant to Jim McInally for a short spell eleven years later.

His more tangible success as a coach came during his 28 years as a PE teacher at Summerhill College, where his teams won eighteen Connacht titles and five All-Irelands. More than a dozen of his protégés went on to play in the League of Ireland and further afield.

As he reflects on an amazing sporting life well lived, Pugh has only one lingering regret.

> I've been very lucky. As a young child, I could never have imagined I'd get to do so much in so many different sports, and I'm thankful for all of that. But, if I could change one thing, it would be to have won something with Sligo Rovers. That would have been the pinnacle.

Even now, he hasn't grasped the reality; he will always be regarded as a winner, the ultimate Sligo sports star.

Rovers' European Odyssey 2022

"You can smell the football in this town"

"You can smell the football in this town." It takes a Dutch referee to articulate it, to find the words which are unreachable for the thousands of us caught up in this perfect storm of love of place and ancient belonging to a beguiling soccer tradition. We've grown up with mythical tales of 'big European nights' at football temples like Old Trafford or San Siro or the Bernabéu, but now we have our own, and not just for one token, random occasion, but through a historic consistency of three proper rounds of the Europa Conference League. We've gone toe-to-toe with the big and not-so-big, we've been the architects of, and almost victims of, seismic shocks. The rickety old Showgrounds is throbbing, the town is heaving with rare excitement, the Red Army is on a dreamlike odyssey, the team, moderate in several of its domestic performances, is magically transformed into a cohesive European force, capable of toppling those who would normally be considered well beyond our reach.

At a time when the world is gripped by a series of crippling crises, the effects of which invade Sligo families with the same devastating fall-out as anywhere else, Sligo Rovers are the unlikely bearers of an exhilarating antidote. The capacity of sport to rise above both the mundane and the monstrous, to provide feel-good distraction, is everywhere to be seen – from the lived-in faces of veteran supporters who thought they had seen it all to the giddy excitement of exuberant youngsters who, no matter how often their future lives will bring them here, might never experience the likes of it again.

The unique connection between the club and its public has always been palpable. Because the supporters do the heavy-lifting in the grim days – and there have been a multitude – their raucously joyful celebration of the genuinely glorious occasions is borne of real depth, endowed with near religious fervour. It is neither faked nor manufactured, because Sligo Rovers is a community-owned club, and that means literally owning the bad days and, like any shareholders in a successful company, extravagantly embracing the good ones.

And so, during one of the most breath-taking vignettes in the club's history, rich in high drama and manifested in unprecedented demand for match tickets, Sligo Rovers is both big news and good news. "Na, na, na, na, hey, hey, Sligo Rovers."

For three sun-splashed nights at the Showgrounds in what became a summer soccer festival, generations of Rovers' supporters, from the very young to elderly pensioners, gathered in tribal celebration of their magnificent team. Lifetime memories were forged in historic victories over Bala Town, Motherwell and Viking. The fact that the Norwegians knocked us out on an aggregate score of 5–2 was but a slight dent in the general euphoria gripping the town and county.

If the home support – a combined attendance of more than 12,000 over the three scintillating games – served as a reminder of the team's exalted place in the community at large, the significant numbers who travelled to the away games illustrated the unparalleled loyalty which has kept the club afloat during good times and bad.

The march of the club's 'Red Army' through European football was mobilised with military-like precision, their artillery comprised only of scarves and replica jerseys and unquenchable good humour. The friendliest invasion ever of the UK was launched over three glorious weeks in July 2022.

From Wrexham to Motherwell and on to the Norwegian city of Stavanger – and a host of welcoming towns in between – Sligo Rovers' legion of devoted pilgrims blazed a novel trail of carefree abandon, following their team with pride and passion on a football odyssey which confirmed the Bit O'Red faithful as the greatest supporters in Irish soccer.

They travelled by boat, by air, by train. Two hardy fans even cycled from Sligo to Wales. They set up camp in Wrexham, Liverpool, Glasgow, Edinburgh, Oswestry on the English/Wales border, and Motherwell. For the third round, an intrepid crew made their way through various circuitous routes to Norway, for many a third expensive trip in less than a month. Undaunted by a crash-bang-wallop back-to-earth result, they stood by their team.

Throughout the European excursions, Rovers' fans partied enthusiastically, day and night. They sang, danced, laughed and cried. They spent a fortune – so much it would be impossible to calculate, according to one hardened supporter. But the economics of the experience were irrelevant. How do you put a price on overwhelming joy?

Everywhere they went, they left behind a wonderful impression. Locals were enchanted by their exemplary behaviour.

"We brought a different culture", says Shane McGoldrick, a member of the Bit O'Red Supporters' Trust (BORST) who organised some of the travel arrangements for the trips to Wales and Scotland.

> Football fans generally have a bad reputation. A lot of towns hate to see them coming. But everybody loved us. We were there to have a good time, to support our team, but we were also determined to do Sligo proud. We wanted to create a good impression, respect our hosts, to represent our club and town in the best way possible.

When the draw for the first round pitted Rovers against Welsh side Bala Town, with the first leg played in the market town of Oswestry in Shropshire, close to the Welsh border, Gary McLean of the Sligo Rovers' Dublin Supporters' Club began work on a painstaking plan to ensure the Rovers family could come together as one 'army of fans' for the big game.

Together with RTE journalist and die-hard Rovers' fan Rory Houston, they sought out bus companies and pubs in Wrexham which could accommodate their requirements. Many of the 500 supporters were based in Wrexham so the first priority was to establish a base in the city.

> We made numerous calls to bus operators and eventually nailed down an arrangement with one company to ferry our fans from Wrexham to Oswestry for the game. Rory worked on the social side of things and set us up in the Hill Street Social venue in Wrexham.
>
> Thankfully, everything worked out perfectly. We even managed to get a third bus organised for the night of the match. Our fans took over the Hill Street Social and enjoyed a couple of great nights there. The staff looked after us brilliantly and we converted them to the Bit O'Red. It was like Christmas for them. They made a fortune.

Rovers' fans even persuaded legendary social media sensation 'Bootlegger' to join in the fun in Wrexham. He has over 330,000 followers on Twitter and when word got out that he was ripping it up with the Irish supporters, crowds of locals flocked to the venue.

The scenes in Wrexham were replicated at Fitzgerald's pub in Liverpool, where many of the fans who travelled with the BORST group were billeted. Gerry O'Connor and Conor Lynch organised travel arrangements from Liverpool to Oswestry for the game. The battalions joined forces at the quaint stadium hours before kick-off. "The atmosphere was incredible," reports Gary McLean. "I've followed Rovers all over Ireland and Europe and I don't think I've ever seen anything like it. Our fans were in full voice from start to finish. The place was hopping."

Bala proved stubborn opposition, though. It eventually required a nerve-shattering penalty shoot-out at a packed Showgrounds to set up a second-round meeting with Scottish Premier League team Motherwell.

And, so, with sweet memories and new friendships established from the occupation of North Wales, the 'Red Army' next swept north to Scotland. Once more the Dublin Supporters' Club and BORST spearheaded the travel, accommodation and social arrangements. Most of the fans settled in Glasgow for the clash with Motherwell. Grace's famous pub, renowned as a favourite hostelry for Celtic supporters, became the HQ.

Gary McLean organised three buses to take fans from Glasgow to Fir Park stadium. Everybody was full of excitement and expectation on the way to the ground. The return journey was chaotically jubilant after Rovers' thrilling 1–0 victory.

"There seemed to be twice as many people on the buses on the way home," reports McLean.

> Everybody wanted to get back to Glasgow as quickly as possible so that the party could begin in earnest. Beating a team from the SPL in their own backyard was the stuff of dreams. We knew we were witnessing history in the making.

Shane McGoldrick has supported Rovers for more than thirty years. The trip to Scotland, culminating in that spellbinding victory over Motherwell, was one of the greatest experiences ever, he maintains.

"It embodied what Rovers are all about," he declares. "We had the time of our lives, defied the odds and got an incredible result, and most of all we did Sligo proud on and off the pitch. It doesn't get much better than that."

It did get better, though. On what many considered to be the greatest ever night in the Showgrounds, Rovers recorded a famous 2–0 second-leg victory, sending them into the third round of European competition for the first time.

About 100 hardy souls made the trek to Norway, where not even the setback of a 5–1 defeat and a number of cancelled return flights could dampen their enthusiasm. They returned with golden memories and new friendships, as had been the case on all of their travels.

The excitement, of course, was not confined to the supporters. Those who fashioned those memorable occasions were also caught up in the infectious passion of it all.

"Magic, wasn't it." John Russell, eight weeks into his first managerial job, is a serious student of the game, not given to hyperbole. But it's less than 24 hours since his side dumped Scottish Premier Division side Motherwell, out of Europe in front of a sold-out Showgrounds. He's entitled to his moment of disequilibrium. Anyway, his use of the word 'magic' is a perfect summation of Rovers' unprecedented European achievement.

A former FAI Regional Development Officer for Sligo, and a veteran of Rovers' glory years during which he won two FAI Cups, the League Cup and the Setanta Cup (he's also won the League title with St Patrick's Athletic), Russell served his managerial apprenticeship as assistant to Liam Buckley for 18 months before replacing the Dubliner in the top job in June 2022. As a rookie manager, the European success has provided a window into his philosophy, his self-belief and his vision for the future of the team.

The European journey 2002 is just the beginning as far as the Galway native is concerned. "Even as a player, I relished European football. It was always a big thing for me, testing myself against so-called better opposition, seeing how far we could go," he explains.

> It's exactly the same as a manager. Motherwell was a big step up for us, but that's how you progress as a team, step by step. You build confidence and belief by beating these teams and it gives everybody a lift. The big crowds, the excitement – it shows the players what this club means and they buy into it and feed off it.
>
> In my interview for the manager's job, I told the committee I wanted to dream big. This club needs to be ambitious. In Europe, we've taken that first step. I want to build on it. I want us to strive not just to qualify for Europe but, in time, to be capable of reaching the group stages. I want the fans to go away happy from the Showgrounds, to want to come back. There's a real football buzz in Sligo, and it was great to be part of creating a bit of history in Europe. It was something special for all of us. But it has to be the beginning and not the end. There's huge potential here.

For ambitious club chairman Tommie Higgins, the €850,000 financial windfall will help further his dream of building a new stadium and academy, but the former CEO and founder of Ticketmaster Ireland knows there is no panacea for the unrelenting cash demands of a community-owned professional club.

"We can't afford to get carried away," he emphasises.

> Of course, the financial injection from Europe is a terrific boost, but there are plenty of holes for it. Bonuses and travel expenses will take a large slice, and there's huge expense involved in running eight teams. We have to maintain our various fund-raisers to make sure there's always enough in the kitty to fund our ambition, both on and off the pitch.

Higgins and his committee colleagues who travelled to the various European matches did so at their own expense, underlining the voluntary nature of their involvement.

"We are merely the custodians of a proud tradition. We're in it only for the love of the club," says the man who's been going to the Showgrounds, as man and boy, for an astonishing 69 years.

As a successful businessman, he sees the bigger picture – the club's place in the evolving prominence of Sligo as a sports tourism destination and the potential for the Showgrounds to become a magnet for family entertainment.

> For our European games, all the local hotels were full. The bars and restaurants were packed. Everybody benefitted. That's exactly the model we want to build, where the club becomes an integral part of the community. We want the Showgrounds to be a place where families come for a good night out, where visitors are made feel welcome, where everybody feels part of the excitement. The experience in Europe shows how it can be done.

The enchanting adventure ended with heavy defeat to a much better equipped Norwegian side, the quaintly named Viking FK, modern-day plunderers of our hopes and dreams. But, with the Showgrounds once again packed to the rafters and in typically celebratory mood for a second-leg 1–0 victory, nobody got too down-hearted, relishing instead the history-making nature of the journey and the treasure trove of memories it evoked.

Dutch referee Jochem Kamphuis has been to many of the football strongholds of Europe, both for club and international assignments. On his visit to Sligo to take charge of Rovers' first-round Europa Conference League tie with Bala Town, he was bowled over both by the town and the club, mesmerised by the football umbilical cord which unites both.

He summed it up in his immortal observation to a local official: "you can smell the football in this town." Never a truer word spoken.

Soccer (Youth)

Barry Cogan

Close encounters with Keano in FA Cup final

It's the seventy-seventh minute of the FA Cup final. The game is meandering to its predictable conclusion as Manchester United canter to their eleventh triumph, against rank outsiders Millwall. But Roy Keane is not for resting. He scuttles to contest a throw-in near the halfway line when he feels the menacing presence of an opponent's hand attempting to curtail his movement. Nonchalantly warding off the unwanted attention, he turns and directs his infamous withering stare directly into the gaze of his crestfallen adversary. The recipient is teenager Barry Cogan.

Cogan is the only Sligo footballer ever to play in an FA Cup final. Apart from his prized runners-up medal and John O'Shea's shirt, that brief encounter with his boyhood idol is his abiding memory.

Most parts of the biggest game of his life are but a blur these days, but the Riverstown native retains a few precious nuggets from that momentous day, 22 May 2004. At 19 years old, he had played less than a handful of games for Millwall in the English Championship that season and hadn't featured at all in their fairytale march to the Cup final. Yet here he was, less than two years a professional player, on the team bus to Cardiff's Millennium Stadium to face the mighty Manchester United on one of the world's most famous football occasions.

Millwall's first ever FA Cup final appearance was watched by a crowd of more than 70,000, among them 30 of Barry's family, relatives and friends who had made the trip from Sligo in the hope of watching history being made.

The mid-table championship club had the former Chelsea and England player Dennis Wise as player–manager, and he had taken a shine to the Sligo youngster, regularly including him in match squads and giving him the occasional start. With his Cup final squad depleted by injuries, Wise was relying heavily on his younger players, so Cogan was quietly confident he'd be there on the big day.

> I didn't sleep a wink the night before. I'd grown up watching the Cup final on telly – the big build-up and all that – and here I was being part of it. It just seemed a bit unreal. Hundreds of Millwall fans had gathered around the hotel and I could hear their excitement outside. There was no chance of getting any sleep.

He was quite relaxed about the game itself, though:

> As a young lad, not much would have been expected of me. Some players had played maybe 400 games for the club and never got near a Cup final, and outside our club some of the best players ever to play the game had never been to a Cup final. So, all I really wanted to do was get on the pitch and enjoy it.

His chance came in the seventy-fourth minute when he replaced injured fellow Irishman Robbie Ryan. United were already two goals to the good and cruising. Young Cogan felt he had nothing to lose.

The nod came from Millwall's coach, Ray 'Butch' Wilkins, who'd played in World Cups for England and FA Cup finals for Manchester United. This was familiar territory for him, but for the young lad to whom he'd just motioned, it was the making of history.

As he warmed up on the sideline, stretching nervous limbs, he was suddenly aware of the thunderous noise still engulfing the giant stadium. Butterflies somersaulted in his tight tummy. He allowed himself a brief glimpse into the ocean of faces encircling the arena, like a scene from a Lowry painting. He knew his parents would be among them, their hearts beating even faster than his own. One step across that white line, not only into a game of football, but into an indelible page of immortality – the history of a football club, his county, his parish, his family. Seldom would less than 20 minutes of football mean so much.

"I couldn't wait to get on. It was late in the game so it was just a matter of trying to get a few touches, see if I could influence things somehow," he recalls.

> I remember Roy Keane, though. Who wouldn't? I'd been a United fan since childhood and being Irish, I adored Keane. Here I was rubbing

> shoulders with him in the biggest game in the world. I wasn't long on when we got a throw-in and he challenged for it. I got as close as I could, reached my hand towards his groin area, just to try to prevent him getting control of the ball. Of course, he took it easily, shrugged me off almost, and then turned and killed me with that famous stare. I swear I nearly melted, but I think I smiled back. That bit stands out. I remember going to him after the game, you know, shaking hands and all that stuff. I said something like "hey Keano", and he just smiled at me. He was going up to collect the Cup, and here's this scrawny little Irish kid greeting him like a long-lost pal. I think he was amused by it.

Irish international John O'Shea, who'd been marking Cogan during his time on the field, was a bit more receptive, willingly handing over his shirt, now a treasured souvenir.

With players like Keane, Ronaldo, Scholes and Giggs, United added a third goal near the end, playing to script and leaving Millwall to return to the relatively obscurity from which they'd surprisingly emerged. But there was one last sniff of the big time.

Because United had already qualified for the Champions League, it meant Millwall would feature in the 2004/05 UEFA Cup. Cogan played in both legs against Hungarian side Ferencváros, drawing the first game 1–1 and losing the second 3–1.

Such exalted experiences while still a teenager could have been the springboard to a dazzling career. Instead, Cogan was destined to become something of a footballing gypsy, fleeting to and from clubs in the lower leagues and non-leagues, his career hampered by the vagaries of football – injuries, change of managers, loss of form. He reflects:

> In as much as I got lucky at Millwall, being in the right place at the right time, that good fortune didn't stick around too long. That can happen in football. You go with the flow.

The trouble started with a stress fracture in his back which went undiagnosed for too long, leading to more time spent in the treatment room than on the pitch. Suddenly the season was over, and he'd missed most of it. The following season, Dennis Wise, who'd been a valued advocate, left the club, and Millwall subsequently went into free-fall, lunging towards Division One.

> Sometimes your face just doesn't fit. A new manager came in, didn't fancy me, didn't play a style that suited me, that sort of thing. Players

> were coming and going, and basically everybody's looking out for themselves. That's the way it works.

After Millwall, he played a full season at Barnet, then moved up a division to Gillingham, where, by his own admission, he had a bad time. The manager who signed him left the club, old injuries flared up, and the club was relegated to the bottom tier.

Next stop was at Grays Athletic, then Crawley Town, both full-time professional contracts, and then finally to Dover Athletic, where he became a part-time player for the first time.

In a short number of years, he had gone from being the Cup final teenager to struggling for game time at some of the game's smaller clubs. But he's refreshingly honest and philosophical about it.

> You have to realise there are hundreds of Barry Cogans out there. The lower down you go, the more you see these players. Really talented lads, many of them still holding out for that one shot at the big time. Then, there's the lads on the way down, who might harbour a bit of residual bitterness. It's a bit of a rat race where everybody, players, managers, directors, are looking out for themselves. You just accept that and make the most of it.

> I have absolutely no regrets about not making it at a higher level. I don't blame anybody. I played as long as I enjoyed it, and when I stopped enjoying it, I packed it in. I knew when it was time to stop chasing the dream.

It's all a long way from his roots in the townland of Heapstown, where his precocious talent was nurtured initially in his local Arrow Harps club and then at Boyle Celtic. He moved to Dublin nursery club Belvedere when he was 13, travelling by train from Sligo each weekend. He was one of a litter of exciting young Irish players who moved to Millwall two years later. The group included Tim Clancy and Mark Quigley, who would later play for Sligo Rovers, and Steve Elliott, who enjoyed an outstanding career at top clubs in Scotland and England.

Millwall is a notoriously tough place and the club's supporters have a reputation associated with the worst of English football hooliganism. It couldn't be further removed from the idyllic rural setting in which Cogan was reared the youngest of six siblings. But he won't hear a bad word said about the London Docklands club.

> Going to live in a tough part of London as a 15-year-old was a huge culture shock. Maybe I'd been prepared a bit by having gone to Dublin as a kid, because that, too, was a massive change from my rural upbringing. I missed my family and friends back home, but I knew I was getting this great opportunity to live the dream. I knuckled down and got on with it. I was lucky. A lot of young lads go through that and never get a career.

Following a short-term job with London Underground, Cogan now works as contracts manager with his father-in-law's firm, Victoria Flooring Company.

A few months ago, relaxing at home and indulging the promptings of his seven-year-old son, Louis, who is now beginning to take a keen interest in football, Barry slipped on a recording of the 2004 Cup final and watched it for the first time.

"You know, I didn't play too badly at all against some of the top players in the world at that time. I did alright", is his assessment.

The same could be said for Barry Cogan's career in general – not bad for a lad reared a stone's throw from the ancient Heapstown Cairn who went on to build something of a football monument of his own.

Youth Soccer

European medal reflects value of grassroots

An Irish international soccer team winning a European Championship, beating powerhouse nations such as Spain, Portugal and Italy along the way. Couldn't happen, of course. Except it did, and a young Sligoman was at the heart of the unprecedented success.

Ian Rossiter was a member of the groundbreaking squad who became known as Kerr's Kids, in honour of the master tactician Brian Kerr, who guided Ireland to glory in the under-16 European Championships in Scotland in 1998.

As the only Sligo footballer to win a European Championship medal, Rossiter is an illuminous example of the prodigious production line of young players whose impressive careers began as raw fledglings in the Sligo–Leitrim Youth Leagues.

The unheralded work at grassroots level in Sligo over many decades has given youngsters like Rossiter and countless others the opportunity to nurture natural talent and to hone life skills which prove beneficial well beyond the confines of a playing pitch.

Reflecting on a career which had its foundations in the local youth leagues long before Brian Kerr's exciting crop of young players captured the imagination of the country's soccer public, Rossiter confirms the value of his grassroots education:

> I was raised in a council estate. Along with my friends, we'd play street football from one end of the day to the next. Many of us went on to play professionally; people like my brother, Mark, neighbours Lee Marshall, Keith Carty, Alan Cawley, Paddy Conlon. That couldn't have happened if the local leagues hadn't given us a structure.

His first experience of organised football was with the local Cranmore-based team Abbey United, where volunteer coaches Seánie McGuire and Martin Dunbar organised the teams from under-11 to under-16 grades. Selection for the Sligo–Leitrim representative teams soon followed and further success arrived in the shape of an All-Ireland title with Summerhill College, under the expert tuition of the legendary David Pugh.

> Winning an All-Ireland colleges title was a massive achievement. Practically every member of our squad that year would have graduated from the local youth leagues. That illustrates the power of the good work being done at local level.

Signing for Galway United at just 15 years of age and becoming the club's youngest ever player when making his League of Ireland debut less than a year later, Rossiter went on to build a successful career which included spells at Sligo Rovers, Finn Harps, Athlone Town and Newry Town. His younger brother, Mark, whose promising career at Sunderland was cut short by an unfortunate knee injury, carved his own legacy by winning League and FAI Cup doubles with Bohemians, and also had a successful spell at Dundalk. Both brothers won European medals with Ireland, Ian the gold in 1998 and Mark a bronze two years later.

Naturally, it is that magical summer of 1998, when the Irish youngsters conquered the best Europe could offer, which provide the golden memories for Rossiter. Under Kerr's meticulous management, Ireland drew with hosts Scotland, before beating Spain and Finland to qualify for a semi-final against Portugal, who were similarly dispatched. Unusually, but as an indication of the growing swell of interest back home, RTE screened the final live as Kerr's Kids shocked the highly fancied Italians to write their names in sporting history.

The elite squad included players who would go on to become full Irish internationals – John O'Shea, Graham Barrett, Andy Reid, Jonathan Douglas, Joe Murphy, Jim Goodwin and the late Liam Miller all made substantial careers at the top flight of English football. But back then, when teenage heads were filled with extravagant dreams, there was no star mentality. Rossiter recalls:

> Brian Kerr would not have tolerated any arrogance. We were a very tight group who were prepared to do anything Kerr or his coach, Noel O'Reilly, asked of us. To this day, we're still very close and stay in regular contact. We were all part of a little bit of Irish soccer history, and nobody can take that away from us.

If Rossiter's European exploits provide one of the more tangible examples of the incredible work of an army of Sligo volunteers, there are countless other youth league alumni in an endless list of League of Ireland winners, both players and managers, FAI Cup captains, Irish League winners, FAI coaches, and record goalscorers.

There have been youth leagues in Sligo dating back to the 1960s, when men such as Fr Gerry Donnelly, Fr Michael Donnelly, Frank Ballantyne and Christy Conway were to the fore in organising street leagues, mainly based around the Catholic Boys' Club based in O'Connell Street.

The first formal league structure was established in 1976 when early administrators like Seán Coyle and T.J. McManamon did trojan work in recruiting teams and facilitating matches. From those raw beginnings has grown an amazing organisation which now caters for 164 boys' and 49 girls' teams from under-11 to under-18 grades, with up to 45 games being played in every corner of the county each weekend.

The League's representative teams have achieved significant success at national level over the years. One of the early milestones was winning the SFAI Kennedy Cup Shield in 1995, with a team which included soon to be household names like Raff Cretaro, Alan Cawley and Mark Rossiter. Two years later, the League's under-18 team won the FAI Inter-League Cup against a Wexford team managed by Mick Wallace and including future Irish international Kevin Doyle in its ranks. A noteworthy feature of that campaign was a semi-final victory over Waterford, in which Seán Flannery scored a hat-trick despite being marked by John O'Shea, who would sign for Manchester United a couple of months later. The Inter-League trophy was won again in 2001 when Gino O'Boyle, a future mayor of Sligo, scored the winner against Tipperary. More recently, a Sligo–Leitrim league team managed by John McAteer showed huge potential in reaching the final of the coveted SFAI Kennedy Cup.

The girls' league representative teams have also been making their mark at national level in recent years. In 2022, the under-14s reached the semi-final of the prestigious Gaynor Cup tournament and the under-13s made it all the way to the final of the national inter-league competition.

Another noteworthy victory was recorded by local youth club Cartron United in 2001, when they won the FAI under-16 Barry Cup at a time when teams outside of Dublin rarely made a mark at national level. The big city soccer nurseries of St Kevin's Boys, Stella Maris and Home Farm couldn't hold a candle to a multi-talented Sligo team superbly coached by the late John Gaffney.

Michael Mulvaney has served as vice-chairman and secretary of the Sligo–Leitrim Schoolboys' and Girls' Youth League for several years. He has witnessed at first hand the abundance of selfless work of generations of volunteers and the dividends which that work has reaped in terms of producing top class players:

> There's an endless list of players who've emerged from our leagues and gone on to successful senior careers. There's a lot of emphasis these days on League of Ireland academies, where great work is being done, but the process starts much earlier at clubs in our youth leagues.
>
> It's a massive organisation. Brilliant work by FAI development coaches like John Russell and Niall Harrison help develop our players, and it's up to us to provide the structure, not just for potential elite players but for youngsters who want to play for the recreational value. To that end, people like our administrator, Terry Hayes, and chairman, John Healy, and the long-serving Paul Hynes, amongst many others, have done unbelievable work. They always have their fingers on the pulse.

Others to whom a huge debt is owed for their contribution to the development of youth football over the years include John O'Donoghue, Francie Kelly, Michael Gilmartin, Charlie Kavanagh (RIP) and Charlie Conlon.

In recent years, a unique showcase for local youth football was provided by an elite international competition, the Sligo Super Cup, which brought several top-class young teams to Sligo. The brainchild of former League of Ireland title winner Packie Lynch, the prestigious tournament ran for three years and attracted high-profile clubs such as Celtic, Leeds United, Derby County, Aberdeen and Sheffield Wednesday, giving young local players a rare opportunity to measure their talents against some of the best academy players from across Ireland and the UK, while at the same time highlighting the town's ever-improving sports facilities.

With such ambitious projects and the ongoing success of representative teams enhancing the image of the local youth leagues, allied to the ongoing selfless dedication of administrators, coaches and volunteers, the potential for another European medal winner to follow in the footsteps of Ian Rossiter has never been greater.

Top left: Olympian Mona McSharry on her triumphant homecoming to Grange in 2021. Pic *Sligo Champion*

Top right: 2022 Irish 200m sprint champion, Lauren Cadden from Sligo Athletic Club

Bottom: Sligo's promising young cyclist, Matthew Devins

Top left: Giselle Gallagher in action for Sligo Rugby Club U18s. Pic courtesy Sligo Rugby Club

Top right: Brian Colsh, winner of a bronze medal at the World Under-23 Rowing Championships 2022 in Italy, pictred with his mum, Rosaleen

Bottom: Johnny Kenny (centre) celebrates Celtic's 2022 League title success with Liam Scales and Michael Johnstone

Top: Tubbercurry's Liam Kerrigan greets Spanish soccer legend and World Cup winner Cesc Fabregas at their Italian club, Como 1907

Bottom: Sligo under-20 captain, Jack Lavin. Pic Eamonn McMunn

Top: RTE commentator Adrian Eames at the London Olympics

Bottom: *Sunday World* journalist Seán McGoldrick interviews world boxing champion Katie Taylor. Pic Stephen McCarthy, Sportsfile

Top left: Sligo-based broadcaster Micheál Ó Domhnaill. Pic TG4

Top right: The late Ray Flynn pictured with his daughter, Zola. Pic *Sligo Champion*

Bottom: RTE soccer pundit Alan Cawley. Pic Stephen McCarthy, Sportsfile

Top: Sligo-born racing commentator Richard Pugh. Pic Healy Racing (courtesy Richard Pugh)

Bottom: The late Red Óg Murphy. Pic Eamonn McMunn

Top: Authors Jim Gray (left) and Leo Gray. Pic Darren Carr

Bottom: The late John McGowan, who devoted more than 50 years to the promotion of basketball in the Sligo region

Sligoman Roddy Gaynor, winner of the national 800m in 1982, before going on to become one of the country's leading athletics coaches

Surfing

Gearóid McDaid

Chasing waves all over the world

As Ireland's top professional surfer, Calry native Gearóid McDaid is used to chasing giant waves all over the world, but he's also hot in pursuit of a dream goal: to be Ireland's first Olympics surfer.

Surfing became an Olympic sport for the first time at Tokyo 2020 and McDaid is determined to represent his country in Paris in two years' time:

> It's great that surfing is now an Olympic sport. It will make it more mainstream and create a wider audience. In Tokyo, it was a bit of a tester, so they only allowed 20 qualifiers, which made it extremely difficult. Still, I thought I had a chance. I got through the first qualifying tournament, but luck went against me in the second, and Covid interfered with preparations as well. Although the qualification process for Paris 2024 is still unclear, it's definitely a big goal for me. The prospect of becoming Ireland's first Olympic surfer is a massive incentive.

His aptitude for high adventure and tall waves was evident from a very early age. Like most youngsters, he dabbled in a variety of sports, displaying a raw talent in soccer, basketball and tennis, but once he discovered the exhilaration of the thunderous waves at Strandhill, nothing else even came close.

"I played all sports, liked all of them, but I just figured out from about ten years old that I loved surfing and that I was good at it," the 24-year-old confirms. "One by one, as the other sports interfered with surfing, they were dropped. Really, from that age on, nothing else mattered very much."

McDaid, a globe-trotting professional surfer who literally chases waves to the end of the earth, is regarded as Ireland's top competitive surfer, one of the best in Europe, with a string of honours and awards every bit as impressive as the swells he masters in some of the most demanding surf locations on the planet.

A 'performance' surfer rather than a big waves operator – though he has tackled some dynamic breaks in his time – McDaid competes in what is known as the Qualifying Series (QS), where he's currently ranked amongst the best 200 in the world. His speciality is showing technique – the thrilling power, flow, carves and flourishes – in competitions across the globe and in specially made promotional videos and still photography for sponsors who've been backing his potential since his teenage years.

Growing up the youngest of three siblings in Calry, McDaid's interest in surfing was nurtured by his father, Ray, who had surfed for Ireland and had run his own surf school in Strandhill for a number of years. McDaid recalls:

> Dad got us into it from an early age, maybe six when I started. My older siblings, Tony and Carol, were good too but they were more interested in basketball. Dad had his own school, so he was a really good teacher. A big advantage was that he would video me in action and that made it easier to see the mistakes and to learn and improve all the time.

From the age of twelve, he was representing Ireland at European and World Junior Surfing Championships. In the beginning, scarcely more than 4-foot tall, the adult size-surf and often rogue sets would tower over his slight frame, and sometimes he'd be scared at the prospect of the dangers they posed. But unwavering belief in his own ability carried him through. His newly acquired passport would soon bear stamps from exotic locations such as South Africa, Japan, Ecuador, the Azores, Portugal, France, Spain and Nicaragua as he chased his dreams and the waves across the continents of the world.

By the time he was 16, he had set a unique record in Irish surfing, becoming the youngest person ever to win both the junior and senior Irish titles in the same year.

High rankings in junior and senior championships on the European circuit boosted his burgeoning reputation, and soon sponsors were taking a keen interest. When energy drink companies Ripcurl and Monster came on board, the dream of professional surfing became a reality. McDaid explains:

> In the early years, my parents had to fund a lot of it, and some local companies were very good to me in helping with expenses. But the major sponsorship allowed me to go straight from school in Summerhill College into surfing as my full-time job. I had never even considered

> what third-level course I might follow or anything like that, because I knew from about sixteen years onwards that all I wanted to do with my life was surfing. Luckily, my parents backed me all the way.

His job as a full-time pro has two distinct features - competition, and creating videos and social media content and advertisements for his sponsors. It involves a lot of travelling, often to some exceptionally exotic places, and often at short notice. He's lost count of the number of countries he's visited. And yet, it can sometimes be an incongruous mix of the thrilling and the tedious.

> Because the sport is so weather-dependent, you can't really do a lot of forward planning. During the summer I would be away for months on end in a lot of really cool places, locations where I could not have imagined I'd ever be in, but it's still nice to be home for the winter. But it's never cut and dried. I'm potentially on the go all the time, because you could literally be in a place one day and then have to pack up and rush off somewhere else the next day to chase a swell or try some competition.
>
> It sounds glamorous, and sometimes it is. But it can be hard work, too. We'd not be in too many swish hotels. Airbnb most of the time, and sometimes I've even slept in my car. But in a way that adds to the fun of it all.

Candidly, McDaid admits that the fear which gripped his early interaction with the sport has not fully dissipated, but he's learning to master it.

> There was a bit of fear there in the early years, definitely. There's obviously a bigger risk of danger with the bigger waves, but you could be unlucky in any type of waves, so you have to be conscious of that all the time. But I've become more comfortable as I've become more experienced. It's a learning process really, and I think surfers generally look to the challenges and the competitive edge rather than the potential dangers.

Competing in the QS, which is a tier below the World Surf League Championship (WSL), where the best 38 competitive surfers in the world compete, McDaid reveals it's all about rankings, endlessly trying to pick up the points that will improve grades and get him closer to the big time:

> Good results get you up the ranking ladder, and that's the goal. Getting into the top 100 on the QS tour would be amazing. The ultimate aim would be to get on the WSL tour, where the real superstars compete. It's a huge ask, because there's only 38 surfers allowed on the tour. Most of these guys are millionaires, which shows how lucrative the sport is at the highest level. I'm nowhere near that, of course, but I make a reasonable living from doing something I love, so I can't complain.

Having crisscrossed the globe as one of Europe's top professionals, McDaid is still enamoured by the lure of the local waves, spending as much 'down' time as possible surfing with old pals at Strandhill or Mullaghmore. He has an almost evangelical zeal for spreading the news of Ireland's fertile surfing waters.

> Abroad sometimes, people will be amazed to meet surfers from Ireland, wondering if we've really got any waves at all. But that's been changing in recent years; Ireland is now on the map for surfing, and a lot of the best surfers in the world are coming here. We really have some of the best waves in the world, and I think you'll see a huge increase in surf tourism in the years ahead.

In Sligo, people like Stan Burns and Tom Hickey were early pioneers of the sport, sparking a tradition which has produced a string of top-class surfers in recent decades. McDaid respects the heritage which has produced an ever-developing surf culture in the county, and is hoping his career can help maintain the progress:

> Surfing is huge in Sligo now, and that's as it should be. We are the surf capital of Ireland as far as I'm concerned. As a kid, I looked up to locals like Colin O'Hare and the Kilfeather brothers, Stephen and Andrew, and learned a lot from them. We still surf together. That's part of this ongoing tradition, and hopefully, my success can inspire others.

Over the years, many Irish surfers have dabbled in the pro circuit without ever making a major impact, but with youth on his side, McDaid is contemplating a long career, joking:

> The greatest surfer of all time, Kelly Slater, is still going strong at 50, so that gives me another quarter of a century at least. It's been my life so far, and hopefully will continue to be so for many years to come.

Swimming

Mona McSharry

"I can't wait to get lost in Thailand"

There's an engaging ebullience about Mona McSharry. She's cheerful, chatty, comical. It's clear that the beaming smile and easy manner which captivated the country in her post-Olympic interviews were unrehearsed, rather a purely natural reflection of the happy person she is. It's such a refreshing antidote to the often sullen, vacuous attitude of some elite sports people.

For instance, how many other world-class athletes would nominate talking to the media as the favourite part of their first Olympics?

"I loved the media interviews," she enthuses, recalling her encounters with the world's press at the delayed Olympic Games in Tokyo 2021. "I love talking about swimming anyway, but the opportunity to talk about my race, knowing that I was communicating directly with family and friends back home was so cool. It was crazy because so many people wanted to talk to me, but I really enjoyed it."

But inside that seemingly carefree exterior burns an unapologetic desire to create new records, embrace new horizons, win brig prizes. The breath-taking magnitude of what the 21-year-old Sligo swimmer has already achieved reflects not only her prodigious talent but her utterly selfless commitment to her sport. The sweet 'girl-next-door' persona quickly evaporates in the heat of battle.

Becoming Ireland's first Olympic swimming finalist in 25 years at Tokyo 2021 would be an astonishing milestone in itself, but in McSharry's case it was merely the latest in a glittering catalogue of eye-catching triumphs. She had already become the country's first gold medal winner at the World Junior Championships and had amassed a clutter of gold, silver and bronze over two European Junior Championships. National and college records had been regularly demolished along the way.

The Grange native's first recollection of interaction with water was less than encouraging, however. She recalls a family holiday in Austria with her parents, Aidan and Viola, and brother, Mouric, when she was five years old.

> I fell into a lake off a pontoon and dad had to dive in to save me. That's when my parents decided it was time for swim lessons.

She joined the Marlin's Swim Club, based in Ballyshannon Leisure Centre, and although she's adamant that she initially didn't stand out as "anything special", she had an early inkling that it might all lead to some excitement.

A visiting coach from Belfast asked his class after a session in the pool if any of them would one day like to swim at the Olympics. Every hand in the room shot skywards. Mona remembers:

> It's what we all wanted at that stage. Whether we were old enough to realise what it even meant is another thing. But I do remember that moment as a first conscious awareness of the possibility of swimming in the Olympics.

She was thirteen years old when her first national recognition arrived, being selected on an underage Irish team for a tournament in Canada, but even then it was more about the excitement than any highfalutin idea of greatness. She confides:

> It was the first time anyone had really taken any notice of me as a swimmer, but, for me, it was just about getting away to Canada without my parents. It was my first time travelling out of the country to compete, and it was exciting. But it was new to me. I had no idea of the process of becoming a good swimmer.

Nonetheless, the three medals she brought home, allied to two national Community Games golds, provided the growing evidence of a special talent. Her commitment to swimming began in earnest as she made the transition from Carns National School in north Sligo to Coláiste Cholmcille in Ballyshannon, choosing the school primarily because of its proximity to the Ballyshannon club in which she was now undergoing a more measured training regime under the guidance of coach Grace Meade.

Her first European Junior Championships in 2015 in Baku, Azerbaijan, yielded no medals but bucketloads of invaluable experience. Although meeting boxer Katie Taylor, who won a European medal at the same event, remains a standout highlight, it was the aura of a top-class competitive environment which stoked her fires.

> That's where it really started to get serious for me. For the first time, I began to figure out how this works. I sat down with Grace and we worked on a targeted new training regime. I was thinking about competing and that whole process of preparing to win. Things changed from there.

She described the European Juniors in Hungary the following year as the 'lightbulb' moment, when she brought home a silver in the 100m and bronze in the 50m breaststroke.

"Winning those medals helped me realise I was as good as anyone else. I could compete with the best. I was no longer there just to make up the numbers", she declares.

The graph was on an unstoppable upward curve. In 2017 at the European Juniors in Hungary, McSharry secured double gold in the 50m and 100m breaststroke and silver in the 200m breaststroke as Ireland finished joint fifth in the medals' tables.

History beckoned, and seven weeks later, in Indianapolis, the Sligo girl announced herself on the world stage, becoming the first Irish swimmer to win a World Championship gold medal with a stunning triumph in the 100m breaststroke. For good measure, she added a bronze in the 50m breaststroke.

She recalls:

> It was hard to take it in. Achieving something that had never been done before was awesome. All the hard work, the early morning sessions, the sacrifices, it seems like this is the dividend. On the podium, listening to the national anthem, and knowing my parents and family and Grace were there, was so special. There's always the next event of course, but you get to live in that glory for a while.

But being a sports prodigy has its challenges. McSharry concedes she found the transition from junior to senior ranks a difficult proposition. Compounding the problems were a debilitating bout of glandular fever, a loss of form, and the onset of the Covid pandemic.

Her analysis is typically honest:

> I had probably begun to find the junior ranks relatively easy, and maybe I took it for granted a bit. Nobody knew who I was, there were few expectations, other than those I brought on myself, and I was pretty much in control.
>
> The senior ranks were a lot more challenging than I had expected, and for the first time, I began to feel a bit of pressure. I dropped three seconds in the space of two years, and I let that worry me. In one 365-day period during that time I was out of the country travelling for thirteen solid weeks. I don't think that helped either. It was a lot for a seventeen-year-old to deal with, and then there was the expectation building up around the Olympics. I was probably crippled by the stress of trying to live up to unrealistic expectations. They were challenging years, but I learned a lot from them.

She began her freshman year at the University of Tennessee in Knoxville in 2020, and found her love of the sport rejuvenated. She loves the family atmosphere, competitive but convivial, and a coaching system which helps her attain her goals. She has broken Tennessee college records in both the 100- and 200-yard breaststroke, winning silver and bronze medals in the prestigious collegiate NCAA Championships.

Qualifying for the delayed Tokyo Olympics and reaching the 100m final, where she finished eighth, propelled her into the spotlight. Now, everybody knew or wanted to know Mona McSharry, but she remained quite philosophical about it.

> Don't get me wrong, it's such a thrill to be an Olympian, and it's something I'll always have. But on another level, in a weird way maybe, it's just another competition. I don't recall feeling particularly nervous before any race, or getting uptight about all the attention. Maybe the lack of spectators had something to do with it, but I'm pretty good at blocking out noise anyway. As a competitor, it's always about doing your best, swimming as fast as you can, and the pleasing thing for me about the Olympics is that I achieved those goals.

Her abiding memory from the Olympics is the groundswell of goodwill which cascaded in from Sligo and beyond, and the frenzied excitement of her homecoming.

> Getting all the updates from my parents at home was terrific. Because local athlete Chris O'Donnell was also at the Olympics, the whole village of Grange seemed to go mad, and it was such a buzz knowing we were making people so happy back home. Then, the homecoming, driving through Grange and Ballyshannon, seeing the bonfires, waving an Irish flag out the car window, it was just crazy and sort of strange, too. The joy of it all will remain with me forever.

The goal now, of course, is to qualify for Paris 2024. Somewhat surprisingly, McSharry suggests she hasn't begun to focus that far ahead:

> I try not to think about it too much and to concentrate on more immediate targets. Obviously, the goal would be to do better than Tokyo. It's understandable if people see me as a medal contender, but that's not on my mind right now. There are so many steps before that. Maybe Tokyo came a bit too early for me. The expectations this time are a bit more realistic.

Beyond Paris, she's not so sure. Maybe a few years as a professional and then retirement to catch up on the things she has missed out on. To borrow her own favourite word, she has some pretty 'cool' ambitions.

> I honestly have no idea what I'll do when I finish swimming, because it's been such a huge part of my life. I want to travel, see the world. People might say I've already been to so many exotic places, but all I get to see is an airport, a hotel and a pool. Not much fun in that.
>
> I want to go skiing and hiking and take some mad road trips. I want to get lost in Thailand. These are things I couldn't possibly attempt while I'm still competing, so I'm counting down the days to my freedom!

The young girl with the world at her feet but whose toes remain firmly planted on the ground hopes more than anything, she says, that her story will inspire other youngsters to become involved in sport.

> Hopefully, young people might look at my journey and think it's something that would be possible for them, in whatever sport. I'd be a different person if not for swimming. Through the good and the bad, it has shaped the person I am. Sport can do that in a positive way. It genuinely excites me to think young children might be inspired by that.

> There is nothing better than sport, making friends, having a healthy lifestyle, learning life lessons.

Already confirmed as one of Sligo's greatest ever sportspeople, the tantalising prospect is that there is still so much more to come from Mona McSharry. Dust down the podiums.

Next Generation

Exciting crop of young stars ready to shine

Lauren Cadden (Athletics)

Sligo AC's Lauren Cadden has been described as 'Sligo's sprint sensation', and there's no doubt the talented Atlantic Technological University scholarship student has a hugely impressive CV and the potential to add even more illustrious achievements in the years ahead.

The 22-year-old Sligo AC runner has enjoyed a stunning spell of success in 2022, having been hampered by injury in recent years.

A glorious season was crowned in June 2022 when she struck gold in the senior women's 200m final at the Irish Life Health National Senior Championship Track and Field Championships in Santry. As a lightning-fast bunch powered off the bend, Cadden found herself 3 metres behind the fancied Sarah Leahy of Killarney AC. But in a storming finish, the Sligo speedster clicked into overdrive, clawing back the Kerry girl inch by inch. As they approached the line, Cadden even had time for a celebratory air punch as she became national senior champion for the first time.

Earlier in the season, she had won gold in the women's 200 metres at the Irish Universities' Athletics Association Indoor Track & Field Championships in January and followed up with a bronze in the 200 metres Senior Women's Indoor Championship. She finished out her indoor season as the national under-23s 200m champion.

Coached by Dermot McDermott, the Skreen native also struck gold in the 200m event at the Connacht Senior Women's Championship.

A formidable underage runner, Cadden illustrated her promise on the national stage when winning the girls 200m at the National Juvenile Championships in 2018, setting a new Irish record in the process.

Her star continued to rise in 2022 when she was selected as part of the Ireland team for an international athletics competition in Athens. She was part of the Irish 4×100-metre women's relay team and also competed individually in the 200 metres.

Dean Clancy (Boxing)

Already a European under-22 champion, Sligo's Dean Clancy is firmly established as one of the country's up and coming young boxers.

The 20-year-old light welterweight fighter confirmed his exciting potential when he claimed the European title in clinical fashion in Roseto degli Abruzzi, Italy, in June 2021.

Despite not having had a fight in eighteen months because of Covid restrictions, and the fact that he was competing at the weight division for the first time in his career, Clancy emerged as an impressive champion.

The young Sligoman, a product of the progressive Seán McDermott Boxing Club in Manorhamilton, where his father, Jason, is a highly respected coach, ruthlessly dismissed the challenge of four of the continent's top fighters on his way to the final. He was ready to deliver the performance of his life in the decider but, bizarrely, his opponent, Ahmad Shtiwi, failed to show for the contest. It meant Clancy was declared champion without having to break sweat in the ring.

The strange circumstances surrounding the conclusion of the Championship didn't in any way diminish the scale of Clancy's achievement, however.

Olympic and World Champion Kellie Harrington is among a growing list of admirers, outlining her endorsement of the Sligo fighter on social media. She tweeted: "One to watch, I'm tellin ye, this lad is special."

Brian Colsh (Rowing)

Among an impressive list of high achievers at Sligo Rowing Club is Brian Colsh, a young man whose progress through the underage ranks has been so prolific he's entitled to harbour realistic ambitions of competing at the Olympic Games in years to come.

The 20-year-old Ballymote student underlined his exciting potential by winning a bronze medal at the World Under-23 Rowing Championships in Varese, Italy, in 2022. He finished third in the men's double sculls with his teammate, Konan Pazzaia (Queen's).

It followed on from his silver medal as part of a four-man Irish team at the European Junior Championships in Serbia in 2020. He also competed at the World Under-23 Championships in the Czech Republic.

Colsh inherited a love of rowing from his father, Tom, himself an international rower of renown, and his athletics prowess from his mother, Rosaleen.

A student at NUI Galway where he is studying Accountancy and Commerce, he displays almost obsessive devotion to his chosen sport. A typical day begins with a gruelling 6 a.m. training session on the Corrib River and ends with a punishing few hours in the gym. It's a six-day-a-week cycle, with academic studies squeezed into a frantic schedule.

Regularly in contention for coveted medals at the annual national championships in Cork, Colsh is eagerly looking forward to the qualifying races for the 2024 Olympics. Colsh was in top form again at the Senior World Rowing Championships in the Czech Republic in September 2022, reaching the final of the single sculls event.

The Ballymote teenager is quick to acknowledge the enormous influence of his coaches at Sligo Rowing Club, stalwarts like Rory Clarke, Ray Murtagh and Malua Donohoe. The club was formed in 2006, thereby extending the town's proud tradition in the sport, and has claimed a substantial haul of silverware at home and abroad over the years.

Rowing in the Sligo region has a rich history dating back to the 1800s, when there were several clubs along the shores of Lough Gill. Back in the day, there were many competitive regattas on the lake, the most famous of which was the Aughamore regatta, one of the sporting highlights on the local sporting calendar for many years.

Matthew Devins (Cycling)

Ambitious young Collooney man Matthew Devins is on track for an exciting career in professional cycling.

The 20-year-old road rider is attached to the English-based Trinity Cycling team, a professional development outfit. He has competed in the European under-23 championships in Italy and the Tour de Bretagne, as well as several other prestige races in recent years.

The Sligo rider is a member of the Irish team which took part in a series of European stage races in 2022. It's all part of Cycling Ireland's under-23 Road Programme, which acts as a springboard for talented young riders to progress to senior professional teams.

Devins declares:

> I want to make it all the way the top. There are different stages to negotiate along the way, and I believe my involvement with the Trinity team affords me an opportunity to showcase all I have to offer. If

> everything goes to plan, the target would be to join a top professional team and compete in some of the iconic events such as the Tour de France and the Olympics. All that is a long way down the line, but I'm pleased with the progress I've made so far.

His determination to further his career is all-consuming. He estimates he puts in 36 hours training every week, averaging about 700km. In the last year alone, he's clocked up a staggering 30,000km in training and competitions.

Although he rides with a professional club, the Sligo cyclist isn't paid, meaning he relies on the support of local sponsors and his parents, Michael and Rachel, to finance his involvement in the sport.

"It's a tricky existence and sponsorship is always welcome," he confirms.

The former Ballisodare NS and Summerhill College student began his cycling career with the Yeats' Country Cycling Club in Sligo and spent a year with a Spanish team before joining Trinity.

Away from cycling, he's undertaking an online psychology course with DCU.

Cormac Finn (Handball)

In a victory laced with poignancy, Cormac Finn wrote his name into the history books when he became the first Sligo player to win an All-Ireland 40x20 minor handball singles title in March 2022.

Less than a fortnight before the epic final at Kingscourt, Co. Cavan, the Ballymote youngster's preparations were thrown into disarray by the sudden death of his long-time mentor and friend, Gerry Coleman from Curry.

The late Mr Coleman had been an influential driving force in the growth of handball in the county and had regularly gone out of his way to steer generations of young handballers towards ambitious targets. In his hour of glory, young Finn displayed remarkable maturity in dedicating his victory to the memory of the man who had done so much to help him attain his place in history:

> Gerry was one of the key men in handball in the county. He had done so much for me personally and for the sport in general. He played a huge role in developing the handball centre in Collooney. The day I won the All-Ireland it struck me hard that without him I probably would never have come this far, might not have even had a place to train.

The gesture spoke volumes about the character of an impressive young sportsman, who was also delighted to share the glory with his parents, Michael and Colette, and people like Francie McCann and Martin Golden, who introduced him to the sport as a youngster.

The 18-year-old, who's been playing handball at an intensely competitive level for over for ten years, had previously won an All-Ireland under-15 softball title, but was still considered an outsider when he faced Kilkenny ace Kyle Jordan in the minor singles final.

"When lockdown allowed us back training, I went at it full throttle," he says. "The result might have been a shock to most people, but for myself and those who knew the work I'd put in, it was what we expected."

Giselle Gallagher (Rugby)

A career in international rugby is the target for Tubbercurry teenager Giselle Gallagher, who has just begun a four-year rugby scholarship at the renowned Lindenwood University in Missouri.

A relative latecomer to the sport – she didn't play rugby at all until her first year at St Attracta's Community School – Giselle quickly emerged as one of the county's most promising young stars.

Now she's hoping her spell in Lindenwood, where she is studying Exercise Science, will pave the way for a career in rugby:

> I'm hugely excited by the prospect of completing my scholarship in Missouri and making the most of the opportunities which come from that. A career in professional rugby is the ultimate ambition.

The nineteen-year-old has a strong sporting pedigree. Her uncle Brian Curran was on the Sligo GAA team which won the Connacht Championship in 2007, while another uncle, Gary Curran, played for a number of clubs in the League of Ireland, including Sligo Rovers.

"Sport was a big part of my childhood," says Giselle. "I played soccer with Real Tubber and GAA with Tubbercurry. I never even watched a game of rugby. It's funny the way things have worked out."

Introduced to rugby by Jean McConnell, a teacher at St Attracta's, she was a member of the Sligo Rugby Club team which won the Connacht Cup in 2022.

With the support of her father, David Curran, and mother, Jennifer Gallagher, Giselle explored the possibility of securing a rugby scholarship abroad and was thrilled to be accepted by Lindenwood University.

Johnny Kenny (Soccer)

Scenes of unbridled joy flashed across TV screens on the day Glasgow Celtic received the Scottish Premier League title in 2022. There amid the glorious mayhem and manic celebrations was a familiar face.

Nineteen-year-old Johnny Kenny, the exciting young striker signed from Sligo Rovers just four months earlier, was soaking in the adulation of Celtic's ecstatic fans, his Championship medal a glorious confirmation of his rapid progress at the world-famous club.

Fast-tracked to the first team squad by Celtic boss Ange Postecoglou, Kenny is eagerly looking forward to progressing his career at Parkhead.

"Training with the first team lads, all top-class players, has been an important part of my development", he reports.

Hot-shot Kenny hit 13 goals in his debut season for Sligo Rovers, alerting several top cross-channel clubs to his explosive potential. Hibs led the chase but once Celtic entered the frame, there was only one choice for the striker. He admits:

> I couldn't turn down the chance to join Celtic. I was very happy at Rovers where Liam Buckley and Conor O'Grady were hugely influential in my career, but it was always my ambition to play at a higher level.

A back injury, which came to light during his medical with the Scottish club, sidelined him for nine weeks but even that setback failed to hinder his progress. He got valuable match time with the reserve team, bagging five goals in a handful of games.

The Riverstown youngster has already made his mark at international level, scoring five goals in six games for the Irish under-19s.

"Nothing beats the thrill of pulling on the green jersey," he beams. "Hopefully, I can continue to develop at club and international level over the coming years."

The Sligo teenager furthered his development during a productive loan spell at Scottish Championship club Queen's Park in 2022.

Liam Kerrigan (Soccer)

One of Ireland's most exciting young soccer prospects, Liam Kerrigan broke new ground in July 2022 when he signed a three-year contract with Italian Serie B team Como 1907.

The 22-year-old Tubbercurry native burst onto the international scene in 2022 when playing a major role in Ireland's bid for a first-ever appearance at an under-21 European Championship. In a team laden with cross-channel professionals, many attached to Premier League clubs, Kerrigan's League of Ireland pedigree proved to be no impediment as he emerged as one of the stars of the qualifying campaign. He was named as Ireland's man of the match when scoring in a key qualifier against Montenegro in June 2022.

Kerrigan admits:

> It was a big surprise to be called into the squad initially because I was playing with UCD in the first division whereas most of the lads were attached to English clubs. But once I settled in, I felt right at home. It's a great thrill to represent your country, valuable experience for the future and, hopefully, a shop window to show what I can do.

A member of the UCD-promotion winning team in 2021, Kerrigan had been on the books of Sligo Rovers since he was 15 years old, having played youth football with his hometown club, Real Tubber. He played Kennedy Cup football for the Sligo–Leitrim under-14 representative team and was also a talented Gaelic footballer with his local club and his school, St Attracta's, with whom he won a number of Connacht titles.

A first cousin of Celtic's rising star Johnny Kenny, Kerrigan clocked up 25 senior appearances with Rovers before moving to pursue a scholarship at UCD, where he graduated with a Commerce degree.

His outstanding performances for UCD and the under-21 national team brought him many admirers and it's understood a number of English clubs were eyeing up a move before the Italian second division team moved in to open an exciting new chapter for the amiable Tubbercurry youngster.

Keelan Kilrehill (Athletics)

West Sligo's European gold medal winner Keelan Kilrehill has his sights set on the Olympics. Even if Paris 2024 might come too soon for the 21-year-old Dromore West athlete, he's still young enough to contemplate participation in Los Angeles four years later:

> It's something that's always at the back of an athlete's mind. In this sport, even a few seconds or fractions of a second make all the difference, so it's about constantly improving my times. The aim is to get closer to a qualifying time and to be in a good place to take advantage when the opportunity comes.

Kilrehill was part of the six-man gold-medal-winning Irish under-23 team at the European Cross-Country Championships in December 2021, finishing sixth in front of home supporters at the Sport Ireland Campus in Abbotstown. Darragh McElhinney's second-place finish and Michael Power crossing in thirteenth secured the gold for Ireland. Kilrehill reports:

> We weren't expected to pull it off but that made all the more enjoyable. There was a big homecoming in Dromore West, which was great craic. It was unbelievable to be posing for photographs and signing autographs. It felt like the big time, although it only lasted for a few days and then it was back to work.

With an Economics degree from DCU, Kilrehill is hoping to link up with a sponsor who can help accelerate his career, but for now he's happy to count his blessings after a freak accident almost left him paralysed a few years ago. Aged fourteen, he was cycling downhill near his home when he collided head-on with a car driven by a neighbour.

Initially treated at Sligo University Hospital, he was subsequently transferred to Crumlin Children's Hospital where severe damage was confirmed: three broken vertebrae in his back and a C1 fracture in his neck. Had it been a break rather than a fracture, it was likely he would never walk again.

"It was very worrying. It could have been far more serious, but what annoyed me most was that I missed the Community Games National Finals. Luckily, I was fit enough the following year to go back and win a gold, and I've never looked back," he says.

Jack Lavin (Gaelic football)

At just 20 years of age, Jack Lavin has already claimed a cherished place in Sligo GAA folklore. The Ballymote wingback was captain of the Sligo under-20 team which won the Connacht Championship for the first time in 2022. And he further embellished the historic achievement by grabbing a dramatic winning goal with the last kick of the game in a thrilling final against Mayo at Markievicz Park.

Although Sligo's bid for All-Ireland glory came to an end in a semi-final showdown with Kildare, Lavin believes the breakthrough in Connacht provides a solid platform for substantial progress at senior level:

> There are several talented players coming through the underage grades in the county. The breakthrough success of the under-20s can be the

> springboard for a bright new era for Sligo football. I had three great years with the under-20s and having tasted success at that level, my next target is to try to break into the senior squad.

The Ballymote man was a promising soccer player too but committed exclusively to Gaelic football, winning a Manning Cup medal with Sligo under-16s before graduating to the minor and under-20 ranks.

He comes from a strong sporting background. His father, John, is among a select group of players who lined out for both Sligo GAA seniors and Sligo Rovers, while his younger brothers, Michael and James, are in the Rovers academy, playing for the under-19s and under-14s respectively. His grandfather, the late Tommy Lavin, was a keen sportsman and a noted GAA player in his day. Lavin's uncle Nigel Keady was one of the youngest players to captain Galway United in the League of Ireland.

"There's a strong sporting pedigree in the family," he says. "We all encourage and support each other and there's always a good bit of banter between us."

John Mahon (Soccer)

Towering centre-back John Mahon was only 18 years old when Sligo Rovers' manager, Ger Lyttle, plucked him for the club's academy and threw him headlong into the cauldron of League of Ireland football. He could not have imagined how quickly his career would blossom.

Within three seasons he was off to Scottish Premier League club St Johnstone, rated as one of the most promising defenders in the country. Having settled in well at the Perth-based club, he is confident of becoming a permanent fixture in their first team.

A native of Collooney, Mahon's natural talent was nurtured in the nearby Ballisodare United underage teams. He was also a gifted Gaelic football midfielder and represented the county at under-14 and under-16 grades before progressing to the minor squad. At that stage, however, his attention turned full-time to soccer when Sligo Rovers recruited him to their under-17s panel.

Having progressed to the under-19s, he got his chance in the senior team when regular centre-back Kyle McFadden suffered a long-term injury. Mahon took to it like the proverbial duck to water:

> I'm a big lad, so the physicality of the League of Ireland wasn't a problem. Technically, I had a bit to learn, but I got up to speed quickly and managed to retain my place in the team. As a local lad, playing for Rovers as a professional was a bit of a dream come true.

Such was his progress that rumours soon began to grow about possible cross-channel interest. With a number of options, Mahon plumped for St Johnstone, making the move in January 2022. He has featured in Premier League and League Cup matches and was given his first full game against Inverness in a crucial relegation play-off.

"It was a high-pressure game to come into, because so much was riding on it. For the manager to put his faith in me in such an important game gave me a lot of confidence", he reports.

Mahon's immediate ambition is to nail down a permanent first-team place in a League he describes as not dissimilar to the top section of the League of Ireland. Ultimately, a senior cap for the Republic of Ireland would be the main target.

"To get this chance of a professional career is something I value greatly. To play for Ireland one day would be the icing on the cake", he confirms.

Grace Foley (Athletics)

Nine-year-old Grace Foley has the distinction of being the youngest sports star featured in this book. The promising athlete from Sligo AC created quite a stir when she won the All-Ireland 300m event, having come through local and provincial championships, leading to her participation in the acclaimed Millrose Games in New York in January 2022.

The Millrose Games is an international indoors event which attracts some of the world's top athletes – but one of its novel features is the 'World's Fastest Kid' race, which is always hotly contested by some of the most promising youngsters from across the globe.

Well-known athletics coach Dermot McDermott, who has been nurturing Grace's talent at Sligo AC, felt she would be up to the test. And how right he was. The schoolgirl produced an astonishing performance to finish in third place, taking just 9.01 seconds to run the 55 metres, watched from the stands by proud parents, Heather and Desi, and her twin brother, Oliver.

The third fastest kid in the world didn't take her talent off the stones, either. Mum Heather is a former full-time triathlete and cyclist who represented Northern Ireland at the Commonwealth Games in 2006 and was a member of the Irish cycling team at the Games in Delhi in 2010. Dad Desi also has a background in athletics and is a keen cyclist.

Having celebrated so many Sligo sports stars, personalities and events from a wide range of sports in this book, how lovely it is to spotlight a nine-year-old girl who might someday be the greatest of them all. Well done Grace.

Media

Alan Cawley

Passionate pundit pulling no punches

By his own admission, Alan Cawley was a 'brier' on a football pitch, berating colleagues, criticising referees, niggling opponents. The debonair pundit whose insightful analysis is becoming a staple of RTE's soccer coverage is more restrained these days, but his assertive passion for the game is no less compelling.

Intelligent and insightful, Cawley's forthright analysis can sometimes be an incongruous mix of critic and advocate. He can appear pugnacious when standing his ground on a firmly held view and yet displays remarkable sensitivity in a masterful interviewing technique on his popular podcast, *Cawley's Call*.

Whether as a television match analyst, co-commentator, radio panelist or podcast host, what you see is what you get – and what you get is a proud Sligoman unafraid to ventilate strong and sometimes unpopular opinions, informed by meticulous research and backed by a varied playing career at the coalface of the League of Ireland.

Cawley grew up in the Cranmore area of Sligo, a council housing estate which has spawned a remarkable number of top-class sportsmen, including world cycling champion Mark Scanlon and European Championship-winning underage soccer international Ian Rossiter, as well as a host of professional soccer players. He would have heard many an opinion and not a few football arguments in his childhood.

At sixteen, he was signed by Leeds United, who agreed to allow him finish out his fourth year at Summerhill College on condition that he play at the highest level possible in the Irish youth system. So, he left his boyhood club

Merville United to spend a year at the Dublin nursery club Belvedere, where he played alongside the wizardly Wes Hoolihan.

On joining Leeds, who were then managed by George Graham, he quickly progressed to the reserve team under the management of former Celtic great Roy Atkin. Future Premier League players such as Darren Huckerby and Alf-Inge Haaland were amongst his teammates while opponents would have included the likes of Jamie Redknapp, Gary McAllister and the enigmatic Paul Gascoigne.

His inherent self-confidence was already on display:

> There's a perception that, going over from Ireland, you couldn't possibly be as good as the lads at the bigger clubs. But when you get to train and play with them, you soon realise you're every bit as good. As a young lad away from home for the first time, it was difficult on a personal level, but the football side of things was never a problem.

Under David O'Leary, Leeds were flying high. Money appeared to be no object. Transfer records were broken to sign Rio Ferdinand from West Ham to augment home-grown youngsters like Harry Kewell and Alan Smith as the Yorkshire club reached the Champions League semi-final. Starry-eyed kids lower down the ranks were finding it increasingly difficult to catch the eye.

"It was almost impossible to break through. Hardly any of my group actually made it to the first team. It was time to move on," he recalls. He had trials with Hearts and Preston but opted for Championship club Sheffield Wednesday on an 18-month contract. Having made a couple of appearances for the first team during a pre-season tour in Scotland, he felt he was on the verge of the big breakthrough. But, for reasons he has never fathomed, he suddenly became the forgotten man. He recalls:

> With the club's permission, I came home to Sligo for a few days to attend my granny's funeral. When I got back to Sheffield, everything had changed. I went from being on the verge of the first team to being cast aside. I was back at the bottom of the pile. The manager never spoke to me, I got no explanation. It was very hard to deal with. To this day, I have no idea why it happened.

Disenchanted by the experience, the young playmaker decided he'd had enough of the undergrowth of the English football jungle. He came home to enjoy a distinguished League of Ireland career with UCD, Longford, Bray, St Patrick's Athletic, Dundalk and Shelbourne, with whom he won the League title. His only regret is that he never had the opportunity of playing for his hometown club.

He'd already retired in 2008 when a chance meeting with Sligo-born RTE sports journalist Rory Houston ignited what has become a hugely successful media career. Houston offered Cawley the opportunity to write a weekly League of Ireland blog on the RTE website – both were pleasantly surprised with the reaction.

Unlike a lot of footballers, Cawley always had an interest in newspaper coverage of his sport, so much so his dressing room name was 'Quotesy', so often were his opinions featured in the media. So, the chance to formally express those opinions in print was immediately appealing:

> Although I wasn't quite sure what a blog was to begin with, once I got writing it, I felt at home. There was hardly any money in it initially, but it opened so many doors. I had strong opinions, and I wasn't afraid to express them. Because it was so different, people took to it, and everything took off from there.

Radio work followed with 2FM's *Game On* programme, while *Monday Night Soccer* brought more TV exposure for the enthusiastic analysist. He's covered women's internationals, League of Ireland, European Championship qualifiers, the European Super Cup, and an Olympics final featuring Argentina and Germany.

During lockdown, he launched his podcast, *Cawley's Call*, to a hugely positive reaction. Co-presented with partner-in-crime Stuey Byrne, the show pulls no punches, taking a scalpel to the inner workings of the League of Ireland and diving deep into the personalities of some of the top players in the domestic league. Revealing and sensitive interviews with Chris Forrester and Jack Byrne have garnered particularly glowing responses. Cawley explains:

> We like to get fellas who wouldn't normally do interviews. It's amazing the way some of the lads have opened up to us, and the audience reaction to their stories has been overwhelmingly positive. While it's mostly League of Ireland, we've had guests from other sports, too. I particularly enjoyed Ken Doherty, as I'm a massive snooker fan ever since my dad used to run tournaments for the CYMS in the town hall in Sligo when I was a kid.

Often controversial and always provocative, Cawley lives his professional life by two straight-forward rules:

> It's never personal, even if sometimes it might come across as being harsh. Secondly, I'm meticulous about research. I never go on any programme without being fully researched. That's not to say I'm always right. The nature of it is that I'm sometimes wrong, but it's never personal and it's never badly researched. I'm never argumentative just for the sake of it. Being so forthright has cost me a few friendships along the way, but my job is to call it as I see it.

An accounts manager with the Dublin-based industrial detergents manufacturer Diversey, Cawley is anxious to expand his media career.

> I've always been ambitious, and I'm relentless in my media work. I'm very happy with what I've done so far, but I'm always looking for the next thing. On my radar now is the World Cup. To be on a panel for such a major tournament and get to analyse some of the top players in the world would be amazing. That's the immediate target.

Adrian Eames

Sligo voice painting word pictures

It's an early autumn night in Moscow. A game of football which has become embedded in the national psyche. The unforgettable night when lion-hearted Irish defender Richard Dunne, battered and bloodied, almost single-handedly repelled a mighty Russian invasion. Heroic goal-line clearances, juggernaut-headed interventions, and thundering tackles helped Ireland secure an unlikely scoreless draw which ultimately led to their qualification for the 2012 European Championships. In the wake of one monstrous challenge on an unsuspecting Russian forward, Dunne clattered into a running track surrounding the pitch, his face scratched and smothered in blood as he re-entered the fray with a fresh white jersey. Bizarrely, in the midst of the frantic maelstrom, Irish officials had to scribble the number five in a felt-tip marker on the back of the new shirt. It was all happening.

But high up in the RTE radio commentary box, nothing was happening. In a real-life incarnation of a dreaded nightmare, the transmission lines had disappeared. Commentator Gabriel Egan was in full flow, but radio listeners back home weren't hearing a single word. At the command wheel, producer Adrian Eames was beginning to learn how Titanic skipper Edward Smith must have felt when he first spotted that giant iceberg.

"It was an absolute, panic-stricken nightmare", Eames confirms, now able to allow himself a contented smile. But, in the heat of a Moscow crisis, he had to draw on the depths of calm calculations which years of work in pirate and local radio had taught him.

> In pirate radio, and maybe to a lesser extent on local radio, lots of things often go wrong in a live broadcast, and you have to deal with it.

> That night in Moscow was, of course, a much bigger deal, but you draw on whatever experience you can to stay calm and retain the hope that everything will be alright.
>
> The lines just suddenly went dead. We were off air during one of the most exciting matches Ireland had played in years. The technicians were mostly Russian, with very little English, so there was a bit of panic, a lot of head-scratching and shrugging of shoulders. We initially switched to the television commentary, which was a useful stop gap, and got on with the mechanics of trying to sort out our own problems. And all the time, you're trying to keep an eye on the match so that you miss nothing for when you do get back on air.
>
> Everyone remembers that night for Richard Dunne's heroics, as do I. But I will never forget it for very different reasons. Thankfully, it all came good in the end, both for our commentary team and the Irish team.

If the Moscow calamity represented a prime example of the perils of live broadcasting, there has been an abundance of far better experiences for the Sligo native, who has travelled the world covering a raft of high-profile sports events as producer, commentator and reporter for RTE.

He has barely finished relating his Russian experience when his mind rushes to Iran, and the vociferous reception he and co-commentator Eoin Hand received from 100,000 fanatical supporters in Tehran. They were covering the second leg of a World Cup qualification play-off in November 2001, in which Ireland held the upper hand thanks to a 2–0 first-leg victory. He relates:

> We decided to walk the pitch before kick-off. We came out to a cauldron of hostility. There must have been 100,000 people in the stadium. They'd been there since 9 a.m., and they were in a frenzy of excitement. I remember the huge image of the Ayatollah and Islamic music blasting from massive speakers. It was a steaming hot day and Eoin had rolled up his shirt sleeves, and as we walked around, we were subjected to deafening jeers and boos. We were told later that the animosity from the crowd was because he was exposing his arms. I like to think they were just having the craic, the way a crowd would on a big match day at the Aviva. They were in better form at the end, as Iran won 1–0, but, thankfully, Ireland went through.

A sports fanatic from a very early age – he has vivid memories of childhood visits to the Showgrounds with his parents, Brendan and Josie – Eames recalls listening to commentaries on RTE and the BBC and marvelling at how people were getting paid for doing something they would probably have done for nothing.

With his interest stirred, he started working long hours, mostly on a voluntary basis, in pirate radio, and when independent radio was finally legalised he wrote to every station in the country seeking work. He was taken on by Midwest Radio before moving to his hometown station, North West Radio (now OceanFM). Stints followed at Century Radio and Dublin's FM104, where his aptitude for sports coverage was given full vent.

He joined RTE in 1998, where an initial six-month contract has become a lengthy career, jam-packed with illustrious opportunities. The Ballinode native has presented all of RTE radio's flagship sports programmes, including *Saturday Sport* and *Sunday Sport*, *Sport at 7*, *Drivetime Sport* and *Game On*. He has worked as a television commentator at three World Cups, South Africa (2010), Rio (2014) and Russia (2018). He has also worked on the Euros in 2012 in Poland and 2016 in France, where he commentated on all of Ireland's games for RTE radio, and has covered the 2020 Euros in England.

Away from football, Eames has covered three Olympic Games, being team leader of the RTE radio crews at both London 2012 and Rio 2016, and has been to the Paralympics in Beijing, London and Rio. He has lost count of the number of Cheltenham Racing Festivals he covered as producer.

While big-match commentaries offer the more glamorous side of the business, Eames is more readily intoxicated by the adrenalin rush of producing marathon shows, keeping the listening audience up to date with all the breaking news of the day:

> Producing the Saturday or Sunday sports shows is a real buzz, particularly on busy days, where you might have a big rugby or soccer match and a full programme of important GAA games. We'd have reporters and commentators at all the venues, and the producer's job is to ensure we don't miss anything, that we're on top of the breaking action, and that we get the balance right between the mix of the various sports.
>
> Then there are the quiet days where there's not as much happening or where bad weather has decimated the fixture list. You've still got four or five hours' airtime to fill, so that calls for a bit of imagination and creativity, and very often that leads to great radio, too, if slightly more challenging.

Despite being an avid soccer fan, and having covered some of the game's biggest tournaments, he regards the Olympics and Paralympics work as the highlights of his career.

> With the Olympics, there's always this sense of the entire world gathering in one city, which is slightly surreal. It's a massive event, and yet there's a sense of community about it which I find very satisfying. Also, I find athletes tend to be much more open and accessible, whereas football is far more controlled and the players are practically inaccessible these days.
>
> The Paralympics would probably be my favourite of all the events I've covered. There's such a genuine sense of joy and fulfillment. The participants radiate pure joy from start to finish, and that comes across so well in their interviews. It's great to be able to relay such positive feel-good stories back to an Irish audience.

Despite the emergence of new media, ever-changing technology and the readily available information offered by top-quality podcasts and social media, Eames believes traditional radio will continue to enjoy steadfast loyalty from the Irish public.

Of all the extraordinary challenges and opportunities he has encountered as a globe-trotting intrepid reporter, Eames still finds covering his beloved Sligo Rovers among the more difficult tasks. He explains:

> Doing a Rovers game is difficult because it's who I am. Since childhood, I've been going to Rovers matches wanting them to win. Covering a game, I'm elated when they score and disappointed if they concede, but I can't let that come through in the commentary. I have to be completely dispassionate, and sometimes that can be very challenging.

Reflecting on what he admits is a 'dream job', Eames concedes he's been very lucky.

"It never feels like work. It's been a lot of fun making a living from a boyhood dream", he happily confirms.

Seán McGoldrick

The night Katie Taylor saved my bacon

On the worst night of her amateur career, her last fight before turning professional, Katie Taylor, the sweetheart of Irish sport, was entitled to be at war with the world. She had just surrendered her Olympic champion status, losing by a split decision in the lightweight quarter-finals to Finland's Mira Potkonen, and now the baying press corps, lightbulbs flashing and microphones thrust forward like threatening bayonets, were in the mood for a clinical autopsy. They were doing their job.

Taylor, for so long a beacon of smiling gravitas who wore her greatness with beguiling ease, was not in a good place. Her preparations for Rio 2016 had been hampered by injury and personal trauma. Her parents' marriage had disintegrated and her long-time coach and ally, her dad, Peter, was no longer in her corner. The last place on earth she would have wished to be at that moment was standing in front of an inquisition, trying to explain how she had lost a fight she came so close to winning.

It must have been tempting to bolt when a direct question enquiring if she thought she had won the fight sent her coach into angry convulsions. He urged her to abandon the press conference, to return to the sanctuary of her dressing room. But she recognised the reporter whose honest query had caused the furore. She stood her ground. The reporter, who had been covering her career for 27 years, was Seán McGoldrick from the *Sunday World*, a veteran of three previous Olympics, multiple European Championships, and every All-Ireland football and hurling final since 1986. He'd cut his journalism chops on the news and sports circuit with his local paper, the *Sligo Champion*.

In the tense uproarious few minutes between his question and Taylor's answer, he wondered if he had just blown the press conference asunder. He would have faced a furious backlash from his assembled colleagues had the boxer exited stage left. Katie Taylor saved his bacon. McGoldrick recalls:

> She was extremely upset and very tearful when she came into the room. It had been a tough fight decided by a split decision. Many people thought she had won it. Once she composed herself, I asked her if she felt she'd won the fight. Immediately, her coach went ballistic and tore into me. I'd never experienced anything like it. He was urging Katie to leave the stage, to abandon the press conference. I'm not saying she stayed because I was the one who asked, but she would have known me. We'd worked together a lot over the years. Anyway, she stood her ground, and when things calmed down, she answered the question in a very measured way, as is her style.
>
> But it was very tense for a while. I'd say we came within seconds of losing her. I'd have been lynched by the other press people if that had happened. We were all working to tight deadlines and they needed Katie's reaction. I hate to think what would have happened if my question had caused her to walk away. I'll always be thankful she didn't.

McGoldrick, a seasoned GAA writer with the *Irish Press* for eleven years before the paper's demise, and latterly with the *Sunday World*, began covering boxing at the European Amateur Championships in Greece in 1989.

He has had a ring-side seat as Taylor emerged as the public face of female boxing. He remembers her entering tournaments as K. Taylor, so her gender would not be an issue when fighting against boys of a similar age, and he was present when, as a 15-year-old schoolgirl, she fought her first legally sanctioned all-female fight in Dublin's National Stadium, when she beat Alanna Audley-Murphy from Belfast.

But by far his most memorable Katie Taylor experience was her historic fight at the Madison Square Garden in New York in 2022, when she beat Amanda Serrano in what has been hailed as the 'fight of the century'. He recalls:

> Halfway through the epic fight, I was composing a story of how her 20-fight unbeaten run in professional boxing was coming to an end. Although she didn't quite hit the canvas in the fifth round, metaphorically she rose from the canvas to record one of the most famous wins ever achieved by an Irish sports person on foreign soil.

> Such was the adrenalin rush, I found it impossible to sleep that night. Unless Leitrim win an All-Ireland, I don't think there'll be a comparable sporting moment in my lifetime.

According to McGoldrick, Taylor and her father took a big risk in devoting their lives full-time to boxing, with Katie giving up a promising soccer career - she had played internationally for Ireland - and dropping out of secondary school.

"She was a game-changer. Winning European and world titles, she transformed female boxing. Women would never have had the chance of fighting at Olympic level had it not been for Katie Taylor", he insists.

The Olympics in London 2012 provided some of his best memories in a distinguished career stretching back more than 40 years:

> To be there, recording Katie's Olympic debut, was something really special. Her opening fight against GB's Natasha Jones in the ExCel Arena in London's Dockland area was simply incredible. Afterwards it was confirmed that record noise levels had been recorded that night. Although the British audience accounted for a lot of it, I can tell you the Irish were no shrinking violets, either, particularly when Katie won.

Having learned the nuts and bolts of the trade during five years on the *Sligo Champion*, the golden rule of journalistic objectivity would have been enshrined in McGoldrick's armour from an early age, but it was sorely tested on Thursday, 9 August 2012 when Katie Taylor beat Russia's Sofya Ochigava to win the Olympic Gold.

> The place went wild. I have to admit objectivity went out the window for a while. I'd known Katie personally, I knew precisely how much she had put in to get to this position, and to see that gold medal around her neck was quite emotional.

Outside the ring, McGoldrick has found Taylor to be a "very humble and shy person", who would rather do six rounds of sparring than sit down for a media interview:

> She's a genuinely lovely person with a sharp sense of humour. But she can be quite guarded. Since turning professional, she seems to be pre-prepared for interviews. She'll have stock answers prepared and she rarely deviates from that. I get on well with her in the sense of a good working relationship but there is a genuine shyness about her.

When Taylor retired from amateur boxing after her defeat in Rio, it opened the door for a new hero of female boxing. Kellie Harrington has, according to McGoldrick, been like a breath of fresh air.

"She's so humble and so very funny. What you see is what you get with Kellie", he reports. "She's a dream to work with, so much so, you now have all these hardened, cynical reporters actually looking forward to her press conferences."

On a personal level, Harrington's Gold at the delayed 2020 Olympics in Tokyo in August 2021 provided McGoldrick with the most emotional night of his career. He confirms:

> You're not supposed to get emotionally involved, of course, but I found the medal ceremony in Tokyo incredibly emotional on a personal level. My mother, who was in her 90s and had been a great sports fan and would always watch events she knew I would be working at, had died a month before the Olympics. So, seeing Kellie being so deliriously happy getting her gold medal, and the national anthem playing and the tricolour being raised – I don't know, it just got to me. It's one of the memories that will live with me.

After an eventful career which also included working on that unforgettable night in Sydney 2000 when Sonia O'Sullivan finally won her richly deserved silver medal, McGoldrick laments the changed environment around GAA coverage.

> When I first started, I probably had a phone number for every GAA player in the country. We used to get fellas out of bed early in the morning for a chat or ring schools where lads would be teaching and get them out of class. You'd nearly be arrested if you tried that now. There has been a complete disengagement between footballers/managers and the media. Reporters are barely tolerated. However bad it is that they won't engage with the national media, it's absolutely outrageous that county teams won't talk to their local papers. It's utter madness, and the sooner people come to their senses on that one, the better.

It's a long way from Fivemilebourne near the Sligo–Leitrim border, where McGoldrick was raised on a small farm, to some of the greatest sports stadia and iconic events in the world.

"There have been some 'pinch me' moments alright," he concurs. "But you just get on with the job. I'm very privileged to have been present at so many big sports occasions."

Micheál Ó Domhnaill

From Barcelona to Ballygunner

He's presented high-profile soccer programmes from some of the most iconic stadiums in the world, interviewed a host of box-office superstars and witnessed the glitz and glamour of the beautiful game at first hand.

But for Sligo-based broadcaster Micheál Ó Domhnaill, nothing compares to relaying the passion and drama of GAA football and hurling games to hundreds of thousands of TG4 viewers.

A native of Ring in the Waterford Gaeltacht, he has been the anchorman of TG4's increasingly popular GAA coverage for over 20 years, embellishing the role with an enthusiastic, informative style of presentation. An engaging interviewer, his relaxed, ultra-professional approach to the job brings viewers to the very heart of the action, ensuring a fascinating production which appeals not just to an Irish-speaking audience but to the wider GAA community.

It's a measure of TG4's ever expanding appeal that while the channel remains steadfastly committed to its remit of providing a programme schedule principally for Irish speakers, it draws respectable viewing figures throughout the country.

"Our GAA coverage was a bit of slow burner, but we've been growing our figures steadily over the years and the current audience share is impressive. Obviously, we're getting it right but we're not resting on our laurels. We're always striving to do better", says Ó Domhnaill.

His career path into sports broadcasting took an unusual but interesting route. After graduating from St Patrick's teacher training college in Drumcondra, he taught for two years in Ireland before taking up an offer to teach in Pamplona in northern Spain, the city famous for its annual bull-running festival. He recalls:

> I hadn't studied Spanish at college, so I had to learn the language on the hoof. As a young person, it was very exciting to be living in such a vibrant city. There was a lot going on there, politically and culturally, but it was a great experience.

Back in Ireland, a progressive production company, Nemeton, set up by an old school friend, secured the rights to broadcast Spanish soccer in Ireland. Ó Domhnaill was tempted by an opportunity to get involved in the project and returned to Ireland.

His first job in Irish broadcasting was as a camera man, working at many of the top sporting events in the country. Eventually, he moved to front of camera, becoming the main presenter of an exciting new Spanish soccer programme on Teilifís na Gaeilge called *Olé, Olé*. It was an hour-long weekly magazine show which, despite some pessimistic forecasts to the contrary, quickly built up a solid following.

The first match Ó Domhnaill covered live was a derby clash between Barcelona and Espanyol at a packed Nou Camp stadium in September 1996. The famous ground was throbbing in anticipation of a masterclass from Barcelona's new recruit, the Brazilian superstar Ronaldo. The teenager didn't disappoint. The Sligo-based broadcaster reminisces:

> It was a magical night. The pitch cut up badly. It was like trying to play football in a bog, but still the genius of Ronaldo was irresistible. He set up one goal with a mesmerising run through the heart of the Espanyol defence, virtually laying it on a plate for his teammate to tap into an empty net. The stadium erupted and the thunderous noise of 90,000 Barcelona fans raising up in triumphant celebration was something to behold. It was the night the legend of Ronaldo was born, and it was a privilege to be there to cover it for an Irish audience.

During his time covering Spanish soccer, he also broadcast from the Bernabeu Stadium on many occasions and interviewed several of the world's leading players of the time. He explains:

> Unlike the situation which pertains now, access to players was quite relaxed. All the big names were willing to do after-match interviews. I'd explain to them I was working for an Irish-speaking TV channel and 99% of the time they were more than happy to do an interview. It's extraordinary looking back on it now, given how inaccessible some of the big names in sport are these days.

Ó Domhnaill also worked on several top games in the Scottish League, the most memorable of which was a clash between Celtic and St Johnstone at Parkhead on the closing day of the 1997/98 season. Celtic had to win the game to clinch the title and deny their fierce rivals, Rangers, their tenth League crown in a row.

"The atmosphere was incredible," he recalls. "The destination of the title came down to this last game and Celtic were desperate to stop Rangers' all-conquering run. They won 2–0 and the place went mad."

The introduction of GAA into TG4's schedule in the late 1990s offered new opportunities for Ó Domhnaill and he relished the challenge.

A typical Sunday afternoon programme includes two games, usually at different venues, and runs for up to five hours of live broadcasting.

It's a hectic and demanding schedule and Ó Domhnaill is the man tasked with stitching it all together, conducting pre- and post-match interviews, scene-setting the day's action and capturing the agony and ecstasy of the big occasions:

> It's a labour of love. I enjoy everything about it – the research during the week, the build-up on the day of the match and then presenting the programme. It's a way of life. I don't regard it as work at all. Once a programme is finished, I can't wait to get started on the next one.

Initially, TG4's arrangement with the GAA was confined to club championships – the first one they covered was the 1999 Donegal final – but their remit now includes provincial club championships, football and hurling National League games, a range of underage championship fixtures and extensive coverage of ladies' competitions.

Ó Domhnaill believes their schedule of games has enormous appeal to GAA fans up and down the country. And there's also the satisfaction of providing a showcase for club competitions which are the lifeblood of the GAA and which receive no more than passing coverage elsewhere.

He says:

> The club games are particularly relevant in that they are the very essence of what the GAA is all about. So much is invested by so many people at club level and to give them the platform to portray all that to a national television audience is a special privilege. In many cases, the men and women playing in club finals would only get one chance to play in a game covered live on television. For them, it's the most important day in their careers. There is always the possibility of a David v Goliath

> clash in club championships, a chance for the underdogs to have their big day out. That doesn't happen so much on the inter-county scene. So, it's wonderful to be part of all that, bringing those stories to life for television viewers.

The 2022 All-Ireland club finals underlined the point, with Ballygunner in the hurling and Kilcoo in the football taking the titles in dramatic circumstances.

> Those two games were extraordinary. I thought I'd seen it all in my broadcasting career and then the club championships produce two finals which went right down to the wire with Ballygunner and Kilcoo winning their first titles. You couldn't make it up. They are the sort of occasions which make sport so compelling and underline why it is such a privilege to do this the job.

A proud Waterford man, Ó Domhnaill has been living in Sligo since 1999. He is married to Sligo native Michelle Davitt, and the couple have three children, Niamh, Calum and Ella. The family is deeply immersed in the sporting, cultural and social life of the county.

He is heavily involved in the Sligo Spanish Armada Society and Sligo Comhaltas and is passionate about the county's tourism potential.

"The various organisations and groups involved in tourism promotion are now on the same page and if they all keep working together the possibilities for Sligo are endless. It's a wonderful county with so much to offer," he declares.

Richard Pugh

Calling the horses

Fairyhouse, Easter Monday, 2022. At last free from the soul-destroying grip of the Covid pandemic, carefree revelers and hardened punters find common cause in a blissful expression of liberation, transforming the usually refined County Meath venue into a throbbing cauldron of unbridled joy.

As 27 horses make their way to the start for the year's showcase event, the Irish Grand National, a thundering rendition of 'Olé, Olé, Olé' fills the air with the sort of feverish adulation normally reserved for raucous football stadiums.

It's gloriously chaotic. Far from holding its breath, the nation is puffing out a collective air of overdue celebration.

High up in the commentary box, Richard Pugh surveys the biggest party Irish racing has seen in over two years, thrilled the days of empty stands, ghostly parade rings and eerie winners' enclosures are a thing of the past. The crowds are back. He's always subscribed to the creed that Grand National day is the mecca of Irish racing. Now he's witnessing the word made flesh.

It's his job to convey the unique thrill of the big race to an expectant television audience. He's on top of every move, relating the emotion and spectacle of the unfolding drama, spotting the fallers, the stragglers, the quiet progress of the improvers, the unsparing courage of the front runners. Down to the last fence, the punishing surge to the line, the agony and ecstasy of a typically relentless battle for supremacy, the moment of triumph for the winner, the extravagant celebrations of the winning connections. The whole package, delivered with unconditional neutrality, descriptive and informative, is a classic example of perfect race-calling.

The Sligoman is the voice of Irish racing for TV viewers, having succeeded Tony O'Hehir as RTE's top racing commentator in 2019. He's now an integral part of the national broadcaster's superb racing team, joining Ruby Walsh, Jane Mangan, Barry Geraghty, Ted Walsh and a host of other high-profile personalities in a panel of analysts who has elevated coverage of the sport to a level of unrivalled excellence.

Coming from a family steeped in equestrian pursuits – his parents, Derek and Bernadette, were actively involved in Sligo Harriers for a long number of years – Richard was fascinated by the sport from an early age.

"When I was a young boy, I used to watch the horse boxes passing by our house on their way to Sligo races and I was utterly fascinated. Nothing captured my imagination in the same way", he remembers.

Although he enjoyed playing Gaelic football, soccer and rugby, nothing matched the compelling thrill of horse riding.

"I first rode in a point-to-point meeting when I was 16 years old and I'd never known a buzz like it", he confirms. "From that day on, it was horses for me."

Francie Kerins from Tubberbride gave him his first ride in a point-to-point race aboard Carrigan's Lad and the McGarry family in Coolera and Billy Boyers at Rosses Point were others who offered invaluable support.

He achieved a particularly noteworthy win aboard Liam Clancy's Handy Fellow in the Ladies Cup over the cross-country course at the Punchestown festival in 1995, thereby gaining the distinction of being one of the first jockeys to ride a winner over the now famous 'Ruby's Double', one of the most iconic obstacles at the track.

Managing his weight became an issue, however. He'd run three times every day, but it proved to be an unwinnable battle.

He went out with a bang, driving home two winners on his last day riding in 1996. He rode Drop the Act for his father and Hope's Delight for Enda Bolger at a point-to-point meeting in Sligo. The fact he clocked up the spectacular double at his local track, literally down the road from the family home, added further substance to the occasion.

When his fledgling riding career was cut short, Pugh was determined to explore other opportunities within the industry. He explains:

> I had been immersed in racing since I was a young boy so there was no way I was going to settle for just being a spare part. I had a huge interest in reading form. For me, it wasn't about which horses won or didn't win, but why horses won or didn't win. I was always looking to put the pieces of the jigsaw together.

That almost obsessive yearning for knowledge of the ins and outs of the sport proved the perfect grounding for a career in race-calling, although it was as much by accident as design that he followed that path.

"My father suggested I try doing some commentary on a point-to-point meeting at Sligo in 1997. I absolutely loved it. I can't really describe why, it just came naturally", he says.

Determined to further his education in the art of race-calling, Pugh was acutely aware there were many aspects of the craft which required to be mastered. He recounts:

> I had to perfect a commentary accent. Whenever I was driving from Sligo to Dublin, I would commentate on everything, the traffic, the houses on the side of the road, the cattle in the fields, the most random of things. It was crazy but I did it all the time, developing a consistent commentary voice.

His first break came at a point-to-point meeting at Down Royal on St Stephen's Day, 1998. And to say it was a baptism of fire would be putting it mildly:

> The weather was horrific, snow and sleet and rain. I could see about a furlong of the two-mile circuit and then the horses would disappear. I was there saying absolutely nothing. I didn't have the experience to fill in the commentary when the horses were out of view. And even when they came back into my sightline, I still couldn't pick them out. Fortunately, there was one in pink colours which I could identify. So, I concentrated on that one. I kept calling the one name I could pick out, Mrs Battle. And guess what? The horse went and won the race. Talk about luck. I was so bad; I was convinced my race-calling career started and finished that day.

Having survived that sharp learning curve, Pugh continued to work tirelessly at meetings all around the country. One point-to-point race in particular stands out in his memory. It was at Belclare in 1999 and there were only two runners. One of them was Best Mate, later to win three Cheltenham Gold Cups.

He started doing radio commentaries for RTE in 2012, a role which presented its own peculiar challenges:

> When you're doing radio, you have to be conscious of the fact that many of those listening aren't necessarily racing fans. So, you have to paint

> a picture, tell a story in a way that perhaps you wouldn't when you're commentating at racetracks. I enjoyed that.

Now firmly established as RTE's main commentator on television coverage, Pugh spends endless hours in forensic research, accumulating deep knowledge of runners and riders, and basically being on top of every single detail associated with the sport.

"Sometimes, the most important moments for a race commentator are the thirty seconds before the race and the thirty seconds after the race. What happens in between looks after itself in some respects," he explains.

He believes the job of race-calling is infinitely easier now that when he first started out in the business:

> These days, there are about ten or fifteen cameras at the big meetings and the commentator has a monitor. Also, we now get the list of runners about 48 hours in advance of the races so there's plenty of time to do the necessary homework. That all helps.

His favourite race to call is the Irish Grand National and the horse he enjoyed commentating on most was the all-conquering Hurricane Fly, winner of five Irish Champion Hurdles and two Cheltenham Champion Hurdles.

He is married to Dr Jennifer Pugh, the senior medical officer with the Irish Horseracing Regulatory Board, and the couple live in County Kildare with their two children, Christopher and Conor.

He is the owner of the point-to-point racing website p2p.ie and is a member of the board of Tattersalls Ireland.

Eamonn Sweeney

Red Army book was "labour of love"

Eamonn Sweeney was in the Showgrounds two days before he was born. His mother, Evelyn, therefore, knew all about a labour of love 29 years before her firstborn son experienced the same cliched emotion when writing the Sligo Rovers' masterpiece, *There's Only One Red Army*.

A brilliantly told autobiographical essay of the author's journey through Rovers' unforgettable but totally unexpected treble-winning 1993/94 season, *There's Only One Red Army* is laced with love, laughter and intellectual lucidity, and could only have been written by a true disciple of the club's incongruous history of trauma and triumph.

And Gurteen-born Sweeney is as true a disciple as any of the Gospel writers. His parents, Joe and Evelyn, were the prophets. As a young couple, they rarely missed a Sunday match in the Showgrounds; two days after one such excursion in 1968, Evelyn gave birth to Eamonn, the first of her four children. As the young family grew, it merely meant extra clicks at the Showgrounds rusty turnstiles. Sweeney ponders:

> My dad was from Kilkenny and my mum was born and reared in the Connemara Gaeltacht, so I'm not sure where the soccer came from. Dad had played a bit in Kilkenny, though hurling would have been his first love. Maybe, when he came to live in Sligo he was smitten by that Rovers bug. It's fairly contagious. Whatever it was, it stuck with him, and us, all our lives.

He recalls travelling the 20 miles into the Showgrounds as a "natural thing to do" on a Sunday afternoon, but they would often be late arrivals, missing the first few minutes and enduring the mischievous slagging of his dad's pals who would tease that they had missed a couple of goals. Typically, Rovers would end up on the wrong side of a hefty scoreline, but heroes were invading the soul nonetheless.

"I was besotted with a pre-beard Fago and I loved our goalie, Gary Scothorn, mainly because of that unusual name. I remember John Minnock scoring against us for Athlone Town and the great Bobby Tambling, who'd played for Chelsea and England, running out against us for Cork Celtic", he happily remembers.

The Sweeneys loved the GAA, too, and a literary seed may have been sewn in young Eamonn's mind when his father, a national school teacher, penned a celebratory poem after their team, Eastern Harps, had beaten the mighty Croabh Rua in the 1975 County Senior final. Sweeney quips:

> It was a great little poem, but there was a bit of poetic license taken, too. One of their lads blasted a penalty high and wide, but my dad described it as a great save by our goalkeeper. I learned a lot about accurate reporting from that poem.

The young Sweeney played Gaelic football with Harps and soccer with Ballymote Celtic and won county badminton titles with his brother, Eoghan, as well as winning performances in Community Games in table tennis and athletics.

But his real flair was demonstrated as a wordsmith. Utilising words with the delicacy of a stonemason, he crafted beautifully constructed articles on everything from non-league football to cricket and speedway during a "highest of craic" four years with the *Thurrock Gazette* in the Essex town of Grays.

"There were four non-league football teams in our circulation area, so there was no shortage of matches to be covered. It was a terrific learning ground. I adored every minute of it", he testifies.

Having served his apprenticeship on local papers like the *Roscommon Herald* and *Roscommon Champion*, Sweeney returned to the local scene after his spell in England, settling in at the *Longford News* before heading to the big smoke and the *Irish Press*. He subsequently worked as a researcher with RTE before moving to the *Cork Examiner* and then to the *Irish Independent* group, where his award-winning twice-weekly columns have become compulsory reading for sports fans.

But it is his groundbreaking book on the unforgettable Rovers' treble-winning season which has endeared him to soccer fans, not only in Sligo, but throughout the country and beyond. He had already written a well-received novel, *Waiting for the Healer*, as well as plays and short stories, when the opportunity came to pen the soccer masterpiece in 1997. Sweeney explains:

> It was around the time when Roddy Doyle was having all the success with his Barrytown trilogy, and publishers were throwing money at Irish authors. New Island Books, which had been set up by the acclaimed writer Dermot Bolger, gave me a few quid to write about anything I wanted. Following the rule you should always write about something you know, I immediately thought about Rovers and decided to go for it.

So, he took himself off to a house "in the middle of nowhere" in Achill, Co. Mayo, and wrote for eight hours a day because "there was nothing else to do". He finished the book in a month. It was, as his mother might have told him 29 years earlier, that cliched labour of love. He recalls:

> You couldn't click onto the internet in those days, so it was mostly from memory. What I liked about it was that it didn't pretend to be a definitive history of the events of that era. It was one person's experience of an unprecedented season in the life of a football club that didn't usually end up winning three trophies, or indeed, any trophies.
>
> And it was the first of its type. Nobody had ever written about the League of Ireland in that way. I've often heard my book compared to Nick Hornby's Fever Pitch, and people wondering if I'd been influenced by it. Quite honestly, I hadn't read Hornby's book. I'm not sure I'd even heard of it. I have read it since, but I'm not sure the comparison stands up. There's a radical difference between describing a trip with 40,000 people to watch Arsenal every week and going to the Showgrounds where, sometimes, there might be less than a few hundred in the ground. It's a totally different experience, a totally different story.

For the uninitiated, the narrative centres primarily on Willie McStay's young team, who recovered from relegation the previous season to take the League of Ireland by storm. They won the Shield tournament early in the season, before marching to promotion by winning the First Division title. They were seven points adrift of leaders Athlone Town at the halfway stage, before the historic switching-on of the town's first ever floodlights literally illuminated the season as the team glided regally through a fifteen-match unbeaten run. Then, stretching imagination to the limit, they won the FAI Cup for only the second time in the club's history, beating Premier League hotshots Derry City in a Lansdowne Road final.

All the material was there for a gripping, fairytale epic, and Sweeney captures it all magnificently in a book which has sold several thousand copies and continues to be in high demand.

The author is delighted with the positive reaction, particularly as a huge portion of praise has come from people associated with clubs other than Sligo Rovers, and indeed from people who might not otherwise take much notice of the League of Ireland.

> You honestly never know when writing something whether anyone will bother reading it. It's a step into the unknown. Naturally, I was hoping Rovers fans would enjoy it, but it was lovely when people from other clubs started saying nice things about it. I think people identified with it because it was true. I wasn't pretending that this club meant so much to me. I was telling the truth about that. I still have great affection for the book and for the club.

Now living in West Cork, he concedes he doesn't get to watch Rovers as much as he would like these days, but he's glad he got the chance to bring his young daughter, Lara, to all the games during the 2012 League-winning season. She's still an avid Rovers fan.

"I like the idea of passing it on," he insists. "Just as my parents gave me this great love of a football club, I can honour that memory by making sure my own children are aware of that identity. Sport gets into your soul, and for Sligo people, Sligo Rovers opens that door", he says.

Local Scribes Who Record Our History

Sligo has a long tradition of quality sports journalism, dating back nearly 200 years to the foundation of the county's early newspapers, the *Sligo Champion* and *Sligo Independent*, and through 26 different papers since then. In more recent times, the advent of local radio has brought an exciting new dimension to coverage of sports in the county, while the emergence of several successful local podcasts have offered unique opportunities for analysis and comment.

One of the longest serving local scribes is Michael Moran, who covered sport, in particular the Sligo Rovers and junior soccer beat, for over 30 years with the *Sligo Champion*. Now retired, he has maintained his journalism instincts as co-producer of two highly acclaimed Rovers documentaries. Co-produced with his cousin, cameraman Oisín Moran, *Shine* documented Rovers' successes in the 1970s, 80s and 90s, while the more recent *2012* examined the phenomenal march to the League of Ireland Championship that year.

Moran can trace his love of Rovers all the way back to his toddler's pram. He recalls:

> Not many people had cars in those days, so for most families, Sunday recreation was an afternoon stroll. I vividly recall my parents used to place an old green-and-white transistor radio in my pram and it always seemed to be a Rovers commentary they listened to. With that kind of upbringing, I couldn't escape the Rovers' bug.

A regular spectator at the Showgrounds since childhood, he began reporting on Rovers shortly after joining the *Champion* in 1979. As a wide-eyed young supporter he had known only heartbreak, but that was all about to change in his professional life:

> The Champion is nearly 200 years old, and for the majority of that time, local reporters would have had hardly any success to write about. I was blessed I got to cover so many historic League and Cup victories in my time there. I appreciated it all the more because I knew from my own experience how locals had waited so long for any hint of success. Those were great years, memories to last a lifetime.

The two Rovers documentaries will ensure the perseverance of those memories, and a third, planned to coincide with the fortieth anniversary of the first FAI Cup victory in 1983, will complete an impressive trilogy for the Moran cousins, whose respective families are steeped in support for soccer over many generations.

Jessica Farry has become synonymous with coverage of soccer in recent years. She has the notable distinction of being the first woman to be lead commentator on a Premier League game for Newstalk.

A native of Coolaney, she started writing a weekly column about Sligo Rovers in the *Sligo Champion* while still studying for a journalism degree, before taking up a full-time position with the paper in 2015. She later worked briefly for Setanta Sport before becoming well known for live video reports and previews of games during Eir Sport's coverage of the League of Ireland. She is currently a regular commentator on Rovers games for Ocean FM and LOITV. She reflects:

> The commentaries were challenging in the beginning, and it took some time to adjust, but I've always been the type of person to try anything.
>
> While people are genuinely delighted to see a 'female' doing commentaries, I like to think of myself as just a commentator, rather than a 'female commentator', which feels like a tag I've grown. It's been full-on these past few years, but thoroughly enjoyable.

Another relatively new voice in the commentary box is Enniscrone native Cathal Mullaney, who is a regular contributor to flagship RTE programmes such as *The Sunday Game* and *Saturday and Sunday Sport*.

Like Farry, Mullaney cut his journalism chops covering matches for the *Sligo Champion* at the invitation of then sports editor Leo Gray. His radio introduction came via Ocean FM, where Darragh Cox and Austin O'Callaghan were early mentors.

His national breakthrough came on Newstalk's *Off the Ball*, where his voice has become familiar on sports news builletins across Newstalk, Today FM and 98FM. He has worked for RTE across both television and radio. He says:

> A chance to be a small part of the Sunday Game team or having an input into Saturday or Sunday Sport is a real thrill and a genuine privilege. Like any line of work, one of the perks is the many great people you meet as you make your way in a chosen career. I am very lucky to have had such supportive colleagues both in Sligo and Dublin and to have made many friends along the way.

West Sligo has another emerging sports voice in the person of Skreen native Kathleen McNamee, whose impressive portfolio includes coverage for ESPN of major events such as Wimbledon, the Carabao Cup, November internationals, the Six Nations, Women's Champions League, Olympics Games and the FA Cup final.

A graduate of Trinity College, where she studied Law and was assistant editor of the college paper, the *University Times*, McNamee covered the European elections for *TheJournal.ie* before joining ESPN, initially as a graduate intern and then as a freelancer.

In addition to her work with ESPN, the former Ursuline College student hosts the COYGIG (Come on You Girls in Green) podcast with *Off the Ball*, and is passionate about promoting women's sport.

"On COYGIG, we focus on Irish women's football as well as the Women's Super League. I'd like to keep growing the profile of women's sport and proving there is space for us at the table", she says.

The advent of local radio in 1990 brought an entirely new dimension to sports coverage in the region. The current sports editor at Ocean FM, which covers County Sligo, north Leitrim, and south Donegal, is Drumcliffe native Austin O'Callaghan, who says the importance of local coverage should never be underestimated.

"We never underestimate the impact that getting coverage or even a mention on a local radio station can have on a young athlete, team or community", he maintains.

> While the buzz around Sligo Gaelic footballers reaching a Connacht final or Rovers getting to a Cup final is enjoyable stuff, it's often the less

> obvious stories that resonate most with our audience. For instance, the most listened-to piece of sports audio broadcast by the station is a live interview with Sligo marathon runner Karen Mulrooney immediately after she had set a new record for a Sligo female athlete in Seville. That interview has reached an online audience of thousands.

O'Callaghan, a self-confessed sports fanatic whose career has included work with Eurosport, EuroNews and the BBC, insists some of the most satisfying moments have come from covering local sport:

> If there's a perception out there that local means smaller or less important, it's a wrong one. There are hundreds of sports stories out there. We'll only get to cover a fraction of them, but they are stories which matter.

Transferring from local to global is Achonry native J.J. Devaney, now based in New York, where he hosts a popular bi-weekly soccer podcast, *Caught Offside*, for ESPN.

For the past eight years, Devaney and his co-host, Andrew Gundling, have covered the English Premier League, the US national team, the Champions League, and whatever else is grabbing the headlines in the global soccer community.

Citing early work experience at the *Sligo Weekender*, under the guidance of sports editor Liam Maloney, and MidWest Radio as huge influences, Devaney says:

> We've built up a large listenership at a time when soccer is booming in the United States and the demand for content has never been higher. I was lucky enough to cover the Champions League final between Liverpool and Real Madrid in Paris, and the privilege of being able to work in this environment is not lost on me.

Podcasts have opened up an entirely new way to consume sports debate and analysis. Locally, *The Sligo Way* podcast, hosted by sports aficionados Ronan Moriarity, Ross O'Boyle and Adrian McPartland, takes a unique and often hilarious view of the local sports world, while former county footballer and musician Kieran Quinn, offers a more mellow take in his *In the Lamplight* series. Sligo Rovers fans are catered for by the BORST (*Bit O'Red Supporters Trust*) podcast, hosted by die-hard fans Gerry O'Connor, Shaun Dunne, Shane McGoldrick and Conor Lynch.

The current generation set to establish further links in the time-honoured chain of local sports journalism includes writers and broadcasters such as Emma Gallagher, Liam Maloney, Alan Finn, Gerry McLoughlin, Rory Houston, Arthur James O'Dea, Alanna Cunnane, David Goulden, Gavin Cawley, Rian Bailey, Mark Halton, Donal Ryan and Keith O'Dwyer. Michael McGarry is another long-serving scribe who gave years of dedicated service to the coverage of sport in Sligo.

So, from Tourlestrane to the Tour de France, from Community Games to Olympic Games, from a windswept sideline of a Junior B Championship game to a Champions League press box, the honourable profession of local Sligo scribes continues to flourish. They are, as famed publisher of the *Washington Post* Philip L. Graham so succinctly put it, the recorders of the first draft of history.

Special Olympics

"Let me win, but if I cannot win, let me be brave in the attempt"

It's a motto which should probably govern every sport, but it belongs uniquely to Special Olympics, and it encapsulates the ethos of a movement which showcases the enormous talents of the world's bravest and most-loved athletes.

This celebration of Sligo sport would not be complete without a massive bow to hundreds of Special Olympics athletes from this region who have not only brightened up all our lives but who have brought home an Aladdin's cave full of national, European and world medals, more than justifying their place on any pantheon of all-time Sligo greats.

Myra Merrick is the regional director for Special Olympics in Connacht. She has witnessed first-hand the massive impact of the movement not only for the athletes but for their families and the wider community. She explains:

> The real value of Special Olympics is that it shines a light on the athlete's abilities rather than disabilities. They go off to training or competition with a bag on their back and their heads full of dreams just the same as any other athlete.
>
> The competitions give children and adults with intellectual disability the opportunity to train and compete in fifteen different sports, initially in their own communities and then on to a national and international stage.
>
> It goes well beyond sport, though. It provides a brilliant social outlet, where people can make new friends, build confidence, assume

> leadership roles. It has made such a huge positive difference to the athletes and their families. The sense of pride that the competitors generate is almost indescribable.

The first international Special Olympics Games were held in Chicago, Illinois, USA, in 1968, in the home state of its founder, Eunice Kennedy Shriver.

Ten years later, Special Olympics Ireland was formed by a number of volunteers, with Mary Davis at the forefront. It established Special Olympics within intellectual disability services and special schools in Dublin but as the interest grew, other disability services from around the country joined the movement. Regional offices were soon developed with sports coordinators employed to develop the programme at regional level.

Cregg House, Cloonamahon Services and Gallagher House, Tubbercurry were among the first services to take on Special Olympics in Sligo, with the movement growing rapidly locally from 1982 onwards. In the important early years, Tommy and Annie Killoran from Tubbercurry were synonymous with Special Olympics, having their daughter, Margaret (RIP), involved in all community activities. Margaret became one of the most recognisable representatives of what Special Olympics was all about in the formative years.

With the support of the Office of Public Works, the first Connacht office was opened in Sligo to develop Special Olympics throughout the region. Pioneer clubs locally included Nightriders Special Olympics Club, Splashin' Penguins Special Olympics Club and Sligo Fairways Special Olympics Golf Club.

As the appeal of the Games widened, Sligo Resource Centre and RehabCare Sligo subsequently joined the Special Olympics programme while Sligo Shuttle Stars and Sligo All-Stars community clubs were soon established to give athletes experience in badminton and basketball.

When Ireland became the first country outside of America to host a Special Olympics World Summer Games in 2003, Sligo played its part in a global event which captured the imagination of millions of television viewers. As part of the Host Town Programme, Sligo hosted 31 athletes and coaches from Gibraltar and a team of 18 from Benin, West Africa. It was a huge success as athletes and coaches got time to acclimatise and soak in the Irish culture, food and weather, and many returned home with very happy memories of their time in the Yeats County.

Sligo wasn't found wanting in the competition either, as five sports athletes and fifteen motor activities training programme athletes from the county were selected for Team Ireland, bringing home gold, silver and bronze medals.

In golf, Bairbre Callagy took gold, Batty Colligan won silver, and Ursula Scully placed fifth, while Catriona Ryan took fourth in Pitch & Putt and Mary Swift won a silver and fourth in Equestrian.

Motor activities athletes from Cregg House who represented Ireland at the Games included Bridie Byrnes, Bernie Horkan, William Montgomery, Teresa McDonagh, Amanda McGuinness, Jacinta Fleming, Maureen Small, Sharon Watson, Clodagh Gallagher, Geraldine Harte, Kathleen Keavney, Carmel Ann Doocey, Annette Finan, Geraldine Mahon, and Fiona Gallagher. All the athletes achieved their Challenge Award Medal.

The remarkable run of success for local athletes continued at the 2007 World Games in Shanghai, China, where Tony Lynagh won a silver and bronze in athletics; Edel Hannon took a bronze in football; in golf, Antonia Casey captured a silver while Paul Kilgannon and his partner Liam Hyland won bronze; and Gerard McCormack seized gold, bronze and a fifth place in table tennis.

At the 2011 World Games in Greece, there was a further haul of medals, Joseph Cullen winning gold in swimming and Adrian Cornwall bringing home a gold, silver and bronze in badminton. Four years later in Los Angeles, Sligo athletes were again to the fore, Thomas Connolly winning gold and silver in equestrian and Margaret Carr claiming a gold in 18 holes golf.

Athletes from the region have competed with great distinction at a series of international events in the intervening years, and although the Covid pandemic disrupted the movement in recent years, the machine is now well-oiled and ready to roar back into action.

Myra Merrick reports:

> Loads of stuff is going on in the background and a lot of our clubs are beginning to get back up and running. The priority at the moment is to ensure that the athletes have the opportunity to return to training, to re-build the connection with their clubs and with their friends, and to be in a position where they'll be considered for selection for the next World Games in Berlin in 2023. Hopefully, Sligo athletes will continue the county's proud record on the biggest stage.

It's estimated that over five million athletes across the globe benefit from their involvement in Special Olympics. Sligo might seem like a relatively small cog in such a massive wheel, but for those involved it is the greatest thing in their lives. As Myra confirms:

> It means absolutely everything. The dedication of an army of volunteers, the support and goodwill of the wider community, and the giant smiles on the faces of every athlete is such a pure joy. For us, and for the athletes and families involved, the Special Olympics is the home of real superstars.

There could scarcely be a more fitting way to conclude this celebration of Sligo sport.

Eternal Stars

Ray Flynn

Centurion 512 has left an indelible mark

A month before his untimely death on 26 April 2022, in an interview for this book, the late Ray Flynn recalled his life and times in an eventful athletics career. With the endorsement of his family, we are honoured to include his last ever interview, telling his remarkable story in his own words.

Ray Flynn has had a ringside seat and the inside track at some of the greatest moments in Ireland's sporting history, from cheering home Sonia O'Sullivan's historic silver in Sydney to welcoming his close friend Rob Heffernan over the line as world race-walking champion in Moscow.

As chairman of high performance with Athletics Ireland and coach and mentor to the country's elite race-walkers, the Calry man has been at the coalface of athletic endeavour at no fewer than six Olympic Games and countless European and World Championships. He has travelled the world in the company of some the country's greatest athletes, shared their highs and lows, and has enjoyed substantial success himself at local, national and international level.

Sometimes, he admits, he wonders if it's too good to be true. He reflects:

> You're sitting in an Olympic stadium, up close to some of the world's best athletes. You're watching history being made and sometimes you're actually part of it. Coming from my background, a working-class farm family in rural Sligo, that can be hard to take in. I've been very lucky.

It's all a world away from his humble beginnings in sport. It's hard to imagine now when every road in the country is dotted with supremely toned joggers, but Ray can recall a time when aspiring athletes would only feel comfortable training under the cover of darkness for fear of being subjected to sarcastic criticism:

> I believe I might have been the first Sligo athlete to train in daylight. Farmers in roadside fields would look at me distainfully. You could see them wondering if I had nothing better to do with my time. Crazy to think of that now, but in the 1960s it was something of an unusual sight to see fellas out running the roads.

When he began race-walking with his local Calry AC, inspired by men like Jackie McGowan and Tommy Casey, who were pioneers of the sport in the Sligo region, Flynn could never have imagined how massively popular athletics would become over the next four decades, nor indeed his own rise to one of the most demanding and challenging jobs in Irish sport. With Athletics Ireland, he plays a key role in devising programmes, policies and strategies to ensure the country's top athletes have the best possible preparation for major championships.

His coaching instincts were honed during his own race-walking and marathon career, when the quest for constant improvement convinced him that the route to the top could only be attained by meticulous preparation. He explains:

> Roy Keane popularised the mindset: fail to prepare; prepare to fail. In my day, we didn't articulate it so perfectly, but that awareness was always there. I was an addicted trainer, always doing my best to be better, but maybe I wasn't blessed with natural ability. But I was always aware there were people out there who could be so much better if they had better preparation systems and facilities. That was in my mind from early on.

His analysis of his own career is cloaked in modesty. In fact, although he never made it to any major games, he has represented Ireland at various international events and has clocked up an amazing 42 marathons.

He was a member of the first Irish race-walking team to compete in international competition, the Lugano Cup (now the World Cup), in Sweden in 1974, where his fellow Sligoman and early mentor, Tommy Casey from Doorly Park, was a valued team member. He went on to represent Ireland at a number of smaller international events over the years, before concentrating on long-distance running, specialising in the marathon and travelling all over the world to compete at major events.

One of his proudest achievements was becoming 'Centurion 512' in June 1971. The ultramarathon consists of a 100-mile non-stop walk race along the River Thames from Richmond, London, to Oxford, which must be competed in a 24-hour time limit. Finishers are given their classified number which can never be taken from them. Hence, when it comes to that gruelling event, Ray Flynn from Calry will be forever known simply as 'Centurion 512.'

At just 18, he was the youngest athlete to complete the course, coming home in a respectable time of 21 hours, 40 minutes. He explains:

> I was so proud of myself, feeling really happy that I had this record of being the youngest ever centurion. Then, a few years ago, when I went to the House of Commons to celebrate the 100th year of the Centurion Club, I was introduced to a 17-year-old lad who had just broken my record. It was a bit of a shock, but we had a laugh about it, too. The great thing is, no matter what happens in the event in the future, I'll always be Centurion 512. Nobody can take that from me.

As his own career began to slow down, his growing interest in coaching included a range of courses designed specifically for race-walkers. This would lead him into the rarified air of high-performance coaching.

In the late 1990s, after so many barren years in the sport, a glut of high-performance race-walkers began to emerge in Ireland. Three of them would become world-class medalists: Gillian O'Sullivan won a World silver, Olive Loughnane won a World gold, while Rob Heffernan won both a World gold and Olympic bronze.

Flynn was deeply involved in all of their careers and successes.

> I was fortunate enough to be the coach who accompanied them on training camps, mainly at altitude, in places such as Johannesburg, Mexico City and Sierra Nevada in Spain, and at the big championships.
>
> During that time, I was also serving on the board of the old BLE, later to become Athletics Ireland, so I would have travelled with Irish teams as either manager or coach to major competitions all around the world. It was a fabulous time.

Those travels included coaching and mentoring duties at half-a-dozen Olympic Games, starting in Sydney in 2000, through Athens 2004, Beijing 2008, London 2012, Rio 2016 and the delayed 2020 Games in Tokyo 2021. One of his stand-out memories is 25 September 2000, in the Olympic Stadium, Sydney, when Sonia O'Sullivan raced her heart out to become the country's first female track-and field medalist, winning silver in a titanic 5,000-metre final.

He recalls:

> That was truly a hairs-standing-on-the-back-of-my-head moment. It's such a brilliant stadium and it was packed with 120,000 people. In all the big venues I've been at all over the world, in whatever sport, I have never heard noise like that night. It was deafening, unreal.
>
> I was lucky enough to be sitting in one of the front rows. I could see the runners charging up the home straight. When I saw Sonia challenging so hard inside the final 200 metres, my heart was in my mouth. It was like I was running the race with her. I was thinking of all the excitement at home, people glued to televisions all over the country, willing her to win, and here I was, a small farmer's son from Calry, stuck in the middle of it all, watching history unfold before my eyes. I have never known emotion like it. I don't often cry, but I'll tell you, I shed some tears that night. Sonia had so many ups and downs in her career, but this was her moment. She deserved it so much, and she was mightily unlucky not to get the gold. An unforgettable night.

But an even more momentous occasion lay ahead. Over the years, Flynn had built up a strong friendship with Cork race-walker Rob Heffernan. He had been to many tournaments with him as coach and mentor, had been groomsman at his wedding and had shared too many disappointments along the way. Vindication came on a bright Moscow morning in August 2013, when Heffernan powered his way to gold in the 50km final at the IAAF World Track & Field Championships.

On duty at one of the many water stations out on the course, the Sligoman had an up-close view of the progress of the athletes as they passed. He knew his old friend would not be beaten. He recalls:

> From about the half-way stage, Rob began to pull away from the Russian Mikhail Ryzhov, who was, naturally enough, the home-town favourite. As I made my way back inside the stadium I could hear the excitement from a very boisterous Irish contingent, and I knew our boy had done it. I will always remember the way the Russian fans embraced me and congratulated me once they saw the Irish colours. Even Ryzhov's supporters seemed genuinely delighted for Rob.

> He'd come so close to big victories throughout his career, but we always knew he had it in him. I don't think I've ever wanted an athlete to win as much as I did for Rob that day. We'd been through so much together. Meeting him in the stadium after the race was incredible. I'm not sure I've ever hugged anyone so tightly.

No sooner does he contend that nothing could ever beat the thrill of eye-witness accounts of O'Sullivan's and Heffernan's heroics when he remembers something that does. It's a small family triumph which neatly illustrates his long-held contention that all success grows organically from the local seed.

His daughter, Zola, a talented underage athlete before life took her on a different path, felt she would like to return to running and targeted the Cork Marathon in 2014. Although in his early 60s, her dad decided he would run with her. They finished together in around the four hours mark. He was shattered; Zola was hooked.

"She got the notion of taking it seriously, so I came on board as her trainer, and we worked bloody hard over the next few years. In 2018, she won the Cork Marathon. I have to say, for me, that topped even Heffernan and O'Sullivan", he insists.

Now tipping towards 70 years of age, he retains an almost child-like love of sport. These days, far from the glitz and glory of an Olympics, he enjoys nothing better than his Tuesday evenings spent in the company of young athletes from Sligo AC, where he still coaches.

Whatever the future holds for the next generation of Irish athletes, Ray Flynn's indelible place in the pantheon of Sligo sporting legends is assured. A Sligoman at six Olympic Games is a record unlikely ever to be equalled.

***Other outstanding Sligo athletes who have brought honour to their respective clubs and county over the years and up to the present time include:**

Mickey Kearns

Mickey hailed from the Goolwrappers in Calry and was a famous road and cross-country runner in the late 1950s and 1960s.

John McDermott

John's longevity as an athlete is truly remarkable. An All-Ireland champion in the late 1960s, he won numerous Masters titles in every decade since, ranging from 200 metres to 800 metres, and has also been prolific as a hurdler and decathlete. Remarkably, in 2022, he won both the 200-metre and 400-metre over-70 indoor titles and, aged 76, he ran a phenomenal 71 seconds for 400 metres. The Strandhill-based athlete followed up with a gold medal at the World Masters Athletics Championships in Finland, clinching the men's over-75s 300-metre title.

Tommy Casey

A native of Mohill, Co. Leitrim, Tommy was a pioneer of the sport of race-walking in Sligo. He won numerous national titles and gained representative honours in 1974, competing in Boris, Sweden. He died tragically in a road accident in 1978, while travelling to an athletics event. His son, Michael, carried the baton in the sport thereafter, winning an athletics scholarship to the USA. Michael represented Ireland in European championships during the 1990s and won many Irish titles as a runner and race-walker. Tommy's grandchildren, Tommy and Aisling, also gained American athletics scholarships, with Tommy winning many school and national juvenile titles.

Brendan Mooney

Brendan was a prolific winner of road and cross-country titles in the late 1960s and 1970s. Deemed by many to be the toughest athlete to ever come out of Sligo, he holds many local records and cross-country championships in his beloved local racecourse, where he often trained alone and barefoot on cold winter nights.

Jackie McGowan

Another Calry race-walker who also excelled in marathon and ultra-marathon events. He ran the first Dublin Marathon and went on to compete in the event consecutively for the next 25 years. He gained international honours when representing Ireland in a 100-kilometre race walk in France in the early 1980s.

Roddy Gaynor

A Sligo town native who won a national title in the ultra-competitive 800 metres in 1982. He represented Ireland at numerous events and went on to become a highly successful and inspirational coach to a new generation of outstanding athletes.

Feidhlim McGowan

The north Sligo runner gained school international vests and has excelled as a marathon runner. He holds the Sligo marathon record of 2 hours, 22 minutes.

Karen Mulrooney

The Ballisodare runner created her own slice of history in 2022 when she created an all-time record for a Sligo AC female athlete in a women's marathon, finishing the Seville event in an astonishing time of 2.41.25. The run secured her thirty-eighth place on the fastest Irish all-time women's marathon list and put her among the top five female marathon runners in Connacht. A late-comer to the sport, she broke the record established by Lucy Brennan nineteen years earlier.

Aoife Kilgallon

From a family steeped in local athletics, the 32-year-old Sligo AC athlete grabbed national headlines in 2022 when winning the 10km Women's Mini Marathon in Dublin in an impressive time of 33.07 seconds. It was Aoife's second major success, following her victory in the 5,000-metre race in the 2021 Athletics Ireland Senior Track & Field Championships.

Terry Hayes (Administrator)

A native of Inchicore, Dublin, Terry has been a stalwart of athletics in Sligo since taking up residence here in 1979. Initially associated with North Sligo AC, he was one of the motivators behind the revival of Sligo AC alongside loyal servants such as Tommy Casey and Kay Crocock. He has served as chairperson, secretary and treasurer over four decades of dedicated service.

John McGowan

Basketball legend's legacy will endure

Reared on the same street as contemporaries Tony Fagan and Dessie Gallagher, who both fulfilled boyhood dreams of playing for Sligo Rovers, and just across the road from one of the town's iconic soccer legends, Johnny Armstrong, John McGowan would have gown up inhaling deeply the inescapable football air which lingers perennially over urban Sligo. But in the early 1960s, a new sporting craze was sweeping across the town, providing a novel outlet for aspiring young athletes. John McGowan bought in early to the basketball fraternity and, over six decades, became one of the sport's greatest luminaries.

As a player, coach and administrator, the St Brigid's Place native became the backbone of Sligo All-Stars, the club he helped form with early pioneers of the game locally such as Joe Palmer, Brian McHugh, Stan Burns and Tom O'Brien. At the time of his sudden death on 31 July 2022, he was the club's honorary president.

His playing career included a dozen caps for the Irish international senior team, representing his country in pre-Olympic qualifying rounds, while as an innovative coach he helped scores of teams to win national titles, notably alongside his sister, Therese, for the hugely successful Mercy College teams over many years.

As his lifelong friend Gerry Monaghan observed: "There is hardly a family in Sligo that hasn't had a member coached by John, and he became a friend to each and every one of those he encountered."

Remarkably, given his lifelong devotion to basketball, John was also an accomplished Gaelic footballer, winning six senior county titles and two Connacht Championships with St Mary's, as well as an All-Ireland Sevens title.

Unwilling to shed entirely his love of soccer, he lined out regularly for Sligo Rovers reserves and remained a loyal supporter of the club throughout his life.

The esteem in which he was held throughout Sligo's vast sporting community was evidenced by massive attendances at his wake and funeral and in the thousands of tribute messages which flowed in from all over the world.

In a touching eulogy at his funeral Mass, John's son, Colin, told how the basketball court was John's 'second home'.

> Dad travelled the world playing basketball. He achieved so much for his beloved Sligo All-Stars and was proud to represent his country. He loved the game so much, it's safe to say the court was his second home.

Local priest Fr Pat Lombard, who celebrated the funeral Mass, touched on the wider influence of John's commitment to sport. "He understood the importance and potential for good which sport offers us," Fr Pat told mourners.

> John knew that sport, be it GAA, Sligo All-Stars or Sligo Rovers, helped people to be their best, lifted people up and gave people enjoyment, competition, purpose and helped build community. Having received so much from sport, he was always anxious to give back as much as he could and to help others, be it through coaching, management or just support from the sidelines.

Gerry Monaghan, who soldiered alongside John in successful basketball and Gaelic football careers, described his friend as the "best point guard I have ever seen" and said he was the 'rock' of the basketball community in Sligo.

> John played with and coached All-Stars, Mercy College and Eircom teams for over 50 years. He was a leader, a coach and a friend to so many, and was highly respected all over Ireland. As a person, he was a very genuine, straight and loyal friend. You always knew where you stood with John. For all he achieved, he always remained humble and private. He probably never fully realised just how popular and respected he was.

For all his sporting achievements, John was first and foremost a loving family man, proud of his children and young grandchildren. "Dad seemed happiest in the company of his grandchildren. He was such a kind man who was always there for us," Colin confirmed.

By any yardstick, John McGowan deserves the accolade of a legend of Sligo sport. His sudden passing has left a huge void, particularly in the basketball community, but his contribution to the sport and Sligo's sporting arena generally will never be forgotten.

Red Óg Murphy – A Tribute

When we sat down in the early days of 2022 to consider the contents of this book, we decided that as well as the established legends across as many sports as possible we should also include a chapter on the next generation of potential sporting heroes. The first name we pencilled in on this list was Red Óg Murphy, an up-and-coming GAA footballer who was already forging a huge reputation as a certain star of the future. Red Óg's untimely death on 1 April 2022 shocked and saddened the entire country. Our conviction is that a book of this nature would be incomplete without his inclusion. So, following consultation with his family, and as a permanent tribute to a young man who brightened so many lives, we include here the magnificent eulogy delivered at Red Óg's funeral Mass by his friend, teacher and mentor, Colm McGee.

I coached Red for five years, where we spent countless hours kicking and coaching and laughing on the pitch, and where he always won the free kick competitions between us. I taught him English for three years (before and after he was in Australia) and came to regard him and the Murphy family as close friends.

It's an honour to be asked to speak on behalf of Red Óg's parents, Redmond and Geraldine, and his brothers, Oisín and Daithí.

There are only two men in Ireland known by their first name, Red Óg and Bono – James McDonagh came up with that one.

It's difficult to know where to begin when trying to sum up Red Óg. He was so many things to so many people. First and foremost, he was a Murphy (and let's not forget the Lavin side of the family too). He was a son, a brother, grandson, nephew, a boyfriend to Rachel, a friend to countless people, a teammate, classmate, college mate, an exemplary student. A role model.

He had a great network of friends from all walks of life, young and old - a true sign of the affection everyone had for him.

As WB Yeats put it: "Think where man's glory most begins and ends, and say my glory was I had such friends".

I can nearly hear him giving out saying, "Jaysus, is McGee still going on about bloody poetry?" Knowing him, he'd probably have the poem learned off by heart.

We have read and heard all week the beautiful tributes being paid to him and the talent he possessed on the football field. But the immense player he was isn't a patch on the beautiful human being he was.

The words I've heard repeated all week are: humble, charismatic, warm, genuine, kind, gentle. We can all learn a great lesson from how he treated people, with kindness, humility, no ego, and of course that big beaming smile.

Being in his presence automatically lifted you. He made you the centre point of a conversation and was always genuinely interested in your story, not just telling his.

He was relentless in his pursuit of improvement and perfection in sport. Self-driven. Always wanted feedback. "Where can I improve?" One of my most special memories of this was after a junior final he played for St Attracta's. He kicked 3-11 out of 3-15 but his first comment afterwards was to ask, "what can I do better?" Other clubs and school coaches have told similar stories this week.

He had an elegance and ease on the ball as he toyed with opposition and weaved his magic. One of his club mates phrased it: "Some of the things he did had to be seen to be believed."

His beautiful left foot, his ability to stay in the air and field high balls, his fitness levels, his squeaky-clean boots and questionable haircuts were his trademarks.

Red Óg just didn't accept mediocrity from himself. He propelled himself and the teams he was a part of to new heights. His teams included Moylough NS, his club Curry (2020 intermediate), St Attracta's Community School (13 finals, winning 8), Sligo (0-11 v Derry in an All-Ireland minor quarter-final back in 2017), under-17 and under-20 captain, and he played two seasons in the senior team, and most recently in DCU (Sigerson Team of the Year).

He reached heights that most of us can only have ever aspired to, and he inspired everyone he came in contact with. Young and old.

In DCU/St Pat's he was studying to become a primary school teacher. From reading some of the online comments it is already clear that he has left a lasting impression on those young lives.

Just this time last year, while on teaching practice in his old primary school in Moylough, he bought an Easter egg for each student in his class. Another example of his generosity was when he was in Paris earlier this year with Rachel. He had the presence of mind to think of his former French teacher and bought her a gift. Fittingly, it was a small diamond figurine.

Words are all I am able to offer here but words for us all can be the most important tool to try and process this.

During the week I looked back at a video that Curry GAA compiled as a send-off when Red Óg departed for North Melbourne. In the video, the words of the song read, "so wake me up when it's all over." It seems somehow poignant today. We all wish we could wake up from this nightmare and that it could be "all over", but unfortunately that isn't the case.

The song continues: "I wish that I could stay forever this young", and in a way that's comforting too, to realise that all the memories we will have of him will be of the happy, smiling, forever young Red Óg!

Words for us all can be the most important tool. Let's use our words for good. Let us use words to build people up instead of knock them down. We need to be ultra-cautious with how we use our words in what we say, or in what we type on social media. In any conversation around mental health, we need to tread carefully. Communicate. Talk but also listen. Empathise with people. Share your thoughts and time. Care for one another.

Your thoughts aren't always facts. But if you never share them, you can never see another point of view. If you are dwelling on something for too long, a fresh opinion or another way of looking at it might be needed. Another perspective. Please share your nagging thoughts. Lean on someone in your time of need.

The great people of Moylough and Curry and the wider South Sligo community have been in deep mourning over the last number of weeks and months, and even recent years. You've shown huge togetherness and unity. You have been and will need to continue to be each other's support network going forward.

Tough times show you what people are made of and you are all in the thoughts and prayers of your South Sligo friends and those from much further afield.

To Geraldine and Redmond, thank you for the three beautiful gifts you gave us, Red Óg, Oisín and Daithí.

Mr McGee then read the following poem in tribute to Red Óg:

Close up every place,
Bring all action to an end,
We have gathered here
To mourn our friend.

Our dear friend Red Óg,
Your memory will be great,
The fact that you were in our lives,
We will cherish and celebrate.

At just 21, becoming a man,
He packed so much into his years.
It's a mark of his great character,
That he has prompted so many tears.

From the Land of Heart's desire.
His craft and class were clear to all.
So many he did inspire,
Endless magic with the ball.

Very few like him could soar through the air,
Always playing with passion, skill and flair.
Off his left or off his right or a sweetly struck 45,
With him in your team hope and belief would thrive.

He wrote his story and blazed a trail,
From Moylough to the land down under.
It is so cruel, why we're gathered here,
Our lives all torn asunder.

But do not share your weight alone,
Do not have a heart of stone.
Do not judge with haste or speed,
But be there in this great time of need.

Pause and wisely consider your words,
Forget rumour and gossip you may have heard.
Give your best to his family,
Being certain that they'd do the same for you.

One thing in common that we all share
Is our love for him and deep despair.
Our thoughts of him will long remain,
Our heavy loss is heaven's gain.

Our Travelling Soldier we're blessed to have found.
Our love for you knows no bounds.
Privileged to have known him is what we all are,
Rest in peace Red, our shining star.